Sydney Smith

Wit and Wisdom of the Reverend Sydney Smith

Sydney Smith

Wit and Wisdom of the Reverend Sydney Smith

ISBN/EAN: 9783337812799

Printed in Europe, USA, Canada, Australia, Japan

Cover: Foto ©Lupo / pixelio.de

More available books at **www.hansebooks.com**

WIT AND WISDOM

OF THE

REV SYDNEY SMITH

BEING

SELECTIONS FROM HIS WRITINGS

AND PASSAGES OF HIS

LETTERS AND TABLE-TALK

WITH A BIOGRAPHICAL MEMOIR AND NOTES

BY

EVERT A. DUYCKINCK

AND A PREFATORY MEMOIR OF E. A. DUYCKINCK
BY R. H. STODDARD

NEW YORK:
A. C. ARMSTRONG & SON
714 BROADWAY
1880.

Entered, according to Act of Congress, in the year 1856,
BY J. S. REDFIELD,
in the Clerk's Office of the District Court of the United States, in and for the Southern District of New York.

COPYRIGHT,
1879,
BY A. C. ARMSTRONG & SON.

NEW YORK: J. J. LITTLE & CO., PRINTERS,
10 TO 20 ASTOR PLACE.

EVERT AUGUSTUS DUYCKINCK.

The family of Evert Augustus Duyckinck was conspicuous among the early Dutch settlers of New Amsterdam, one of its members, an Evert Duyckinck (who figures in old records as Ever Duckings) having suffered violence at the hands of the Connecticut colonists to the extent of having a hole struck in his head with a stick, "so that the bloode ran downe, very strongly downe, upon his body." Another Evert Duyckinck, the second of the name, settled early in the last century at Raritan Landing, New Jersey. He was the father of nine children, the third of whom, Christopher, was engaged during the Revolutionary War in the struggle for independence. This pugnacious Duyckinck was the father of seven children, the eldest of whom, Evert, the third of the name, became a resident of New York about the beginning of the present century, and was known as a publisher and bookseller. The difference between the New York of to-day and the New York of seventy years ago may be inferred from the neighborhood in which Mr. Duyckinck lived, moved, and had his being, for his house was in Old Slip, and his store, which adjoined it on the rear, was in Water Street. No publisher of that day had a higher reputation. He gave the young firm of J. & J. Harper the first order they ever received for a printed book, and he was so well known to Mr. Diedrich Knickerbocker, that that veracious writer regretted his famous "History of New York" had not been published by him, he being a "lineal descendant from one of the ancient heroes of the Manhattoes, whose grandfather and my grandfather were just like brothers." Only two of Mr. Duyckinck's children attained their majority, Evert Augustus, who was born in New York, November, 23d, 1816, and George Long, who was about seven years his junior, and was named after his uncle, who was also known as a publisher. The Masters Duyckinck grew up in an atmosphere of books; Evert was graduated at Columbia College, in 1835, and afterward spent two years in the law office of Mr. John Anthon. He was admitted to the bar in 1837, but like many another young gentleman who had mistaken his profession, literature had marked him for her own; and if he did not exactly pen a stanza when he should have engrossed, he penned a great many prose contributions for leading literary periodicals, among others a series of papers for Mr. Park Benjamin's *American Monthly*, entitled "Felix Merry's Fireside Essays." These papers were remembered by Poe, when he was writing his "Literati of New York City," and not at all to the discredit of their author. "Mr. Duyckinck," he remarked, "has slyly acquired much fame and numerous admirers under the *nom de plume* of 'Felix Merry.' The various essays thus signed have attracted attention everywhere from the judicious. The style is remarkable for its very unusual blending of purity and care, with a seemingly inconsistent originality, force, and independence." About this time, or possibly a little earlier, he furnished an essay on "The Old Prose Writers" to a little publication called the *Literary;* and soon afterward became a regular contributor to the *New York Review and Quarterly Church Journal*, for which he wrote notices of the poetical works of Crabbe, Mrs. Hemans, George Herbert, and Goldsmith.

In the autumn of 1838, Mr. Duyckinck visited the Old World, to look upon it with the eye of the Past, as Howell, or Evelyn, or Wotton traveled in the seventeenth century. He was fortunate enough to make the acquaintance at Paris of Mr. Harmanus Bleeker, of Albany, a descendant, like himself, of good Holland stock, who was well known in Holland, and was versed in the Dutch language and literature. Mr. Bleeker persuaded the young lawyer to accompany him to the land of their ancestors. They had a private audience with the King; attended a ball at the palace of the Prince of Orange; and received fraternal welcome at the hospitable tables of the burghers of Amsterdam and the Hague. They remained in Holland until the following spring, when Mr. Duyckinck set his face homeward, and after spending the summer and autumn in England and Scotland, returned to New York and to literature.

Mr. Duyckinck's next literary enterprise was a monthly periodical entitled *Arcturus*, which he edited in conjunction with Mr. Cornelius Matthews, and which ran through three volumes. Poe declared (in his "Literati") that it was decidedly the very best magazine, in many respects, ever published in the United States, and added, in his sneering way, "The magazine was, upon the whole, a little *too good* to enjoy extensive popularity—although I am here using an equivocal phrase, for a *better* journal might have been far more acceptable to the public."

It was to Mr. Duyckinck, I believe, that readers of thirty years ago were indebted for the "Library of Choice Reading," a collection of belles-lettres volumes, consisting of reprints and original works, of which he was the editor, and which fully bore out the pithy motto of Lamb that was prefixed to them—"Books which are Books." He was also the editor, if not the projector, of the *Literary World*, which was commenced in the early part of 1847, though it soon passed into the hands of Mr. Charles Fenno Hoffman, who was assisted for a time, if I remember rightly, by Mr. Bayard Taylor, who made his debut in its columns as a metropolitan journalist. In the fall of the following year Mr. Duyckinck resumed control of it in connection with his brother George, who in his turn had made a European tour, and between them it occupied the field of literary criticism until the close of 1853. It was the forerunner of the *Round Table* and the *Nation*, and, if not quite so critical as the latter, was a paper to be depended upon for its impartiality as well as its intelligence.

The demise of the *Literary World* left the brothers Duyckinck leisure to undertake the "Cyclopædia of American Literature," a painstaking, voluminous work, which covered the history of intellectual effort in the New World from the early Colonial period,—ground which had been carelessly gone over by Dr. Griswold, in three solid octavos, and which he was loath to resign to any other pen. After the completion of this important work, which is still an authority on the subject of which it treats, Mr. Evert Duyckinck edited "The Wit and Wisdom of Sydney Smith," which was published in 1856, and at once took a prominent place among volumes of similar character. "Where are the rest of them?" Sheridan is said to have asked, on being shown a book entitled "The Beauties of Shakespeare,"—a query not likely to be repeated by any possessor of this entertaining compilation who happens to be familiar with the miscellaneous writings of the author, who is here represented at his best; much better, indeed, than a volume issued in England two or three years later, under the same title, a scrappy collection by some anonymous writer, who may be briefly described as a snapper-up of unconsidered trifles.

The later writings of Mr. Duyckinck consisted of the letter-press to two volumes entitled the "National Portrait Gallery of Eminent Americans;" of a contemporary "History of the War for the Union," in three volumes; and "Biographies of Eminent Men and Women of Europe and America," in three volumes. He also edited, with a memoir and notes, the "Poems of Philip Freneau;" the American edition of the "Poets of the Nineteenth Century;" a memorial of John Allan, a well-known American book collector; and commemorative sketches of the Rev. Dr. Hawks, Henry T. Tuckerman, and James W. Beckman, read before the New York Historical Society, and similar memorials of John David Wolfe and Samuel G. Drake, read before the American Ethnological Society. He was a member of the Societies just named, of the American Geographical Society and the New York Society Library, a trustee of Columbia College, and a corresponding member of other learned bodies.

Mr. Duyckinck died on August 13th, 1878, in his sixty-second year, and was buried in the graveyard at Tarrytown, beside the old church of Sleepy Hollow, a spot which had been selected by himself and his brother on account of its loveliness of situation, and the associations which have been woven about it by the hand of Irving, whose grave is near theirs.

The life and life-work of Mr. Duyckinck have been carefully summed up by Mr. William Allen Butler, in a memorial sketch read before the New York Historical Society on January 7th, 1879. I am indebted to this thoughtful paper for the materials of this memoir of this estimable man of letters, and I fully concur in the estimate which his friend has placed upon his literary character. "He was fully equipped for the best critical and biographical work. He knew the whole field of English literature, ' as seamen know the sea.' The authors of the Elizabethan age were as familiar to him as any of their successors of the Victorian era. Those 'old fields,' out of which comes so much of the 'new corn' of modern thought and expression, were to him like the woodland and meadow around an ancestral homestead. In the general range of literature and on most of its special subjects his knowledge was complete as to authors, and the proper critical estimate of their works, and the various editions through which they had passed, and thus, as scholar, critic, and bibliographer, he was a standard authority. I know of no one to whom any vexed questions on points of literary inquiry could have been as safely referred for decision without further appeal as in a tribunal of last resort. Nor do I know any scholar of our country better fitted, by natural disposition and temperament, by study and research, by constant practice as a writer, by experience as journalist and editor, and by thorough magnanimity and impartiality of judgment, to discharge the duty and fulfill the trust of a literary critic."

R. H. S.

CONTENTS.

BIOGRAPHICAL MEMOIR	PAGE 9
PASSAGES FROM THE EDINBURGH REVIEW	107
SKETCHES OF MORAL PHILOSOPHY	195
PASSAGES FROM SERMONS	256
ESSAYS AND SKETCHES	278
PASSAGES FROM PETER PLYMLEY LETTERS	297
REFORM SPEECHES	314
LETTERS TO ARCHDEACON SINGLETON	329
LETTERS ON RAILWAYS	344
LETTERS ON AMERICAN DEBTS	353
A FRAGMENT ON THE IRISH ROMAN CATHOLIC CHURCH	363
LETTER ON THE CHARACTER OF SIR JAMES MACKINTOSH	379
RECOLLECTIONS OF FRANCIS HORNER	387
PASSAGES FROM LETTERS	392
TABLE TALK — ANECDOTES	417

WHEN WIT IS COMBINED WITH SENSE AND INFORMATION; WHEN IT IS SOFTENED BY BENEVOLENCE AND RESTRAINED BY STRONG PRINCIPLE; WHEN IT IS IN THE HANDS OF A MAN WHO CAN USE IT AND DESPISE IT, WHO CAN BE WITTY AND SOMETHING MUCH BETTER THAN WITTY, WHO LOVES HONOUR, JUSTICE, DECENCY, GOOD-NATURE, MORALITY AND RELIGION, TEN THOUSAND TIMES BETTER THAN WIT;—WIT IS THEN A BEAUTIFUL AND DELIGHTFUL PART OF OUR NATURE.

SYDNEY SMITH.

BIOGRAPHICAL MEMOIR.

SYDNEY SMITH* was born at Woodford, Essex, in the vicinity of London, June 3, 1771, of a respectable family in the middle class of English society. His parents, as will commonly be found with the immediate ancestors of those who have risen to eminence in the world, were persons of marked character. Robert Smith, the father, was a man of curious talents and impulses, with a passion for foreign travel, and a mania, not a little destructive to his finances, for building and altering country-houses in various parts of England. He married a lady of beauty and accomplishments, Miss Olier, of Huguenot birth, her father having been one of the refugees driven to England in the great expatriation consequent on the bigoted tyranny of Louis XIV. This infusion of French blood was afterward called to mind to account for certain peculiarities of disposition, the humours and the mercurial vivacity, associated with strength of purpose, of their son, the subject of the present memoir.

* The union of the honourable name of Sydney with the generic patronymic Smith, which has been illustrated by several distinguished personages, would appear to have been adopted in this extensive family from the marriage, in the seventeenth century, of Sir Thomas Smythe, created Viscount Strangford, with a niece of Sir Philip Sydney. It was one of the jests and humours of the Rev. Sydney Smith's life, to confound himself and be confounded with his contemporary, the British admiral, Sir Sidney Smith. George Sydney Smythe, the member of the short-lived Young England party who published a volume of poems, "Historic Fancies," is another instance of the association of these names.

1*

Five children were the fruit of the marriage, four sons and a daughter: all of them, we are told, "remarkable for their talents."*

The eldest of the family, one year the senior of his brother Sydney, was Robert, known amongst his contemporaries in the London society of wits and statesmen, from a familiar handling of his Christian name at school, as Bobus Smith. Educated at Eton, he there, at the age of eighteen, was associated with the future statesman George Canning, and the fastidious, fine poet, and finished classical scholar of after life, John Hookham Frere, in the composition of the Microcosm. This periodical, of the prolific family of the Spectator, appeared in forty weekly numbers be-

---

* Memoir of the Rev. Sydney Smith, by his daughter, Lady Holland, Am. ed. p. 13. We take the first opportunity to notice the sentiment, propriety, and faithfulness which characterize this filial work. It furnishes ample materials for a knowledge of the man, particularly in his domestic and social relations. The development of his fortunes and position in the world is of especial biographical value.

Immediately after the death of Sydney Smith, the material for the Memoir was begun to be collected by his widow, who was about intrusting the work to the poet Moore, when his broken health defeated the plan. Mrs. Sydney then requested her friend Mrs. Sarah Austin, the accomplished German translator, to undertake the narrative and edit the Letters which had been brought together. Ill health limited Mrs. Austin's subsequent performance of the work to the Selection from the Correspondence which constitutes the second volume of the Memoirs.

Much as the genius of the biographer of Sheridan and Byron is to be respected, and with every consideration of the feeling with which he would have entered on the "life," in its political, social, and personal aspects, it is a matter for congratulation that the Memoirs have fallen into female hands. Woman alone could have interpreted so gracefully and truly the kindly virtues of the man. His keen, consistent, brilliant writings need no particular exhibition of his political and public life. They speak for themselves. Mrs. Austin, in her preface finds another appropriate reason for the participation of the sex in the work: in gratitude for what Sydney Smith had accomplished, by his arguments, for female education. "Within our times," she remarks, "no man has done so much to obtain for women toleration for the exercise of their understandings, and for the culture of their talents, as Sydney Smith." Mrs. Jameson, in her "Ethical Fragments," makes a similar acknowledgment: "See what he has done for humanity & society, for liberty, for truth — for us women!"

tween November, 1786, and July of the following year. Nine of its papers, chiefly grave studies of history or serious reflections, are set down to Robert Smith. He was, also, joint author with Canning, of one of the essays. Leaving Eton, he became a student of King's College, Cambridge, where he distinguished himself by the excellence of his Latin verses, amongst which were some admired compositions after the manner of Lucretius on the systems of Plato, Descartes and Newton.* He received his degree of Master of Arts, in 1797, and was the same year called to the bar by the Honourable Society of Lincoln's Inn. It was also the year of his marriage to Miss Caroline Vernon, daughter of Richard Vernon and Lady Ossory, aunt of Lord Lansdowne. The ceremony was performed by Sydney Smith, then a needy

* A number of Robert Smith's Latin compositions are preserved in the *Musæ Etonenses*, where we find this elegant Latin version of the exquisite Danae of Simonides.

EX SIMONIDE.

" Ventus quum fremeret, superque cymbam
Horrentis furor immineret undæ,
Non siccis Danaë genis puellum
Circumfusa suum, ' Miselle,' dixit,
' O quæ sustineo ! sopore dulci
Dum tu solveris, insciâque dormis
Securus requie ; neque has per undas
Illætabile, luce sub malignâ,
Formidas iter ; impetumque fluctûs
Supra cæsariem tuam profundam
Nil curas salientis (ipso molli
Porrectus tunicâ, venustus infans)
Nec venti fremitum. Sed o miselle,
Si mecum poteras dolere, saltem
Junxisses lacrymas meis querelis.
Dormi, care puer ! gravesque fluctus,
Dormite ! o utinam mei Dolores
Dormirent simul ! o Pater Deorum,
Cassum hoc consilium sit et quod ultra
(Forte audacius) oro, tu parentis
Ultorem puerum, supremo, serves."

Some fine and eloquent Latin lines on Death, found in his desk, after his decease, are printed in Lady Holland's Memoir.

young curate, who wrote in a letter to his mother: "The marriage took place in the library at Bowood, and all I can tell you of it is, that he cried, she cried, and I cried."* This alliance was afterward of use in the introduction of Sydney to the leading whig families.

Robert became highly esteemed as a barrister, and was sent to India with the profitable appointment of Advocate-General of Bengal. Eight years of official duty, performed to the admiration of the natives, secured to him a considerable fortune,† with which he returned to London, in 1812. He soon after entered the House of Commons, as member for Grantham; but, notwithstanding his acute argumentative turn is said to have failed in his maiden speech.‡ He spoke seldom and briefly afterward, during his extended parliamentary career; while his talents were exerted as a valuable business member of committees. In 1818, he contested, unsuccessfully, the city of Lincoln; but carried that place in the election of 1820, finally, retiring from Parliament at the dissolution in 1826. The concluding period of his life was passed in lettered and social ease and in retirement. His sympathies were intimately associated with those of his brother Sydney. The death of one followed closely that of the other. Robert survived the canon of St. Paul's but a fortnight. Thirty years

---

* Lady Holland's Memoir, 4th Eng. ed., p. 14.

† His personal estate was sworn, at his death, in 1845, as not exceeding £180,000.

‡ De Quincey has a curious reminiscence of this circumstance in his Essay on Dr. Parr, to be found at page 137 of vol. II., of "Essays on Philosophical Writers and other Men of Letters," published by Ticknor and Fields. Sydney Smith, who wrote of his brother Robert about this time, as "a capital personage; full of sense, genius, dignity, virtue, and wit," addressed to him, in his manly, courageous way, a felicitous letter on this subject, in which personal chagrin and disappointment are smothered under kindness, and a genuine solicitude. "Whether," he writes, "you turn out a consummate orator or not, will neither increase nor diminish my admiration for your talents, or my respect for your character; but when a man is strong, it is pleasant to make that strength respected; and you will be happier for it, if you can do so, as I have no doubt you will soon." (Letter 93 in Mrs Austin's Collection, March 17, 1813.)

before, when the former had been attacked by a serious illness Sydney wrote to him, "Dear Bobus, pray take care of yourself. We shall both be a brown infragrant powder in thirty or forty years. Let us contrive to last out for the same, or nearly the same time. Weary will the latter half of my pilgrimage be, if you leave me in the lurch."*

Robert was a man of high honour and integrity. Those who knew him intimately spoke in strong terms of his wit and powers of mind. Moore tells us, in his Diary, of his agreeable qualities, and of his being ranked, in his best time, by some people, superior to Sydney.† The remark is not unusual in such cases. Friendship readily exaggerates a question of capacity; but the execution must decide. As the ability to succeed with the public in exhibitions of mental power generally brings the desire along with it, it may, in most instances be taken for granted—certainly with the healthiest of developments—that all is claimed from the world which can be enforced. There is sometimes, perhaps, in imputing these extraordinary merits to the less-known brothers of eminent authors a compensation to self-love for the honours which are grudgingly paid to acknowledged attainments.

The testimonies, however, to the intellectual strength and charm of polished conversation of Robert Smith are not to be discredited. Dr. Parr bestowed upon him, while both were living, a Latin inscription, in his famous lapidary style, written in the presentation copy of a book. He commended his fertile and skilful Latinity; his strong, manly, vehement mode of pleading, free from captiousness or cunning, and, when the occasion demanded, even magnificent and splendid; his integrity and humanity in the regulation of life; his greatness of mind in public affairs.‡ Sir James Mackintosh

---

* Lady Holland's Memoir, p. 361.
† Diary, March 13, 1833.
‡ The inscription is given in the Gentleman's Magazine for April, 1845, p. 441. Dr. Parr, in the enumeration of college worthies, in a note to his Spital Sermon, pays this compliment to Robert Smith, τῇ ἀκριβείᾳ, καὶ δεινοτῆτι, καὶ μεγαλοπρεπείᾳ εὐδοκιμοῦντος.—(*Parr's Works*, ii. 543.)

bears witness, in his Diary, to the eclat of his legal career in India, and to his social qualities. "His fame," he records, "among the natives is greater than that of any pundit since the days of Menu;" and again: "I hear from Bobus; always merry and always kind. Long live Bobus!" The sincere strength of expression of his conversation was held in esteem. "Bobus's language," said Canning, "is the essence of English." His old friend, Lord Carlisle, remarks, in a careful memorial in the Gentleman's Magazine: "There was much in him of the sturdy Saxon, combined with the refined and thoroughly finished scholar. No one was ever so clear of all frippery, and the only thing for which he probably felt no toleration, was a prig."* Rogers, the poet and fastidious critic of society, pronounced Sir James Mackintosh, Malthus, and Bobus Smith, the three acutest men with whom he was ever acquainted.† The sound mind was enclosed in a fair body, as we learn from a pleasant anecdote related by Lady Holland. "When Talleyrand," she writes, "was an emigrant in England, he was on very intimate terms with Robert Smith. The conversation turned on the beauty often transmitted from parents to their children. My uncle, who was singularly handsome (indeed, I think I have seldom seen a finer specimen of manly beauty, or a countenance more expressive of the high moral qualities he possessed), perhaps, with a little youthful vanity, spoke of the great beauty of his mother, on which Talleyrand, with a shrug and a sly disparaging look at his fine face, as if he saw nothing to admire, exclaimed, 'Ah, mon ami, c'était donc apparemment monsieur votre père qui n'était pas bien.'"

The younger brothers of Sydney were Cecil and Courtenay. The former was educated with Robert at Eton, the latter with Sydney at Winchester. Both were fitted out for India. Courtenay gained distinction there in the Judiciary as Supreme Judge of the Adawlut Court at Calcutta. He was also a good oriental

---

* Obituary, Gentleman's Magazine, April, 1845.
† Dyce's Recollections of the Table Talk of Samuel Rogers, p. 194.

scholar. Having accumulated a large fortune, he returned to England late in life and died suddenly in London, in 1843, at the age of sixty-nine.

Maria, the only sister lived unmarried. She died in 1816 at her father's residence at Bath. Delicate in constitution, ill health did not obscure the good temper and amiability of her disposition. Her brother Sydney spoke of her as one whom he would have cultivated as a friend, if nature had not given her to him as a relative.

Robert Smith, the father, lived to an advanced age. His son Sydney, visited him, at his residence at Bishop's Lydiard in Somersetshire, in 1821. A letter to Jeffrey has this picture of the old man:—"I have travelled all across the country with my family, to see my father, now eighty-two years of age. I wish, at such an age, you, and all like you, may have as much enjoyment of life; more, you can hardly have at any age. My father is one of the very few people I have ever seen improved by age. He is become careless, indulgent, and anacreontic."

The mother of Sydney Smith died many years earlier at the beginning of the century. In feeble health, she devoted herself, in the absence of her husband, to the care of her children; wrote letters to her sons at Winchester which the school-boys "gathered round to hear read aloud;" lived to see Robert and Sydney married, and left to her descendants a pathetic memory of her grace, and virtues.

The boyhood of Sydney Smith was passed at school at Southampton and Winchester. At the celebrated foundation of William of Wykeham he acquired a good classical education and became the leader of the school, entitling himself by his position to a scholarship and afterward a fellowship at New College, Oxford. But though he was thus indebted to Winchester for an early and important move in life, his impression of the habits and conduct of the place fastened upon him a permanent dislike to that boasted institution of learning and manliness, the English public school

Years after, in an article in the Edinburgh Review, he wrote against the cruel and oppressive system of fagging pursued in such places; the false notion of hardening youth by exposing it to privations which were positive evils, under plea of inuring to hardships which there was little probability of meeting in after-life; the heartless exposure to premature vice and the almost inevitable neglect of instruction, with so great a number of pupils.* As captain of the school, Sydney was of course an adept in the composition of Latin verses, one of the chief benefits of which was the inexhaustible subject of ridicule it afforded to him through life. The brothers Sydney and Courtenay were such proficients at Winchester, that a round robin was sent up by the pupils to the effect that it was useless to contend for the prizes as the Smiths always gained them. Another anecdote places the young Sydney in a picturesque light. A visiter of distinction came to the school and found him reading Virgil under a tree while his schoolfellows

* Though learning and academic honours seem readily to have been acquired at these institutions by the members of the Smith family, their personal experience was by no means favourable. "Even in old age," says his daughter of her father Sydney, "I have heard him speak with horrour of the misery of the years he spent at Winchester. He suffered there many years of misery and positive starvation." Courtenay was compelled by ill usage to run away twice from the same school. At a later day Sydney's son Douglas became King's scholar at Westminster. When he was sent to the school in 1820 his father writes to a lady correspondent: "Douglas is gone to school; not with a light heart, for the first year of Westminster in College is severe — an intense system of tyranny, of which the English are very fond, and think it fits a boy for the world; but the world, bad as it is, has nothing half so bad." "The hardships and cruelties Douglas suffered as a junior boy from his master," his mother tells us, "were such as at one time very nearly to compel us to remove him from the school. He was taken home for a short period, to recover from his bruises and restore his eye. His first act, on becoming captain himself, was to endeavour to ameliorate the condition of the juniors, and to obtain additional comforts for them from the head master."

Rogers tells us in illustration of the system (Dyce's Table Talk) that "when Lord Holland was a school-boy, he was forced, as a fag, to toast bread with his fingers for the breakfast of another boy. Lord H.'s mother sent him a toasting-fork. His fagger broke it over his head, and still compelled him to prepare the toast in the old way. In consequence of this his fingers suffered so much that they always retained a withered appearance."

were at play. He took the book from the boy's hand, patted his head, uttered the words: "Clever boy! clever boy! that is the way to conquer the world," and clinched the encouraging aphorism with the gift of a shilling. The encomium and prophecy are said to have produced a strong impression on the youthful scholar.*

A brief interval was passed by Sydney between Winchester and Oxford. He was for six months in a boarding-school in France, at Mont Villiers in Normandy, where he acquired a familiar knowledge of the language, which he ever afterward retained, and saw something of the troubled scenes of the French Revolution. Plain Sydney, for obvious prudential reasons, became "Le Citoyen Smit", affiliated member of the Club of Jacobins of Mont Villiers. At New College, Oxford, his career, of which little has been told the public, was one of industry and its rewards. He was safe, in his constitutional temperance and sense of independence, from the usual temptations to dissipation and expense. He received his degree of Bachelor of Arts, Oct. 10, 1792, and that of Master of Arts exactly four years later. He secured his fellowship at the earliest moment, with its perquisite of a hundred pounds a year, out of which he managed to support himself and magnanimously pay a debt of thirty pounds which his brother Courtenay had contracted at Westminster school.

The world was now before Sydney for the choice of a profession. His father at one time meditated sending him in the track of his brothers to the East, in the mercantile line as supercargo to China; the youth himself naturally thought of carrying his powers of mind, well suited to the profession, to the bar; his father settled the matter by choosing for him the church. Sydney, who was a practical optimist, acquiesced and was installed in 1794 as a humble curate in the parish of Netheravon near Amesbury in the middle of Salisbury Plain. His parochial domain was limited to a few cottagers and farmers, relieved by the Sunday dinner with the parish squire, Mr. Hicks Beach, who fortunately apprehended

* Lady Holland's Memoir, p. 19.

the sagacity and education of his visiter, "took a fancy" to him, and at the close of a second year engaged him as teacher to his eldest son.* A course at the university of Weimar was determined upon; but the wars of the continent put an end to the plan: and, "in stress of politics," as Sydney Smith himself has related, "he put into Edinburgh." This was in 1797.

The incidents of Sydney Smith's domestic life with his pupil at Edinburgh are happily related in his correspondence with the family of Mr. Beach.† He took lodgings in an excellent quarter of the town and kept up a bachelor's establishment with his pupil Michael and a German courier, Mithoffer, the companion of the journey. All sorts of domestic difficulties were encountered. He conquered the susceptibility of his housemaid and kept her in his service, safe from the attacks of "seven sweethearts;" went to market himself till Mithoffer became a better "judge of meat;' failed lamentably in a joint attempt with cook and courier to "make a pie;" laid in beef in the salting tub and "looked into the family affairs like a fat old lady of forty." At the coming on of winter the female owner of the premises attempted to raise the rent. Sydney resisted the imposition and held his ground notwithstanding the landlady called him "a Levite, a scourge of human nature and an extortioner," and ordered him out "instantly, bag and baggage, without beat of drum or colours flying."

Judging from the candid reports sent home, which by no means exhibit the usual flattery of such relations, Sydney Smith was a

* Mr. Hicks Beach at one time represented Cirencester in Parliament. Cobbett, in his Rural Rides in the Counties of England, gives an account of a visit in 1826 to Netheravon. He speaks of the valley of the Avon in which the village is situated as of great beauty — and the population as having deteriorated. "There is a church, large enough to hold a thousand or two of people, and the whole parish contains only three hundred and fifty souls men, women, and children. This Netheravon was formerly a great lordship, and in the parish there were three considerable mansion-houses, besides the one near the church."

† The letters of Sydney Smith, chiefly addressed to Mrs. Beach appear in the later English editions of Lady Holland's Memoir.

faithful guardian. While he stimulated mental exertion and exacted personal respect he was, no doubt, a very agreeable one. His admirable art of conveying information, must have made instruction very much a pastime. The tuition was moreover relieved by summer excursions in the Highlands and Wales, and winter advances into the attractive circles of Edinburgh society.

A passage of the Highland experiences is characteristic in its double consciousness of sublimity and inconvenience. "He knows not the earth," Sydney writes, "who has only seen it swelling into the moderate elevation, or sinking to the gentle descent of southern hills and valleys. He has never trod on the margin of the fearful precipice, journeyed over the silent wilderness, and gazed at the torrent hiding itself in the profound glen. He has never viewed Nature but as she is associated with human industry; and is unacquainted with large tracts of the earth from which the care of man can hope for no return; which seem never to have been quickened with the principle of vegetation, or to have participated in the bounties of Him whose providence is over all. This we have seen in the Highlands; but we have mortified the body in gratifying the mind. We have been forced to associate oat-cakes and whiskey with rocks and waterfalls, and humble in a dirty room the conceptions we indulged in a romantic glen."

Edinburgh society was then on the verge of a new intellectual development. It was rich in honour and promise. Taking the year of Sydney Smith's arrival for a glance at its celebrities, we find Jeffrey, his future intimate and associate in friendship and letters, at the age of twenty-four, recently entered at the bar, fresh from his energetic, youthful studies, and the invigorating, mental exercises of the Speculative Society. Brougham, a young man, just entered at the Speculative, was laying the foundation of his great public career. Walter Scott, the mention of whose name gives a glow to the time, was twenty-six, an advocate—his head filled with as yet undeveloped studies of romantic history, which was all living reality in the heart of the young lover at the feet of the future Lady Scott. Francis Horner, one of the youngest members of the whig circle of the town, destined to become honourably distinguished in a brief, public career, was that year absent from his native place, polishing off in England the asperities of his native dialect. Sydney Smith, attracted to him by his personal worth and liberal politics, sought his acquaintance on his return, and formed a noble friendship interrupted only by death. John Allen who, not long after, was recommended by Sydney Smith to Lord Holland as his travelling-companion in Spain, whose historical studies and personal qualities secured for him a forty years' residence at Holland House, was a physician and reform politician, at the age of twenty-seven; highly distinguished for his Edinburgh Lectures on the Animal Economy.* Lord Webb Seymour, brother of the Duke of Somerset, attracted by the opportunities of study afforded by the University, came from Christ Church, Oxford, to Edinburgh about the same time. He was then at the age of twenty, a young man of singular worth of character, and distinguished by conscientious application to the mathematical and metaphysical sciences, which, had he possessed more vivacious powers of mind, would have doubtless produced some lasting literary monument for the world. Before he had completed the studies, which, indeed, would have been life long with one of his tastes and temper, he fell into ill health and died at Edinburgh,

* Allen, who frequently figures in the Sydney Smith Letters, was one of those useful students whose conversation is more productive to the world than their writings. He assisted Lord Holland in his historical speeches, and was a great authority at Holland House on matters of physical and moral science, politics and metaphysics. Lord Brougham, in his "British Statesmen," speaks of his "combination of general views with details of fact," with warm admiration. He published an article in the Edinburgh Review for June, 1816, on the Constitution of Parliament, which was highly spoken of by Mackintosh. He wrote the Life of Fox in the Encyclopædia Britannica; "An Inquiry into the Rise and Growth of the Royal Prerogative in England," "A Vindication of the Independence of Scotland," and a reply to Lingard, whose history he had reviewed in the Edinburgh. He was made Master of Dulwich College He died in 1843, at the age of seventy three leaving property of about seven or eight thousand pounds.

which he had continued to make his home, at the age of forty-two, in 1819. He was the intimate friend of Horner, and an important member of the youthful society from England which had then gathered in the Scottish metropolis.* Dugald Stewart was at that time in the full enjoyment of his great reputation, at once popular and profound, in his lectures and books, at the University and with the public. Thomas Brown, his successor in the chair of Moral Philosophy, uniting much of the poetical with more of the philosophic mind, was a keen, sensitive youth of twenty, already becoming distinguished by his scientific attainments. Smith afterward recalled the Sunday dinner in Edinburgh with this intimate friend; and added the eulogy: "He was a Lake-poet, a profound metaphysician, and one of the most virtuous men that ever lived."† John Murray, afterward Lord Murray, eminent in political and judicial life, was one of the early esteemed companions of Sydney Smith; a friendship which lasted to the end. John Thomson, subsequently known to the world as one of the most learned physicians of his day, was also on Sydney's select list of intimates. Another early acquaintance was Charles Hope, afterward Lord President of the Court of Session, whose judicial eloquence and weight of character are celebrated in the eulogy of Lockhart.‡ The sweet, Scottish poet, and zealous oriental scholar, John Leyden, remarkable in the annals of self-educated men, had come up to Edinburgh from the wilds of Roxburghshire, was detected by Scott as a poet, appreciated by Smith, and not long after liberally aided out of the narrow income of the latter, with a handsome contribution of forty pounds to his outfit for India. There he perished, a devotee to science, leaving a few verses, still admired, as the Ode to an Indian Gold Coin, the memorial of his toil and sen-

* Biographical notice of Lord Webb Seymour, by Henry Hallam, in the Appendix to vol. i. of the Memoirs of Horner; a carefully-elaborated composition which Lord Cockburn, in his Life of Jeffrey, characterizes as "one of the best portraits of a character in writing that exists."
† Letter to Sir George Philips, Feb. 28, 1836.
‡ Peter's Letters to his Kinsfolk, ii. 102

sibility. It wa. at this season, too, that Thomas Campbell, having established himself in Edinburgh the year of Smith's arrival, published, in 1799, the first edition of his Pleasures of Hope, a literary advent of mark in the annals of that metropolis. We do not hear of any particular intimacy at the time between Campbell and Smith, but they must have been well acquainted. In a list of the Friday Club which grew up at Edinburgh, about the time Smith left for London, both his name and Campbell's are among the members.* When Campbell went to London, Sydney Smith did him some "kind offices," and in later life they met on pleasant terms as brother wits.† Amongst the older members of the society, Playfair, Professor of Mathematics at the University was in the maturity of his powers, ripening at the close of middle life. Of an elder generation, Dr. Hugh Blair, an octogenarian, was approaching the term of his prolonged career. Henry Mackenzie, whose extended existence brought down almost to the present day the literary association of a century ago, was then warm in the es-

---

* Cockburn's Life of Jeffrey, i. 119.

† Campbell, in a letter, Jan. 1808 (Beattie's Life and Letters of Campbell, i. 485), says: "Off I marched [from his first dinner at Holland House] with Sydney Smith; Sydney is an excellent subject—but he too has done me some *kind offices*, and that is enough to produce a most green-eyed jealousy in my noble and heroic disposition! I was determined I should make as many good jokes, and speak as much as himself; and so I did, for though I was dressed at the dinner-table much like a barber's clerk, I arrogated greatly, talked quizzically, metaphorically; Sydney said a few *good* things, I said many! Saul slew his thousands, David his tens of thousands." Thirty years later, when Campbell was sixty, there is an entry in his Diary of a street rencontre with Sydney Smith, a passing glimpse of these venerable wits:—"June 16, 1838—I met Sydney Smith the other day. 'Campbell,' he said, 'we met last, two years ago, in Fleet street; and, as you may remember, we got into a violent argument, but were separated by a wagon, and have never met since. Let us have out that argument now. Do you recollect the subject?' 'No,' I said; 'I have clean forgotten the subject; but I remember that I was in the *right* and that you were violent and in the wrong!' I had scarcely uttered these words when a violent shower came on. I took refuge in a shop, and he in a cab. He parted with a proud threat that he would renew the argument the next time we met. 'Very well,' I said; 'but you sha'r't get off again, either in a wagon or a cab.'"

teem of a new generation of the admirers of the Man of Feeling and Julia de Roubigné. He was a genial, bustling man, who put his melancholy in his books and gave his mirth to his friends.

Such was the society into which the young Sydney Smith was introduced—a society abounding in intellectual activity, living on its acquired honours in British literature, teeming with elements of further progress. It was remarked that, in after-life, while the genial humourist indulged his wit freely—after the example of Dr. Samuel Johnson—at the expense of Scottish characteristics of manners and conversation, and the peculiarities of some of his intimates, he looked back upon this time with respect and affection. It is at least a proof that he had been well received. His poverty, united with his susceptible nature, might readily have made him sensitive in the matter.

He passed five years at Edinburgh, at the end of the second making a short visit to London, to marry a lady to whom he had been engaged some time before, Miss Catherine Amelia Pybus, an intimate friend of his sister. The connection was a most happy one, enduring through nearly half a century, supported by many virtues and felicities. It may be mentioned, for the consolation of those who enter upon married life under similar difficulties, that this union, though approved of by the lady's mother, was violently opposed by her brother, Mr. Charles Pybus, a member of Parliament, and commissioner of the treasury in Pitt's administration.* A poor curate, the tutor to the son of a

---

* Charles Small Pybus acquired some literary notoriety at the beginning of the century, from the publication (in 1800) of a peculiarly ill-timed poem, entitled "The Sovereign; Addressed to his Imperial Majesty Paul, Emperor of all the Russias." It was a eulogy of the Emperor as a member of the coalition against France; but, unhappily, at the time of publication, Paul broke off from the alliance, and appeared in all his hideous insanity to the English public. Mr. Pybus' mode of publication, too, was unfortunate. He issued his flat heroic couplets in a folio of sixty pages, with his own portrait prefixed—at the price of a guinea. The Gentleman's Magazine (September, 1800) gave it a brief and significant notice: "Unfortunate experience has shown, that the subject of this poem was unhappily chosen. What

country squire, was probably no very lofty object in the considerations of a family alliance. Mr. Pybus did not see the potentialities of the future Edinburgh Reviewer, popular London preacher, caustic political essayist, brilliant wit of Holland House, canon of St. Paul's, who might have had a bishopric, but who could not fail, as an author, of being read and admired wherever the English literature of the nineteenth century was known. It is not to the credit of Mr. Pybus, once Lord of the Admiralty, that he failed to set greater store by what was more immediately within his view, the generous, warm-hearted soul of his brother-in-law.

His wife brought Sydney a small property, which he honourably can we say more on this delicate subject?" The "Sovereign" was squibbed in a travesty, "The Mince Pye, an Heroic Epistle," in 4to. (Monthly Review xxxiv., 421). Porson reviewed "The Sovereign" in a pungent critique in the Monthly Review (xxxiii., 378, December, 1800): "The happy alliteration resulting from the title, 'A Poem to Paul by the Poet Pybus,' reminds us of a Latin work, entitled, 'Pugna porcorum per Publium Porcium, poetam.' Though this work is addressed to the Emperor Paul, it is, with inimitable dexterity, dedicated to our own king." On first looking into this magnificent production, Porson (Kidd's Tracts and Miscellaneous Criticisms, quoted in Barker's Lit. Anecdotes) is said to have sung:—

  And when the pie was opened,
  The birds began to sing,
  And is not this a dainty dish
  To set before the KING?"

Pybus has also a share in an epigram by Porson, of which three more or less correct versions are given, in Notes and Queries (xi., 263, xii., 53). The best is that in Dyce's Porsoniana:—

  Poetis nos lætamur tribus,
  Pye, *Petro* Pindar, *parvo* Pybus:
  Si ulterius ire pergis,
  Adde his Sir James Bland Burges.

Pye was the well-known laureate before Southey. His Alfred; an Epic Poem, in six books, is now almost forgotten. Burges wrote The Birth and Triumph of Love, and Richard the First, an Epic, the tenth book of which, Byron asserted he had read at Malta, in the lining of a trunk. "If any one doubts it," he added, "I shall buy a portmanteau to quote from." Burges had a share in another Epic, The Exodiad, written in association with the dramatist Cumberland.

Pybus died unmarried, in 1810, at the age of forty-four.

secured to her and his children; his own contribution to the family settlement being six small, well-worn silver teaspoons. Throwing these into his wife's lap, he exclaimed, in his riotous fun, "There, Kate, you lucky girl, I give you all my fortune!" He had, however, his profession to look to; while his friend, Mr. Beach, of whose second son he had now charge, made him a liberal payment of seven hundred and fifty pounds.* That his talents in the pulpit at this period gave him strong claims to attention is witnessed by a passage in the journal of Francis Horner, who tells us, that after passing the forenoon of April 26, 1801, with Lord Webb, in a five-hours' study of Bacon's *De Augmentis Scientiarum*, the two friends "went afterward to hear Sydney Smith preach, who delivered a most admirable sermon on the true religion of practical justice and benevolence, as distinguished from ceremonial devotion, from fanaticism, and from theology. It was forcibly distinguished by that liberality of sentiment, and that boldness of eloquence, which do so much credit to Smith's talents. I may add, that the popularity of his style does equal honour to the audience to whom it is addressed, or, at least, to that diffusion of liberal opinions and knowledge, to which the members of so mixed an audience are indebted for the fashion and temper of their sentiments."†

The great event of Sydney Smith's northern residence was the commencement of the Edinburgh Review. He has given so graphic an account of this, in his peculiar manner, in the Preface to his collected writings, that his biographers will generally be compelled to repeat the passage:—

"The principles of the French Revolution were then fully afloat, and it is impossible to conceive a more violent and agitated state of society. Among the first persons with whom I became acquainted were, Lord Jeffrey, Lord Murray (late Lord-Advocate for Scotland), and Lord Brougham; all of them maintaining

---

* Lady Holland's Memoir, fourth Eng. ed. i., 52.
† Memoir and Correspondence of Francis Horner i., 157.

opinions upon political subjects a little too liberal for the dynasty of Dundas, then exercising supreme power over the northern division of the island.

"One day we happened to meet in the eighth or ninth story or flat in Buccleugh-place, the elevated residence of the then Mr. Jeffrey. I proposed that we should set up a Review; this was acceded to with acclamation. I was appointed editor, and remained long enough in Edinburgh to edit the first number of the Edinburgh Review. The motto I proposed for the review was,

"'*Tenui musam meditamur avena.*'
"'We cultivate literature upon a little oatmeal.'

But this was too near the truth to be admitted, and so we took our present grave motto from *Publius Syrus*, of whom none of us had, I am sure, ever read a single line; and so began what has since turned out to be a very important and able journal."*

Jeffrey wrote a more circumstantial account of the origin of the Review, in a letter to Mr. Robert Chambers, which corroborates this statement. It was not, however, quite the extempore undertaking which might be inferred from the language in which Sydney Smith lightly speaks of his apparently off-hand proposition. There were "serious consultations" about it, we are told by Jeffrey, which "were attended by Sydney Smith, Horner, Dr. Thomas Brown, Lord Murray, and some of them, also by Lord Webb Seymour, Dr. John Thomson and Thomas Thomson." Smith and Jeffrey were the leaders of the set; they had the best capacity for, and took the largest share in, the enterprise, and it was probably due to the superior hopefulness of the former, united with his constitutional energy, that the work was undertaken at all. Jeffrey whose habit of mind was to be, as his biographer, Lord Cockburn, has given the description, "generally in a state of lively, argumentative despair," croaked dismally over the affair, before the

* Preface to Works of the Rev. Sydney Smith. Longmans, 1839.

first number was out of the press-room.* Sydney, through all difficulties, seems to have held to the opinion, that if conducted fairly and with discretion the success was certain.

When Jeffrey collected his Contributions to the Review for publication in 1844, he dedicated them to Sydney Smith, as "the original projector of the Edinburgh Review." To Jeffrey who brought considerable experience as a trained reviewer to the work, belongs the honour of having written the first article—a discussion of the share borne by the French philosophers in producing their great national Revolution—thus striking at once into the main question of the troubled times. For thirty-eight years he continued to contribute to it compositions, distinguished at once by subtlety and enthusiasm; opening to the public stores of acute, philosophical thinking; and widening this influence by disclosing novel methods of criticism and historical description, for a new school of writers. He was the prince of modern reviewers; full, ready, ingenious, expert, rational and eloquent. Readers of the present day owe him a monument for originating and developing

---

* There is a letter from Jeffrey to Horner, giving a lively account of the various dispositions of the parties to the undertaking, dated April, 1802; the Review appearing the following November: "We are in a miserable state of backwardness, you must know, and have been giving some symptoms of despondency. . . . . Something is done, however, and a good deal, I hope, is doing. Smith has gone through more than half his task. So has Hamilton (Alexander, afterward Professor of Sanscrit at Hayleybury). Allen has made some progress: and Murray (John A., afterward Lord Murray) and myself, I believe, have studied our parts, and tuned our instruments; and are almost ready to begin. On the other hand Thomson (Dr. John) is sick. Brown (Dr. Thomas, the metaphysician) has engaged for nothing but Miss Baillie's Plays; and Timothy (Thomas Thomson, the lawyer) has engaged for nothing, but professed it to be his opinion, the other day, that he would never put pen to paper in our cause. Brougham must have a sentence to himself; and I am afraid you will not think it a pleasant one. You remember how cheerfully he approved of our plan at first, and agreed to give us an article or two without hesitation. Three or four days ago I proposed two or three books that I thought would suit him; he answered, with perfect good humour, that he had changed his view of our plan a little, and rather thought, now, that he should decline to have any connection with it."—*Horner's Correspondence*, i. 186.

that intellectual luxury, the speculative, appreciative, picturesque Article — a profound and entertaining compound of metaphysics, biography, history and criticism of the highest gusto.

The momentum of Jeffrey increased as he proceeded, his treatment growing more easy, varied and commanding; Smith struck his peculiar vein at the outset. The latter wrote seven articles for the first number of the Edinburgh. His first paragraph was a famous description of Dr. Parr's wig, humourously turned into a quiz on the arrangement of his text and notes. A few pages further on he despatched, in two or three sentences of witty drollery, an Anniversary Sermon before the Humane Society, by a Doctor in Divinity. There are also some grave words of counsel administered to Dr. Rennell, Master of the Temple, for his aptness "to put on the appearance of a holy bully, an evangelical swaggerer, as if he could carry his point against infidelity by big words and strong abuse, and kick and cuff men into Christians." A Mr. John Bowles is also pungently rebuked for his vulgar style of writing on the affairs of France. In fine, there is proof in this very first number, of that moral courage, and of most of those brilliant powers of thought and expression which, for nearly half a century after, were the delight of Smith's intimates among the brightest and most cultivated men of England. His style appears to have been fully formed: nor is it any marvel, as, with the favourable natural disposition which he inherited, he had been a precocious youth in his studies; had been well disciplined at Oxford; since sluggish fortune had afforded him opportunity for meditation on the silent desert of Salisbury Plain, and the habit of teaching had brought all his faculties promptly to the surface; and he had, moreover, enjoyed, for several years, the sharp contests of the Edinburgh wits, to give the keenest edge to his understanding. In October, 1802, the date of the first publication of the Edinburgh Review, he was in his thirty-second year, a mature age for his work. His contributions to the first three volumes were numerous; they were then intermitted, for a time, till they were rigorously resumed in 1807, and continued, with little interruption, for the next twenty years. There were occasional conflicts between Sydney's humourous style and the editor's more sober judgment; but, happily for the Review, and for posterity, the wit had pretty much his own way, in spite of the snubbing. "I think," Smith writes, in 1807, to Jeffrey, "you have spoilt many of my jokes;" and we find the humourist, even after he had established a reputation, restricted "on the subject of raillery."*

The prospects of the Review did not, at the outset, promise a fortune to the contributors and projectors. Indeed, at the commencement, the literary services rendered to it were voluntary and unpaid. It was only after some consideration, and the abandonment of false notions on the subject, that it was found essential to establish the work on a sound mercantile basis, with a paid editor, and paid writers. In this period of indecision, with the purse held aloof, and with the fortunes of the Review yet to make, Sydney Smith, whose profitable pupils had now outgrown his services, taking counsel from his wife, resolved to carry his talents to London, as the best mart of intellect and literature, doubtless looking for a better field for his pulpit oratory, with better chances of church promotion than the scant episcopacy of Scotland afforded. He had preached frequently in the Edinburgh chapel, the assistant of its regular occupant, Bishop Sandford, with success, and had published a first collection of "Six Sermons,"† with a striking preface, commenting freely on the not uncommon lethargy, and other defects of the pulpit. He took with him, from Edinburgh, in addition, a respectable knowledge of medicine, acquired by attending the hospitals—sufficient, at least, to enrich his vocabulary with anatomical and other professional terms, occasionally employed in his writings with felicity; and practical enough to alleviate the imaginary or real ailments of his country parishioners. He became quite fond of the practice in an amateur

* Letter to Jeffrey, March 17, 1822.
† Six Sermons. Edinburgh, 1800. 12mo.

way, stirring up wit with his prescriptions, and playing a merry jingle with his pestle.

Arriving in London, he at first occupied a small house in Doughty street, Russell Square, which he chose, we are told, for the legal society of the neighbourhood. His habits of mind qualified him to enjoy the best points of the profession. Romilly and Mackintosh were among his acquaintances at the time, and he rapidly found his way into the brilliant circle of wits and diners-out who centred about Holland House. The family alliance of his brother facilitated this social connection, which common political views and congenial powers of mind firmly cemented. Among the wits and statesmen who have gathered in those historical halls, sacred to literature and freedom, in the group of Lansdowne, Russell, Horner, Mackintosh, Allen, Sharp, Rogers, Moore, Luttrell, Dudley, and all that gifted race of beings, the figure of Sydney Smith will always be remembered.

But the brilliant young divine had something else to attend to, at this time, besides forming distinguished friendships. A narrow purse had to be expanded and filled, to meet the wants of an increasing family, which now included a son and daughter; Saba (his recent biographer, Lady Holland), born at Edinburgh, and Douglas. He applied himself to his profession, preaching several occasional sermons, one of which, before a company of volunteers when a French invasion seemed imminent, attracted some attention from the public. He was soon recommended by the friendship of Sir Thomas Bernard,* to an evening preachership at the

---

* This eminent philanthropist was the son of Sir Francis Bernard, the Colonial Governor of New Jersey and Massachusetts. He was an Alumnus of Harvard College, of the class of 1767. Returning to England, he was called to the bar in 1780, by the Society of the Middle Temple. Having become wealthy by marriage, and the practice of his profession, he devoted himself to measures of philanthropy. In 1795, he was elected treasurer of the Foundling Hospital, and adopted Count Rumford's plans for economy in food and fuel. He projected the Society for Bettering the Condition of the Poor, and was one of the originators, in 1799, of the Royal Institution, intended for the "improvement of the means of industry and domestic comfort

Foundling Hospital, worth fifty pounds a year, which was an important addition to his limited income. An effort made by himself to secure another position was less successful. A friend who was the owner of a chapel, at that time occupied by a congregation of Swedenborgians, offered the lease of the building to Sydney Smith. To secure the privilege of preaching in it, it was necessary to obtain the consent of the rector of the Parish. The letters addressed him on the occasion by Smith, afford the clearest proof of the necessity and poverty to which he was at this time reduced. His pride stooped to a plea for the admissibility of his talents and virtues to such a post, while he ingeniously complimented the rector, and warded off the objection to a divided interest, by reminding him that the mere surplus of his over-crowded church would fill the few seats of the chapel, which would, moreover, thus be rescued from what both considered the vulgar and injurious doctrines of the New Jerusalemites. The rector saw in the proposal violation of church precedents, danger to the parochial establishment, and may have been naturally disinclined to admit a rival near his throne. He refused the application. Sydney, who thought it a grievance that any ranter might preach, as a matter of course, where a well-educated clergyman, with the noblest intention, could not gain admission, plied him with pleas and arguments; but without avail. The rector was determined to protect his parochial interests; and the more admirably the applicant argued, the more danger was probably seen in the request. Annoyed by the correspondence, the dignitary took refuge in an affectation of Christian submission to the logic of his opponent. Considering the position of the parties, the doctor in power and the curate in

among the poor," as well as "the advancement of taste and science." Care of the chimney sweepers, a Free Chapel in the neighbourhood of the Seven Dials, Hospitals, the British Institution for the Fine Arts, the Alfred Club, were among his spirited and benevolent projects and labours. Besides his Philanthropic Reports, he wrote a little volume, Spurinna; or, the Comforts of Old Age, with Biographical Illustrations. He died in 1818, at the age of sixty-eight. A memoir of Bernard, written by his nephew, the Rev. James Baker, was published the next year.

poverty, it is but a pitiable illustration of the "pride which apes humility," which is presented by a sentence of his closing letter. "I hope never to be offended, sir," he writes, "at the freedom of any who are so kind as to teach me to know myself; and the inconsistency of my letter to you, which you are so good as to point out, is, alas! an addition to the many inconsistencies of which, I fear, I have been too often guilty through life."

In an article in the Edinburgh Review, Sydney Smith subsequently argued the general question of the allowance of free competition of preachers within the parishes, with an express allusion to his own case. He saw, in the deprivation, a great loss of peculiar talents and efficiency to church interests, and admitted, as well, the improbability of gaining his point. "We hope nobody," he writes, "will rate our sagacity so very low, as to imagine we have much hope that any measure of the kind will ever be adopted. All establishments die of dignity. They are too proud to think themselves ill, and to take a little physic."*

Besides the poorly-paid duty at the Foundling Hospital, a favourite resort of the Londoners, for its excellent music, and the neat display of its charities, Sydney Smith also secured a morning preachership at Berkeley Chapel, where his genius and emphasis soon succeeded in covering empty benches with a flock of intelligent hearers. He afterward alternated this service with a similar duty at Fitzroy Chapel, with equal acceptability to the public. The character of these pulpit discourses, may be judged of by the "Two Volumes of Sermons" which he published under that title, at the close of this, his first London period, in 1809. They are terse in expression, marked generally by strength, propriety and dignity. There is underneath, rather than lying on the surface, a vein of genuine feeling. The occasional discourses for public charities are manly, vigorous appeals; full of sympathy for human infirmity, and confident reliance on Christian duty. Enforced by the preacher's full sonorous tones, their popular effect may

* Article on Toleration. Ed. Rev., Feb., 1811.

readily be accounted for. They have, what may be remarked attending all superior minds, an air, a voice of authority.

Though setting out with the zeal of a reformer in the pulpit, Sydney Smith really attempted little innovation upon its habitual practice His published sermons have nothing special to distinguish them from many others of their class. He probably found, on experiment, that there was little room for originality in compositions of necessity circumscribed by various limitations; and had the good sense to recognise the boundary. In the Church of England, the admirable liturgy leaves little to be asked of the sermon. Sydney Smith was content that the Church should be her own expounder in matters of doctrine; and directed his attention to the practical religious obligations of life. His sermons, subsequently preached at St. Paul's, and to his country congregations, of which a volume was published after his death,* are grave and earnest, instinct with the solemnities of life and death.

* Sermons Preached at St. Paul's Cathedral, the Foundling Hospital, and several churches in London; together with others addressed to a country congregation, by the late Rev. Sydney Smith, Canon Residentiary of St. Paul's Cathedral. London, 1846. Two of the sermons in this collection, "On the Excellence of the Christian Gospel," and "On the Necessity of Prayer," were freely borrowed from Dr. Barrow. The usage of the English pulpit would seem to allow some liberty in this particular. Sydney Smith himself tells us, in one of his letters (No. 545 in the collection) that he preached Dr. Channing's sermon on war in St. Paul's Cathedral: "I thought I could not write anything half so good, so I preached Channing." Channing's direct, manly self-reliance pleased him, the pith of his style, and his separation of great moral themes from disabling exceptions. These qualities are all to be observed as belonging to Sydney Smith himself.

The Christian Observer for June, 1846, makes a grave representation of Sydney Smith's obligation to Barrow. The publication, it should be remembered, was not an act of Smith but of his executors. A similar negligence occurred in the posthumous publication of the sermons of the American Bishop Ravenscroft, one of the most esteemed divines of the Protestant Episcopal Church. Sydney Smith, but little indebted to the books of others for the honours of his writings, cannot be supposed to have practised any wilful deception to heighten his reputation. Writing of the imputation of receiving attention for articles in the Edinburgh Review not from his pen, he says: "I should have considered myself the lowest of created beings to have disguised myself in another man's wit and sense, and to have received

If the world was indebted to the residence of Sydney Smith at Edinburgh for the establishment of the Review, and the series of brilliant articles with which he followed up its first successes, London was also immediately a gainer by the courses of lectures on Moral Philosophy, which he delivered during three successive seasons, upon his arrival in the great metropolis. These popular discourses, as well on abstract as familiar topics, were doubtless suggested by his attendance upon the thoughtful and stimulating lectures of Dugald Stewart, his intimacy with the Scottish ratiocinators generally, and with the original and inquiring Thomas Brown. But if he was under obligations to these men for the choice of subject, and a certain speculative habit in the technical portions of his course, there was a wide field lying all around these intellectual barriers which he made entirely his own. This was in what may be called the practical moralities of his text —the quick, genial, kindly introspection with which he penetrated to the heart of his subject, and brought to the world noble and charitable thoughts, full of liberality of opinion, zeal for virtue and human sympathy with his kind. The term moral philosophy truly characterizes them; for their subtle niceties of the intellect, their keen distinctions, and rapid play of wit, are subordinate to their healthy sentiment, and a certain ardent perception of the beautiful.

There were twenty-seven lectures, in all, before the Royal Institution. Sydney Smith was led to undertake them by the proposals and encouragement of his friend Sir Thomas Bernard, who

a reward to which I was not entitled." After this we may conclude that, in preaching the sermons of Barrow or Channing, he was doing nothing considered out of the way or dishonourable in the English Church. In this respect he would appear to have followed the practice of the chaplain so judiciously chosen by Sir Roger de Coverley, who, upon being asked of a Saturday night, who preached on the morrow, replied the Bishop of St. Asaph in the morning, and Dr. South in the afternoon. Another important qualification insisted upon by the good knight was possessed by the Reverend Sydney in perfection. He had "a good aspect and a clear voice." (Spectator, No. 106.

had been associated a few years before with the American Count Rumford, in the foundation of the society. The success was immediate. An audience assembled, composed of the most intelligent society of the metropolis, large in numbers for a popular lecturer in London even at the present day, numbering six to eight hundred persons. This, though far below that of the company on any distinguished occasion of the kind in New York or Boston, of late years, was held to be an immense achievement. Ladies and philosophers were alike entrapped into admiration. A long time after, the lecturer, who was accustomed to speak lightly of the performance as a matter of literature, remembered with pleasure the brilliant result. Toward the close of his life he was applied to by Dr. Whewell for some information on the subject discussed, when he replied, "My lectures are gone to the dogs and are utterly forgotten. I knew nothing of moral philosophy, but I was thoroughly aware that I wanted two hundred pounds to furnish my house. The success, however, was prodigious; all Albemarle street blocked up with carriages, and such an uproar as I never remember to have been excited by any other literary imposture."* His friend Horner, who was in London, writes to Lady Mackintosh, at Bombay, that there were but two topics in London that winter, the young Roscius and the lectures of "the Right Reverend, our Bishop of Mickleham," which, as we learn from Lady Holland's Memoir was a familiar title given to Sydney Smith, from the seat of Conversation Sharp's cottage in Surrey, where the friendly circle frequently met.† It was something, in the popular way, to en-

* Letter to Dr. Whewell, April 8, 1843. Memoirs, ii. 456.
† Richard Sharp was distinguished in the conversational circles of the metropolis. Hence his sobriquet. His forte lay in metaphysics. There is an anecdote of Rogers having proposed to him some question of this kind, when he somewhat discourteously replied, " There are only two men in England [probably Mackintosh and Bobus Smith] with whom I ever talk on metaphysics." (Dyce's Table-Talk of Rogers.) Sharp was a careful, refined writer. His single volume, "Letters and Essays in Prose and Verse," is the book of a scholar — thoughtful and polished. He was from 1806 till 1820 in Parliament. He died in 1835, at the age of seventy-six, leaving a

joy a fashionable mania at the same time with Master Betty who reaped that season, from his first London engagements, no less than eight thousand pounds.* The literary journal which gives us an account of the latter with a portrait of the triumphant prodigy, has not a word of the lecturer at the Royal Institution. We remember how, not many years since, disappointment and chagrin at the success of Tom Thumb ended the career of the artist Haydon. Sydney Smith was made of other stuff. Had his fortune been different, had Roscius carried away his audience, the lecturer would have consoled himself with his own philosophy, laughed at the folly of the town, and kept his head on his shoulders for a more lucky time.

Sydney Smith, following the definition of Moral Philosophy in use in the Scottish Universities where he had found it comprehending mental philosophy as well, ran over the history of ancient and modern theories, discussed the faculties of the mind, laws of conception, the memory, imagination, judgment; the theories of the beautiful and the sublime; the escaping essences of wit and humour; the qualities and methods of the more direct moral affections; the practical conduct of the understanding, and the everyday virtues of life. "Every week," he writes, in the letter to Dr. Whewell, which we have cited, "I had a new theory about conception and perception; and supported by a natural manner, a torrent of words, and an impudence scarcely credible in this prudent age. Still, in justice to myself, I must say there were some good things in them. But good and bad are all gone." He did not publish them at the time or afterward. Resorting to them as a quarry, he drew forth some passages on education for his arti-

---

fortune of a quarter of a million sterling, which he acquired in business, as a wholesale hatter. There is a pleasing anecdote of Grattan in connection with Sharp's seat at Mickleham. In the old age of the Irish statesman, Horner took him down there on a visit, in the spring, "on purpose to hear the nightingales, for he loves music like an Italian, and the country like a true-born Englishman." (Horner Correspondence, May, 1816 ii. 355.)

* European Magazine, xlvii. 374.

cles in the Edinburgh Review, destroyed many of the remaining pages, and would have burnt the whole had not his wife interposed and saved the mutilated manuscripts for posthumous publication. Enough fortunately survived to fill an octavo of four hundred pages, which was published in London, in 1850.* Though incomplete as a view of mental science, it is not without considerable merit on that score. It is a mine of pleasantries and subtleties, of sound thinking in eloquent terms, of description and sentiment, of human nature and natural history, of quips and cranks, familiarities and profundities, theories of morality, equally below the clouds and above the earth. The style was well adapted to the purposes of the popular lecturer with whom it is a necessity to mix entertainment with instruction; though there are few who can equal Sydney Smith in a laughing course of morals and metaphysics.†

The house, situated in Orchard street, *was* furnished with the proceeds, and Sydney Smith continued to occupy it during his early

* Elementary Sketches of Moral Philosophy, delivered at the Royal Institution, in the years 1804, 1805, and 1806, by the late Rev. Sydney Smith, M.A. London: Longmans, 1850, 8vo. pp. 424.

† Henry Rogers, the metaphysician, author of the essay on "Reason and Faith," in an article in the Edinburgh Review says of the Lectures:—"Inexhaustible vivacity and variety of illustration, one would, of course, expect from such a mind; but this is far from being all. The sound judgment and discrimination with which he often treats very difficult topics — the equilibrium of mind which he maintains when discussing those on which his own idiosyncracy might be supposed to have led him astray — of which an instance is seen in his temperate estimate of the value of wit and humour — the union of independence and modesty with which he canvasses the opinions of those from whom he differs — the comprehensiveness of many of his speculations and the ingenuity of others — the masterly ease and perspicuity with which even abstruse thoughts are expressed, and the frequently original, and sometimes profound remarks on human nature, to which he gives utterance — remarks hardly to be expected from *any* young metaphysician, and least of all from one of so lively and mercurial a temperament — all render these lectures very profitable as well as very pleasant reading; and show conclusively that the author might, if he had pleased, have acquired no mean reputation as an expositor of the very arduous branch of science to which they relate." (Ed. Rev April, 1850.)

residence in London. The sketchers of his biography have dwelt with pleasure upon his mode of living at this time. With an increasing family, his means were narrow and required the practice of rigid economy. Still he supported his family with honour, and enjoyed, in their essentials, the delights of English hospitality. Costly entertainments he could not, and, what was more to the purpose of virtuous independence, would not give; but he encouraged a weekly meeting of friends at his house by the entertainment of a frugal supper, and when such men as Horner, Mackintosh, Romilly, Luttrell, Lord Holland, and others of that stamp, came, each guest, as Goldsmith says in the Retaliation, brought the best dish in himself. We are not to suppose, however, that the company ever went away hungry or thirsty. We find him, too, member of a weekly dining "King of Clubs," where the intellect justified the name. There never was a time in his life, apparently, when the social powers of Smith were not in requisition. He was eminently what Dr. Johnson said Sir John Hawkins was not, *a clubable man*. In after-life, in London, he became a member of Johnson's own famous Literary Club. Pity that no Boswell bore him company in these resorts!*

When, in those early London days, the host made his way on foot to the dinner parties of the wealthy, he neutralized the astonishment of the lackeys in the hall, as he released his grimed overshoes, by his humourous remarks on the occasion. Far preferable was this cheerful encounter with the world, this adroit turning of its conventionalities, this healthy share in its activity, to the

* The King of Clubs was founded about the end of the last century by a party at Sir James Mackintosh's house consisting of himself and Mr. Rogers, Mr. Sharp, Mr. Robert Smith (who gave the name to the club) Mr. Scarlett and Mr. John Allen. To these original members were afterward added the names of many of the most distinguished men of the time, amongst others, Lords Lansdowne, Holland, Brougham, Cooper, King and Selkirk; Messrs. Porson, Romilly, Payne Knight, Horner, Bryan Edwards, Sydney Smith, Dumont, Jeffrey, Smithson, Tennant, Whishaw, Alexander Baring, Luttrell, Blake, Hallam, Ricardo, Hoppner. Mr. Windham was to be balloted for on the Saturday succeeding his lamented death. The King of Clubs came to a sudden dissolution in the year 1824.—*Life of Sir James Mackintosh*, i. 137.

too frequent morosity which repines at the unequal distribution of fortune, and eats its heart (a much inferior banquet to a good dinner) in solitude. Sydney Smith, by virtue of his clerical profession, the family connection with Lord Holland, his talents, had a just right of entry into the best London society. That he enjoyed its privileges without paying for them the price exacted from Moore and Theodore Hook is to be set down to the courage and good sense of his nature. That it was not without an effort he overcame the inequality of fortune between him and his wealthy friends, "in a country," where, as he insisted, "poverty is infamous,"* is witnessed by a remark he let fall in after-life, when he had tasted the emoluments of church preferment. "Moralists tell you of the evils of wealth and station, and the happiness of poverty. I have been very poor the greatest part of my life, and have borne it as well, I believe, as most people, but I can safely say that I have been happier every guinea I have gained. I well remember when Mrs. Sydney and I were young, in London, with no other equipage than my umbrella, when we went out to dinner in a hackney coach, when the rattling step was let down, and the proud, powdered red plushes grinned, and her gown was fringed with straw, how the iron entered into my soul."† There was but a short period in Sydney Smith's life, however, in which he is to be looked upon as a very poor man, though for a considerable period he remained a very ill-rewarded one. In the first years of his London residence, when he was making his way, he was assisted by a hundred pounds a year from his brother; but his chapel preaching and lecturing provided him the means of a limited independence. A turn in politics, on the death of Pitt, brought Smith's friends, the Whigs, into office in 1806, and the prompt efforts of Lord, or rather, Lady Holland, secured him a slice of church patronage from the Chancellor, Lord Erskine,‡ in the living of Foston-le-Clay.

* First letter to Archdeacon Singleton.   † Lady Holland's memoir, p. 200.

‡ Smith went to thank Erskine for the appointment. "Oh," said Erskine, "don't thank *me*, Mr. Smith. I gave you the living because Lady Holland

in Yorkshire, a parish embracing a small, rude farmer population, some eleven miles from York. It seems to have been a sinecure when it was presented, since at that time there had not been a resident clergyman for a hundred and fifty years, and Smith through the indulgence of his diocesan Archbishop Markham, and by virtue of his preachership at the Foundling, enjoyed the first year or two of his incumbency quietly in London, while a curate performed the duty for him at the north.

The year 1807 gave birth to the *Letters on the Subject of the Catholics, to my Brother Abraham, who lives in the Country, by Peter Plymley*. They were ten in number, and followed in quick succession, disturbing not a little the equanimity of the ministry of Canning and Perceval, by their sharp, pungent attacks, while strengthening the cause of liberal reform by their enormous popular success.* Though published anonymously, they who knew Sydney Smith knew Peter Plymley. No more caustic wit had been expended on politics since the productions of Swift. Peter Plymley's object was to rescue the claims of the Irish Catholics from the vast mass of prejudice, unsound political economy, and false reasoning which, as he justly thought, overlaid justice and judgment in the minds of well-disposed but bigoted and unthinking Englishmen. The vehicle chosen for the discussion, a series of expostulatory letters on the affairs of the day, addressed by a man of the world to a clergyman in the country, gave the author an opportunity to play off his knowledge of clerical habitudes, and the peculiar idiosyncracies of the Establishment. The main scope

---

insisted on my doing so: and if she had desired me to give it to the devil, *he* must have had it."—*Dyce's Table Talk of Rogers*.

* "The Government of that day," says Sydney Smith, in the preface to his writings, "took great pains to find out the author; all that they *could* find was, that they were brought to Mr. Budd, the publisher, by the Earl of Lauderdale. Somehow or another, it came to be conjectured that I was that author: I have always denied it; but, finding that I denied it in vain, I have thought it might be as well to include the Letters in this Collection: they had an immense circulation at the time, and I think above twenty thousand copies were sold."

of his arguments was expediency; the practical effect of continuing wrongs, which would throw the population of Ireland into the arms of the French; and, on the other hand, the practical effect of freedom, and free intercourse in repressing differences, the chief nutriment of which was oppression. Wit, irony, logic, the author's peculiar weapons of the *argumentum ad hominem*, and the *reductio ad absurdum*, are freely employed in illustration of these views. Though the letters have lost some of their interest since the local absurdities of the day which they refuted have been forgotten, they remain the completest exhibition of the author's powers, in his favourite method of conquering prejudice, and substituting perennial wit and wisdom for darkness and error. Lessons of universal interest in religious toleration may still be learnt by the world, from this partisan skirmish in behalf of a cause which has since been nobly established in England.

Smith further assisted the question in this year, by a sermon on Toleration, preached before the influential audience, chiefly of barristers, at the Temple church. It was, also, printed at the time, and is included in his collection of sermons of 1809. Following the outline of Paley, he defines in it the essentials of a Church establishment: "An order of men set apart for the ministerial office; a regular provision made for them; and a particular creed containing the articles of their faith." His maintenance of these points though they probably fell short of the views of the High-Church party, go beyond what would be asserted in America. Indeed, it would be a sorry fact in the world's history, if America had not fully disproved what he chose to anticipate of the fate of Christianity in this hemisphere: " Homely and coarse," he somewhat gratuitously interpolates in this discourse, " as these principles may appear, to many speculative men, they are the only ones by which the existence of any religion can be secured to the community; and we have now too much reason to believe that the system of greater latitude, attempted naturally enough in the new world, will end fatally for the Christian religion, and for good practical morality." Sydney Smith was a valiant man when he offended his friends and brother churchmen by his plea for the Catholics; but he himself here needs the mantle of indulgence cast by the poet over the "fears of the brave and follies of the wise." His main positions are, that the Roman Church is to be judged, not by its past history, but its present conduct; that the Established Church of England, with a proper respect for its powers and advantages, should be magnanimous to those who differ from it, should prove its superiority by charity, and maintain the lesson of his text from St. Paul, that "God is not the author of confusion, but of peace, in all the churches."

At the same time he enforced his views of the Catholic Question by an article in the Edinburgh Review,* in which he separated the historical causes of the disaffection of Ireland growing out of the political conquest, and those attributable to religious hostilities—assigning a slight proportional weight to the latter. To these views he held till the close of his life. Thirty-two years later he wrote, in reviving this article, in reference to agitations which survived Catholic emancipation: "It is now only difficult to tranquillize Ireland, before it was impossible. As to the danger from Catholic doctrines, I must leave such apprehensions to the respectable anility of these realms."† One of the latest and most vigorous of Sydney Smith's productions was devoted to this cause. Among his papers, after his death, was found an unfinished pamphlet, that "startling and matchless Fragment," as Jeffrey called it, which was published in 1845, with the title, *A Fragment on the Irish Roman Catholic Church*. None of his earlier writings surpass it in wit and felicity of illustration. Every sentence is a jest or an epigram worthy the fame of a Pascal or a Swift. It is an advocacy of the appropriation of the Irish tithes by the state, to the regular payment of the Roman Catholic clergy, as an effective cure of the prevalent wrangling and disaffection— the O'Connellism of the time. Upon that arch-agitator himself,

* July, 1807. † Works, 1st ed., i. 84.

he bestows some memorable counsel, not the less wisdom for the humour in which it is sheathed. He also recommends the establishment of diplomatic relations with the Roman Pontiff.*

To return from this continuous sketch of Sydney Smith's literary efforts in the cause of Catholic Emancipation, to the year 1808. By a new residence bill, clerical incumbents were compelled to build or restore and inhabit the parsonage houses, which, under the prevalent absenteeism, had very numerously gone to decay throughout England. The parochial establishment of Foston-le-Clay, though with capabilities of improved fortune to its new possessor, was one of the least inviting for a restoration or a residence. The parsonage, bounded by a foalyard and a churchyard, was simply a kitchen with a room above it, ready to tumble upon the occupant. Sydney Smith surveyed the premises, the shambling hovel and three hundred acres of glebe land without tithe, to be farmed by himself, and hesitated. To gain time for consideration, and to effect, if possible, an exchange, he secured from the archbishop, Dr. Vernon Harcourt, a respite of three years, during which he established himself at Heslington, a village in the immediate vicinity of York. The proceeds of his two volumes of sermons, and a loan from his brother Robert of about five hundred pounds, assisted his removal from London to the north in the summer of 1809.

Heslington mitigated the descent from London to Foston, or, in Smith's words, "the change from the aurelia to the grub state."† With the resources of York at his elbow, he lived in comparative retirement, visiting his parish, concocting plans of study, reading much, writing for the Edinburgh Review and familiarizing himself with the occupations of his farm land. In truth, though the society of

---

* Sydney Smith also prepared an account of English misrule in Ireland from the earliest date of English possession, which Lady Holland tells us, "formed so fearful a picture that he hesitated to give it to the world when done." It still exists in manuscript. Macaulay, who was consulted on its publication as a posthumous work, by Mrs. Sydney Smith, recommended its suppression. His letter is given in Lady Holland's Memoir.

† To Lady Holland, June 24. 1809.

London was the natural home of his talents, he liked the practical demands of his new life, the management of crops and cattle and peasants, the contrivances of building and the regulation of his parish. The loss of London society to an already established diner-out, who watched with eagerness the political and social movements of the day, was a privation; but these things had brought with them something of satiety, and they were relinquished cheerfully, as he expresses it in a letter to Jeffrey, "for more quiet, more leisure, less expense and more space for his children,"* while he adds, "Mrs. Sydney is delighted with her rustication. She has suffered all the evils of London, and enjoyed none of its goods." In his philosophical way he writes the next year to Lady Holland: "I am not leading precisely the life I should choose, but that which (all things considered as well as I could consider them) appeared to me the most eligible. I am resolved, therefore, to like it, and to reconcile myself to it; which is more manly than to feign myself above it, and to send up complaints by the post, of being thrown away, and being desolate, and such like trash. . . . . . . If, with a pleasant wife, three children, a good house and farm, many books, and many friends, who wish me well, I cannot be happy, I am a very silly, foolish fellow, and what becomes of me is of very little consequence. I have, at least, this chance of doing well in Yorkshire, that I am heartily tired of London."† "Instead of being unamused by trifles," he writes to Jeffrey, drawing on his fund of happiness, "I am, as I well knew I should be, amused by them a great deal too much; I feel an ungovernable interest about my horses, or my pigs, or my plants; I am forced, and always was forced, to task myself up into an interest for any higher objects."‡ Of his reading, he tells Jeffrey that, "having scarcely looked at a book for five years, I am rather hungry."‖ Burke, Homer, Suetonius, Godwin's Enquirer, agricul-

* York, Nov. 20, 1808.
† To Lady Holland, Heslington, Sept. 9, 1809.
‡ To Jeffrey, Heslington, Sept. 3, 1809.
‖ To Jeffrey, Heslington. 1810.

tural matters, and "a great deal of Adam Smith," were thrown in to fill the vacuum. "I am," he writes to his friend John Murray, the lawyer of Edinburgh, "reading Locke in my old age, never having read him thoroughly in my youth: a fine, satisfactory sort of fellow, but very long-winded."* These transition years at Heslington supplied to the Edinburgh Review a series of articles on Education of Women, Public Schools and the Universities, a Vindication of Fox's Historical Work, an account of the Walcheren Expedition, and a paper on Indian affairs. "I am about," he writes to Lady Holland, "to open the subject of classical learning, in the Review, from which, by some accident or other, it has hitherto abstained. It will give great offence, and therefore be more fit for this journal, the genius of which seems to consist in stroking the animal the contrary way to that which the hair lies."

The Edinburgh Review united its forces against the Oxford system of education. The University was attacked in several articles by various writers, on the score of its devotion to Aristotle, the inefficiency of its press, particularly in an edition of Strabo, and the excessive employment of its students in the minutiæ of Latin and Greek. The general assault was made by Sydney Smith. The University was compelled to defend itself; and its renowned champion, Edward Copleston, Provost of Oriel, afterward Bishop of Llandaff, published "A Reply to the Calumnies of the Edinburgh Review against Oxford." This was met in the Edinburgh by an article evidently proceeding from the three authors of the original remarks on Aristotle, the edition of Strabo, and Professional Education. "A Second Reply to the Edinburgh Review," also from the pen of Copleston, commenting on the triple article, closed the controversy.† Sydney Smith, always an excel-

* To John Murray, Heslington, Dec. 6, 1811.
† The Edinburgh Review articles alluded to are an Analysis of Laplace's Mecuanique Celeste, in its concluding pages, January, 1808; the Oxford Edition of Strabo, Jan. 1809; Edgeworth's Professional Education, Oct 1809; Calumnies against Oxford, April, 1810. Copleston's publications are entitled, "A Reply to the Calumnies of the Edinburgh Review against Ox

lent partisan skirmisher, with enough of the philosopher in his generalizations, and of the jury lawyer in the skill of his management of points, held the ear of the public on the question. In the edition of his writings, the paper on Professional Education is one of the most complete, and certainly not the least brilliant of his essays. The exclusive pedantry of Oxford was fair game for a satirist; the attack, since grown familiar, and followed by various degrees of reform, was then a novelty; it was something to invade the dignity of the ancient University, and compel it to a defence: the public was entertained, and Sydney Smith had his revenge upon the Busbys of his school-boy days for their infliction of longs and shorts. It was a capital subject of mirth with him, of which he never tired. The reply to Copleston was not over-delicate in its choice of terms. It was, in fact, a specimen of the old Edinburgh swagger, relieved by some excellent passes of humour.

While thus continuing his literary pursuits, Sydney Smith was not altogether cut off from politics and society. In sympathy with the times he projected "Common Sense for 1810," a pamphlet which it is to be regretted he never accomplished as it would doubtless have formed a brilliant companion to the Plymley Letters. He paid visits to Lord Grey, whom he greatly admired, at Howick, and made flying journeys to London and Holland House. Romilly, Mackintosh, Horner, and others, visited him — among the rest, Jeffrey, "who came with an American gentleman, Mr. Simond, and his niece, Miss Wilkes. We little suspected," adds Lady Holland, "that this lady, great niece to the agitator Wilkes, was so soon after to become Mrs. Jeffrey.*

ford, containing an Account of Studies pursued in that University," and "A Second Reply to the Edinburgh Review," both in 1810. The Quarterly Review for August, 1810, reviews the whole discussion.

* "About the close of 1810, Mons. Simond, a French gentleman, who had left his country early in the revolution, came with his wife and a niece to visit some friends in Edinburgh, where they remained some weeks. Madame Simond was a sister of Charles Wilkes, Esq., banker in New York, a nephew of the famous John; and the niece was Miss Charlotte Wilkes, a daughter of this Charles. It was during this visit, I believe, that she and Jeffrey first

Having given up all hopes of exchanging his undesirable living of Foston, he commenced the reconstruction of the parsonage-house. His account of the proceedings is too characteristic to be given in other terms than his own. "All my efforts for an exchange having failed, I asked and obtained from my friend the Archbishop another year to build in. And I then set my shoulder to the wheel in good earnest; sent for an architect; he produced plans which would have ruined me. I made him my bow: 'You build for glory, sir; I, for use.' I returned him his plans, with five-and-twenty pounds, and sat down in my thinking-chair, and in a few hours Mrs. Sydney and I concocted a plan which has produced what I call the model of parsonage-houses.

"I then took to horse to provide bricks and timber; was advised to make my own bricks, of my own clay; of course, when the kiln was opened, all bad; mounted my horse again, and in twenty-four hours had bought thousands of bricks and tons of timber. Was advised by neighbouring gentlemen to employ oxen: bought four —Tug and Lug, Hawl and Crawl; but Tug and Lug took to fainting, and required buckets of sal-volatile, and Hawl and Crawl to lie down in the mud. So I did as I ought to have done at first —took the advice of the farmer instead of the gentleman; sold my oxen, bought a team of horses, and at last, in spite of a frost which delayed me six weeks, in spite of walls running down with wet, in spite of the advice and remonstrances of friends who predicted our death, in spite of an infant of six months old, who had never been out of the house, I landed my family in my new house nine months after laying the first stone, on the 20th of March; and performed

met."— Cockburn's Life of Jeffrey, i. 168, where an account of the great reviewer's subsequent visit to America, in the midst of the war in 1813, and of his marriage to the lady in America, is given. Louis Simond published several books of travel, highly esteemed for their political and economical social studies. His "Journal of a Tour and Residence in Great Britain in 1810-11," appeared, translated from the French, in 1816. In 1822 he published his "Travels in Switzerland," performed in 1817-18-19. "Travels in Italy and Sicily appeared at Paris in 1827. He passed the latter years of his life at Geneva, where he died in July, 1831.

my promise to the letter to the Archbishop, by issuing forth at midnight with a lantern to meet the last cart, with the cook and the cat, which had stuck in the mud, and fairly established them before twelve o'clock at night in the new parsonage-house — a feat, taking ignorance, inexperience, and poverty, into consideration, requiring, I assure you, no small degree of energy.

"It made me a very poor man for many years, but I never repented it. I turned schoolmaster, to educate my son, as I could not afford to send him to school. Mrs. Sydney turned schoolmistress, to educate my girls, as I could not afford a governess. I turned farmer, as I could not let my land. A man-servant was too expensive; so I caught up a little garden-girl, made like a milestone, christened her Bunch, put a napkin in her hand, and made her my butler. The girls taught her to read, Mrs. Sydney, to wait, and I undertook her morals; Bunch became the best butler in the county.

"I had little furniture, so I bought a cart-load of deals; took a carpenter (who came to me for parish relief, called Jack Robinson), with a face like a full-moon, into my service; established him in a barn, and said, 'Jack, furnish my house.' You see the result!

"At last it was suggested that a carriage was much wanted in the establishment; after diligent search, I discovered in the back settlements of a York coachmaker an ancient green chariot, supposed to have been the earliest invention of the kind. I brought it home in triumph to my admiring family. Being somewhat dilapidated, the village tailor lined it, the village blacksmith repaired it; nay (but for Mrs. Sydney's earnest entreaties), we believe the village painter would have exercised his genius upon the exterior; it escaped this danger, however, and the result was wonderful. Each year added to its charms: it grew younger and younger; a new wheel, a new spring; I christened it the *Immortal;* it was known all over the neighbourhood; the village boys cheered it, and the village dogs barked at it; but 'Faber meæ fortunæ' was my motto, and we had no false shame.

"Added to all these domestic cares, I was village parson, village doctor, village comforter, village magistrate, and Edinburgh Reviewer; so you see I had not much time left on my hands to regret London.

"My house was considered the ugliest in the county, but all admitted it was one of the most comfortable; and we did not die, as our friends had predicted, of the damp walls of the parsonage."

The establishment, with its farm appurtenances, into which Sydney Smith thus inducted himself, cost him some four thousand pounds in all, and of course seriously hampered his fortunes during his protracted, involuntary, though not unhappy residence. The income of Foston was five hundred pounds; increased for the last two or three years to eight hundred.*

Lady Holland, with a woman's feeling for the details of domestic life, has given a genial sketch of this new flitting—it was in the spring of 1814—with the accessories of character and homely incident.

"It was a cold, bright March day, with a biting east wind. The beds we left in the morning had to be packed up and slept on at night; wagon after wagon of furniture poured in every minute; the roads were so cut up that the carriage could not reach the door; and my mother lost her shoe in the mud, which was ankle-deep, while bringing her infant up to the house in her arms.

"But oh, the shout of joy as we entered and took possession!— the first time in our lives that we had inhabited a house of our own. How we admired it, ugly as it was! With what pride my dear father welcomed us, and took us from room to room; old Molly Mills, the milk-woman, who had had charge of the house, grinning with delight in the background. We thought it a palace; yet the drawing-room had no door, the bare plaster walls ran down with wet, the windows were like ground-glass, from the moisture which had to be wiped up several times a day by the housemaid. No carpets, no chairs, nothing unpacked; rough men bringing in

* First Letter to Archdeacon Singleton.

rougher packages at every moment. But then was the time to behold my father!—amidst the confusion, he thought for everybody, cared for everybody, encouraged everybody, kept everybody in good humour. How he exerted himself! how his loud, rich voice might be heard in all directions, ordering, arranging, explaining, till the household storm gradually subsided! Each half-hour improved our condition; fires blazed in every room; at last we all sat down to our tea, spread by ourselves on a huge package before the drawing-room fire, sitting on boxes round it; and retired to sleep on our beds placed on the floor—the happiest, merriest, and busiest family in Christendom. In a few days, under my father's active exertions, everything was arranged with tolerable comfort in the little household, and it began to assume its wonted appearance.

"In speaking of the establishment of Foston, Annie Kay must not be forgotten. She entered our service at nineteen years of age, but possessing a degree of sense and lady-like feeling not often found in her situation of life—first as nurse, then as lady's-maid, then housekeeper, apothecary's boy, factotum, and friend. All who have been much at Foston or Combe Florey know Annie Kay; she was called into consultation on every family event, and proved herself a worthy oracle. Her counsels were delivered in the softest voice, with the sweetest smile, and in the broadest Yorkshire. She ended by nursing her old master through his long and painful illness, night and day; she was with him at his death; she followed him to his grave; she was remembered in his will; she survived him but two years, which she spent in my mother's house; and, after her long and faithful service of thirty years, was buried by my mother in the same cemetery as her master, respected and lamented by all his family, as the most faithful of servants and friends.

"So much for the interior of the establishment. Out-of-doors reigned Molly Mills—cow, pig, poultry, garden, and post-woman; with her short red petticoat, her legs like millposts, her high cheek-bones red and shrivelled like winter apples; a perfect specimen of a 'yeowoman;' a sort of kindred spirit, too; for she was the wit of the village, and delighted in a crack with her master, when she could get it. She was as important in her vocation as Annie Kay in hers; and Molly here, and Molly there, might be heard in every direction. Molly was always merry, willing, active, and true as gold; she had little book-learning, but enough to bring up two fine athletic sons, as honest as herself; though, unlike her, they were never seen to smile, but were as solemn as two owls, and would not have said a civil thing to save their lives. They ruled the farm. Add to these the pet donkey, Bitty, already introduced to the public; a tame fawn, at last dismissed for eating the maid's clothes, which he preferred to any other diet; and a lame goose, condemned at last to be roasted for eating all the fruit in the garden; together with Bunch and Jack Robinson—and you have the establishment."

An anecdote of Smith's first visit to Foston, preserved by Lady Holland, is a good index of his character at all times, and of his subsequent position in the village. The house and grounds presented the most forbidding appearance. To shed light upon the scene: "The clerk, the most important man in the village, was summoned; a man who had numbered eighty years, looking, with his long gray hair, his threadbare coat, deep wrinkles, stooping gait, and crutch-stick, more ancient than the parsonage-house. He looked at my father for some time from under his gray, shaggy eyebrows, and held a long conversation with him, in which the old clerk showed that age had not quenched the natural shrewdness of the Yorkshireman. At last, after a pause, he said, striking his crutch-stick on the ground, 'Muster Smith, it often stroikes moy moind, that people as comes frae London is such *fools*. . . . But you,' he said (giving him a nudge with his stick), 'I see you are no fool.'" The foraging accommodations of the parish were once feelingly described by Sydney Smith: "My living in Yorkshire was so far out of the way, that it was actually twel' miles from a lemon." In his jesting way, he said, "When I began to thump the cushion of my pulpit, on first coming to Foston, as is my wont when I preach, the accumulated dust of a hundred and fifty years made such a cloud, that for some minutes I lost sight of my congregation."

Sydney Smith was forty-three when he began his residence at Foston. He remained there fourteen years, until his appointment, by Lord Chancellor Lyndhurst, to a vacant stall at Bristol. They were years of some privation, which was overcome by economy, and the incumbent's great mastery of the laws of human happiness. At one time, in a season of the failure of the harvest, the family, with their neighbours, were obliged to dispense with bread, and consume, as best they could, the damaged, sprouted wheat. A malignant fever in the parish was the consequence of this distress, which brought out the medical and humanitary resources of the rector. Courageous in risking life on this, as on similar occasions, he did much to alleviate the general misery. Inability to purchase books at this period, must have been a frequent annoyance. The omniscient Edinburgh Reviewer conscientiously abstained from running in debt for a cyclopædia. His friends, however, and the neighbouring library of Castle Howard, where he enjoyed a warm intimacy with the Earl of Carlisle, in a great measure supplied the deficiency.*

* The Earl of Carlisle of this period was Frederick (grandfather of the present Earl), the relative and guardian of Lord Byron. The poet dedicated to him his Hours of Idleness, vilified him in his famous satire, and apologized in Childe Harold. Lord Carlisle wrote tragedies: The Father's Revenge (which Dr. Johnson and Walpole praised), The St -Mother, and various Poems. He came to America during the Revolutionary war, fellow-commissioner with William Eden (Lord Auckland), and Governor Johnstone, with offers of peace, and was challenged by La Fayette, for terms used in the Address to Congress, derogatory to France. In Jesse's "Selwyn and his Contemporaries," there are numerous agreeable letters of Carlisle — among them two, written from Philadelphia and New York, with notices of "Mr. Washington," and the war, which were pleasantly introduced by Mr. Thackeray, in his recent lecture on George III. Lord Carlisle died in 1825, at the age of seventy-seven.

In the midst of all embarrassments, however, Foston was not an unhappy home. The humours of its lord had full play. He was the hero of domestic life, his resources—his kindness, his wit, his personal humour, never failing. Numerous anecdotes of this nature are preserved in the narrative of his daughter—the charm of whose work is its thoroughly woman's picture of the household habits, which, after all, stamp the man. They may be briefly summed up in his art of happiness; his industry, constant self-culture, a curious fondness for the minutiæ of the menage, attention to the common duties of life, care of his parishioners, attachment of his servants, and the cement of those noble friendships which brought Horner, Mackintosh, Jeffrey, the Hollands, Rogers, to his hospitable home—an inviting baiting-place for these keen appreciators of wit and good-nature, which he characteristically christened the Rector's Head.

Within doors he made good taste and original management do the work of wealth in promoting comfort. He contrived cheap decorations for his windows, his ceilings, and his fireplaces, ingeniously brightening his fires by a ventilating aperture. His bed-rooms were placarded with unframed prints, full of elevating suggestions. The arrangements of his store-room and apothecary's shop were among the curiosities of the place. Out of doors his management was quite as peculiar. He oddly economized time in farming his acres, by the use of "a tremendous speaking trumpet" at his door, with the supplement of a spy-glass, to bring the operations under view. His humanity to his cattle was shown in a way said to have been practised by a Duke of Argyle. in alleviating the distressed cuticles of his irritated tenantry. He set up a skeleton machine in the midst of a field, ingeniously arranged for every four-footed creature to rub against, which he called his Universal Scratcher. He carried his household to church, a mile distant from the parsonage, through the miry clay, more successfully than the family of the Vicar of Wakefield, in the adventure of Blackberry and the pillion, in his old furbished-up carriage, the

Immortal, drawn by his cart-horse in shafts, and guided by the carter on foot. At the barn-like church fifty persons were, on one occasion, probably an average one, present.

The portrait of Bunch, that important portion of the Foston family, is immortal; a sketch from reality equal to the imagination of Dickens. Mrs. Marcet, the author of the Conversations on Political Economy, an old friend of the host, exhibits her in full play:—

"I was coming down stairs one morning, when Mr. Smith suddenly said to Bunch, who was passing, 'Bunch, do you like roast duck or boiled chicken?' Bunch had probably never tasted either the one or the other in her life, but answered, without a moment's hesitation, 'Roast duck, please, sir,' and disappeared. I laughed. 'You may laugh,' said he, 'but you have no idea of the labour it has cost me to give her that decision of character. The Yorkshire peasantry are the quickest and shrewdest in the world, but you can never get a direct answer from them; if you ask them even their own names, they always scratch their heads, and say, 'A's sur ai don't knaw, sir;' but I have brought Bunch to such perfection, that she never hesitates now on any subject, however difficult. I am very strict with her. Would you like to hear her repeat her crimes? She has them by heart, and repeats them every day.' 'Come here, Bunch!' calling out to her, 'come and repeat your crimes to Mrs. Marcet;' and Bunch, a clean, fair, squat, tidy little girl, about ten or twelve years of age, quite as a matter of course, as grave as a judge, without the least hesitation, and with a loud voice, began to repeat: 'Plate-snatching, gravy-spilling, door-slamming, blue-bottle-fly-catching, and courtesy-bobbing.' 'Explain to Mrs. Marcet what blue-bottle-fly-catching is.' 'Standing, with my mouth open and not attending, sir.' 'And what is courtesy-bobbing?' 'Courtesying to the centre of the earth, please, sir.' 'Good girl! now you may go.' 'She makes a capital waiter, I assure you; on *state* occasions Jack Robinson, my carpenter, takes off his apron and waits too, and does pretty well, but he sometimes naturally makes a mistake and sticks a gimlet into the bread instead of a fork.'"

Mrs. Marcet also supplies to the "Memoir" some pleasing anecdotes of those medical traits, the foundation of which had been laid at Edinburgh. Sydney is taking her the rounds of his Foston parsonage :—

"'But I came up to speak to Annie Kay. Where is Annie Kay? Ring the bell for Annie Kay.' Kay appeared. 'Bring me my medicine-book, Annie Kay. Kay is my apothecary's boy, and makes up my medicines.' Kay appears with the book. 'I am a great doctor; would you like to hear some of my medicines?' 'Oh yes, Mr. Sydney.' 'There is the gentlejog, a pleasure to take it—the Bull-dog, for more serious cases—Peter's puke—Heart's delight, the comfort of all the old women in the village—Rub-a-dub, a capital embrocation—Dead-stop, settles the matter at once—Up-with-it-then needs no explanation; and so on. Now, Annie Kay, give Mrs. Spratt a bottle of Rub-a-dub; and to Mr. Coles a dose of Dead-stop and twenty drops of laudanum.'

"'This is the house to be ill in,' turning to us; 'indeed everybody who comes is expected to take a little something; I consider it a delicate compliment when my guests have a slight illness here. We have contrivances for everything. Have you seen my patent armour? No? Annie Kay bring my patent armour. Now, look here: if you have a stiff-neck or swelled-face, here is this sweet case of tin filled with hot water, and covered with flannel, to put round your neck, and you are well directly. Likewise, a patent tin shoulder, in case of rheumatism. There you see a stomach-tin, the greatest comfort in life; and lastly, here is a tin slipper, to be filled with hot water, which you can sit with in the drawing-room, should you come in chilled, without wetting your feet. Come and see my apothecary's shop.'

"We all went down stairs, and entered a room filled entirely on one side with medicines, and on the other with every description of groceries and household or agricultural necessaries; in the centre, a large chest, forming a table, and divided into compartments for soap, candles, salt, and sugar.

"' Here you see,' said he, 'every human want before you :—

"' Man wants but little here below,
 As beef, veal, mutton, pork, lamb, venison show;'

spreading out his arms to exhibit everything, and laughing."

Sydney Smith wrote a great deal about prisons and prisoners, crimes and penalties, and justice's justice. It is of positive value that we have this account of his own management in matters of rural police as a Justice of the Peace :—

"He set vigorously to work to study Blackstone, and made himself master of as much law as possible, instead of blundering on, as many of his neighbours were content to do. Partly by this knowledge, partly by his good-humour, he gained a considerable influence in the quorum, which used to meet once a fortnight at the little inn, called the Lobster-house; and the people used to say they were 'going to get a little of Mr. Smith's lobster-sauce.' By dint of his powerful voice, and a little wooden hammer, he prevailed on Bob and Betty to speak one at a time; he always tried, and often succeeded, in turning foes into friends. Having a horror of the Game laws, then in full force, and knowing, as he states in his speech on the Reform Bill, that for every ten pheasants which fluttered in the wood one English peasant was rotting in jail, he was always secretly on the side of the poacher (much to the indignation of his fellow-magistrates, who in a poacher saw a monster of iniquity), and always contrived, if possible, to let him escape, rather than commit him to jail, with the certainty of his returning to the world an accomplished villain. He endeavoured to avoid exercising his function as magistrate in his own village when possible, as he wished to be at peace with all his parishioners.

"Young delinquents he never could bear to commit; but read them a severe lecture, and in extreme cases called out, 'John bring me my *private gallows!*' which infallibly brought the little urchins weeping on their knees, and, 'Oh! for God's sake, your honour, pray forgive us!' and his honour used graciously to pardon them for this time, and delay the arrival of the private gallows, and seldom had occasion to repeat the threat."*

Such was the life at Foston, the poverty of a scholar and a country clergyman, supported by self-respect. His independence led him to make many sacrifices, but he had no hesitation in honourably accepting a favour. He received a hundred a year from his brother Robert, to support his son Douglas at Westminster school; but "Aunt Mary," an old lady, dying not long after, and unexpectedly leaving him a moderate legacy, he at once released his brother from the obligation.† Other accessions of prosperity followed, those affluent rills which the river is sure to meet with if its course be long continued. The neighbouring living of Londesborough, vacant for a short time, was added to his resources by the Earl of Carlisle, in 1825, which enabled him to visit Paris the next year.

The three weeks' journey, as it is recorded in daily letters to Mrs. Sydney Smith, supplies one of the most delightful and amusing portions of his always profitable and entertaining correspondence. It is full of the novelty, the gusto and enjoyment of the Englishman's or American's first pleasant impressions of the Continent, when everything appears gayer, brighter, better than ever before, and the senses are feasted by the brilliant theatrical display. Sydney Smith had a happy temperment, never above being surprised and delighted. From the moment of his crossing the channel his latent Gallic blood is all of a tingle. Calais is full of fine sensations. The bedroom at Dessein's is superb, and so is

* Lady Holland's Memoir, p. 150.
† To the Countess Grey, Foston, Nov. 21, 1821 :—"An old aunt has died and left me an estate in London; this puts me a little at my ease, and will, in some degree save me from the hitherto necessary, but unpleasant practice of making sixpence perform the functions and assume the importance of a shilling.

"Part of my little estate is the Guildhall Coffee-house, in King street, Cheapside. I mean to give a ball there. Will you come?"

the dinner. "I wish you could see me," he writes, with a husband's and a child: delight, to Mrs. Sydney, "with my wood fire and my little bed-room and fine sitting-room." The streets please him "exceedingly." Calais "is quite another world, and full of the greatest entertainment." As for the propriety and civility of the people, "I have not seen," he says, "a cobbler who is not better bred than an English gentleman." Everything is better than in England. The tea is better, the cookery "admirable;" and after a day's surfeit on the raree show, he throws himself to profound slumber "on a charming bed." One thing only is wanting—the presence of Mrs. Sydney and the family. They are well remembered. "You shall all see France; I am resolved upon that;" and again, "I most sincerely hope, one day or another, to conduct you all over it; the thought of doing so is one of my greatest pleasures in travelling." Paris, at which he arrives in a day or two, is great, but perhaps not quite equal to Calais. Under the influence of those rose-coloured first impressions, a hovel at the seaboard rivals a palace at Versailles, and a signboard a masterpiece at the Louvre. How many thousand Americans have been so overcome, on arriving at Havre, after a sea-voyage, by the raree show, and how human, caustic, witty, Sydney Smith appears in writing down all this nonsensical delusion — this capital trick of the Gallic puppets and scenery. At Paris we see the same process. Sydney takes lodgings in the Rue St. Honoré:—"My sitting-room is superb; my bed-room, close to it, very good; there is a balcony which looks upon the street. * * I am exceedingly pleased with everything I have seen at the hotel, and it will be, I think, [to Mrs. Sydney] here we shall lodge." Rather too fast this. The next letter has an amendment, with an apology for undue haste in locating the future air-castle—"of course, my opinions, from my imperfect information, are likely to change every day; but at present I am inclined to think that I ought to have gone, and that we will go, to the Boulevards." Then comes a course of dinners, under the auspices of the Holland family; talk, gossip, and visits. The wonder becomes less wonderful, and admiration, still kept up, is here and there chilled by criticism. First impressions need revision. A confession of the dinner table has a wider application out-of-doors than its admirable individual lessons within. "I dined with Lord Holland; there was at table Barras, the Ex-Director, in whose countenance I immediately discovered all the signs of blood and cruelty which distinguished his conduct. I found out, however, at the end of dinner, that it was not Barras, but M. de Barente, an historian and man of letters, who, I believe, has never killed anything greater than a flea." Sir Sidney Smith, the Admiral, was then in Paris, and there is some pleasant confusion between the two celebrities. The clerical Sydney meets Talleyrand, Humboldt and Cuvier; sees Mars and Talma at the theatre, attends the opera; finds Charles X. growing very old since he dined with him at the Duke of Buccleugh's, in Scotland, and acting very foolishly in his government, which leads to the prophecy, soon to be fulfilled, that "if this man lives, another revolution is inevitable." The local pictures are exquisite. "It is curious to see in what little apartments a French *savant* lives; you find him at his books, covered with snuff, with a little dog that bites your legs." "The Parisians are very fond of adorning their public fountains: sometimes water pours forth from a rock, sometimes trickles from the jaws of a serpent. The dull and prosaic English turn a brass cock or pull out a plug. What a nation!" He finally leaves France, having purchased for himself the coat-of-arms of a French peer, on a seal, which took his fancy, as he professed, for family use,* a " Cuisinier Bourgeois," and some rolls of French paper, to

* Smith was fond of joking on this subject, as on all others, for that matter. Lady Holland has the following anecdote of Combe Florey, some years later:—" He was writing one morning in his favourite bay-window, when a pompous little man, in rusty black, was ushered in. 'May I ask what procures me the honour of this visit?' said my father. 'Oh,' said the little man, 'I am compounding a history of the distinguished families in Somersetshire, and have called to obtain the Smith arms.' 'I regret, sir,' said my father, 'not to be able to contribute to so valuable a work; but the Smiths never had any arms, and have invariably sealed their letters with their thumbs.' "

add a cheap magnificence to the humble Foston. So closed this charming episode in the life of the north country Rector. It may be here added that Sydney Smith did carry out his good intention of taking Mrs. Sydney to Paris. The visit came off in the autumn of 1835. Dessein's hotel, at Calais, was still magnificent; Rouen afforded a glowing sensation; gentlemen and ladies in blouses and caps were as common on the streets as before; the cookery of Paris had a nicer appreciation from a palate which had been much cultivated by London dinners in the interval:—"I shall not easily," he writes to Lady Grey, "forget a *matelote* at the Rocher de Cancale and almond tart at Montreuil, or a *poulet a la Tartare*, at Grignon's. These are impressions which no change in future life can obliterate."* Sydney Smith crossed the channel once more in 1837, to visit Holland, but the gout was then the companion of his journey, and the rose-coloured atmosphere had vanished. Worldly prosperity had advanced, but youth had receded.

In the beginning of 1828, his youngest daughter was married at York, and in the same month of January, he received the prebendal stall at Bristol, intelligence of which was gracefully communicated to him by Lady Lyndhurst. Thither he at once removed, and inaugurated his labours by preaching a sermon before the startled mayor and corporation, in the Cathedral, on the fifth of November, Guy Faux's day, in support of religious toleration, particularly in reference to the Catholics.†

* Sydney Smith was not an epicure, in the vulgar sense of the word; but he was undoubtedly something of the *gourmet*. He knew the value of flavours and sauces to life. He seasoned his curate's dish of potatoes, on Salisbury Plain, with ketchup; studied, as we see, the mysteries of taste in Paris, and on one occasion (recorded by Dyce, in the Table Talk of Rogers) rose in a bravura of fancy to the declaration that "*his* idea of heaven was eating foie gras to the sound of trumpets!" Smith wrote well on temperance, and practised it. Fine sayings like these, however, the immortal salad receipt, and records of innumerable "dinings out," in the Memoirs and Letters, will render his memory fragrant in the traditions of gastronomy.

† He thus mentions it in a letter to Lord Holland, Bristol, Nov. 5, 1828:—
"MY DEAR LORD HOLLAND, To-day I have preached an honest sermon [5th

It is published in his works, and remains a plain, simple, sincere assertion in the words of its title, of "Those Rules of Christian Charity, by which our Opinions of other Sects should be formed." The Bristol preferment brought with it a living, and Foston-le-Clay was exchanged for the more euphonious Combe Florey, situated in a scene of natural beauty, near Taunton; in Smith's own description, "a most parsonic parsonage, like those described in novels." This increase of prosperity was darkened by the death of his son Douglas, in 1829—a sorrow which accompanied the father through life. In his note book of the time, he writes, "April 14th, My beloved son Douglas died, aged twenty-four. Alas! alas!" And afterward: "So ends this year of my life—a year of sorrow, from the loss of my beloved son Douglas—the first great misfortune of my life, and one which I shall never forget." Lady Holland adds the touching trait, "in his last hours he often called his youngest son by the name of Douglas."

A year after, his friend Lord Grey having become minister, Sydney Smith's cathedral stall at Bristol was exchanged for a similar but more profitable post in London, and he became Canon Residentiary of St. Paul's.* Combe Florey he still continued to hold, and thus, between town and country, "dining with the rich in London, and physicking the poor in the country, passing from the sauces of Dives to the sores of Lazarus,"† he continued his clerical career through life.

of November] before the Mayor and Corporation, in the Cathedral—the most protestant Corporation in England! They stared at me with all their eyes. Several of them could not keep the turtle on their stomachs."

* The following letter to his friend, Mrs. Meynell, records the event:—
"SAVILLE Row, September, 1831.
"MY DEAR G., I am just stepping into the carriage to be installed by the Bishop, but can not lose a post in thanking you. It is, I believe, a very good thing, and puts me at my ease for life. I asked for nothing—never did any thing shabby to procure preferment. These are pleasing recollections. My pleasure is greatly increased by the congratulations of good and excellent friends like yourself. God bless you! "SYDNEY SMITH."
† Letter to M. Eugene Robin. Memoir, ii. 497.

Nor were his duties at either place neglected. He became a most zealous guardian of the church property and affairs at St. Paul's, superintending building accounts and expenses toilfully and skilfully; and preaching in his turn, to the close of his life, with dignity and eloquence; while in the summer months, at Combe Florey, his heart expanded among his parishioners, whom he attended with faithful tenderness; entering into their circumstances, and, what is so rare in the world with persons of superior station, surveying, with heartfelt sympathy, the cares and enjoyments of life on a lower level. Hodge had always, in Sydney Smith, a friend, who understood him, and when it was threatened that Hodge's beer would be cut off by meddling licensers, or Hodge was in danger from the game laws, he had, in his clerical visiter, a useful protector. Sydney Smith's Advice to Parishioners is worthy of the philanthropy, humanity, and good-humoured shrewdness of Poor Richard. For Franklin, indeed, Smith entertained a generous admiration, and the manners of the two sages were, in many things, not unlike.

To the domestic sketches of Foston, must be added, as a pendant, this pencilling, by Lady Holland, of "glorified" Combe Florey:—"I long to give some sketches of these breakfasts, and the mode of life at Combe Florey, where there were often assembled guests that would have made any table agreeable anywhere; but it would be difficult to convey an adequate idea of the beauty, gayety, and happiness of the scene in which they took place, or the charm that he infused into the society assembled round his breakfast-table. The room, an oblong, was, as I have already described, surrounded on three sides by books, and ended in a bay-window, opening into the garden: not brown, dark, dull-looking volumes, but all in the brightest bindings; for he carried his system of furnishing for gayety even to the dress of his books.

"He would come down into this long, low room in the morning like a 'giant refreshed to run his course,' bright and happy as the scene around him. 'Thank God for Combe Florey!' he would exclaim, throwing himself in his red arm-chair, and looking around; 'I feel like a bridegroom in the honeymoon.' And in truth I doubt if ever bridegroom felt so joyous, or at least made others feel so joyous, as he did on these occasions. 'Ring the bell, Saba;' the usual refrain, by-the-by, in every pause, for he contrived to keep every body actively employed around him, and nobody ever objected to be so employed. 'Ring the bell, Saba.' Enter the servant, D——. 'D——, glorify the room.' This meant that the three Venetian windows of the bay were to be flung open, displaying the garden on every side, and letting in a blaze of sunshine and flowers. D—— glorifies the room with the utmost gravity, and departs. 'You would not believe it,' he said, 'to look at him now, but D—— is a reformed Quaker. Yes, he quaked, or did quake; his brother quakes still: but D—— is now thoroughly orthodox. I should not like to be a Dissenter in his way; he is to be one of my vergers at St. Paul's some day. Lady B—— calls them my virgins. She asked me the other day, 'Pray, Mr. Smith, is it true that you walk down St. Paul's with three virgins holding silver pokers before you?' I shook my head, and looked very grave, and bid her come and see. Some enemy of the Church, some Dissenter, had clearly been misleading her.'

"'There now,' sitting down at the breakfast-table, 'take a lesson of economy. You never breakfasted in a parsonage before, did you? There, you see my china is all white, so if broken can always be renewed; the same with my plates at dinner: did you observe my plates? every one a different pattern, some of them *sweet articles;* it was a pleasure to dine upon such a plate as I had last night. It is true, Mrs. Sydney, who is a great herald, is shocked because some of them have the arms of a royal duke or a knight of the garter on them, but that does not signify to me. My plan is to go into a china shop and bid them show me every plate they have which does not cost more than half a crown; you see the result.'"

Smith's London life, at his residence in Charles street, appears to have been attended by "all that should accompany old age, honour, love, obedience, troops of friends," but some faces, alas, were missing. Mackintosh, whose memory he fondly cherished, was no longer living, and others had fallen in the race. He gained, however, the alliance of Dr. Holland,* who married his daughter Saba, in 1834, and new faces came to cheer him in his home-circle.

The fifteen years assigned to the Canon of St. Paul's, bore rich fruits of his preceding culture and discipline. He had ceased contributing to the Edinburgh Review, having penned his last article—it was on the Catholic Question—in 1827. He now thought it decorous that a Church dignitary should appear openly to the world in his writings, and not shelter himself under the anonymous. His pen, however, was not idle, and he stood forth still, as ever, in pamphlets and letters to the newspapers, a champion of liberal interests, and of the rights of his order.

Having been thrown, upon his first arrival at Bristol, in 1830, into the midst of the violent agitations of the times, he met the crisis by his practical earnest advice to the uninstructed laboring classes, and his more resolute warnings to the exclusive politicians. To enlighten the poor on the value of machinery, which they were bent upon destroying, he published several cheap tracts, entitled "Letters to Swing;" while at county Reform meetings at Taunton, he levelled several most vigorous speeches at the pressing evils of the representative system. In one of these occurs his now world renowned introduction of Mrs. Partington.

The most notable of all Sydney Smith's writings on the affairs of the Establishment, were his three Letters addressed to Archdeacon Singleton, the first of which appeared in 1837, and the

* Sir Henry Holland, eminent for his literary and philosophical, as well as professional attainments. He took his degree of M. D. at Edinburgh, in 1809. In the summer of 1810 he visited Iceland, in company with Sir George Mackenzie, to whose book of travels in the island he contributed the Preliminary Dissertation and the article on Education and Literature. His "Travels in the Ionian Isles, Albania, Thessaly, Macedonia, &c., during the years 1812 and 1813," were received with favour on their publication in 1819

others at intervals of about a year. They relate to the affairs of the Whig Ecclesiastical Commission, then sitting, and chiefly to its attempted invasions of Cathedral endowments and patronage. It was proposed, among other things, to assist the revenues of the poorer clergy, by taking from a number of the larger benefices pecuniary advantages, to form a fund for the augmentation of small livings. The prebendal stalls of St. Paul's, in particular, were exposed to the shears of the projected bill. They were to be diminished in number, and their emoluments curtailed. Sydney Smith came forth resolutely to the rescue. As it was a commission of Bishops in which Deans and Chapters were not represented, and as Episcopal revenues were not to be touched, the Bishops were made to feel the full force of his wit and argument. There is some very plain talk addressed to the Bishop of London, the learned Blomfield, whose passion for government is made to appear a virtue in excess. " Here it is," Smith exclaims, citing a charge of rashness against the Bishop's classical emendations, "*qualis ab incepto.* He begins with Æschylus, and ends with the Church of England; begins with profane, and ends with holy innovations—scratching out old readings which every commentator had sanctioned, abolishing ecclesiastical dignities which every reformer had spared; thrusting an anapæst into a verse which will not bear it; and intruding a Canon into a Cathedral which does not want it." The handling of the Bishop of Gloucester, Dr. Monk, who threw into the discussion an attack upon Sydney Smith, as " a scoffer and jester," is excessively severe, retorting personality for personality. There is a very neat example of mingled satire and eulogy in a page on Lord Melbourne. In these papers, too, occurs the celebrated description of Lord John Russell: "There is not a better man in England; but his worst failure is, that he is utterly ignorant of all moral fear; there is nothing he would not undertake. I believe he would perform the operation for the stone—build St. Peter's—or assume (with or without ten minutes' notice), the command of the Channel Fleet; and no one would discover, by his manner, that the patient had died—the Church tumbled down—and the Channel Fleet been knocked to atoms."

The main argument of the Letters, which shows the Canon something of a conservative in the plurality interest, is that the reform would be unjust and injurious to the Church. It would interfere with vested rights, and, though it might tend to equalize the incomes of the clergy, the majority of them would remain very small—the individual gain would be trifling, while the great pecuniary and social rewards of the Church would be destroyed. The English Establishment, he argued, is, upon the whole, poor, but its character is maintained in a country where wealth is essential to secure respect by its high prizes. As in the profession of the bar, many are induced to enter it, and encounter every early privation with the hope of attaining its splendid positions; which also attract many persons of independent incomes, who thus supply the general deficiency of means. Destroy these glittering emoluments, and the ground will be occupied by inferior men, low, badly educated, and fanatical. "You will have a set of ranting, raving Pastors, who will wage war against all the innocent pleasures of life, vie with each other in extravagance of zeal, and plague your heart out with their nonsense and absurdity: cribbage must be played in caverns, and sixpenny whist take refuge in the howling wilderness. In this way low men, doomed to hopeless poverty, and galled by contempt, will endeavour to force themselves into station and significance."

The Chapter rights were gallantly and successfully defended from behind the entrenchments of St. Paul's, with many a dashing sortie and skirmish—without any particular delicacy as to the weapon or its stroke—with the Bishops. That his friends, the Whigs, suffered from the force of his logic was but a proof of his independent character. It was no desertion of his political principles, but evidence of his constancy to what he had always regarded as the practical welfare of the Church; while he had, shortly after, an opportunity of proving to the world how little he was guided, in this defence, by his private pecuniary interests. A perquisite of the Chapter of St. Paul's, the living of Edmonton, worth seven hundred pounds a year, fell to his share, on the death of his associate, Mr. Tate. According to the usage in such matters, it was expected that he would turn the emolument to his own advantage. He generously conferred the whole on the son of the late incumbent. The incident is so characteristically narrated by him, in a letter addressed to his wife, that it would be injustice to the reader not to present the scene in his own words: "I went over, yesterday, to the Tates at Edmonton. The family consists of three delicate daughters, an aunt, the old lady, and her son, then curate of Edmonton; the old lady was in bed. I found there a physician, an old friend of Tate's, attending them from friendship, who had come from London for that purpose. They were in daily expectation of being turned out from house and curacy. . . . I began by inquiring the character of their servant; then turned the conversation upon their affairs, and expressed a hope the Chapter might ultimately do something for them. I then said, 'It is my duty to state to you (they were all assembled) that I have given away the living of Edmonton; and have written to our Chapter clerk this morning, to mention the person to whom I have given it; and I must also tell you, that I am sure he will appoint his curate. (A general silence and dejection.) It is a very odd coincidence,' I added, 'that the gentleman I have selected is a namesake of this family; his name is Tate. Have you any relations of that name?' 'No, we have not.' 'And, by a more singular coincidence, his name is Thomas Tate; in short,' I added, 'there is no use in mincing the matter, you are vicar of Edmonton.' They all burst into tears. It flung me, also, into a great agitation of tears, and I wept and groaned for a long time. Then I rose, and said I thought it was very likely to end in their keeping a buggy, at which we all laughed as violently.

"The poor old lady, who was sleeping in a garret because she could not bear to enter into the room lately inhabited by her husband, sent for me and kissed me, sobbing with a thousand emotions. The charitable physician wept too. . . . I never passed so remarkable a morning, nor was more deeply impressed with the sufferings of human life, and never felt more thoroughly the happiness of doing good."

A pamphlet on the Ballot was the most important of Sydney Smith's later productions. It appeared in 1839, when the subject was much agitated by the liberals. He opposed its introduction with his usual ingenuity and pertinacity of argument, considering it ineffective in reaching the evil, interference with the freedom of voting, it was set forth to cure. He regards it as inimical to moral courage, a foe to just responsibility and good example; citing, with unction, a reply of John Randolph, at a dinner-party in London, to the question whether ballot prevailed in his state of Virginia. "I scarcely believe," replied the American orator, "we have such a fool in all Virginia, as to mention, even, the vote by ballot; and I do not hesitate to say, that the adoption of the ballot would make any nation a nation of scoundrels, if it did not find them so." "John Randolph," continues Sydney Smith, "was right; he felt that it was not necessary that a people should be false in order to be free; universal hypocrisy would be the consequence of ballot; we should soon say, on deliberation, what David only asserted in his haste, *that all men were liars.*" It is curious to note the matter-of-fact way in which it is taken for granted, that the landlord will, in some way, control his tenants. In America, where the ballot, though generally prevalent, is not universal, he asserts, "it is nearly a dead letter; no protection is wanted: if the ballot protects any one it is the master, not the man." One of the difficulties urged, in the use of the ballot, is its defeat of a reliable system of registration, by which contested returns might be settled. At the close of the essay, the argument of which rests, as usual with him, greatly on local expediency, he expresses his distrust of what he regarded as a concomitant of the measure in England, the demand for universal suffrage.

The occurrence of the railway disaster, by fire, at Versailles, in 1842, when a number of lives were lost, in consequence of a regulation by which the passengers were locked in the cars, drew forth from Smith several characteristic letters on the subject, addressed to The Morning Chronicle and Sir Robert Peel.

The year 1843 produced Sydney Smith's famous Petition to Congress, and Letters on American Debts. The failure of several States in the midst of financial embarrassments, to make provision for the payment of interest due on bonds, with whatever extenuating circumstances it may have been attended, was a pressing evil. Judged by the lower test of expediency, it was a political blunder. The delay, fortunately, was soon enough terminated, in most of the cases, to ward off the severe verdict of the world which would have attended upon persistance in the neglect. Smith was the holder of certain Pennsylvania Bonds. He missed his semi-annual interest on pay-day; heard talk of the ill word "repudiation," and took up his pen in illustration of the sound principles of pecuniary obligation and national faith. The cause was just, and his wit was trenchant. He made the most of the subject, as he had a right to do; indeed, he made so much of it, that the laugh was rather turned against him, when it was found over how slight a personal loss he had contrived to raise so loud a storm of indignation. He sold his shares at a discount, and was damaged a small matter by the operation. The principle, however, was the same. If the "drab-coloured men" had taken but two pence in the spirit of robbery, they would have been justly exposed to the vituperatives of all the languages of the civilized world. Sydney Smith's extravagance of statement and exaggerating invective, the riot of his humour, while increasing the efficiency, abated, however, from the acerbity of his denunciations. As to the principle involved, there could be but one opinion for both sides of the Atlantic; and it was generally considered, on this side, that Sydney Smith's Letters did good service. In other days, when America had been in need of English opinion, Sydney Smith, it should not be forgotten, had stood forth her resolute eulogist and champion. It was with him that the very complimentary phrase applied to the United States, originated, "a magnificent spectacle of human happiness."* The entrance of the demon Repudiation on the scene disturbed the show.†

* Article, America, Ed. Rev., July, 1824. Letter to Jeffrey, Nov. 23, 1818.
† There is a stanza in an amusing, though reckless, English squib of the time on the topic, introducing Sydney Smith:—

"A NEW SONG TO AN OLD TUNE.

"Yankee Doodle borrows cash,
  Yankee Doodle spends it,
And then he snaps his fingers at
  The jolly flat who lends it.
Ask him when he means to pay,
  He shows no hesitation,
But says he'll take the shortest way
  And that's Repudiation!
    Chorus: Yankee Doodle borrows cash, &c.

"Yankee vows that every State
  Is free and independent:
And if they paid each other's debts,
  There'd never be an end on't.
They keep distinct till "settling" comes,
  And then throughout the nation
They all become "United States"
  To preach Repudiation!

"Lending cash to Illinois,
  Or to Pennsylvania,
Florida, or Mississippi,
  Once was quite a mania.
Of all the States 'tis hard to say
  Which makes the proudest show, sirs,
But Yankee seems himself to like
  The State of O-I-owe, sirs.

The reverend joker of St. Paul's
  Don't relish much their plunder,
And often at their knavish tricks
  Has hurled his witty thunder.
But Jonathan by nature wears
  A hide of toughest leather,
Which braves the sharpest-pointed darts
  And *canons* put together!

The Pennsylvania bonds supplied a frequent theme to Sydney Smith, in his conversations and letters, grave and gay. He read the American papers, and found himself a well-abused man: "The Americans, I see," he said, "call me a Minor Canon. They are abusing me dreadfully to-day: they call me Xantippe; they might, at least, have known my sex: and they say I am eighty four." To the Countess Grey, he writes: "There is nothing in the crimes of kings worse than this villainy of democracy." To Mrs. Grote: "My bomb has fallen very successfully in America, and the list of killed and wounded is extensive. I have several quires of paper sent me every day, calling me monster, thief, atheist, deist, etc. Duff Green sent me three pounds of cheese, and a Captain Morgan a large barrel of American apples."

A Captain Morgan is *the* Captain Morgan, of New York, late of the packet ship Southampton, whose genial personal qualities,

"He tells 'em they are clapping on
　Their credit quite a stopper,
And when they come to go to war
　They'll never raise a copper.
If that's the case, they coolly say,
　Just as if to spite us,
They'd better stop our dividends,
　And hoard 'em up to fight us!

'What's the use of moneyed friends
　If you mustn't bleed 'em?
Ours, I guess, says Jonathan,
　The country is of freedom!
And what does freedom mean, if not
　To whip our slaves at pleasure
And borrow money when you can,
　To pay it at your leisure?

"Great and free Amerikee
　With all the world is vying,
That she the "land of *promise*" is
　There's surely no denying.
But be it known henceforth to all,
　Who hold their I. O. U. sirs,
A Yankee Doodle *promise* is
　A Yankee *Doodle do*, sirs!"

appreciated by many Atlantic travellers and intimates at home, have long endeared him to such honourable literary and artistic friends and acquaintances abroad, as Dickens, Thackeray, Leslie and his brother-artists of the Sketching Club of London. To Captain Morgan we are indebted for the two following letters, now first published, addressed to him by Sydney Smith—touching the apples aforesaid, and American obligations generally. The first, which we also present, in a fac-simile of the original, is dated at the writer's London residence, in December, 1843. It reads: "Sir: I am much obliged by your present of Apples, which I consider as apples of Concord not discord. I have no longer any pecuniary interest that your countrymen should pay their debts—but as a sincere friend to America, I earnestly hope they may do so." The other is dated Combe Florey, January 14, 1844: "Sir: I should have written long since to have thanked you for your Apples, but unfortunately lost your address. It lately occurred to me, that I could find you by means of our friend, Mr. Bates. The apples have been eaten with universal applause, after I had assured the company that they came from a Solvent State. My opinion (worth something, not much), is, that Pennsylvania will *not* pay. I heard my friend Stokes upon the subject, but his facts and his arguments led me to conclusions very opposite to his own. I sincerely hope that you have only a theoretical interest in the subject."

In spite of skepticism, the apples were doubtless eaten with good will. Sydney Smith, though tenacious of his satire and his jests, listened with interest to the representations of Mr. Edward Everett, then in England, and read with satisfaction the fair-minded letter published by Mr. George Ticknor in the Boston Daily Advertiser.*

It was this year, 1843, which brought to the Canon of St. Paul's, too late in life to add much to his usefulness or enjoyments, a large increase of wealth. His brother Courtenay died without a will,

* It is given in Lady Holland's Memoir, pp. 264-268.

and Sydney, at the age of seventy-two, inherited one third of an estate of a hundred thousand pounds.

Sydney Smith had now arrived at that period of life, in which in general, there is little for a man to do but to fold his robes about him and leave the stage with decorum. Though retaining his faculties to the last with unabated mental vigour, the premonitions of disease warned him of the grave. "I am going slowly," he writes to a friend in 1836, " down the hill of life. One evil in old age is, that as your time is come, you think every little illness is the beginning of the end. When a man expects to be arrested, every knock at the door is an alarm." The gout paid him several such domiciliary visits before the final summons. He was not what is called a martyr to the disease, but he felt its sting. He jests on the subject in his correspondence with his friend and fellow-victim, Sir George Philips,* and bears up bravely under the infliction. In the history of suffering, pain has been no unfrequent stimulant of wit. The season before his death he said "I feel so weak, both in body and mind, that I verily believe, if the knife were put into my hand, I should not have strength or energy enough to stick it into a Dissenter." Under the last regimen of his physician, he said to his friend General Fox, " Ah, Charles! I wish I were allowed even the wing of a roasted butterfly." Such things had once set the table on the roar. The jest cost more now.

It is pleasant to note how kindly the old humourist carries himself to the last in his letters to his female friends. The novels of Dickens, for which he had a genuine appreciation, were among his latest enjoyments. The infirmities of age, with intermissions

---

"* A more benevolent man," says Haydon, in his Diary, "never lived than Sir George Philips." He advanced five hundred guineas to the artist for his picture of Christ in the Garden. Smith visited Philips at his seat near Manchester, when the host revelled in his guest's humour. " He was incessantly stimulating him to attack him," says Lady Holland, " which my father certainly did most vigorously ; yet I believe no one present enjoyed these attacks more than Sir George himself, who laughed at them almost to exhaustion.' Philips died in 1847, at the age of eighty-one.

of comfort, crept steadily on, and in October, 1844, a last attack, an affection of water on the chest, consequent on disease of the heart, seized its victim in the country at Combe Florey. He was removed to town, was attended by his beloved son-in-law, Dr. Holland, and by his nurse, Annie Kay, who had been with him since the old days at Foston. Earl Grey sent him messages of sympathy from his own death-bed. In one of his last hours the wonted fire of the preacher of St. Paul's burst forth in the recitation of a touching and eloquent passage from his sermon on Riches. "One evening," his daughter, Lady Holland, tells us, "when the room was half darkened, and he had been resting long in silence, and I thought him asleep, he suddenly burst forth, in a voice so strong and full that it startled us — 'We talk of human life as a journey, but how variously is that journey performed! There are some who come forth girt, and shod, and mantled, to walk on velvet lawns and smooth terraces, where every gale is arrested, and every beam is tempered. There are others who walk on the Alpine path of life, against driving misery, and through stormy sorrows, over sharp afflictions; walk with bare feet, and naked breast, jaded, mangled, and chilled.'" But these inequalities of life were now over. He had arrived at the common level of mortality. The end had come. He calmly met death the 22d of February, 1845. His remains were laid in the cemetery of Kensal Green. The tomb upon which his epitaph is written has also an inscription to the memory of his son Douglas; and there, too, rests all that was mortal of his wife who soon followed him to the grave.*

In person, Sydney Smith, as he has been described to us by those who knew him, was of the medium height; plethoric in habit though of great activity, of a dense brown complexion, a dark ex-

---

* Sydney Smith's personal property was sworn under £80,000. His wife, for whom liberal provision was made, was sole executrix of his will. There was a legacy of £30,000 to his son Wyndham, and his servants were mentioned in several bequests.

pressive eye, an open countenance, indicative of shrewdness, humour, and benevolence. There is a look, too, in the English engraved portraits, of a thoughtful seriousness. A certain heaviness in his figure was neutralized by constitutional vivacity. His "sense, wit, and clumsiness," said a college companion, gave "the idea of an Athenian carter." He once sat to his friend, Gilbert Stuart Newton, for an abbot, in a painting.

Newton made a portrait of Smith, representing him in the later period of life when all his faculties were mellowed and refined. It was while in attendance upon the artist for this picture, on a warm day, that the wit remarked he would prefer to take off his flesh and sit in his bones!* After Newton's death the portrait was brought to America by his widow. In 1847, a copy was made from it for Captain E. E. Morgan, by Miss Ann Leslie, sister of the well-known artist. Not long after, the original was destroyed by fire. The copy has been kindly lent to us by its owner, and the engraving placed as the frontispiece to the present volume is made after it.

The practical, sound, every-day, working character of Sydney Smith's life, is its greatest lesson. He united in a rare manner

* The jest, a thing not uncommon with humourists, seems to have done duty on another occasion. We have this report of it among various scraps of conversation, in Lady Holland's Memoir (p. 238), with the pleasant addition of Mrs. Jackson's wonderment:—

"Nothing amuses me more than to observe the utter want of perception of a joke in some minds. Mrs. Jackson called the other day, and spoke of the oppressive heat of last week. 'Heat, ma'am!' I said, 'it was so dreadful here, that I found there was nothing left for it but to take off my flesh and sit in my bones.' 'Take off your flesh and sit in your bones, sir! Oh! Mr. Smith! how could you do that?' she exclaimed, with the utmost gravity. 'Nothing more easy, ma'am; come and see next time.' But she ordered her carriage, and evidently thought it a very unorthodox proceeding."

There is another anecdote of Newton's studio. The artist was engaged in painting a portrait of Moore, which the poet took Smith, from a breakfast with Rogers, to see. 'Couldn't you contrive," said Sydney, in his gravest manner to Newton, "to throw into his face somewhat of a stronger expression of hostility to the Church Establishment?" (Moore's Diary, May 27, 1826.)

the virtues of the optimist and the reformer. An ardent devotee of human happiness, he did not destroy life to improve it; nor did he ever cease to oppose evils in the way of its prosperity. While he appears taking his ease in that great inn, the world, enjoying himself and communicating pleasure to others, he is quarrelling with all sorts of injustice in high places; contending for the peasant and the labourer; advocating the rights of accused criminals, with a word for poor chimney-sweeps; reading lessons to squires, parliament men and bishops; battling for religious and political freedom. He fought a long fight with dullness, pedantry, prejudice, private and political interest, and came off conqueror. His honest laugh rang through the whole field. An instinctive genius, the inspiration of common sense, was his weapon. He had an advantage of position too in favour of his wit and his reforms in fighting under the protection and in defence of the established Church; for the best reformer is not all reformer. He must have some point of support, or how can he wage war with success? Where can he deposit the fruits of victory? There are noisy reformers who cut themselves loose from all positive institutions, and, like the poets' "cats in air-pumps," attempt subsistence in a vacuum. Sydney Smith was not one of these empty whims.

The most genial and conciliatory, he was the most independent of men. His independence was, with his other virtues, of a practical character; alike above obsequiousness, indolence and churlishness. He had a just knowledge of the respect due his faculties and attainments, of his claims upon the society to which he belonged, his party and his church. On proper occasions he asserted them in a manly way; when they were not acknowledged he bore the loss philosophically, and even sported with his misfortunes. There was no misanthropy in his disposition.

In the art of getting on in the world, he was certainly not indifferent to the main chance, while his life affords an illustration of the benevolence of men of moderate means. During a considerable part of his career in narrow circumstances, and compelled to economy, whether selling his wife's jewels preaching at chapels, lecturing, reviewing, eking out a curate's humbleness by drafts on humour and imagination, he is constantly doing liberal acts; a man of charity and beneficence; bestowing free-will offerings from a life of self-denial and honourable industry; contributions which a generous nature extorted from a stock almost too small for home necessities.

Independence of opinion and of fortune he valued most highly, and pursued steadily and successfully, the one for the other, the inferior for the superior. In the wisdom of Burns the poet's manly Epistle, he "assiduously waited" upon Fortune and gathered wealth—

> "Not for to hide it in a hedge,
> Nor for a train attendant,
> But for the glorious privilege
> Of being independent."

He had the courage in a luxurious, artificial society, where weak men are crushed by conventionalisms, of appearing what he was and spending no more than he could afford. An instance of his business punctilio in pecuniary obligations occurs in one of his letters to his early friend Mr. Beach. The latter had a small sum of money left in his hands on settlement with his son's tutor. Mr. Beach credits the account with five per cent. interest. Sydney insists positively that it *must* be but four, and will be under no obligation for any more.*

His personal independence was shown in many instances during the period of his alliance with a political party out of office; an association unfriendly to his clerical advancement. In a less public light it was exhibited in the manly freedom of his intercourse with his friends. His wit spared none of their absurdities. His letters, frequently models of courtesy and compliment, are always frank and truthful.

This resolute self-possession, though based on brave, natural

* Fourth English edition of the Memoirs, i. 109

qualities, and developed with freedom, was also an affair of conviction and the will. Bashfulness is one of the last qualities which would be assigned to Sydney Smith, but we read that he was shy even in his early manhood. His acuteness of mind, however, soon corrected the evil. He first discovered, he says, " that all mankind were not solely employed in observing him, as all young people think, and that shamming was of no use, the world being very clear-sighted, and soon estimating a man at his just value. This cured me, and I determined to be natural, and let the world find me out."*

Subsidiary to this personal courage was his hopeful way of looking at the world. He was always practising and inculcating the disposition. " Some very excellent people," he said, "tell you they dare not hope. To me it seems much more impious to dare to despair." He had an excellent rule for the happiness and wisdom of life as to the future, not to look too far into it for inevitable though probably distant disaster. " Take *short views*, hope for the best, and trust in God."† Inclined by temperament to anticipate coming evils—for our wit, spite of his many jests, was a serious man—he resisted the atrabilious tendency, and avoided drawing drafts on the misery of futurity. "Never," he said, "give way to melancholy; nothing encroaches more: I fight against it vigorously. One great remedy is, to take short views of life. Are you happy now? Are you likely to remain so till this evening? or next week? or next month? or next year? Then why destroy present happiness by a distant misery, which may never come at all, or you may never live to see it? for every substantial grief has twenty shadows, and most of them shadows of your own making." It was said of the happy nature of Oliver Goldsmith that he had a knack at hoping: with Sydney Smith it was a principle. Cheerfulness he made an art. He liked household illuminations of a good English coal fire, "the living thing," he said, "in a dead room," abundance of lights, flowers on his

* Mem. i. 77, 324. † Ib. i. 167, 117.

table, prints and pictures on his walls. He was no connoisseur in the latter, and if he had been, could not have afforded the gratification of the taste, but he made poor and cheap pictures do the work of good ones by filling up the gap between with his sport and imagination.

There is a highly characteristic anecdote of the man, illustrating his habitual regard to human happiness, and his frequent solicitude for the natural welfare of children. The story is thus told by his daughter, Lady Holland: "One of his little children, then in delicate health, had for some time been in the habit of waking suddenly every evening; sobbing, anticipating the death of parents, and all the sorrows of life, almost before life had begun. He could not bear this unnatural union of childhood and sorrow, and for a long period, I have heard my mother say, each evening found him, at the waking of his child, with a toy, a picture-book, a bunch of grapes, or a joyous tale, mixed with a little strengthening advice and the tenderest caresses, till the habit was broken, and the child woke to joy and not to sorrow."

The intellectual habits of Sydney Smith were those of a quick, keen, sensitive nature, prompt to receive impressions, apt to decide upon them, cautious of its convictions, never driven at random. Impatient of restraint, ardent and vivacious, he was remarkable for his self-knowledge, and the discriminating use of his powers. He did not over-estimate them or under-estimate them; he knew precisely what he could do; the weight of the projectile, the momentum, the effect.

His habits of reading were somewhat peculiar. He read many books, and was content, on principle, to secure the best use of his faculties, to remain ignorant of many others. He was constantly looking into his stock of knowledge and strengthening his defences on the weak points. In this way he laid up a large store of practical, working information. His directness and vivacity of mind led him at once to the essential points of a subject. He plucked out the heart of a series of volumes, in a morning. The happy result may be seen in his reviews, in the Edinburgh, of books of travels—his favourite reading.

He wrote rapidly, making few corrections, a proof of his exact discipline of mind, for his writings have that conciseness which may be supposed to have required frequent revision. His handwriting, a sign of his impatience, was villainously bad. He described it, in a letter to a gentleman who wished to borrow one of his sermons: "I would send it to you with pleasure, but my writing is as if a swarm of ants, escaping from an ink-bottle, had walked over a sheet of paper without wiping their legs."* It is amusing to notice his lectures to Jeffrey, on his cacography, which may be attributed to a similar restlessness of mind.

The clearness and purity of his style are noticeable. It is direct, forcible, manly English; brief without obscurity; rich without any extravagance of ornament; the unaffected language of a gentleman and a scholar. It has a constant tendency to the aphorism—the ripe fruit hanging on the tree of knowledge—noticeable in the writings of the higher order of men of genius; the great dramatists, the poets generally, Bacon, Burke, Franklin, Landor, and indeed most of the classic authors who pass current in the world in quotation. Wit, indeed, of all the faculties, is the most rapid and powerful condenser; it puts volumes into apophthegms; has a patent for proverbs; contracts an essay to an aphorism; bottles an argument in a jest.

Unless where peculiar Latinized expressions or technical terms are intentionally introduced for their witty effect, Smith's language is of the purest Saxon. His method is very direct. His meaning reaches us pure of all superfluities and pruned of all tediousness. It is a style, too, which is essentially his own, a reflex of his keen, impulsive, straight-forward character. In his first published sermons he has been charged with imitating the efforts of Jeremy Taylor and others of the old divines; but this transfusion, which appears very slightly, is rather a beauty. When he advanced into

* Memoirs, i. 174.

the conflict of life he borrowed no weapons from others, but relied on his own manly vigour. His style, consequently, is inimitable. It is capable of no transpositions or changes. The same meaning can be conveyed only in the same words. They are those picturesque, truthful words; ready, inevitable to a man of genius; coy of their presence to the dullard.

The most pervading characteristic of Sydney Smith's writings is his wit; wit blended with the genial humour of the man. It breathes from him as the very atmosphere of his nature.

Lord John Russell, in the preface to one of the volumes of his Memoirs of the poet Moore, has happily discriminated the peculiarities of this omnipresent faculty, as it was developed in society. "There are," he says, "two kinds of colloquial wit, which equally contribute to fame, though not equally to agreeable conversation. The one is like a rocket in a dark air, which shoots at once into the sky, and is the more surprising from the previous silence and gloom; the other is like that kind of firework which blazes and bursts out in every direction, exploding at one moment, and shining brilliantly at another, eccentric in its course, and changing its shape and colour to many forms and many hues. Or, as a dinner is set out with two kinds of champagne, so these two kinds of wit, the still and the sparkling, are to be found in good company. Sheridan and Talleyrand were among the best examples of the first. Hare* (as I have heard) and Sydney Smith were brilliant instances of the second. Hare I knew only by tradition, but with Sydney Smith I long lived intimately. His great delight was to produce a succession of ludicrous images: these followed each other with a rapidity that scarcely left time to laugh; he himself

---

* James Hare, the intimate of Charles James Fox and his circle, the friend and correspondent of Selwyn. Few passages of his wit survive his personal memory. Jesse (Selwyn and his contemporaries, iii. 285) gives the following neat specimen : "He was one day conversing with General Fitzpatrick, when the latter affected to discredit the report of General Burgoyne having been defeated at Saratoga. "Perhaps you may be right in your opinion," said Hare, "but take t from me as a flying rumour."

laughing loudest and with more enjoyment than any one. This electric contact of mirth came and went with the occasion; it cannot be repeated or reproduced. Anything would give occasion to it. For instance, having seen in the newspapers that Sir Æneas Mackintosh* was come to town, he drew such a ludicrous caricature of Sir Æneas and Lady Dido, for the amusement of their namesake, that Sir James Mackintosh rolled on the floor in fits of laughter, and Sydney Smith, striding across him, exclaimed, 'Ruat Justitia!' His powers of fun were at the same time united with the strongest and most practical common sense. So that while he laughed away seriousness at one minute, he destroyed in the next some rooted prejudice which had braved for a thousand years the battle of reason and the breeze of ridicule. The letters of Peter Plymley bear the greatest likeness to his conversation; the description of Mr. Isaac Hawkins Brown dining at the Court of Naples in a volcano coat with lava buttons, and the comparison of Mr. Canning to a large blue-bottle fly with its parasites, most resemble the pictures he raised up in social conversation. It may be averred for certain that in this style he has never been equalled, and I do not suppose he will ever be surpassed."†

In the occasional passages of Moore's Diary in which Sydney Smith is mentioned, always under agreeable circumstances, there are numerous instances of this peculiar vein of humour, " huddling jest upon jest with impossible conveyance," the sagacity apparently not inspiring the wit, but the extravagance giving birth to the wisdom. At a breakfast at Rogers's, "Smith, full of comicality and fancy, kept us all in roars of laughter. In talking of the stories about dram-drinkers catching fire, pursued the idea in every possible shape. The inconvenience of a man coming too near the candle when he was speaking, 'Sir, your observation has caught

---

* Twenty-third laird of the Mackintoshes of that ilk, was created a Baronet in 1812. He died in the sixty-ninth year of his age, in 1820, when the Baronetcy became extinct. " He was a gentleman of the greatest worth," says his obituary in the Gentleman's Magazine.

† Preface to the Sixth Volume of Memoirs of Thomas Moore, pp. xii-xiv

fire.' Then imagined a person breaking into a blaze in the pulpit; the engines called to put him out; no water to be had, the man at the waterworks being a Unitarian or an Atheist." This was mostly pure fun. On the same occasion, one of his apparently ludicrous sayings displayed a keen wit, with matter for profound thought, when he said of some one—" He has no command over his understanding; it is always getting between his legs and tripping him up."* Another instance of this humourous amplification in his table talk, which is happily related in Lady Holland's Memoir, brings the very man before us, "in his habit as he lived:"— " Some one mentioned that a young Scotchman, who had been lately in the neighbourhood, was about to marry an Irish widow, double his age and of considerable dimensions. ' Going to marry her!' he exclaimed, bursting out laughing; 'going to marry her! impossible! you mean a part of her; he could not marry her all himself. It would be a case, not of bigamy, but trigamy; the neighbourhood or the magistrates should interfere. There is enough of her to furnish wives for a whole parish. One man marry her! it is monstrous. You might people a colony with her; or give an assembly with her; or perhaps take your morning's walk round her, always provided there were frequent resting-places, and you were in rude health. I once was rash enough to try walking round her before breakfast, but only got half-way and gave it up exhausted. Or you might read the Riot Act and disperse her; in short, you might do anything with her but marry her.' 'Oh, Mr. Sydney!' said a young lady, recovering from the general laugh, ' did you make all that yourself?' ' Yes, Lucy,' throwing himself back in his chair and shaking with laughter, ' all myself, child; all my own thunder. Do you think, when I am about to make a joke, I send for my neighbours C. and G., or consult the clerk and church-wardens upon it? But let us go into the garden;' and, all laughing till we cried, without hats or bonnets, we sallied forth out of his glorified window into the garden."†

* Moore's Diary, May 27, '826. † Memoir, i. 304-5.

The best proof of the kindliness of Sydney Smith's wit is, that it did not offend the friends upon whom it was played off. It was truthful without bitterness: its playful brightness cleared the atmosphere, but the bolt never scathed. His jests upon Jeffrey, the "maximus minimus," were incessant, but they did not interrupt mutual friendship and esteem. The strongest recognition of the kindliness which underlay the mirth, is in a compliment paid by the Earl of Dudley, whose eccentricities, based on physical infirmity, might have excused sensitiveness. When Smith took leave of him, on going from London to Yorkshire, Dudley said, "You have been laughing at me constantly, Sydney, for the last seven years, and yet, in all that time, you never said a single thing to me that I wished unsaid." The fact is, that the humour of Sydney Smith was a relief from the usual social impertinences, the chief ingredient of which is malevolence, which pass, in society, under the name of wit. Take away the malignity, the spite, the perversions, the irreligion, the indecorum of most witty sayings, and how small a residuum is left. There was nothing of the slow, stealthy approach of the sarcastic, biting sayer of "good things" in Sydney Smith. His jests were in a rollicking vein of extravaganza. The tendency of this humour is to license, but Smith's conversation was innocent. Moore, who had the best opportunity of knowing the range of Smith's social moods, says, " in his gayest flights, though boisterous, he is never vulgar."[*] Rogers described his style to the life: " Whenever the conversation is getting dull, he throws in some touch which makes it rebound and rise again as light as ever. There is this difference between Luttrell and Smith: after Luttrell, you remember what good things he said — after Smith, you remember how much you laughed."[†]

[*] Diary, March 13, 1833.
[†] Moore's Diary, April 10, 1823. On the same occasion Moore writes: "Smith particularly amusing. Have rather held out against him hitherto; but this day he conquered me; and I am now his victim, in the laughing way, for life. His imagination of a duel between two doctors, with oil of Croton on the tips of their fingers, trying to touch each other's lips, highly ludicrous "

In his own Essay on Wit, Smith fearlessly quoted the multifarious and exhaustive definition of Barrow. He may be tried on each of its counts, and be found honourably guilty of perpetrating every jest enumerated in the indictment. The "pat allusion to a known story," is exemplified in the case of memorable Mrs. Partington; the "forging an apposite tale," in the passage from the Synod of Dort and the story of "the Village;" while the "dress of humourous expression," the "odd similitude," the "bold scheme of speech," the "tart irony," the "lusty hyperbole," the "acute nonsense," were peculiarly Sydney Smith's own. The *reductio ad absurdum* was his favourite method. He gave his fish line, and swam it to death. He well knew how "affinity of sound and words and phrases" enriched expression, and practised the art in his style, but the perversion of these things in puns he despised. We have noticed only two instances in all his writings.*

If the form of his wit indicated something of levity, its spirit was sound and earnest. There was a grave thought always at the bottom. This has given his writings a permanent value, while brilliant contemporary reputations have fluttered and died. On this point an acute critic, Mrs. Jameson, remarks—and her testimony may be taken for the greater value, since she complains, that "her nature feels the want of the artistic and imaginative in his nature"—that "the wit of Sydney Smith almost always involved a thought worth remembering for its own sake, as well as worth remembering for its brilliant vehicle: the value of ten thousand pounds sterling of sense concentrated into a cut and polished diamond. It is not true, as I have heard it said," she continues, "that after leaving the society of Sydney Smith, you only remembered how much you had laughed, not the good things at which

---

* One of Napoleon, in 1798, "Ireland safe; and Buonaparte embayed in Egypt; that is, surrounded by Beys!" The other, in a note to the Countess Grey: "If any one bearing the name of Grey comes this way (to Combe Florey), send him to us: I am *Grey-men-iverous!*"

you had laughed. Few men—wits by profession—ever said so many memorable things as those recorded of Sydney Smith."*

The Letters of Sydney Smith have little pretension in their form as epistolary compositions; but they are rare specimens of a rare class; ranking, for their terseness and witty flavour, with the notes and "notelets" of Charles Lamb. They are generally brief, never attempt any regular or didactic exposition of a subject, but contain, in virtue of their epigrammatic truthfulness—to say nothing of the constant entertainment—profitable matter of general wisdom and information of the men and affairs of his day, to take their place with the published correspondence of the greatest of his contemporaries. In a few lines he settles a moral question, draws the portrait of a public man, pleasantly corrects a defect, or rallies the spirits of a friend. He wrote often to Jeffrey, and to John Murray; less frequently to Allen, Lord Holland, Earl Grey, and in the latter part of his life exchanged a gouty correspondence with Sir George Philips, and wrote warm complimentary notes to Dickens. But most of his letters are addressed to ladies; to Lady Holland, to Mrs, Meynell, to Miss Georgiana Harcourt, daughter of the Archbishop of York, the Countess Grey, Lady Mary Bennett, and others. Playful and sincerely affectionate, they are the perfection of ingenious flattery, the sweetness of the adulation being taken off by the humourous extravagance.

A paragraph is due to Holland House, a seat sacred in the history of Letters, the centre of the important social, literary, and political circle with which Sydney Smith revolved during the greater part of his life. Its traditions go back to the early years of the seventeenth century, when it was built by Sir Walter Cope.† The grounds had belonged to the noble family of the De

---

* Common-Place Book of Thoughts, Memories and Fancies, p. 49.

† There is a pleasant account of the historical incidents connected with Holland House, in two papers by Leigh Hunt, in Nos. 204 and 205 of Household Words.

Vere's since the Conquest. The house was bequeathed by Cope to his son-in-law, Henry Rich, first Earl of Holland, a son of the first Earl of Warwick. Rich was a gallant man, a favourite at the court of Charles I. In the beginning of the civil war he sided with the Parliament, then took up arms for the King—was taken prisoner and executed in 1648. Fairfax, the Parliamentary general, next occupied the mansion; when, as tradition goes, it was privy to the deliberations of Cromwell. After the Restoration it had various occupants, Pope's "downright Shippen" among them. Before establishing himself at Kensington, King William, as we learn, from Macaulay's History, thought of the House as a residence, and occupied it a few weeks.* The second Earl of Holland, the elder branch of his family failing, united the titles of Warwick and Holland. Marriage with the widow of his son, the Countess of Warwick, in 1716, made Addison an inmate of Holland House. The poet passed there the last three years of his life, not very happily, as Johnson would have us infer, who represents him as a slave to the rank of the Countess. He gained new titles of his own to honour, however, at the time, for it was in the second year of his marriage that he was made Secretary of State. There is a doubtful story of his meditating Spectators in the library, refreshed by a bottle of wine at either end of the room. This, if it occurred at all, must have been before his marriage, since the Spectator closed with the year 1714. It was in a chamber of Holland House that the death scene occurred, when Addison called to him his step-son, the young Earl of Warwick, to "see how a Christian can die." The family of the Earls of Holland becoming extinct, in 1759, the house became, soon after, by purchase, the property of Henry Fox, the crafty politician of the Walpole era, who was created Lord Holland, the first of the present line. His father was Sir Stephen Fox, who, from being a chorister boy at Salisbury Cathedral, was called to an inferior situation at court, attended Charles II. in exile, and on his return

* Chapter xi., vol. iii.

secured an honourable fortune by his financial skill and integrity. "In a word,' says Evelyn, in his Diary, "never was man more fortunate than Sir Stephen; he is a handsome person, virtuous, and very religious."* He was seventy-six years old when he married a second time, and became the father of Henry Fox. A son of the latter, Stephen Fox, was the second Lord Holland, elder brother of Charles James Fox. Stephen Fox died young, and left the title to the late Lord Holland, who restored the literary prestige of the house, not only by his own writings, but by his patronage of merit. His liberal parliamentary career is matter of recent history. His chief writings are, Lives of Lope de Vega and Guillem de Castro, a translation of three Spanish comedies, and of a Canto of the Orlando Furioso, the Preface to Fox's History of James II., for the copyright of which Murray paid the magnificent sum of four thousand pounds, the Prefaces to his editions, from the original MSS., of Earl Waldegrave's Memoirs, and Horace Walpole's Last Ten Years of the Reign of George II., and posthumous Recollections of Foreign Courts, and Memoirs of the Whig party. He was a clever writer of occasional verses. His couplet to the poet Rogers, affixed to a garden-seat in the grounds of Holland House, is very neat:—

"Here Rogers sat; and here for ever dwell
To me, those Pleasures that he sang so well."

The lines which were found on his dressing-table at his death, are as finely conceived:—

"Nephew of Fox and friend of Grey—
Enough my meed of fame,
If those who deigned to observe me say
I injured neither name."

The amiable character of Lord Holland, no less than his intellectual characteristics, endeared him to Sydney Smith. Lady Holland celebrates their conversation:—"short, varied, interspersed with wit, illustration and anecdote on both sides; the perfection of so-

* Diary, September, 6, 1680.

cial intercourse, a sort of mental dram-drinking, rare as it was delightful."*

An important position in the literary annals of Holland House belongs to Lady Holland. She was the daughter and heir of Richard Vassall and the divorced wife of Sir Godfrey Webster. Lord Holland, previous to his marriage to her, in 1797, paid to her husband six thousand pounds damages in a criminal action. He took, at the marriage, the name of Vassall. Lady Holland had talent, knew how to shine among the wits, be fascinating and influential, was often a warm friend, while her domineering patronage appears at times to have been sufficiently offensive. It is curious to note Sydney Smith's recognition of a *Hollandophobia* visiting all new guests at the house. The poet Campbell, at the age of thirty, went there with dread. "Lady Holland," he writes to a friend, " is a formidable woman. She is cleverer, by several degrees, than Buonaparte." Rogers told a characteristic story of her manner :—" When Lady Holland wanted to get rid of a fop, she used to say, 'I beg your pardon, but I wish you would sit a little further off; there is something on your handkerchief which I don't quite like.' "† Very unlike this was Sydney Smith's description of the kind and intellectual Miss Fox, Lord Holland's sister:— " Oh, she is perfection: she always gives me the idea of an aged angel."

Byron gave some caustic touches to the literary set at Holland House, in his English Bards and Scotch Reviewers, with a cutting glance at "My lady." There are some instances of her rule in Rogers' Table Talk,‡ and an occasional glimpse, in Moore's Diary, of her

* Memoirs, i. 78.
† Dyce's Table Talk, p. 273.
‡ Take one for the sake of the adroitly-turned compliment at the close .- "Lord Holland never ventured to ask any one to dinner (not even me, whom he had known so long and so intimately) without previously consulting Lady H. Shortly before his death I called at Holland House, and found only Lady H. within. As I was coming out I met Lord Holland, who said, 'Well, do you return to dinner?' I answered, 'No; I have not been invited.' Perhaps this deference to Lady H. was not to be regretted; for Lord Holland was so

"rather *bravura* mood." A Sunday garden scene, in that record, is picturesque: "Breakfasted with Rogers. Went out to Holland House. The levee there of a Sunday always delightful. My Lord on his stock-still pony, taking exercise, as he thinks: and my Lady in her whiskey, surrounded by *savans*. There were to-day Sydney Smith, Brougham, Jeffrey, &c. Sydney Smith praised my 'Byron,' the first book of mine (or indeed any one else's) I ever heard him give a good word to; seemed to do it, too, with sincerity."* Elsewhere Moore chronicles Lord Holland at breakfast "in his gouty chair, but with a face as gay and shining as that of a schoolboy." He has a happy look in Leslie's picture of the Library at Holland House, where he is introduced with full lengths of Lady Holland and their constant companion, Allen; who appears as well filled out in person and beneficent in countenance as his Lordship.

There are some very pleasant glimpses of Holland House in Sydney Smith's Letters. Writing to Lady Holland, he says:—"I am sure it is better for Lord Holland and you to be at Holland House, because you both hate exercise (as every person of sense does), and you must be put in situations where it can be easily and pleasantly taken. Even Allen gets some exercise at Holland House, for Horner, Sheridan, and Lord Lauderdale take him out on the gravel-walk, to milk him for bullion, Spain, America, and India; whereas, in London, he is milked in that stall below stairs."†

In another letter to Lady Holland, without date, Allen reappears:—"I know nothing more agreeable than a dinner at Holland House; but it must not begin at ten in the morning, and last till six. I should be incapable, for the last four hours, of laughing at Lord Holland's jokes, eating Raffaelle's cakes, or repelling Mr Allen's attacks upon the church."

hospitable and good-natured, that, had he been left to himself, he would have had a crowd at his table daily."—(Dyce's Recollections, p. 275.)

* Moore's Diary, May 2, 1830.
† Heslington, April 21, 1810.

Allen's chemistry and opinions were always a resource for Sydney Smith. Moore has one of these occasions; dining at Holland House, he enters in his Diary:—" Sydney Smith very comical about the remedy that Lady Holland is going to use for the bookworm, which is making great ravages in the library. She is about to have them washed with some mercurial preparation; and Smith says it is Davy's opinion that the air will become charged with the mercury, and that the whole family will be salivated. 'I shall see Allen,' says Smith, 'some day, with his tongue hanging out, speechless, and shall take the opportunity to stick a few principles into him.'"*

The finest tribute to the literary glories of Holland House, under the long reign of its late master, is in an article on Lord Holland, by Macaulay, in the Edinburgh Review for July, 1841—where, in most musical periods, are painted the reminiscences of "a few old men" visiting the locality on which the great city is so rapidly encroaching. "With peculiar fondness they will recall that venerable chamber, in which all the antique gravity of a college library was so singularly blended with all that female grace and wit could devise to embellish a drawing-room. They will recollect, not unmoved, those shelves, loaded with the varied learning of many lands and many ages; those portraits in which were preserved the features of the best and wisest Englishmen of two generations. They will recollect how many men who have guided the politics of Europe—who have moved great assemblies by reason and eloquence—who have put life into bronze or canvass, or who have left to posterity things so written as it shall not willingly let them die—were there mixed with all that was loveliest and gayest in the society of the most splendid of capitals. They will remember the singular character which belonged to that circle, in which every talent and accomplishment, every art and science, had its place. They will remember how the last debate was discussed in one corner, and the last comedy of Scribe in another; while Wilkie

* Diary, April 6, 1823.

gazed with modest admiration on Reynolds' Baretti; while Mackintosh turned over Thomas Aquinas, to verify a quotation; while Talleyrand related his conversations with Barras at the Luxemburg, or his ride with Lannes over the field of Austerlitz. They will remember, above all, the grace—and the kindness, far more admirable than grace—with which the princely hospitality of that ancient mansion was dispensed."

Whilst honouring these associations of Sydney Smith's manly and noble friendships, it is but justice to the society of his age, to remind the reader, that there were brilliant thinkers and writers outside of the charmed circle and visiting list of Holland House, of whose existence we are scarcely reminded in the letters and conversations of this clever divine. "We should never discover," remarks the North American Review, "from this chronicle that Coleridge also talked, Carlyle reasoned, Lamb jested, Hazlitt criticised, and Shelley and Keats sang in those days. Within the sensible zone of English life, as that term is usually understood, Sydney lived. His scope was within the Whig ranks in politics, and the Established Church pale in religion. The iron horizon of caste is the framework of this attractive picture."*

It is to be noticed also, in this connection, how little Smith's reputation was promoted by the arts of the press of the present day. His associates avoided mere literary notoriety. The Edinburgh Review was anonymous, and it was only in his latter days, when he wrote, occasionally, to the newspapers, and his "works"

---

* N. A. Rev. Jan., 1856. An appreciative view of the essential personal character of Sydney Smith, by Mr. H. T. Tuckerman. The list of omissions might be enlarged by many honoured names. It is not to be supposed, however, that Smith was or would have been insensible to the merit of the great authors just named, or that the "Chronicle" tells the whole story of his tastes and acquisitions. Preoccupied with his own duties, he was slow or indifferent in making new acquaintances. In 1848, ten years after Carlyle had published his Sartor Resartus, and three years after the publication of his French Revolution, Smith writes to a lady friend: "I have not read Carlyle, though I have got him on my list. I am rather curious about him." But had any man ever nobler friends, or did any ever honour such friends more ?

had been collected, that Sydney Smith's name was much before the public. There are few early notices of him by his brother authors.

Byron has an allusion in "English Bards and Scotch Reviewers," to "Smug Sydney," and in his sixteenth Canto of Don Juan, in the description of the banquet:—

> "And lo! upon that day it came to pass,
>   I sat next that o'erwhelming son of heaven,
> The very powerful parson, Peter Pith,
>   The loudest wit I e'er was deafened with.
>
> "I knew him in his livelier London days,
>   A brilliant diner-out, though but a curate;
> And not joke he cut but earned its praise,
>   Until preferment, coming at a sure rate,
> (O Providence! how wondrous are thy ways!
>   Who would suppose thy gifts sometimes obdurate?)
> Gave him, to lay the devil who looks o'er Lincoln,
>   A fat fen vicarage, and nought to think on.
>
> "His jokes were sermons, and his sermons jokes;
>   But both were thrown away amongst the fens;
> For wit hath no great friend in aguish folks.
>   No longer ready ears and short-hand pens
> Imbibed the gay bon-mot, or happy hoax:
>   The poor priest was reduced to common sense,
> Or to coarse efforts very loud and long,
> To hammer a hoarse laugh from the thick throng."

Moore compliments him in some verses written about 1840 entitled, "The Triumphs of Farce."

> "And still let us laugh, preach the world as it may,
>   Where the cream of the joke is, the swarm will soon follow;
> Heroics are very fine things in their way,
>   But the laugh, at the long-run, will carry it hollow.
>
> "Yes, Jocus! gay god, whom the Gentiles supplied,
>   And whose worship not even among Christians declines;
> In our senates thou'st languished, since Sheridan died,
>   But Sydney still keeps thee alive in our shrines.
>
> "Rare Sydney! thrice honoured the stall where he sits,
>   And be his every honour he deigneth to climb at!
> Had England a hierarchy formed all of wits,
>   Whom, but Sydney, would England proclaim as it primate?

> "And long may he flourish, frank, merry, and brave,
> A Horace to feast with, a Pascal to read!
> While he *laughs*, all is safe; but, when Sydney grows grave,
> We shall then think the Church is in danger indeed."

There are one or two notices of Smith in the *Noctes Ambrosianæ*, where his old Edinburgh friends took good care of him. *Tickler* pronounces him "a formidable enemy to pomposity and pretension. No man can wear a big wig comfortably in his presence; the absurdity of such enormous fizzle is felt; and the dignitary would fain exchange all that horsehair for a few scattered locks of another animal." To which Christopher North sagely replies, "He would make a lively interlocutor at a Noctes." Sydney is introduced again, in 1831, when there was talk of making him a Bishop. North thinks that, at the first vacancy, he should be made Dean of St. Patrick's, as a witty successor, of course, of Swift. Tickler suggests, that we should then have the charges in rhyme, e. g.:—

> "Reverend brethren, fish not, shoot not,
> Reel not, quadrille not, fiddle not, flute not,
> But of all things, it is my devoutest desire, sirs,
> That the parson on Sunday should dine with the Squire, sirs.*

In 1838, there was a lively notice of "the Reverend Sydney Smith," in Fraser's "Gallery of Literary Characters," with a

---

* Smith, by the way, was himself no sportsman. When he settled in the country he formed a resolution never to shoot, and gave these conclusive reasons: "First, because I found, on trying at Lord Grey's, that the birds seemed to consider the muzzle of my gun as their safest position; secondly, because I never could help shutting my eyes when I fired my gun, so was not likely to improve; and thirdly, because, if you do shoot, the squire and the poacher both consider you as their natural enemy, and I thought it more clerical to be at peace with both." (Lady Holland's Memoir, p. 133.) He was quite too careless a rider for the chase, and had far too little patience for the angle. Dancing seems to have had a peculiar effect upon him. When his pupil was under his charge at Edinburgh, he wrote to Mrs. Beach: "Michael takes a lesson in dancing every day. I get him, now and then, to show me a step or two. I cannot bear the repetition of this spectacle every day, as it never fails to throw me into a fit of laughing little short of suffocation." (Memoir, 4th Eng. ed., p. 25.) Of theatres, oratorios and the like, he was always impatient.

wicked caricature, by Maclise, which, however, taken with the other engraved portraits, may help, materially, to a knowledge of the personal appearance of the man.

Much has been said concerning the irreverence of Sydney Smith, and his incapacity, in consequence of the social freedom, the license of the intellect, which he indulged in, to discharge the sober duties of the Church. As there is, apparently, some colour for this objection, it may be worth while to look into its nature. It is undoubtedly right that a clergyman should be required to make some sacrifices of matters allowable enough in themselves, to sustain the distinct professional character of his calling. The world exacts something from the lawyer, the physician, and the merchant, on this point. These classes are bound under various social penalties, to sustain, to a certain extent, a conventional propriety and decorum. The pleader is expected by his client to be calm and collected, and play no mountebank tricks in court. A physician who indulges in any great levity of manner should not be disappointed at the slender list of his patients. The great merchant is a grave man, for he is intrusted with the millions of other people, and pecuniary responsibility of this kind must needs occupy his attention seriously. In a higher degree and to a greater extent, the vocation of the divine demands and inspires solemnity. There is, however, parallel with all these requirements, a natural, healthy, free development of the individual man. Gravity is a good thing in its place, but it may be asked for in excess. The cheap gravity of the fool, whose stagnant countenance is the index of the unstirred mind within, may be purchased in every market; and very frequently finds purchasers who pay dear for the commodity. Gravity may be the cloak of hypocrisy; it is a garment easily made up, and its wear deceives many. Get the genuine article, and it is invaluable. "There is," says Doctor South, "the silence of an Archimedes in the study of a problem, and the stillness of a sow at her wash." Lest we confound exhibitions so diverse, we must look underneath to the elements of character. The man, after all, is the basis of the worth, and as it is upon the development of what Nature has implanted, care must be taken not to thwart or defeat her movements. She, the mighty mother, will assert herself rightfully, and overrule or be revenged upon the conventionalisms. If your grave lawyer does not possess liveliness or quickness of mind, he will not see promptly into your case, or will hazard it where readiness is required, in the brief, dramatic action of the court. The physician should have great vivacity of perception, for he has frequently but a moment to choose between life and death. The merchant needs a nimble understanding, else his staid formulas of trade will leave him in poverty. Is it any ground of objection with an intelligent mind, that the lawyer is a man of humour, that he makes an excellent after-dinner speech, that he enjoys a dramatic entertainment; that the physician contrasts the pretensions of intellect with his knowledge of physical necessities, and laughs loudly and frequently over the incongruities brought to his knowledge; or that the merchant, out of his counting-house, makes himself as jocose and agreeable as it is possible for him to be? To state the objection is to refute it. How is the case, then, different with a clergyman? Does wit incapacitate him for the work of a Christian minister? Because he may be said, unlike the lawyer, physician, or merchant, to be always practising his profession, is he, on that account, never to relax the muscles of his face, or shake the midriff of his neighbour by laughter-compelling jest? An Apostle has borne his testimony against dullness in conversation, by recommending that speech be seasoned with salt. No one can reasonably question the good gifts of wit and humour, in their beneficence to one in the clerical relation, or in any other. It becomes, then, a question of degree, when Sydney Smith is arraigned as too great a jester for the pulpit. But how can this question of moderation be decided? Who shall set the limit where wit transcends decorum and commences to be anti-clerical? If one jest or a dozen are permissible, why not twenty or thirty? Or, is it to be regulated by time? If the latter, the standard is unequal, for your Sydney Smith will let off a hundred witticisms while your dullard is feebly labouring at one, and voluble nonsense will triumph when wise meditation is silenced. At what precise moment must the wrinkled grin be smoothed down into the platitude of propriety? Is the sin in the strength of the article? Is a smile orthodox, and is a laugh heretical? May a good man, without violation of his goodness, cause his companion to shake in his chair, with gentle titillations, while it becomes sinful to inflict the acuter displays of wit, the inextinguishable laughter of the immortals. Gentle dullness, we know on good poetical authority, ever loves a joke, but must all jokes be conformed to the standard of dullness? "You are always aiming at wit," said some one of the class of objectors to Charles Lamb. "It is better, at any rate," was the retort, "than always aiming at dullness." It was in reference to the same race of critics that the eminent divine, Dr. Samuel Clarke, being once engaged in a game of romps, seeing a mere formalist approaching, exclaimed, "Let us give over, there's a fool coming." The common sense of the world sets any objection at rest. Practically, we have never known any one to possess wit and despise it. On the contrary, we have seen very pious clergymen exult at the perpetration of very feeble jokes. We have observed them also, at a loss for a witticism, run to the Bible for a text. Indeed, they frequently fall into the error of a familiar and irreverent use of Scripture texts in conversation and on public occasions, from lack of that very culture of wit and literature which would place other and more appropriate weapons at their disposal.

There were clerical wits before Smith in the English Church; Latimer, with his rough, homely, vigorous way; the quaint humourist, Dr. Thomas Fuller, the Church historian, whose incessant quips and cranks were always subservient to his much reading and a sound, healthy understanding; Echard, whose "Letters on the Grounds and Occasions of the Contempt of the Clergy," were the godfathers of Sydney Smith's papers on clerical topics; the rich, mellow wit of South, in his pure-toned, eloquent discourses; the scornful mood of Swift; the pulpit attitudinarianism of Sterne. Some of the sermons of these men must have tempted the laughter of their congregations; a natural tribute to honest convictions of truth which would seldom be tolerated within modern church walls. Much might be said in defence of the pulpit wit of South, and his example might be commended as a resource to preachers who cannot afford, at this time of day, to lose a single potent instrument of arousing the susceptibility of their hearers. Sydney Smith, however, does not ask this vindication or indulgence. His published sermons are as solemn, as free from unseemly jesting, as those of the gravest and dullest of his brethren. He drew the line distinctly between levity and sanctity; never confounding the choir of St. Paul's with the dining-room of Holland House. His friend, Mrs. Austin, when she first heard him preach at the London Cathedral, confesses that she had "some misgivings as to the effect which that well-known face and voice, ever associated with wit and mirth, might have upon her, even in the sacred place. Never (she adds) were misgivings more quickly and entirely dissipated. The moment he appeared in the pulpit, all the weight of his duty, all the authority of his office, were written on his countenance; and without a particle of affectation (of which he was incapable), his whole demeanor bespoke the gravity of his purpose."* This was the habitual effect of his ministerial duties, and it might have been looked for. Nor was this gravity confined to the pulpit. After leaving one of Rogers' breakfasts, with Sydney, Moore tells us, "I found him (as I have often done before) change at once from the gay, uproarious way, into as solemn, grave, and austere a person as any bench of judges or bishops could supply: *this I rather think his natural character.*"† The topics of these wits were not always the lightest, as another striking entry in Moore's Diary witnesses. It was in London, in June, 1831:—

* Memoir, p. 273.   † Moore's Diary, May 27, 1826.

"Walked with Sydney Smith; told me his age; turned sixty. Asked me how I felt about dying. Answered that if my mind was but at ease about the comfort of those I left behind, I should leave the world without much regret, having passed a very happy life, and enjoyed (as much, perhaps, as ever man did yet) all that is enjoyable in it; the only single thing I have had to complain of being want of money. I could, therefore, die with the same words that Jortin died, 'I have had enough of everything.'" What the reply of the divine was we are not informed.

True wit is a precious commodity, the distillation of a generous, richly-gifted nature, and such a disposition must be founded on seriousness. There is a light, frivolous wit, a melancholy, scoffing wit; but these do not belong to the nature to which we allude. We hold it to be utterly impossible that a man should possess the honest mirth of Sydney Smith and be insensible to the gravities of life; that he should penetrate to the heart of social abuses, of conventionalisms, of cant of every kind with a loving eye to the real welfare of his race, and should want at the same time sympathy with sadness, tears for grief, or a sacred regard for religious obligations.

What is thus true between man and man does not become false when a clergyman is the subject. It is only where a low, injurious view of the clerical character is taken, that there can be any misconception of the matter. It is as absurd to say that a minister of any religious denomination shall not laugh, and that loudly and frequently too, if he please, because his duty is to worship and to pray, as it would be to forbid a healthy-lunged layman joining in the litanies of the church on account of his gay temperament, and his faculty of enjoying himself prodigiously at festive entertainments.

There is a popular delusion among good men on the matter. The clergyman, whatever his natural disposition may be, is expected by many people, not accustomed to get to the heart of a subject, to wear always the externals of piety and to relax nothing from the rigours of a ghastly white cravat, an unbending, facial muscle, and a stolid, glazed eye. There is consequently a struggle of nature against him. Humanity keeps at a distance from him; and humanity, in the end, will have the advantage over him; for it is too much for any one man or any set of men. If a clergyman assumes a conventional dress and manner, he invites and is pretty sure to receive from the world a conventional treatment. A thousand social hypocrisies start up to meet him. His sanctities are admitted as a matter of fashion; it is respectable to speak well of the cloth, as it is termed, but how is the influence of the man within the garment abated! In another way, also occasional and too frequent injury is sustained. Professional decorum, once established, becomes a mask which it is easier to wear than to challenge the rewards of holiness by practising rigorously its duties; the genial, active life of mental and personal industry, of courage, liberality, and honour; mingling freely with the world, at once in it and above it; the true friendship of publicans and sinners, of the poor and the contemned.

It is to be considered, in illustration of these remarks, in the case of Sydney Smith, how greatly his wit enlarged his influence with the world in the cause of truth; how it pointed and feathered the arrows which were to carry conviction to dull understandings; how it was constantly and uniformly exerted in levelling oppression and injustice; how much it added to the power of the great practical reformer. We may add that it sometimes gave him an authority in rebuking infidelity itself, where a heavier weapon would have failed. At a dinner once at Holland House he met a French savant who took it upon himself to annoy the best disposed of the company by a variety of free-thinking speculations. He ended by avowing himself a materialist. "Very good soup this," struck in Mr. Smith. "*Oui, Monsieur, c'est excellente.*" "Pray, sir," was the retort which for that time and place was worth a library of argument, "do you believe in a cook?"*

* Memoir of Rev. Richard Barham, p. 105.

The Rev. Sydney Smith was sound at heart on this subject. When he saw some signs of unseemly levity, as he thought, in an article* in the Edinburgh Review, he wrote to the editor, Jeffrey, rebuking the license as injurious, by its indiscretion, and rendering it "perilous to a clergyman in particular to be concerned in the Review." Ten years later he wrote again to Jeffrey—"I must beg the favour of you to be explicit on one point. Do you mean to take care that the Review shall not profess or encourage infidel principles? Unless this is the case I must absolutely give up all thoughts of connecting myself with it."†

Sydney Smith must thus be absolved from the charge of employing his wit to the injury of sound religious principle. As a matter of taste he sometimes, it must be admitted, pushed his jest to an extremity with professional ecclesiastical arrangements, and, in a few instances, as in his description of Rogers' dining-room, with "a blaze of light above, and below nothing but darkness and gnashing of teeth,"‡ may be rebuked by the censure of Dr

---

* It was an article in the Review for Jan., 1808, making sport of a heavy and absurd epic poem, by Charles Hoyle, of Cambridge, on the departure of the Israelites from Egypt, entitled Exodus, an example of the not uncommon delusion of crude imitators of Homer and Milton. The article follows one of Sydney Smith on Methodism, which at least to those who winced under it, would appear far more reprehensible than speaking lightly of Pharaoh and the jugglers of his court. Smith's objection to the latter article showed his sensitiveness as a wit as well as his sense of the proprieties. "The levities," he says, "are ponderous and vulgar, as well as indiscreet." Scripture was one thing in the eyes of Sydney Smith, and the Methodism of the beginning of the century quite another. His treatment of what he considered the eccentricities of the latter was vigorous and unsparing. In reading his reply to Mr. John Styles, who ventured a retort, we feel that it is "excellent to have a giant's strength," and perhaps, "tyrannous to use it like a giant."

† Letter 141.

‡ Dyce's Table Talk of Rogers. Rogers arrays the poetical authorities on the distribution of light, in a note to his "Epistle to a Friend," citing Homer, Lucretius, Virgil, Leonardo da Vinci, and Milton. A Quarterly Reviewer remarks upon this: "There are few precepts of taste that are not practised in Mr. Rogers' establishment, as well as recommended in his works; but he has hit upon a novel and ingenious mode of lighting a dining-room. Lamps above, or candles on the table, there are none: all the light is reflected

Johnson on the employment of "idle and indecent applications of sentences taken from the Scriptures; a mode of merriment which a good man dreads for its profaneness, and a witty man disdains for its easiness and vulgarity."* Another is readily pardonable, the oft-mentioned reply to Landseer's request that he should sit to him for his picture—"Is thy servant a dog that he should do this thing?" There is another of the same class attributed to him on receiving, at the time of the Pennsylvania grievance, a visiter who congratulated him on his happy circumstances. "Yes," said Sydney, in the words of St. Paul, "I would that you were almost and altogether such as I am, except these bonds." Sydney Smith, however, appears seldom to have transgressed in this direction. The defence of a friendly writer on this subject must be admitted in his favour. "Some of the happiest jests of Smith were ecclesiastical. But such sallies were too professional to be profane. They seemed to rebound upon himself, or they played about his order: they certainly scorched nothing. If there was satire in them, it was directed only at hypocrisy or corruption. If he could lightly touch the terrene and external part of religion—its secularized institutions—its drowsy dignitaries; he paid lowliest obeisance (wherever he could discern it) to its heavenly spirit. He could play with the tassel of his cushion; never with the leaves of his Bible."†

In one or two instances there is a freedom of expression indulged in by Sydney Smith, allowable perhaps, among the liberties of social life of Europe, where conversation and literature are less

by Titians, Reynolds, &c., from lamps projecting out of the frames of the pictures and screened from the company." (Quar. Rev., lv., 457.)

* Life of Pope. The witty Dr. Thomas Fuller had anticipated Johnson in this remark. In the chapter "Of Jesting," in his Holy State, he says: "Jest not with the two-edged sword of God's word. Will nothing please thee to wash thy hands in but the font? or to drink healths in but the church chalice? And know, the whole art is learnt at the first admission, and profane jests will come without calling."

† An admirable article on the Life of Sydney Smith in the British Quarterly Review for July, 1851

restricted in these respects than in America. Addressing Lady Holland in 1811 in a note, in a reply to an invitation to dinner, his witticism seems bold as addressed to a lady; satirical person ally, considering the antecedents of his honourable hostess:—

"How very odd, dear Lady Holland, to ask me to dine with you on Sunday, the 9th, when I am coming to stay with you from the 5th to the 12th! It is like giving a gentleman an assignation for Wednesday, when you are going to marry him on the preceding Sunday—an attempt to combine the stimulus of gallantry with the security of connubial relations. I do not propose to be guilty of the slightest infidelity to you while I am at Holland House, except you dine in town; and then it will not be infidelity, but spirited recrimination. Ever the sincere and affectionate friend of Lady Holland."

These, however, if pressed as defects, would be but slight blemishes in a lifetime passed in kindliness,* charity, truthfulness and honour. If his wit or humour occasionally appear in excess in his memoirs, it is to be remembered how largely these relaxations of his life have been chronicled, and that all the while he was pursuing a serious, noble, useful career. The jests of Sydney Smith should be passed to his credit, as supererogatory gifts to the world, contributed after he had performed the usual duties of a valuable man. Men of worth and integrity are always to be honoured, but how little would we give for the table-talk of most of them, in comparison with that of this ingenious social benefactor.

Sydney Smith was not, indeed, a profound spiritualist; he was

* There is a rare instance of forbearance for a wit, which comes to light in one of Sydney Smith's letters to Lady Holland, in 1839: "I have written against —— one of the cleverest pamphlets I ever read, which I think would cover —— and him with ridicule. At least it made me laugh very much in reading it; and there I stood, with the printer's devil, and the real devil close to me; and then I said, 'After all, this is very funny, and very well written, but it will give great pain to people who have been very kind and good to me through life; and what can I do to show my sense of that kindness, if it is not by flinging this pamphlet into the fire?' So I flung it in, and there was an end. My sense of ill-usage remains, of course, the same."

not a great philosopher; there have been deeper thinkers, more earnest divines. He was a dogmatist from his impulses and position in society. Fortunately his nature was broad and liberal, and his lot was cast among whigs and reformers. He was for expediency; but his expediency implied courage for the right and true. It was not vulgar temporizing, but an enlarged conformity to the well-being of society.

It is for few to round the outer circle, broken as it is, of human excellence. Sydney Smith, like most of the best of men, was but a parcel man. But how complete within his limits, how perfect in his segment! He took a healthy view of life, as it must practically come home to the greater part of the world; saw its necessities, and complied with its duties, while he embroidered this plainness with his delightful humours.

Such men should be cultivated at the present day from their rarity, for modern levelling is not favourable to their growth. They enlarge the freedom of life, add to its faculties as well as its enjoyments, clear the intellectual and warm the moral atmosphere. Characters there are enough, excrescences on society, oddities, in the sense of perversions of human nature, anomalous churls, crude, hard-hearted and repulsive; but there are few such illustrations of the kindly powers of life as this brave humourist—the man of generous humour and humours.

SELECTIONS.

PASSAGES FROM THE EDINBURGH REVIEW.

DR. PARR'S SPITAL SERMON.*

WHOEVER has had the good fortune to see Dr. Parr's wig, must have observed, that while it trespasses a little on the orthodox magnitude of perukes in the anterior parts, it scorns even Episcopal limits behind, and swells out into boundless convexity of frizz, the μεγα θαυμα of barbers, and the terror of the literary world. After the manner of his wig, the doctor has constructed his sermon, giving us a discourse of no common length, and subjoining an immeasurable mass of notes, which appear to concern every learned man, and almost every unlearned man since the beginning of the world.†

*   *   *   *   *   *   *   *

The style is such as to give a general impression of heaviness to the whole sermon. The Doctor is never simple and natural for a single instant. Everything smells of the rhetorician. He never appears to forget himself, or to be hurried by his subject into obvious language. Every expression seems to be the result of artifice and intention; and as to the worthy dedicatees, the Lord-Mayor and Aldermen, unless the sermon be *done into English by a person of honour*, they may, perhaps, be flattered by the Doctor's politeness, but they can never be much edified by his meaning.

---

* Ed. Rev., Oct., 1802. Spital Sermon, preached at Christ Church upon Easter-Tuesday, April 15, 1800. To which are added, Notes by Samuel Parr, LL.D.

† In the edition of Parr's Works, the sermon occupies fifty pages of pica text; the notes fill two hundred and twelve in brevier.

Dr. Parr seems to think that eloquence consists, not in exuberance of beautiful images — not in simple and sublime conceptions — not in the feelings of the passions; but in a studious arrrangement of *sonorous, exotic, and sesquipedal* words: a very ancient error, which corrupts the style of young, and wearies the patience of sensible men. In some of his combinations of words the Doctor is singularly unhappy. We have the *din of superficial cavillers, the prancings of giddy ostentation, flattering vanity, hissing scorn, dank clod,* &c., &c., &c. The following intrusion of a technical word into a pathetic description renders the whole passage almost ludicrous:—

"Within a few days, mute was the tongue that uttered these celestial sounds, and the hand which signed your indenture lay cold and motionless in the dark and dreary chambers of death."

Dr. Parr, in speaking of the indentures of the hospital, a subject (as we should have thought) little calculated for rhetorical panegyric, says of them:—

"If the writer of whom I am speaking had perused, as I have, your indentures, and your rules, he would have found in them seriousness without austerity, earnestness without extravagance, good sense without the trickeries of art, good language without the trappings of rhetoric, and the firmness of conscious worth, rather than the prancings of giddy ostentation."

The latter member of this eloge would not be wholly unintelligible, if applied to a spirited coach-horse; but we have never yet witnessed the phenomenon of a *prancing indenture.*

DR. LANGFORD'S ANNIVERSARY SERMON OF THE ROYAL HUMANE SOCIETY.*

An accident which happened to the gentleman engaged in reviewing this sermon proves, in the most striking manner, the importance of this charity for restoring to life persons in whom the vital power is suspended. He was discovered, with Dr. Langford's discourse lying open before him, in a state of the most profound sleep; from which he could not, by any means, be awakened for a great length of time. By attending, however, to the rules prescribed by the Humane Society, flinging in the smoke of tobacco,

* Anniversary Sermon of the Royal Humane Society. By W. Langford. D. D. Ed. Rev. Oct. 1802

applying hot flannels, and carefully removing the discourse itself to a great distance, the critic was restored to his disconsolate brothers.

The only account he could give of himself was, that he remembers reading on, regularly, till he came to the following pathetic description of a drowned tradesman; beyond which he recollects nothing.

"But to the individual himself, as a man, let us add the interruption to all the temporal business in which his interest was engaged. To him indeed, now apparently lost, the world is as nothing: but it seldom happens, that man can live for himself alone: society parcels out its concerns in various connections; and from one head issue waters which run down in many channels. The spring being suddenly cut off, what confusion must follow in the streams which have flowed from its source? It may be, that all the expectations reasonably raised of approaching prosperity, to those who have embarked in the same occupation, may at once disappear; and the important interchange of commercial faith be broken off, before it could be brought to any advantageous conclusion."

This extract will suffice for the style of the sermon. The charity itself is above all praise.

BOOKS OF TRAVEL.†

Of all the species of travels, that which has moral observation for its object is the most liable to error, and has the greatest difficulties to overcome, before it can arrive at excellence. Stones, and roots, and leaves, are subjects which may exercise the understanding without rousing the passions. A mineralogical traveller will hardly fall fouler upon the granite and the feldspar of other countries than his own; a botanist will not conceal its non-descripts; and an agricultural tourist will faithfully detail the average crop per acre; but the traveller who observes on the manners, habits, and institutions of other countries, must have emancipated his mind from the extensive and powerful dominions of association, must have extinguished the agreeable and deceitful feelings of national vanity, and cultivated that patient humility which builds general inferences only upon the repetition of individual facts. Everything

† From a review of "Lettres sur l'Angleterre. Par J. Fievée." Ed. Rev. April, 1803.

he sees shocks some passion or flatters it; and he is perpetually seduced to distort facts, so as to render them agreeable to his system and his feelings! Books of travels are now published in such vast abundance, that it may not be useless, perhaps, to state a few of the reasons why their value so commonly happens to be in the inverse ratio of their number.

1st. Travels are bad, from a want of opportunity for observation in those who write them. If the sides of a building are to be measured, and the number of its windows to be counted, a very short space of time may suffice for these operations; but to gain such a knowledge of their prevalent opinions and propensities, as will enable a stranger to comprehend (what is commonly called) the *genius* of people, requires a long residence among them, a familiar acquaintance with their language, and an easy circulation among their various societies. The society into which a transient stranger gains the most easy access in any country, is not often that which ought to stamp the national character; and no criterion can be more fallible, in a people so reserved and inaccessible as the British, who (even when they open their doors to letters of introduction) cannot for years overcome the awkward timidity of their nature. The same expressions are of so different a value in different countries, the same actions proceed from such different causes, and produce such different effects, that a judgment of foreign nations, founded on rapid observation, is almost certainly a mere tissue of ludicrous and disgraceful mistakes; and yet a residence of a month or two seems to entitle a traveller to present the world with a picture of manners in London, Paris, or Vienna, and even to dogmatize upon the political, religious, and legal institutions, as if it were one and the same thing to speak of *abstract* effects of such institutions, and of their effects combined with all the peculiar circumstances in which any nation may be placed.

2dly. An affectation of quickness in observation, an intuitive glance that requires only a *moment*, and a *part*, to judge of a *perpetuity*, and a *whole*. The late Mr. Petion, who was sent over into this country to acquire a knowledge of our criminal law, is said to have declared himself thoroughly informed upon the subject after remaining precisely *two-and-thirty minutes* in the Old Bailey.

3dly. The tendency to found observation on a system, rather

than a system upon observation. The fact is, there are very few original eyes and ears. The great mass see and hear as they are directed by others, and bring back from a residence in foreign countries nothing but the vague and customary notions concerning it, which are carried and brought back for half a century, without verification or change. The most ordinary shape in which this tendency to prejudge makes its appearance among travellers, is by a disposition to exalt, or, a still more absurd disposition to depreciate their native country. They are incapable of considering a foreign people but under one single point of view—the relation in which they stand to their own; and the whole narrative is frequently nothing more than a mere triumph of national vanity, or the ostentation of superiority to so common a failing.

INHABITANTS OF CEYLON.*

Ceylon is now inhabited by the English; the remains of the Dutch and Portuguese, the Cinglese or natives, subject to the dominion of the Europeans; the Candians, subject to the king of their own name; and the Vaddahs, or wild men, subject to no power. A Ceylonese Dutchman is a coarse, grotesque species of animal, whose native apathy and phlegm is animated only by the insolence of a colonial tyrant: his principal amusement appears to consist in smoking; but his pipe, according to Mr. Percival's account, is so seldom out of his mouth, that his smoking appears to be almost as much a necessary function of animal life as his breathing. His day is eked out with gin, ceremonious visits, and prodigious quantities of gross food, dripping with oil and butter; his mind, just able to reach from one meal to another, is incapable of further exertion; and, after the panting and deglutition of a long-protracted dinner, reposes on the sweet expectation that, in a few hours, the carnivorous toil will be renewed. He lives only to digest, and, while the organs of gluttony perform their office, he has not a wish beyond; and is the happy man which Horace describes:—

—— *in seipso totus, teres, atque rotundus.*

The descendants of the Portuguese differ materially from the

* From a review of "An Account of the Island of Ceylon, by Robert Percival." Ed. Rev., April 1803.

Moors, Malabars, and other Mahometans. Their great object is to show the world they are Europeans and Christians. Unfortunately, their ideas of Christianity are so imperfect, that the only mode they can hit upon of displaying their faith, is by wearing hats and breeches, and by these habiliments they consider themselves as showing a proper degree of contempt, on various parts of the body, toward Mahomet and Buddha. They are lazy, treacherous, effeminate, and passionate to excess; and are, in fact, a locomotive and animated farrago of the bad qualities of all tongues, people, and nations on the face of the earth.

The Malays, whom we forgot before to enumerate, form a very considerable portion of the inhabitants of Ceylon. Their original empire lies in the peninsula of Malacca, from whence they have extended themselves over Java, Sumatra, the Moluccas, and a vast number of other islands in the peninsula of India. It has been many years customary for the Dutch to bring them to Ceylon, for the purpose of carrying on various branches of trade and manufacture, and in order also to employ them as soldiers and servants The Malays are the most vindictive and ferocious of living beings. They set little or no value on their own existence, in the prosecution of their odious passions; and having thus broken the great tie which renders man a being capable of being governed, and fit for society, they are a constant source of terror to all those who have any kind of connection or relation with them. A Malay servant, from the apprehension excited by his vindictive disposition, often becomes the master of his master. It is as dangerous to dismiss him as to punish him; and the rightful despot, in order to avoid assassination, is almost compelled to exchange characters with his slave. It is singular, however, that the Malay, incapable of submission on any other occasion, and ever ready to avenge insult with death, submits to the severest military discipline with the utmost resignation and meekness. The truth is, obedience to his officers forms part of his religious creed; and the same man who would repay the most insignificant insult with death, will submit to be lacerated at the halbert with the patience of a martyr. This is truly a tremendous people! When assassins and blood-hounds will fall into rank and file, and the most furious savages submit (with no diminution of their ferocity) to the science and discipline of war, they only want a Malay Buonaparte to lead them to the conquest of the world. Our curiosity has always been very highly excited by the accounts of this singular people; and we cannot help thinking that, one day or another, when they are more full of opium than usual, they *will run a muck* from Cape Comorin to the Caspian.

MADAME DE STAEL'S DELPHINE.*

THIS dismal trash, which has nearly dislocated the jaws of every critic among us with gaping, has so alarmed Buonaparte, that he has seized the whole impression, sent Madame de Staël out of Paris, and, for aught we know, sleeps in a night-cap of steel and dagger-proof blankets. To us it appears rather an attack upon the Ten Commandments than the government of Buonaparte, and calculated not so much to enforce the rights of the Bourbons, as the benefits of adultery, murder, and a great number of other vices, which have been, some how or other, strangely neglected in this country, and too much so (according to the apparent opinion of Madame de Staël) even in France.

It happens, however, fortunately enough, that her book is as dull as it could have been if her intentions had been good; for wit, dexterity, and the pleasant energies of the mind, seldom rank themselves on the side of virtue and social order; while vice is spiritual, eloquent, and alert, ever choice in expression, happy in allusion, and judicious in arrangement.

The story is simply this:—Delphine, a rich young widow, presents her cousin, Matilda de Vernon, with a considerable estate, in order to enable her to marry Leonce Mondeville. To this action she is excited by the arts and the intrigues of Madame de Vernon, a hackneyed Parisian lady, who hopes, by this marriage, to be able to discharge her numerous and pressing debts. Leonce, who, like all other heroes of novels, has fine limbs and fine qualities, comes to Paris—dislikes Matilda—falls in love with Delphine, Delphine with him; and they are upon the eve of jilting poor Matilda, when, from some false reports spread abroad respecting the character of Delphine (which are aggravated by her own imprudences, and by the artifices of Madame de Vernon), Leonce, not in

* Delphine. By Madame de Staël Holstein. London, Mawman. 6 vols. 12mo. Ed. Rev., April, 1803.

a fit of honesty, but of revenge, marries the lady whom he came to marry. Soon after, Madame de Vernon dies—discovers the artifices by which she had prevented the union of Leonce and Delphine—and then, after this catastrophe, which ought to have terminated the novel, come two long volumes of complaint and despair. Delphine becomes a nun—runs away from the nunnery with Leonce, who is taken by some French soldiers, upon the supposition that he has been serving in the French emigrant army against his country—is shot, and upon his dead body falls Delphine, as dead as he.

Making every allowance for reading this book in a translation, and in a very bad translation, we cannot but deem it a heavy performance. The incidents are vulgar; the characters vulgar, too, except those of Delphine and Madame de Vernon. Madame de Staël has not the artifice to hide what is coming. In travelling through a flat country, or a flat book, we see our road before us for half the distance we are going. There are no agreeable sinuosities, and no speculations whether we are to ascend next, or descend; what new sight we are to enjoy, or to which side we are to bend. Leonce is robbed and half-murdered; the apothecary of the place is certain he will not live; we were absolutely certain that he would live, and could predict to an hour the time of his recovery. In the same manner we could have prophesied every event of the book a whole volume before its occurrence.

This novel is a perfect *Alexandrian*. The last two volumes are redundant, and drag their wounded length: it should certainly have terminated where the interest ceases, at the death of Madame de Vernon; but, instead of this, the scene-shifters come and pick up the dead bodies, wash the stage, sweep it, and do everything which the timely fall of the curtain should have excluded from the sight, and left to the imagination of the audience. We humbly apprehend, that young gentlemen do not, in general, make their tutors the confidants of their passion; at least we can find no rule of that kind laid down either by Miss Hamilton or Miss Edgeworth, in their treatises on education. The tutor of Leonce is Mr. Barton, a grave old gentleman, in a peruke and snuff-coloured clothes. Instead of writing to this solemn personage about second causes, the ten categories, and the eternal fitness of things, the young lover raves to him, for whole pages, about the white neck and auburn hair of his Delphine; and, shame to tell! the liquorish old pedagogue seems to think these amorous ebullitions the pleasantest sort of writing *in usum Delphini* that he has yet met with.

By altering one word, and making *only* one false quantity,* we shall change the rule of Horace to

"Nec *febris* intersit nisi dignus vindice r)dus
    Inciderit." ——

Delphine and Leonce have eight very bad *typhus* fevers between them, besides *hæmoptoe, hemorrhage, deliquium animi, singultus, hysteria,* and *fœminei ululatus,* or screams innumerable. Now, that there should be a reasonable allowance of sickness in every novel, we are willing to admit, and will cheerfully permit the heroine to be once given over, and at the point of death; but we cannot consent that the interest which ought to be excited by the feelings of the mind should be transferred to the sufferings of the body, and a crisis of perspiration be substituted for a crisis of passion. Let us see difficulties overcome, if our approbation is required; we cannot grant it to such cheap and sterile artifices as these.

The characters in this novel are all said to be drawn from real life; and the persons for whom they are intended are loudly whispered at Paris. Most of them we have forgotten; but Delphine is said to be intended for the authoress, and *Madame de Vernon* (by a slight sexual metamorphosis) for Talleyrand, minister of the French republic for foreign affairs.† As this lady (once the friend of the authoress) may probably exercise a considerable influence over the destinies of this country, we shall endeavour to make our readers a little better acquainted with her; but we must first remind them that she was once a bishop, a higher dignity in the church than was ever attained by any of her sex since the days of Pope Joan; and that though she swindles Delphine out of her estate with a considerable degree of address, her dexterity some-

---

* Perhaps a fault of all others which the English are least disposed to pardon. A young man who, on a public occasion, makes a false quantity at the outset of life, can seldom or never get over it.—*Author's Note.*

† Madame de Staël, on meeting Talleyrand at an evening party after the publication of this book, was addressed by the ci-devant Bishop with "*Eh, Madame, on dit que nous sommes tous les deux dans votre livre deguisés en femmes.*"

times fails her, as in the memorable instance of the American commissioners. Madame de Staël gives the following description of this pastoral metropolitan female:

"Though she is at least forty, she still appears charming even among the young and beautiful of her own sex. The paleness of her complexion, the slight relaxation of her features, indicate the languor of indisposition, and not the decay of years; the easy negligence of her dress accords with this impression. Every one concludes, that when her health is recovered, and she dresses with more care, she must be completely beautiful: this change, however, never happens, but it is always expected; and that is sufficient to make the imagination still add something more to the natural effect of her charms."— (Vol. i., p. 21.)

Nothing can be more execrable than the manner in which this book is translated. The bookseller has employed one of our countrymen for that purpose, who appears to have been very *lately caught*. The contrast between the passionate exclamations of Madame de Staël, and the barbarous vulgarities of poor Sawney, produces a mighty ludicrous effect. One of the heroes, a man of high fastidious temper, exclaims in a letter to Delphine, "I cannot endure this Paris; I have met *with ever so many people*, whom my soul abhors." And the accomplished and enraptured Leonce terminates one of his letters thus; "*Adieu! Adieu, my dearest Delphine! I will give you a call* to-morrow." We doubt if Grub street ever imported from Caledonia a more abominable translator.

We admit the character of Madame de Vernon to be drawn with considerable skill. There are occasional traits of eloquence and pathos in this novel, and very many of those observations upon manners and character, which are totally out of the reach of all who have not lived long in the world, and observed it well.

The immorality of any book (in our estimation) is to be determined by the general impression it leaves on those minds, whose principles, not yet *ossified*, are capable of affording a less powerful defence to its influence. The most dangerous effect that any fictitious character can produce, is when two or three of its popular vices are varnished over with everything that is captivating and gracious in the exterior, and ennobled by association with splendid virtues; this apology will be more sure of its effect, if the faults are not against nature, but against society. The aversion to murder and cruelty could not perhaps be so overcome; but a regard to the sanctity of marriage vows, to the sacred and sensitive delicacy of the female character, and to numberless restrictions important to the well-being of our species, may easily be relaxed by this subtle and voluptuous confusion of good and evil. It is in vain to say the fable evinces, in the last act, that vice is productive of misery. We may decorate a villain with graces and felicities for nine volumes and hang him in the last page. This is not teaching virtue, but gilding the gallows, and raising up splendid associations in favour of being hanged. In such a union of the *amiable* and the vicious (especially if the vices are such, to the commission of which there is no want of natural disposition), the vice will not degrade the man, but the man will ennoble the vice. We shall wish to be him we admire, *in spite* of his vices, and, if the novel be well written, even in *consequence* of his vice. There exists, through the whole of this novel, a show of exquisite sensibility to the evils which individuals suffer by the inflexible rules of virtue prescribed by society, and an eager disposition to apologize for particular transgressions. Such doctrine is not confined to Madame de Staël; an Arcadian cant is gaining fast upon Spartan gravity; and the happiness diffused, and the beautiful order established in society, by this unbending discipline, are wholly swallowed up in compassion for the unfortunate and interesting individual. Either the exceptions or the rule must be given up : every highwayman who thrusts his pistol into a chaise-window has met with *unforeseen misfortunes;* and every loose matron who flies into the arms of her *Greville* was compelled to marry an old man whom she detested, by an avaricious and unfeeling father. The passions want not accelerating, but retarding machinery. This fatal and foolish sophistry has power enough over every heart, not to need the aid of fine composition, and well-contrived incident—auxiliaries which Madame de Staël intended to bring forward in the cause, though she has fortunately not succeeded.

M. de Serbellone is received as a guest into the house of M. d'Ervins, whose wife he debauches as a recompense for his hospitality. Is it possible to be disgusted with ingratitude and injustice, when united to such an assemblage of talents and virtues as this man of paper possesses? Was there ever a more delightful, fascinating adultress than Madame d'Ervins is intended to be? or a *povero cornuto* less capable of exciting compassion than her husband? The morality of all this is the old morality of Farquhar, Vanburgh, and Congreve—that every witty man may transgress the seventh commandment, which was never meant for the protection of husbands who labour under the incapacity of making repartees. In Matilda, religion is always as unamiable as dissimulation is graceful in Madame de Vernon, and imprudence generous in Delphine. This said Delphine, with her fine auburn hair, and her beautiful blue or green eyes (we forget which), cheats her cousin Matilda out of her lover, alienates the affections of her husband, and keeps a sort of assignation house for Serbellone and his *chère amie*, justifying herself by the most touching complaints against the rigour of the world, and using the customary phrases, *union of souls, married in the eye of heaven*, &c., &c., &c., and such like diction, the types of which Mr. Lane, of the Minerva Press, very prudently keeps ready composed, in order to facilitate the printing of the Adventures of Captain C—— and Miss F——, and other interesting stories, of which he, the said inimitable Mr. Lane, of the Minerva Press, well knows these sentiments must make a part. Another perilous absurdity which this *useful* production tends to cherish, is the common notion, that contempt of rule and order is a proof of greatness of mind. Delphine is everywhere a great spirit struggling with the shackles imposed upon her, in common with the little world around her; and it is managed so that her contempt of restrictions shall always appear to flow from the extent, variety, and splendour of her talents. The vulgarity of this heroism ought, in some degree, to diminish its value. Mr. Colquhoun, in his Police of the Metropolis, reckons up above forty thousand heroines of this species, most of whom, we dare to say, have, at one time or another, reasoned like the sentimental Delphine about the judgments of the world.

To conclude—Our general opinion of this book is, that it is calculated to shed a mild lustre over adultery; by gentle and convenient gradation, to destroy the modesty and the caution of women; to facilitate the acquisition of easy vices, and encumber the difficulty of virtue. What a wretched qualification of this censure to add, that the badness of the principles is alone corrected by the badness of the style, and that this celebrated lady would have been very guilty, if she had not been very dull!

USE OF RIDICULE.*

We are a good deal amused, indeed, with the extreme disrelish which Mr. John Styles† exhibits to the humour and pleasantry with which he admits the Methodists to have been attacked; but Mr. John Styles should remember, that it is not the practice with destroyers of vermin to allow the little victims a *veto* upon the weapons used against them. If this were otherwise, we should have one set of vermin banishing small-tooth combs; another protesting against mouse-traps: a third prohibiting the finger and thumb; a fourth exclaiming against the intolerable infamy of using soap and water. It is impossible, however, to listen to such pleas. They must all be caught, killed, and cracked, in the manner, and by the instruments which are found most efficacious to their destruction; and the more they cry out, the greater, plainly, is the skill used against them. We are convinced a little laughter will do them more harm than all the arguments in the world. Such men as the author before us, cannot understand when they are out-argued; but he has given us a specimen, from his irritability, that he fully comprehends when he has become the object of universal contempt and derision. We agree with him, that ridicule is not exactly the weapon to be used in matters of religion; but the use of it is excusable, when there is no other which can make fools tremble.‡

* From an article on "Methodism." Ed. Rev., 1809.
† Strictures on two Critiques in the Edinburgh Review, on the Subject of Methodism and Missions; with Remarks on the Influence of Reviews, in general, on Morals and Happiness. By John Styles. 8vo. London, 1809.
‡ Smith repeats the "small-tooth comb" illustration in his handling of Dr. Monk, Bishop of Gloucester, in the Third Letter to Archdeacon Singleton. Mr. Styles was again the subject of a literary agitation in 1839, when, having become the Rev. John Styles, D. D., he published, under the auspices of the Society for the Prevention of Cruelty to Animals, a prize Essay entitled, "The Animal Creation, its Claims on our Humanity Stated and Enforced." The tract was replied to in "A Pamphlet, dedicated to the Noblemen, Gentlemen, and Sportsmen of England, Ireland, and Scotland," by the Hon. Grantley Fitzhardinge Berkeley, M. P. The subject is roughly reviewed in an article, "Sydney Smith, John Styles, and Grantley Berkeley," in Fraser's Magazine, August, 1839. The Rev. Dr. Styles was a dissenting clergyman of note, the author of various published discourses of an occasional character. He also published a Life of David Brainerd, and a Family Bible, with illustrative notes, in two volumes quarto.

ANTEDILUVIAN AUTHORSHIP.*

There are occasionally, in Philopatris, a great vigour of style and felicity of expression. His display of classical learning is quite unrivalled—his reading various and good; and we may observe, at intervals, a talent for wit, of which he might have availed himself to excellent purpose, had it been compatible with the dignified style in which he generally conveys his sentiments. With all these excellent qualities of head and heart, we have seldom met with a writer more full of faults than Philopatris. There is an event recorded in the Bible, which men who write books should keep constantly in their remembrance. It is there set forth, that many centuries ago, the earth was covered with a great flood, by which the whole of the human race, with the exception of one family, were destroyed. It appears also, that from thence, a great alteration was made in the longevity of mankind, who, from a range of seven or eight hundred years, which they enjoyed before the flood, were confined to their present period of seventy or eighty years. This epoch in the history of man gave birth to the twofold division of the antediluvian and postdiluvian style of writing, the latter of which naturally contracted itself into those inferior limits which were better accommodated to the abridged duration of human life and literary labour. Now, to forget this event—to write without the fear of the deluge before his eyes, and to handle a subject as if mankind could lounge over a pamphlet for ten years, as before their submersion—is to be guilty of the most grievous error into which a writer can possibly fall.† The author of this book should call in the aid of some brilliant pencil, and cause the distressing scenes of the deluge to be portrayed in the most lively colours for his use. He should gaze at Noah and be brief. The ark should constantly remind him of the little time there is left for reading; and he should learn, as they did in the ark, to crowd a great deal of matter into a very little compass.

* From a review of Characters of the late Charles James Fox, by Philopatris Varvicensis (Dr. Parr). Ed. Rev., 1809.

† Macaulay has borrowed this illustration. In a review (Ed. Rev., 1832) of Nares' Memoirs of Lord Burghley, he has: "Such a book might, before the deluge, have been considered as light reading by Hilpa and Shalum. But, unhappily, the life of man is now three score years and ten : and we cannot but think it somewhat unfair in Dr. Nares to demand from us so large a portion of so short an existence."

ENGLISH CLASSICAL EDUCATION.*

There are two questions which grow out of this subject: 1st, How far is any sort of classical education useful? 2d, How far is that particular classical education adopted in this country useful?

Latin and Greek are, in the first place, useful, as they inure children to intellectual difficulties, and make the life of a young student what it ought to be, a life of considerable labour. We do not, of course, mean to confine this praise exclusively to the study of Latin and Greek; or to suppose that other difficulties might not be found which it would be useful to overcome: but though Latin and Greek have this merit in common with many arts and sciences, still they have it; and, if they do nothing else, they at least secure a solid and vigorous application at a period of life which materially influences all other periods.

To go through the grammar of one language thoroughly is of great use for the mastery of every other grammar; because there obtains, through all languages, a certain analogy to each other in their grammatical construction. Latin and Greek have now mixed themselves etymologically with all the languages of modern Europe—and with none more than our own; so that it is necessary to read these two tongues for other objects than themselves.

The two ancient languages are, as mere inventions—as pieces of mechanism—incomparably more beautiful than any of the modern languages of Europe: their mode of signifying time and case by terminations, instead of auxiliary verbs and particles, would of itself stamp their superiority. Add to this, the copiousness of the Greek language, with the fancy, majesty, and harmony of its compounds; and there are quite sufficient reasons why the classics should be studied for the beauties of language. Compared to them, merely as vehicles of thought and passion, all modern languages are dull, ill-contrived, and barbarous.

That a great part of the Scriptures has come down to us in the Greek language, is of itself a reason, if all others were wanting, why education should be planned so as to produce a supply of Greek scholars.

The cultivation of style is very justly made a part of education.

* From an article "Professional Education." Ed. Rev., Oct., 1809.

Everything which is written is meant either to please or to instruct. The second object it is difficult to effect, without attending to the first; and the cultivation of style is the acquisition of those rules and literary habits which sagacity anticipates, or experience shows, to be the most effectual means of pleasing. Those works are the best which have longest stood the test of time, and pleased the greatest number of exercised minds. Whatever, therefore, our conjectures may be, we cannot be so sure that the best modern writers can afford us as good models as the ancients;—we cannot be certain that they will live through the revolutions of the world, and continue to please in every climate—under every species of government—through every stage of civilization. The moderns have been well taught by their masters; but the time is hardly yet come when the necessity for such instruction no longer exists. We may still borrow descriptive power from Tacitus; dignified perspicuity from Livy; simplicity from Cæsar; and from Homer some portion of that light and heat which, dispersed into ten thousand channels, has filled the world with bright images and illustrious thoughts. Let the cultivator of modern literature addict himself to the purest models of taste which France, Italy, and England could supply, he might still learn from Virgil to be majestic, and from Tibullus to be tender; he might not yet look upon the face of nature as Theocritus saw it; nor might he reach those springs of pathos with which Euripides softened the hearts of his audience. In short, it appears to us, that there are so many excellent reasons why a certain number of scholars should be kept up in this and in every civilized country, that we should consider every system of education from which classical education was excluded, as radically erroneous and completely absurd.

That vast advantages, then, may be derived from classical learning, there can be no doubt. The advantages which are derived from classical learning by the English manner of teaching, involve another and a very different question; and we will venture to say, that there never was a more complete instance in any country of such extravagant and overacted attachment to any branch of knowledge as that which obtains in this country with regard to classical knowledge. A young Englishman goes to school at six or seven years old; and he remains in a course of education till twenty-three or twenty-four years of age. In all that time, his sole and exclusive occupation is learning Latin and Greek:* he has scarcely a notion that there is any other kind of excellence; and the great system of facts with which he is the most perfectly acquainted, are the intrigues of the heathen gods: with whom Pan slept?—with whom Jupiter?—whom Apollo ravished? These facts the English youth get by heart the moment they quit the nursery; and are most sedulously and industriously instructed in them till the best and most active part of life is passed away. Now, this long career of classical learning, we may, if we please, denominate a foundation; but it is a foundation so far above ground, that there is absolutely no room to put anything upon it. If you occupy a man with one thing till he is twenty-four years of age, you have exhausted all his leisure time: he is called into the world, and compelled to act; or is surrounded with pleasures, and thinks and reads no more. If you have neglected to put other things in him, they will never get in afterward;—if you have fed him only with words, he will remain a narrow and limited being to the end of his existence.

The bias given to men's minds is so strong, that it is no uncommon thing to meet with Englishmen, whom, but for their gray hairs and wrinkles, we might easily mistake for schoolboys. Their talk is of Latin verses; and it is quite clear, if men's ages are to be dated from the state of their mental progress, that such men are eighteen years of age, and not a day older. Their minds have been so completely possessed by exaggerated notions of classical learning, that they have not been able, in the great school of the world, to form any other notion of real greatness. Attend, too, to the public feelings—look to all the terms of applause. A learned man!—a scholar!—a man of erudition! Upon whom are these epithets of approbation bestowed? Are they given to men acquainted with the science of government? thoroughly masters of the geographical and commercial relations of Europe? to men who know the properties of bodies, and their action upon each other? No: this is not learning: it is chemistry or political economy— not learning. The distinguishing abstract term, the epithet of scholar, is reserved for him who writes on the Æolic reduplication,

* Unless he goes to the University of Cambridge; and then classics occupy him entirely for about ten years; and divide him with mathematics for four or five more.

and is familiar with the Sylburgian method of arranging defectives in ω and μι. The picture which a young Englishman, addicted to the pursuit of knowledge, draws—his *beau idéal* of human nature—his top and consummation of man's powers—is a knowledge of the Greek language. His object is not to reason, to imagine, or to invent; but to conjugate, decline, and derive. The situations of imaginary glory which he draws for himself, are the detection of an anapæst in the wrong place, or the restoration of a dative case which Cranzius had passed over, and the never-dying Ernesti failed to observe. If a young classic of this kind were to meet the greatest chemist or the greatest mechanician, or the most profound political economist of his time, in company with the greatest Greek scholar, would the slightest comparison between them ever come across his mind?—would he ever dream that such men as Adam Smith or Lavoisier were equal in dignity of understanding to, or of the same utility as, Bentley and Heyne? We are inclined to think, that the feeling excited would be a good deal like that which was expressed by Dr. George about the praises of the great King of Prussia, who entertained considerable doubt whether the King, with all his victories, knew how to conjugate a Greek verb in μι.

Another misfortune of classical learning, as taught in England, is, that scholars have come, in process of time, and from the effects of association, to love the instrument better than the end;—not the luxury which the difficulty encloses, but the difficulty;—not the filbert, but the shell;—not what may be read in Greek, but Greek itself. It is not so much the man who has mastered the wisdom of the ancients, that is valued, as he who displays his knowledge of the vehicle in which that wisdom is conveyed. The glory is to show I am a scholar. The good sense and ingenuity I may gain by my acquaintance with ancient authors is matter of opinion; but if I bestow an immensity of pains upon a point of accent or quantity, this is something positive; I establish my pretensions to the name of a scholar, and gain the credit of learning, while I sacrifice all its utility.

Another evil in the present system of classical education is the extraordinary perfection which is aimed at in teaching those languages; a needless perfection; an accuracy which is sought for in nothing else. There are few boys who remain to the age of eighteen or nineteen at a public school, without making above ten thousand Latin verses :—a greater number than is contained in the *Æneid:* and after he has made this quantity of verses in a dead language, unless the poet should happen to be a very weak man indeed, he never makes another as long as he lives. It may be urged, and it is urged, that this is of use in teaching the delicacies of the language. No doubt it is of use for this purpose, if we put out of view the immense time and trouble sacrificed in gaining these little delicacies. It would be of use that we should go on till fifty years of age making Latin verses, if the price of a whole life were not too much to pay for it. We effect our object; but we do it at the price of something greater than our object. And whence comes it, that the expenditure of life and labour is totally put out of the calculation, when Latin and Greek are to be attained? In every other occupation, the question is fairly stated between the attainment, and the time employed in the pursuit;—but, in classical learning, it seems to be sufficient if the least possible good is gained by the greatest possible exertion; if the end is anything, and the means everything. It is of some importance to speak and write French; and innumerable delicacies would be gained by writing ten thousand French verses: but it makes no part of our education to write French poetry. It is of some importance that there should be good botanists; but no botanist can repeat, by heart, the names of all the plants in the known world; nor is any astronomer acquainted with the appellation and magnitude of every star in the map of the heavens. The only department of human knowledge in which there can be no excess, no arithmetic, no balance of profit and loss, is classical learning.

The prodigious honour in which Latin verses are held at public schools, is surely the most absurd of all absurd distinctions. You rest all reputation upon doing that which is a natural gift, and which no labour can attain. If a lad won't learn the words of a language, his degradation in the school is a very natural punishment for his disobedience, or his indolence; but it would be as reasonable to expect that all boys should be witty, or beautiful, as that they should be poets. In either case, it would be to make an accidental, unattainable, and not a very important gift of nature, the only, or the principal, test of merit. This is the reason why boys, who make a very considerable figure at school, so very often make no figure in the world;—and why other lads, who are passed over without notice, turn out to be valuable, important men. The test established in the world is widely different from that established in a place which is presumed to be a preparation for the world; and the head of a public school, who is a perfect miracle to his contemporaries, finds himself shrink into absolute insignificance, because he has nothing else to command respect or regard, but a talent for fugitive poetry in a dead language.

The present state of classical education cultivates the imagination a great deal too much, and other habits of mind a great deal too little, and trains up many young men in a style of elegant imbecility, utterly unworthy of the talents with which nature has endowed them. It may be said, there are profound investigations, and subjects quite powerful enough for any understanding, to be met with in classical literature. So there are; but no man likes to add the difficulties of a language to the difficulties of a subject; and to study metaphysics, morals, and politics in Greek, when the Greek alone is study enough without them. In all foreign languages, the most popular works are works of imagination. Even in the French language, which we know so well, for one serious work which has any currency in this country, we have twenty which are mere works of imagination. This is still more true in classical literature; because what their poets and orators have left us, is of infinitely greater value than the remains of their philosophy; for, as society advances, men think more accurately and deeply, and imagine more tamely; works of reasoning advance, and works of fancy decay. So that the matter of fact is, that a classical scholar of twenty-three or twenty-four years of age, is a man principally conversant with works of imagination. His feelings are quick, his fancy lively, and his taste good. Talents for speculation and original inquiry he has none; nor has he formed the invaluable habit of pushing things up to their first principles, or of collecting dry and unamusing facts as the materials of reasoning. All the solid and masculine parts of his understanding are left wholly without cultivation; he hates the pain of thinking, and suspects every man whose boldness and originality call upon him to defend his opinions and prove his assertions.

A very curious argument is sometimes employed in justification of the learned minutiæ to which all young men are doomed, whatever be their propensities in future life What are you to do with a young man up to the age of seventeen? Just as if there was such a want of difficulties to overcome, and of important tastes to inspire, that from the mere necessity of doing something, and the impossibility of doing anything else, you were driven to the expedient of metre and poetry; as if a young man within that period might not acquire the modern languages, modern history, experimental philosophy, geography, chronology, and a considerable share of mathematics; as if the memory of things were not more agreeable and more profitable than the memory of words.

The great objection is, that we are not making the most of human life, when we constitute such an extensive, and such minute classical erudition, an indispensable article in education. Up to a certain point we would educate every young man in Latin and Greek; but to a point far short of that to which this species of education is now carried. Afterward, we would grant to classical erudition as high honours as to every other department of knowledge, but not higher. We would place it upon a footing with many other objects of study; but allow it no superiority. Good scholars would be as certainly produced by these means as good chemists, astronomers, and mathematicians are now produced, without any direct provision whatsoever for their production. Why are we to trust to the diversity of human tastes, and the varieties of human ambition in everything else, and distrust it in classics alone? The passion for language is just as strong as any other literary passion. There are very good Persian and Arabic scholars in this country. Large heaps of trash have been dug up from Sanscrit ruins. We have seen, in our own times, a clergyman of the University of Oxford complimenting their majesties in Coptic and Syrophœnician verses; and yet we doubt whether there will be a sufficient avidity in literary men to get at the beauties of the finest writers which the world has yet seen; and though the *Bagvat Gheeta* has (as can be proved) met with human beings to translate, and other human beings to read it, we think that, in order to secure an attention to Homer and Virgil, we must catch up every man—whether he is to be a clergyman or a duke —begin with him at six years of age, and never quit him till he is twenty; making him conjugate and decline for life and death; and so teaching him to estimate his progress in real wisdom as he can scan the verses of the Greek tragedians.

The English clergy, in whose hands education entirely rests, bring up the first young men of the country as if they were all to keep grammar-schools in little country-towns; and a nobleman, upon whose knowledge and liberality the honour and welfare of his country may depend, is diligently worried, for half his life, with the small pedantry of longs and shorts. There is a timid and absurd apprehension, on the part of ecclesiastical tutors, of letting out the minds of youth upon difficult and important subjects. They fancy that mental exertion must end in religious skepticism; and, to preserve the principles of their pupils, they confine them to the safe and elegant imbecility of classical learning. A genuine Oxford tutor would shudder to hear his young men disputing upon moral and political truth, forming and pulling down theories, and indulging in all the boldness of youthful discussion. He would augur nothing from it but impiety to God and treason to kings. And yet, who vilifies both more than the holy poltroon who carefully averts from them the searching eye of reason, and who knows no better method of teaching the highest duties, than by extirpating the finest qualities and habits of the mind? If our religion is a fable the sooner it is exploded the better. If our government is bad, it should be amended. But we have no doubt of the truth of the one, or of the excellence of the other; and are convinced that both will be placed on a firmer basis in proportion as the minds of men are more trained to the investigation of truth. At present, we act with the minds of our young men as the Dutch did with their exuberant spices. An infinite quantity of talent is annually destroyed in the universities of England by the miserable jealousy and littleness of ecclesiastical instructors. It is in vain to say we have produced great men under this system. We have produced great men under all systems. Every Englishman must pass half his life in learning Latin and Greek; and classical learning is supposed to have produced the talents which it has not been able to extinguish. It is scarcely possible to prevent great men from rising up under any system of education, however bad. Teach men demonology or astrology, and you will still have a certain portion of original genius, in spite of these or any other branches of ignorance and folly.

There is a delusive sort of splendour in a vast body of men pursuing one object, and thoroughly obtaining it; and yet, though it be very splendid, it is far from being useful. Classical literature is the great object at Oxford. Many minds so employed have produced many works and much fame in that department; but if all liberal arts and sciences useful to human life had been taught there —if some had dedicated themselves to chemistry, some to mathematics, some to experimental philosophy—and if every attainment had been honoured in the mixed ratio of its difficulty and utility —the system of such a University would have been much more valuable, but the splendour of its name something less.

When a University has been doing useless things for a long time, it appears at first degrading to them to be useful. A set of lectures upon political economy would be discouraged in Oxford,* probably despised, probably not permitted. To discuss the enclosure of commons, and to dwell upon imports and exports—to come so near to common life, would seem to be undignified and contemptible. In the same manner, the Parr or the Bentley of his day, would be scandalized in a University to be put on a level with the discoverer of a neutral salt; and yet, what other measure is there of dignity in intellectual labour, but usefulness and difficulty? And what ought the term University to mean, but a place where every science is taught which is liberal, and at the same time useful to mankind? Nothing would so much tend to bring classical literature within proper bounds, as a steady and invariable appeal to these tests in our appreciation of all human knowledge. The puffed-up pedant would collapse into his proper size, and the maker of verses, and the rememberer of words, would soon assume that station which is the lot of those who go up unbidden to the upper places of the feast.

We should be sorry if what we have said should appear too contemptuous toward classical learning, which we most sincerely hope will always be held in great honour in this country, though we certainly do not wish to it that exclusive honour which it at present enjoys. A great classical scholar is an ornament, and an important acquisition to his country; but, in a place of education, we would give to all knowledge an equal chance for distinction; and would trust to the varieties of human disposition that every science worth cultivation would be cultivated. Looking always to real utility as our guide, we should see, with equal pleasure, a

* They have since been established.

studious and inquisitive mind arranging the productions of nature, investigating the qualities of bodies, or mastering the difficulties of the learned languages. We should not care whether he were chemist, naturalist, or scholar; because we know it to be as necessary that matter should be studied, and subdued to the use of man, as that taste should be gratified, and imagination inflamed.

In those who were destined for the church, we would undoubtedly encourage classical learning more than in any other body of men; but if we had to do with a young man going out into public life, we would exhort him to contemn, or at least not to affect, the reputation of a great scholar, but to educate himself for the offices of civil life. He should learn what the constitution of his country really was—how it had grown into its present state—the perils that had threatened it—the malignity that had attacked it—the courage that had fought for it, and the wisdom that had made it great. We would bring strongly before his mind the characters of those Englishmen who have been the steady friends of the public happiness; and by their examples, would breathe into him a pure public taste which should keep him untainted in all the vicissitudes of political fortune. We would teach him to burst through the well-paid, and the pernicious cant of indiscriminate loyalty; and to know his sovereign only as he discharged those duties, and displayed those qualities, for which the blood and the treasure of his people are confided to his hands. We should deem it of the utmost importance that his attention was directed to the true principles of legislation—what effect laws can produce upon opinions, and opinions upon laws—what subjects are fit for legislative interference, and when men may be left to the management of their own interests. The mischief occasioned by bad laws, and the perplexity which arises from numerous laws—the causes of national wealth—the relations of foreign trade—the encouragement of manufactures and agriculture—the fictitious wealth occasioned by paper credit—the laws of population—the management of poverty and mendicity—the use and abuse of monopoly—the theory of taxation—the consequences of the public debt. These are some of the subjects, and some of the branches of civil education to which we would turn the minds of future judges, future senators, and future noblemen. After the first period of life had been given up to the cultivation of the classics, and the reasoning powers were now beginning to evolve themselves, these are some of the propensities in study which we would endeavour to inspire. Great knowledge, at such a period of life, we could not convey; but we might fix a decided taste for its acquisition, and a strong disposition to respect it in others. The formation of some great scholars we should certainly prevent, and hinder many from learning what, in a few years, they would necessarily forget; but this loss would be well repaid—if we could show the future rulers of the country that thought and labour which it requires to make a nation happy—or if we could inspire them with that love of public virtue, which, after religion, we most solemnly believe to be the brightest ornament of the mind of man.

[The discussion which grew out of the preceding and other articles in the Edinburgh Review, has been already noticed (Memoir ante p. 45). The reader may be interested in a few passages of Smith's reply to the strictures of Copleston. They are taken from the article, "Calumnies Against Oxford." Ed. Rev., April, 1810.]

REPLY TO COPLESTON.

COME we next to the third mould or crucible into which this Oxford gentleman has poured his melted lead,— viz. his reply to our more general observations on the use and abuse of classical learning, and on the undue importance assigned to it in English education; and as this part of his work is more remarkable than the rest for its ostentatious dullness, and its gross departure from the language and manners of a gentleman, we must be excused for bestowing on it a little more of our time than we are in the habit of wasting on such men and such things. . . . . . .

Admitting that a young man, though occupied in overcoming verbal difficulties, has acquired the same real knowledge as if his path had been completely without obstruction—what is all this to the purpose? Our objection is not, that classical knowledge is not a good, but that it is not the only good. We contend that all young men need not be made great classical scholars; that some may be allowed to deviate into mathematical knowledge— some into chemistry, some into natural philosophy—some into political economy—some into modern languages; that all these occupations, though not, perhaps, superior in importance to classical erudition, are not inferior to it; that we are making only one article, when we ought to be making many; that the sole occupation of all young Englishmen, *educated at Oxford*, is to become Latin and Greek scholars. Of the verses so much admired, and so indiscreetly quoted by this gentleman, we shall only say,

> Tale tuum nobis carmen, divine poeta,
> Quale sopor.

The encomiast should remember, that his great model was remarkably careful of committing himself in print: and again and again we warn our author to beware of opportunities; they will, one day or another, prove his ruin.

We did not say that poetry only is read in classical education; but that the most valuable works which the ancients have left us, are their works of fancy; that these are, beyond all comparison, more read than their works either of history or philosophy; and that this, joined to the horrible absurdity of verse-making, does (where classical education does not end in downright pedantry) often make it a mere cultivation of the imagination at the expense of every other faculty. Sometimes, indeed, as in the melancholy instance before us, this price is paid for imagination, and the article never delivered.

Shocked and alarmed as this monk, or rather let us say, this nun, is with the mention of the amours of Pan and Jupiter — we must still maintain, that the loves of the heathen gods and goddesses are the principal subjects by which the attention of young men is engaged in the first years of education. We are sorry to call up a blush into the face of this sly tutor; but the fact is as we state it.

The observations of this writer are, like children's cradles — familiar to old women — sometimes empty — sometimes full of noisy imbecility — and often lulling to sleep. There never, perhaps, was a more striking instance of silly and contemptible pedantry, than the long, dull and serious answer which he has taken the trouble to make to our joke about *Cranzius*, and the *Ernesti*. What can it possibly signify, whether we used the name of one great fool, or of another great fool? Let this writer put his own name to his productions, and it shall take the place of Cranzius in our next edition.......

One who passes for a great man in a little place, generally

makes himself very ridiculous when he ventures out of it. Nothing can exceed the pomp and trash of this gentleman's observations; they can only proceed from the habit of living with third-rate persons; from possessing the right of compelling boys to listen to him; and from making a very cruel use of this privilege. More equal company could never have made him an able man; but they would soon have persuaded him to hold his tongue. That there is something in this gentleman, we do not deny; but he does not appear to us to have the slightest conception how very little that something is, nor in what his moderate talents consist. He is evidently intended for a plain, plodding, everyday personage—to do no foolish things—and to say no wise ones—to walk in the cart-harness that is prepared for him—and to step into every commonplace notion that prevails in the times in which he happens to exist. If he would hold his tongue, and carefully avoid all opportunities of making a display, he is just the description of person to enjoy a very great reputation among those whose good opinion is not worth having. Unfortunately, he must pretend to liberality —to wit—to eloquence—and to fine writing. He must show his brother-tutors that he is not afraid of Edinburgh Reviewers. If he returns rolled in the mud, broken-headed, and bellowing with pain, who has he but himself to blame?

He who has seen a barn-door fowl flying—and only he—can form some conception of this tutor's eloquence. With his neck and hinder parts brought into a line—with loud screams, and all the agony of feathered fatness—the ponderous little glutton flaps himself up into the air, and, soaring four feet above the level of our earth, falls dull and breathless on his native dunghill. Of these sublime excursions, let the following suffice as specimens:

"There are emotions which eloquence can raise, and which lead to loftier thoughts, and nobler aspirings, than commonly spring up in the private intercourse of men : when the latent flame of genius has been kindled by some transient ray, shot perhaps at random, and aimed least where it took the greatest effect, but which has set all the kindred sparks that lay there, in such a heat and stir as that no torpid indolence, or low, earthy-rooted cares, shall ever again smother or keep them down. From this high lineage may spring a never-failing race; few, indeed, but more illustrious because they are few, through whom the royal blood of philosophy shall descend," &c. &c. pp. 148, 149.

"We want not men who are clipped and *espaliered* into any form which the whim of the gardener may dictate, or the narrow limits of his parterre require. Let our saplings take their full spread, and send forth their vigorous shoots in all the boldness and variety of nature. Their luxuriance must be pruned; their distortions rectified; the rust and canker and caterpillar of vice carefully kept from them; we must dig round them, and *water them*, and replenish the exhaustion of the soil by continual dressing." p. 157.

One more, and we have done for ever.

"That finished offspring of genius starts not, like Minerva, from the head of Jupiter, perfect at once in stature, and clad in complete armour; but is the produce of slow birth, *and often of a hard delivery;* the tender nursling of many an infant year — the pupil of a severe school, formed and chastened by a persevering discipline." p. 129.

We question if mere natural dullness, unaided by punch, ever before produced such writing as this......

We have already shown, how very imperfectly this gentleman understands his own silly art of verbal criticism; but when he comes upon subjects of real importance, nothing can well exceed the awkwardness of his movements;—he is like a coach-horse on the trottoir—his feet don't seem made to stand on such places. The objections which he makes to the science of chemistry, are really curious—that it raises and multiplies the means of subsistence, and terminates merely in the bodily wants of man: in other words—*donum rationis divinitus datum in usus humani generis impendit.* And what, we should be glad to know, is the main object of most branches of human knowledge, if it be not to minister to the bodily wants of man? What is the utility of mathematics, but as they are brought to bear upon navigation, astronomy, mechanics, and so upon bodily wants? What is the object of medicine?—what of anatomy?—what greater purposes have law and politics in view, but to consult our bodily wants—to protect those who minister to them—and to arrange the conflicting interests and pretensions which these wants occasion? Here is an exact instance of the mischief of verbal studies. This man has been so long engaged in trifles which have the most remote and faint connection with human affairs, that a science appears to him absolutely undignified and degrading, because it ministers to the bodily wants of mankind—as if one of the greatest objects of human wisdom had not at all times been to turn the properties of matter to the use of man: and then he asks, if ministration to bodily wants is the test of merit in any science, and a reason for its reception in places of education, why the mechanical arts are excluded? But, need this man—need any man—need any boy who has been baptized and breeched, be told, that any single mechanical art is less honoured than chemistry, only because it is less useful, and at the same time less difficult?—or, in other words, that every branch of human knowledge is estimated, not by its utility alone, but in the mixed ratio of its utility and its difficulty; and that it is this very method of deciding upon merit, that renders the publication before us so utterly contemptible as it is?

It is impossible to follow this gentleman into all the ditches into which he tumbles, or through all the sloughs in which he wades. The critic must go on noticing only those effusions of dullness which are the most prominent—*Summa papavera carpens.*

We are quite convinced this instructor confounds together the chemist of the shops and the philosophical chemist: he may be assured, however (whatever he may hear to the contrary), that they are two distinct classes of persons; and that there are actually many ingenious persons engaged in investigating the properties of bodies, who never sold a mercurial powder or an ounce of glauber salts in their lives. By way of exercise, we would wish this writer to reflect, fasting, upon the alteration produced in human affairs by glass and by gunpowder—and then to consider whether chemistry is solely occupied with the bodily wants of mankind, and with the improvement of manufactures; and though we are aware that his first guess will be, that the invention of these two substances has made it more easy to drink port wine, and to kill partridges, yet we can assure him, they have produced effects of still greater importance to mankind. We are not indulging in any pleasantry for the mere sake of misleading him, but honestly stating the plain truth.

The moment an envious pedant sees anything written with pleasantry, he comforts himself that it must be superficial. Whether the Reviewer is or is not considered as a superficial person by competent judges, he neither knows nor cares; but says what he has to say after his own manner—always confident, that, whatever he may be, he shall be found out, and classed as he deserves. The Oxford tutor may very possibly have given a just account of him; but his reasons for that judgment are certainly wrong: for it is by no means impossible to be entertaining and instructive at the same time; and the readers of this pamphlet (if any) can never doubt, after such a specimen, how easy it is to be, in one small production, both very frivolous and very tiresome. ......

We had almost forgotten to state, that this author's substitutes for lectures in moral philosophy, are sermons delivered from the University pulpit. He appears totally ignorant of what the terms *moral philosophy* mean. But enough of him and of his ignorance. We leave him now to his longs and shorts.

I nunc, et versus tecum meditare canoros.

FEMALE EDUCATION.*

A GREAT deal has been said of the original difference of capacity between men and women; as if women were more quick, and men more judicious—as if women were more remarkable for delicacy of association, and men for stronger powers of attention. All this, we confess, appears to us very fanciful. That there is a difference in the understandings of the men and the women we every day meet with, everybody, we suppose, must perceive; but there is none surely which may not be accounted for by the difference of circumstances in which they have been placed, without referring to any conjectural difference of original conformation of mind. As long as boys and girls run about in the dirt, and trundle hoops together, they are both precisely alike. If you catch up one half of these creatures, and train them to a particular set of actions and opinions, and the other half to a perfectly opposite set, of course their understandings will differ, as one or the other sort of occupations has called this or that talent into action. There is surely no occasion to go into any deeper or more abstruse reasoning, in order to explain so very simple a phenomenon. Taking it, then, for granted, that nature has been as bountiful of understanding to one sex as the other, it is incumbent on us to consider what are the principal objections commonly made against the communication of a greater share of knowledge to women than commonly falls to their lot at present: for though it may be doubted whether women should learn all that men learn, the immense disparity which now exists between their knowledge we should hardly think could admit of any rational defence. It is not easy to imagine that there can be any just cause why a woman of forty should be

* Ed. Rev., Jan., 1810.

more ignorant than a boy of twelve years of age. If there be any good at all in female ignorance, this (to use a very colloquial phrase) is surely too much of a good thing.

Something in this question must depend, no doubt, upon the leisure which either sex enjoys for the cultivation of their understandings:—and we can not help thinking, that women have fully as much, if not more, idle time upon their hands than men. Women are excluded from all the serious business of the world; men are lawyers, physicians, clergymen, apothecaries, and justices of the peace—sources of exertion which consume a great deal more time than producing and suckling children; so that, if the thing is a thing that ought to be done—if the attainments of literature are objects really worthy the attention of females, they can not plead the want of leisure as an excuse for indolence and neglect. The lawyer who passes his day in exasperating the bickerings of Roe and Doe, is certainly as much engaged as his lady who has the whole of the morning before her to correct the children and pay the bills. The apothecary, who rushes from an act of phlebotomy in the western parts of the town to insinuate a bolus in the east, is surely as completely absorbed as that fortunate female who is darning the garment, or preparing the repast of her Æsculapius at home: and, in every degree and situation of life, it seems that men must necessarily be exposed to more serious demands upon their time and attention than can possibly be the case with respect to the other sex. We are speaking always of the fair demands which ought to be made upon the time and attention of women; for, as the matter now stands, the time of women is considered as worth nothing at all. Daughters are kept to occupations in sewing, patching, mantua-making, and mending, by which it is impossible they can earn tenpence a day. The intellectual improvement of women is considered to be of such subordinate importance, that twenty pounds paid for needlework would give to a whole family leisure to acquire a fund of real knowledge. They are kept with nimble fingers and vacant understandings till the season for improvement is utterly passed away, and all chance of forming more important habits completely lost. We do not therefore say that women have more leisure than men, if it be necessary that they should lead the life of artisans; but we make this assertion only upon the supposition, that it is of some importance women should be instructed; and that many ordinary occupations, for which a little money will find a better substitute, should be sacrificed to this consideration.

We bar, in this discussion, any objection which proceeds from the mere novelty of teaching women more than they are already taught. It may be useless that their education should be improved, or it may be pernicious; and these are the fair grounds on which the question may be argued. But those who cannot bring their minds to consider such an unusual extension of knowledge, without connecting with it some sensation of the ludicrous, should remember that, in the progress from absolute ignorance, there is a period when cultivation of the mind is new to every rank and description of persons. A century ago, who would have believed that country gentlemen could be brought to read and spell with the ease and accuracy which we now so frequently remark—or supposed that they could be carried up even to the elements of ancient and modern history? Nothing is more common, or more stupid, than to take the actual for the possible—to believe that all which is, is all which can be; first to laugh at every proposed deviation from practice as impossible—then, when it is carried into effect, to be astonished that it did not take place before.

It is said, that the effect of knowledge is to make women pedantic and affected; and that nothing can be more offensive than to see a woman stepping out of the natural modesty of her sex to make an ostentatious display of her literary attainments. This may be true enough; but the answer is so trite and obvious, that we are almost ashamed to make it. All affectation and display proceed from the supposition of possessing something better than the rest of the world possesses. Nobody is vain of possessing two legs and two arms;—because that is the precise quantity of either sort of limb which everybody possesses. Who ever heard a lady boast that she understood French?—for no other reason, that we know of, but because everybody in these days does understand French; and though there may be some disgrace in being ignorant of that language, there is little or no merit in its acquisition. Diffuse knowledge generally among women, and you will at once cure the conceit which knowledge occasions while it is rare. Vanity and conceit we shall of course witness in men and women as long as the world endures: but by multiplying the attainments upon which these feelings are founded, you increase the difficulty of indulging them, and render them much more tolerable, by making them the proofs of a much higher merit. When learning ceases to be uncommon among women, learned women will cease to be affected.

A great many of the lesser and more obscure duties of life necessarily devolve upon the female sex. The arrangement of all household matters, and the care of children in their early infancy, must of course depend upon them. Now, there is a very general notion, that the moment you put the education of women upon a better footing than it is at present, at that moment there will be an end of all domestic economy; and that, if you once suffer women to eat of the tree of knowledge, the rest of the family will very soon be reduced to the same kind of aerial and unsatisfactory diet. These, and all such opinions, are referable to one great and common cause of error; that man does everything, and that nature does nothing; and that everything we see is referable to positive institution rather than to original feeling. Can anything, for example, be more perfectly absurd than to suppose that the care and perpetual solicitude which a mother feels for her children depend upon her ignorance of Greek and mathematics; and that she would desert an infant for a quadratic equation? We seem to imagine that we can break in pieces the solemn institutions of nature, by the little laws of a boarding-school; and that the existence of the human race depends upon teaching women a little more or a little less;—that Cimmerian ignorance can aid parental affection, or the circle of arts and sciences produce its destruction. In the same manner, we forget the principles upon which the love of order, arrangement, and all the arts of economy depend. They depend not upon ignorance nor idleness; but upon the poverty, confusion, and ruin which would ensue for neglecting them. Add to these principles, the love of what is beautiful and magnificent, and the vanity of display;—and there can surely be no reasonable doubt but that the order and economy of private life is amply secured from the perilous inroads of knowledge.

We would fain know, too, if knowledge is to produce such baneful effects upon the material and the household virtues, why this influence has not already been felt? Women are much better educated now than they were a century ago; but they are by no means less remarkable for attention to the arrangements of their household, or less inclined to discharge the offices of parental affection. It would be very easy to show, that the same objection has been made at all times to every improvement in the education of both sexes, and all ranks—and been as uniformly and completely refuted by experience. A great part of the objections made to the education of women, are rather objections made to human nature than to the female sex: for it is surely true, that knowledge, where it produces any bad effects at all, does as much mischief to one sex as to the other—and gives birth to fully as much arrogance, inattention to common affairs, and eccentricity among men, as it does among women. But it by no means follows, that you get rid of vanity and self-conceit because you get rid of learning. Self-complacency can never want an excuse; and the best way to make it more tolerable, and more useful, is to give to it as high and as dignified an object as possible. But at all events it is unfair to bring forward against a part of the world an objection which is equally powerful against the whole. When foolish women think they have any distinction, they are apt to be proud of it; so are foolish men. But we appeal to any one who has lived with cultivated persons of either sex, whether he has not witnessed as much pedantry, as much wrongheadedness, as much arrogance, and certainly a great deal more rudeness, produced by learning in men, than in women; therefore, we should make the accusation general —or dismiss it altogether; though, with respect to pedantry, the learned are certainly a little unfortunate, that so very emphatic a word, which is occasionally applicable to all men embarked eagerly in any pursuit, should be reserved exclusively for them: for, as pedantry is an ostentatious obtrusion of knowledge, in which those who hear us cannot sympathize, it is a fault of which soldiers, sailors, sportsmen, gamesters, cultivators, and all men engaged in a particular occupation, are quite as guilty as scholars; but they have the good fortune to have the vice only of pedantry—while scholars have both the vice and the name for it too.

Some persons are apt to contrast the acquisition of important knowledge with what they call simple pleasures; and deem it more becoming that a woman should educate flowers, make friendships with birds, and pick up plants, than enter into more difficult and fatiguing studies. If a woman have no taste and genius for higher occupations, let her engage in these to be sure rather than remain destitute of any pursuit. But why are we necessarily to doom a girl, whatever be her taste or her capacity, to one unvaried line of petty and frivolous occupation? If she be full of strong sense and elevated curiosity, can there be any reason why she should be diluted and enfeebled down to a mere culler of simples, and fancier of birds—why books of history and reasoning are to be torn out of her hand, and why she is to be sent, like a butterfly, to hover over the idle flowers of the field? Such amusements are innocent to those whom they can occupy; but they are not innocent to those who have too powerful understandings to be occupied by them. Light broths and fruits are innocent food only to weak or to infant stomachs; but they are poison to that organ in its perfect and mature state. But the great charm appears to be in the word *simplicity*—simple pleasure! If by a simple pleasure is meant an innocent pleasure, the observation is best answered by showing, that the pleasure which results from the acquisition of important knowledge is quite as innocent as any pleasure whatever: but if by a simple pleasure is meant one, the cause of which can be easily analyzed, or which does not last long, or which in itself is very faint, then simple pleasures seem to be very nearly synonymous with small pleasures: and if the simplicity were to be a little increased, the pleasure would vanish altogether.

As it is impossible that every man should have industry or activity sufficient to avail himself of the advantages of education, it is natural that men who are ignorant themselves, should view, with some degree of jealousy and alarm, any proposal for improving the education of women. But such men may depend upon it, however the system of female education may be exalted, that there will never be wanting a due proportion of failures; and that after parents, guardians, and preceptors, have done all in their power to make everybody wise, there will still be a plentiful supply of women who have taken special care to remain otherwise; and they may rest assured, if the utter extinction of ignorance and folly be the evil they dread, that their interests will always be effectually protected, in spite of every exertion to the contrary.

We must in candour allow that those women who begin will have something more to overcome than may probably hereafter be the case. We cannot deny the jealousy which exists among pompous and foolish men respecting the education of women. There is a class of pedants who would be cut short in the estimation of the world a whole cubit if it were generally known that a young lady of eighteen could be taught to decline the tenses of the middle voice, or acquaint herself with the Æolic varieties of that celebrated language. Then women have, of course, all ignorant men for enemies to their instruction, who being bound (as they think), in point of sex, to know more, are not well pleased, in point of fact, to know less. But, among men of sense and liberal politeness, a woman who has successfully cultivated her mind, without diminishing the gentleness and propriety of her manners, is always sure to meet with a respect and attention bordering upon enthusiasm.

There is in either sex a strong and permanent disposition to appear agreeable to the other: and this is the fair answer to those who are fond of supposing, that a higher degree of knowledge would make women rather the rivals than the companions of men. Presupposing such a desire to please, it seems much more probable, that a common pursuit should be a fresh source of interest than a cause of contention. Indeed, to suppose that any mode of education can create a general jealousy and rivalry between the sexes, is so very ridiculous, that it requires only to be stated in order to be refuted. The same desire of pleasing secures all that delicacy and reserve which are of such inestimable value to women. We are quite astonished, in hearing men converse on such subjects, to find them attributing such beautiful effects to ignorance. It would appear, from the tenor of such objections, that ignorance had been the great civilizer of the world. Women are delicate and refined only because they are ignorant; they manage their household, only because they are ignorant; they attend to their children, only because they know no better. Now, we must really confess, we have all our lives been so ignorant as not to know the value of ignorance. We have always attributed the modesty and the refined manners of women, to their being well taught in moral and religious duty—to the hazardous situation in which they are placed—to that perpetual vigilance which it is their duty to exercise over thought, word, and action—and to that cultivation of the mild virtues, which those who cultivate the stern and magnanimous virtues expect at their hands. After all, let it be remembered, we are not saying there are no objections to the diffusion of knowledge among the female sex. We would not hazard such a proposition respecting anything; but we are saying, that, upon the whole, it is the best method of employing time; and that there are fewer objections to it than to any other method. There are, perhaps, fifty thousand females in Great Britain who are exempted by circumstances from all necessary labour: but every human being must do something with their existence; and the pursuit of knowledge is, upon the whole, the most innocent, the most dignified, and the most useful method of filling up that idleness, of which there is always so large a portion in nations far advanced in civilization. Let any man reflect, too, upon the solitary situation in which women are placed—the ill-treatment to which they are sometimes exposed, and which they must endure in silence, and without the power of complaining—and he must feel convinced that the happiness of a woman will be materially increased in proportion as education has given to her the habit and the means of drawing her resources from herself.

There are a few common phrases in circulation, respecting the duties of women, to which we wish to pay some degree of attention, because they are rather inimical to those opinions which we have advanced on this subject. Indeed, independently of this, there is nothing which requires more vigilance than the current phrases of the day, of which there are always some resorted to in every dispute, and from the sovereign authority of which it is often vain to make any appeal. "The true theatre for a woman is the sick-chamber;"—"Nothing so honourable to a woman as not to be spoken of at all." These two phrases, the delight of *Noodledom*, are grown into common-places upon the subject; and are not unfrequently employed to extinguish that love of knowledge in women, which, in our humble opinion, it is of so much importance to cherish. Nothing, certainly, is so ornamental and delightful in women as the benevolent affections; but time cannot be filled up, and life employed, with high and impassioned virtues. Some of these feelings are of rare occurrence—all of short duration—or nature would sink under them. A scene of distress and anguish is an occasion where the finest qualities of the female mind may be displayed; but it is a monstrous exaggeration to tell women that they are born only for scenes of distress and anguish

Nurse father, mother, sister, and brother, if they want it; it would be a violation of the plainest duties to neglect them. But, when we are talking of the common occupations of life, do not let us mistake the accidents for the occupations; when we are arguing how the twenty-three hours of the day are to be filled up, it is idle to tell us of those feelings and agitations above the level of common existence, which may employ the remaining hour. Compassion, and every other virtue, are the great objects we all ought to have in view; but no man (and no woman) can fill up the twenty-four hours by acts of virtue. But one is a lawyer, and the other a ploughman, and the third a merchant; and then, acts of goodness, and intervals of compassion and fine feeling, are scattered up and down the common occupations of life. We know women are to be compassionate; but they cannot be compassionate from eight o'clock in the morning till twelve at night: and what are they to do in the interval? This is the only question we have been putting all along, and is all that can be meant by literary education.

Then, again, as to the notoriety which is incurred by literature. The cultivation of knowledge is a very distinct thing from its publication; nor does it follow that a woman is to become an author merely because she has talent enough for it. We do not wish a lady to write books—to defend and reply—to squabble about the tomb of Achilles, or the plain of Troy—any more than we wish her to dance at the opera, to play at a public concert, or to put pictures in the exhibition, because she has learned music, dancing, and drawing. The great use of her knowledge will be that it contributes to her private happiness. She may make it public: but it is not the principal object which the friends of female education have in view. Among men, the few who write bear no comparison to the many who read. We hear most of the former, indeed, because they are, in general, the most ostentatious part of literary men; but there are innumerable persons who, without ever laying themselves before the public, have made use of literature to add to the strength of their understandings, and to improve the happiness of their lives. After all, it may be an evil for ladies to be talked of: but we really think those ladies who are talked of only as Mrs Marcet, Mrs. Somerville, and Miss Martineau, are talked of, may bear their misfortunes with a very great degree of Christian patience.

Their exemption from all the necessary business of life is one of the most powerful motives for the improvement of education in women. Lawyers and physicians have in their professions a constant motive to exertion; if you neglect their education, they must, in a certain degree, educate themselves by their commerce with the world: they must learn caution, accuracy, and judgment, because they must incur responsibility. But if you neglect to educate the mind of a woman, by the speculative difficulties which occur in literature, it can never be educated at all: if you do not effectually rouse it by education, it must remain for ever languid. Uneducated men may escape intellectual degradation; uneducated women cannot. They have nothing to do; and if they come untaught from the schools of education, they will never be instructed in the school of events.

Women have not their livelihood to gain by knowledge; and that is one motive for relaxing all those efforts which are made in the education of men. They certainly have not; but they have happiness to gain, to which knowledge leads as probably as it does to profit; and that is a reason against mistaken indulgence. Besides, we conceive the labour and fatigue of accomplishments to be quite equal to the labour and fatigue of knowledge; and that it takes quite as many years to be charming as it does to be learned.

Another difference of the sexes is, that women are attended to, and men attend. All acts of courtesy and politeness originate from the one sex, and are received by the other. We can see no sort of reason, in this diversity of condition, for giving to women a trifling and insignificant education; but we see in it a very powerful reason for strengthening their judgment, and inspiring them with the habit of employing time usefully. We admit many striking differences in the situation of the two sexes, and many striking differences of understanding, proceeding from the different circumstances in which they are placed: but there is not a single difference of this kind which does not afford a new argument for making the education of women better than it is. They have nothing serious to do; is that a reason why they should be brought up to do nothing but what is trifling? They are exposed to greater dangers; is that a reason why their faculties are to be purposely and industriously weakened? They are to form the characters of future men; is that a cause why their own characters are to be broken and frittered down as they now are? In short, there is not a single trait in that diversity of circumstances, in which the two sexes are placed, that does not decidedly prove the magnitude of the error we commit in neglecting (as we do neglect) the education of women.

If the objections against the better education of women could be overruled, one of the great advantages that would ensue would be the extinction of innumerable follies. A decided and prevailing taste for one or another mode of education there must be. A century past, it was for housewifery—now it is for accomplishments. The object now is, to make women artists—to give them an excellence in drawing, music, painting, and dancing—of which, persons who make these pursuits the occupation of their lives, and derive from them their subsistence, need not be ashamed. Now, one great evil of all this is, that it does not last. If the whole of life were an Olympic game—if we could go on feasting and dancing to the end—this might do; but it is in truth merely a provision for the little interval between coming into life, and settling in it; while it leaves a long and dreary expanse behind, devoid both of dignity and cheerfulness. No mother, no woman who has passed over the few first years of life, sings, or dances, or draws, or plays upon musical instruments. These are merely means for displaying the grace and vivacity of youth, which every woman gives up, as she gives up the dress and manners of eighteen; she has no wish to retain them; or, if she has, she is driven out of them by diameter and derision. The system of female education, as it now stands, aims only at embellishing a few years of life, which are in themselves so full of grace and happiness, that they hardly want it; and then leaves the rest of existence a miserable prey to idle insignificance. No woman of understanding and reflection can possibly conceive she is doing justice to her children by such kind of education. The object is, to give to children resources that will endure as long as life endures—habits that time will ameliorate, not destroy—occupations that will render sickness tolerable, solitude pleasant, age venerable, life more dignified and useful, and therefore death less terrible: and the compensation which is offered for the omission of all this, is a short-lived blaze—a little temporary effect, which has no other consequence than to deprive the remainder of life of all taste and relish. There may be women who have a taste for the fine arts, and who evince a decided talent for drawing, or for music. In that case, there can be no objection to the cultivation of these arts; but the error is, to make such things the grand and universal object—to insist upon it that every woman is to sing, and draw, and dance—with nature, or against nature—to bind her apprentice to some accomplishment, and if she cannot succeed in oil or water-colours, to prefer gilding, varnishing, burnishing, box-making, to real solid improvement in taste, knowledge, and understanding.

A great deal is said in favour of the social nature of the fine arts. Music gives pleasure to others. Drawing is an art, the amusement of which does not centre in him who exercises it, but it is diffused among the rest of the world. This is true; but there is nothing, after all, so social as a cultivated mind. We do not mean to speak slightingly of the fine arts. or to depreciate the good humour with which they are sometimes exhibited; but we appeal to any man, whether a little spirited and sensible conversation—displaying, modestly, useful acquirements—and evincing rational curiosity, is not well worth the highest exertions of musical or graphical skill. A woman of accomplishments may entertain those who have the pleasure of knowing her for half an hour with great brilliancy; but a mind full of ideas, and with that elastic spring which the love of knowledge only can convey, is a perpetual source of exhilaration and amusement to all that come within its reach;—not collecting its force into single and insulated achievements, like the efforts made in the fine arts—but diffusing, equally over the whole of existence, a calm pleasure—better loved as it is longer felt—and suitable to every variety and every period of life. Therefore, instead of hanging the understanding of a woman upon walls. or hearing it vibrate upon strings—instead of seeing it in clouds, or hearing it in the wind, we would make it the first spring and ornament of society, by enriching it with attainments upon which alone such power depends.

If the education of women were improved. the education of men would be improved also. Let any one consider (in order to bring the matter more home by an individual instance) of what immense importance to society it is, whether a nobleman of first-rate fortune and distinction is well or ill brought up;—what a taste and fashion he may inspire for private and for political vice!—and what misery and mischief he may produce to the thousand human beings who are dependent on him! A country contains no such curse within its bosom. Youth, wealth, high rank, and vice, form a combination which baffles all remonstrance and beats down all opposition. A man of high rank who combines these qualifications for corruption, is almost the master of the manners of the age, and has the public happiness within his grasp. But the most beautiful possession which a country can have is a noble and rich man, who loves virtue and knowledge;—who without being feeble or fanatical is pious—and who without being factious is firm and independent;—who, in his political life, is an equitable mediator between king and people; and in his civil life, a firm promoter of all which can shed a lustre upon his country, or promote the peace and order of the world. But if these objects are of the importance which we attribute to them, the education of women must be important, as the formation of character for the first seven or eight years of life seems to depend almost entirely upon them. It is certainly in the power of a sensible and well-educated mother to inspire, within that period, such tastes and propensities as shall nearly decide the destiny of the future man; and this is done, not only by the intentional exertions of the mother, but by the gradual and insensible imitation of the child; for there is something extremely contagious in greatness and rectitude of thinking, even at that age; and the character of the mother with whom he passes his early infancy, is always an event of the utmost importance to the child. A merely accomplished woman cannot infuse her tastes into the minds of her sons; and, if she could, nothing could be more unfortunate than her success. Besides, when her accomplishments are given up, she has nothing left for it but to amuse herself in the best way she can; and, becoming entirely frivolous, either declines altogether the fatigue of attending to her children, or, attending to them, has neither talents nor knowledge to succeed; and, therefore, here is a plain and fair answer to those who ask so triumphantly, why should a woman dedicate herself to this branch of knowledge? or why should she be attached to such science?—Because, by having gained information on these points, she may inspire her son with valuable tastes, which may abide by him through life, and carry him up to all the sublimities of knowledge; because she cannot lay the foundation of a great character, if she is absorbed in frivolous amusements, nor inspire her child with noble desires, when a long course of trifling has destroyed the little talents which were left by a bad education.

It is of great importance to a country, that there should be as many understandings as possible actively employed within it. Mankind are much happier for the discovery of barometers, thermometers, steam-engines, and all the innumerable inventions in the arts and sciences. We are every day and every hour reaping the benefit of such talent and ingenuity. The same observation is true of such works as those of Dryden, Pope, Milton, and Shakespeare. Mankind are much happier that such individuals have lived and written; they add every day to the stock of public enjoyment—and perpetually gladden and embellish life. Now, the number of those who exercise their understandings to any good purpose, is exactly in proportion to those who exercise it at all; but, as the matter stands at present, half the talent in the universe runs to waste, and is totally unprofitable. It would have been almost as well for the world, hitherto, that women, instead of possessing the capacities they do at present, should have been born wholly destitute of wit, genius, and every other attribute of mind, of which men make so eminent a use: and the ideas of use and possession are so united together, that, because it has been the custom in almost all countries to give to women a different and a worse education than to men, the notion has obtained that they do not possess faculties which they do not cultivate. Just as, in breaking up a common, it is sometimes very difficult to make the poor believe it will carry corn, merely because they have been hitherto accustomed to see it produce nothing but weeds and grass—they very naturally mistake present condition for general nature. So completely have the talents of women been kept down, that there is scarcely a single work, either of reason or imagination, written by a woman, which is in general circulation either in the English, French, or Italian literature;—scarcely one that has crept even into the ranks of our minor poets.

If the possession of excellent talents is not a conclusive reason why they should be improved, it at least amounts to a very strong presumption; and, if it can be shown that women may be trained to reason and imagine as well as men, the strongest reasons are certainly necessary to show us why we should not avail ourselves of such rich gifts of nature; and we have a right to call for a clear statement of those perils which make it necessary that such talents should be totally extinguished, or, at most, very partially drawn out. The burthen of proof does not lie with those who say, increase the quantity of talent in any country as much as possible—for such a proposition is in conformity with every man's feelings; but it lies with those who say, take care to keep that understanding weak and trifling, which nature has made capable of becoming strong and powerful. The paradox is with them, not with us. In all human reasoning, knowledge must be taken for a good, till it can be shown to be an evil. But now, nature makes to us rich and magnificent presents; and we say to her—You are too luxuriant and munificent—we must keep you under, and prune you; —we have talents enough in the other half of the creation;—and, if you will not stupify and enfeeble the minds of women to our hands, we ourselves must expose them to a narcotic process, and educate away that fatal redundance with which the world is afflicted, and the order of sublunary things deranged.

One of the greatest pleasures of life is conversation;—and the pleasures of conversation are of course enhanced by every increase of knowledge: not that we should meet together to talk of alkalies and angles, or to add to our stock of history and philology— though a little of these things is no bad ingredient in conversation; but let the subject be what it may, there is always a prodigious difference between the conversation of those who have been well educated and of those who have not enjoyed this advantage. Education gives fecundity of thought, copiousness of illustration, quickness, vigour, fancy, words, images and illustrations—it decorates every common thing, and gives the power of trifling without being undignified and absurd. The subjects themselves may not be wanted, upon which the talents of an educated man have been exercised; but there is always a demand for those talents which his education has rendered strong and quick. Now, really, nothing can be further from our intention than to say anything rude and unpleasant; but we must be excused for observing, that it is not now a very common thing to be interested by the variety and extent of female knowledge, but it is a very common thing to lament, that the finest faculties in the world have been confined to trifles utterly unworthy of their richness and their strength.

The pursuit of knowledge is the most innocent and interesting occupation which can be given to the female sex; nor can there be a better method of checking a spirit of dissipation than by diffusing a taste for literature. The true way to attack vice, is by setting up something else against it. Give to women, in early youth, something to acquire, of sufficient interest and importance to command the application of their mature faculties, and to excite their perseverance in future life;—teach them that happiness is to be derived from the acquisition of knowledge, as well as the gratification of vanity; and you will raise up a much more formidable barrier against dissipation than a host of invectives and exhortations can supply.

It sometimes happens that an unfortunate man gets drunk with very bad wine—not to gratify his palate, but to forget his cares: he does not set any value on what he receives, but on account of what it excludes—it keeps out something worse than itself. Now, though it were denied that the acquisition of serious knowledge is of itself important to a woman, still it prevents a taste for silly and pernicious works of imagination; it keeps away the horrid trash of novels; and, in lieu of that eagerness for emotion and adventure which books of that sort inspire, promotes a calm and steady temperament of mind.

A man who deserves such a piece of good fortune, may generally find an excellent companion for all vicissitudes of his life; but it is not so easy to find a companion for his understanding, who has similar pursuits with himself, or who can comprehend the pleasure he derives from them. We really can see no reason why it should not be otherwise; nor comprehend how the pleasures of domestic life can be promoted by diminishing the number of subjects in which persons who are to spend their lives together take a common interest.

One of the most agreeable consequences of knowledge is the respect and importance which it communicates to old age. Men rise in character often as they increase in years;—they are venerable from what they have acquired, and pleasing from what they can impart. If they outlive their faculties, the mere frame itself is respected for what it once contained; but women (such is their unfortunate style of education) hazard everything upon one cast of the die;—when youth is gone, all is gone. No human creature gives his admiration for nothing; either the eye must be charmed, or the understanding gratified. A woman must talk wisely or look well. Every human being must put up with the coldest civility, who has neither the charms of youth nor the wisdom of age. Neither is there the slightest commiseration for decayed accomplishments;—no man mourns over the fragments of a dancer, or drops a tear on the relics of musical skill. They are flowers destined to perish; but the decay of great talents is always the subject of solemn pity; and, even when their last memorial is over, their ruins and vestiges are regarded with pious affection.

There is no connection between the ignorance in which women are kept, and the preservation of moral and religious principle; and yet certainly there is, in the minds of some timid and respectable persons, a vague, indefinite dread of knowledge, as if it were capable of producing these effects. It might almost be supposed, from the dread which the propagation of knowledge has excited, that there was some great secret which was to be kept in impenetrable obscurity—that all moral rules were a species of delusion and imposture, the detection of which, by the improvement of the understanding, would be attended with the most fatal consequences to all, and particularly to women. If we could possibly understand what these great secrets were, we might perhaps be disposed to concur in their preservation; but believing that all the salutary rules which are imposed on women are the result of true wisdom, and productive of the greatest happiness, we can not understand how they are to become less sensible of this truth in proportion as their power of discovering truth in general is increased, and the habit of viewing questions with accuracy and comprehension established by education. There are men, indeed, who are always exclaiming against every species of power, because it is connected with danger: their dread of abuses is so much stronger than their admiration of uses, that they would cheerfully give up the use of fire, gunpowder, and printing, to be freed from robbers, incendiaries, and libels. It is true, that every increase of knowledge may possibly render depravity more depraved, as well as it may increase the strength of virtue. It is in itself only power; and its value depends on its application. But, trust to the natural love of good where there is no temptation to be bad—it operates nowhere more forcibly than in education. No man, whether he be tutor, guardian, or friend, ever contents himself with infusing the mere ability to acquire; but giving the power, he gives with it a taste for the wise and rational exercise of that power; so that an educated person is not only one with stronger and better faculties than others, but with a more useful propensity—a disposition better cultivated—and associations of a higher and more important class.

In short, and to recapitulate the main points upon which we have insisted: Why the disproportion in knowledge between the two sexes should be so great, when the inequality in natural talents is so small; or why the understanding of women should be lavished upon trifles, when nature has made it capable of better and higher things, we profess ourselves not able to understand. The affectation charged upon female knowledge is best cured by making that knowledge more general: and the economy devolved upon women is best secured by the ruin, disgrace, and inconvenience which proceed from neglecting it. For the care of children, nature has made a direct and powerful provision; and the gentleness and elegance of women is the natural consequence of that desire to please, which is productive of the greatest part of civilization and refinement, and which rests upon a foundation too deep to be shaken by any such modifications in education as we have proposed. If you educate women to attend to dignified and important subjects, you are multiplying beyond measure the chances of human improvement, by preparing and *medicating* those early impressions, which always come from the mother; and which, in a great majority of instances, are quite decisive of character and genius. Nor is it only in the business of education that women would influence the destiny of men. If women knew more, men must learn more—for ignorance would then be shameful—and it would become the fashion to be instructed. The instruction of women improves the stock of national talents, and employs more minds for the instruction and amusement of the world;—it increases the pleasures of society, by multiplying the topics upon which the two sexes take a common interest; and makes marriage an intercourse of understanding as well as of affection, by giving dignity and importance to the female character. The education of women favours public morals; it provides for every season of life, as well as for the brightest and the best; and leaves a woman, when she is stricken by the hand of time, not as she now is, destitute of everything, and neglected by all; but with the full power and the splendid attractions of knowledge—diffusing the elegant pleasures of polite literature, and receiving the just homage of learned and accomplished men.

BOYISH HARDSHIPS AT SCHOOL.*

We are convinced that those young people will turn out to be the best men, who have been guarded most effectually in their childhood, from every species of useless vexation; and experienced, in the greatest degree, the blessings of a wise and rational indulgence. But even if these effects upon future character are not produced, still, four or five years in childhood make a very considerable period of human existence; and it is by no means a trifling consideration whether they are passed happily or unhappily. The wretchedness of school tyranny is trifling enough to a man who only contemplates it in case of body and tranquillity of mind, through the medium of twenty intervening years; but it is quite as real, and quite as acute while it lasts, as any of the sufferings of mature life: and the utility of these sufferings, or the price paid in compensation for them, should be clearly made out to a conscientious parent before he consents to expose his children to them.

MADAME D'EPINAY.—HER FRIENDSHIP WITH ROUSSEAU.†

There used to be in Paris, under the ancient regime, a few women of brilliant talents, who violated all the common duties of life, and gave very pleasant little suppers. Among these supped and sinned Madame d'Epinay—the friend and companion of Rousseau, Diderot, Grimm, Holbach, and many other literary per-

---

* From an article on Public Schools. Ed. Rev., August, 1810.
† Memoires et Correspondence de Madame d'Epinay. 3 vols. 8vo. Ed. Review, Dec., 1818.

sons of distinction of that period. Her principal lover was Grimm; with whom was deposited, written in feigned names, the history of her life. Grimm died—his secretary sold the history—the feigned names have been exchanged for the real ones—and her works now appear abridged in three volumes octavo.

Madame d'Epinay, though far from an immaculate character, has something to say in palliation of her irregularities. Her husband behaved abominably; and alienated, by a series of the most brutal injuries, an attachment which seems to have been very ardent and sincere, and which, with better treatment, would probably have been lasting. For, in all her aberrations, Mad. d'Epinay seems to have had a tendency to be constant. Though extremely young when separated from her husband, she indulged herself with but two lovers for the rest of her life;—to the first of whom she seems to have been perfectly faithful, till he left her at the end of ten or twelve years;—and to Grimm, by whom he was succeeded, she appears to have given no rival till the day of her death. The account of the life she led, both with her husband and her lovers, brings upon the scene a great variety of French characters, and lays open very completely the interior of French life and manners. But there are some letters and passages which ought not to have been published; which a sense of common decency and morality ought to have suppressed; and which, we feel assured, would never have seen the light in this country.

A French woman seems almost always to have wanted the flavour of prohibition, as a necessary condiment to human life. The provided husband was rejected, and the forbidden husband introduced in ambiguous light, through posterns and secret partitions. It was not the union to one man that was objected to—for they dedicated themselves with a constancy which the most household and parturient woman in England could not exceed;—but the thing wanted was the wrong man, the gentleman without the ring —the master unsworn to at the altar—the person unconsecrated by priests—

"Oh! let me taste thee unexcised by kings."

* * * * * * *

The friendship of Madame d'Epinay with Rousseau proceeded to a great degree of intimacy. She admired his genius, and provided him with hats and coats; and, at last, was so far deluded by his declamations about the country, as to fit him up a little hermit cottage, where there were a great many birds, and a great many plants and flowers—and where Rousseau was, as might have been expected, supremely miserable. His friends from Paris did not come to see him. The postman, the butcher, and the baker, hate romantic scenery; duchesses and marchionesses were no longer found to scramble for him. Among the real inhabitants of the country, the reputation of reading and thinking is fatal to character; and Jean Jacques cursed his own successful eloquence which had sent him from the suppers and flattery of Paris, to smell daffodils, watch sparrows, or project idle saliva into the passing stream. Very few men who have gratified, and are gratifying their vanity in a great metropolis, are qualified to quit it. Few have the plain sense to perceive that they must soon inevitably be forgotten—or the fortitude to bear it when they are. They represent to themselves imaginary scenes of deploring friends and dispirited companies—but the ocean might as well regret the drops exhaled by the sunbeams. Life goes on; and whether the absent have retired into a cottage or a grave, is much the same thing.— In London, as in law, *de non apparentibus, et non existentibus eadem est ratio.*

LOCAL ENGLISH MORALS.*

This is very well, considering that seventy years ago, we had scarcely a foot of land in India. But English morals are quite local. Under the meridian of Greenwich, and between the 50th and 58th degrees of latitude, we are an upright, humane, and just people. Between the 6th and 10th degrees of western longitude, we are tyrants and oppressors. On the other side of the Cape, we are ambitious and unprincipled conquerors:—just as the same animal is woolly in one country, hairy in another, and something between both in a third.

A HINT TO TRAVELLERS.†

A traveller who passes through countries little known, should tell us how such countries are cultivated—how they are governed

* From a review of St. Heude's Voyage up the Persian Gulf. Ed. Review, July, 1819.
† From the same.

—what is the face of nature—what is the state of the useful arts—what is the degree of knowledge which exists there. Every reader will be glad to learn these things, or some of them: but few, we imagine, will care to know whether he had a lean horse at this stage, or a fat horse at another—whether his supper at any given village was milk without eggs, or eggs without milk. A little gossip and a few adventures, are very well; but a book of gossip and adventures, especially when related without wit or discretion, had better not be.

USE OF CONQUERORS.*

NOTHING in this world is created in vain: lions, tigers, conquerors, have their use. Ambitious monarchs, who are the curse of civilized nations, are the civilizers of savage people. With a number of little independent hordes, civilization is impossible. They must have a common interest before there can be peace; and be directed by one will, before there can be order. When mankind are prevented from daily quarrelling and fighting, they first begin to improve; and all this, we are afraid, is only to be accomplished, in the first instance, by some great conqueror. We sympathize, therefore, with the victories of the King of Ashantee—and feel ourselves, for the first time, in love with military glory. The ex-Emperor of the French would, at Coomassie, Dogwumba, or Inta, be an eminent benefactor to the human race.

NATURE AT BOTANY BAY.†

BOTANY BAY is situated in a fine climate, rather Asiatic than European—with a great variety of temperature—but favourable, on the whole, to health and life. It, conjointly with Van Diemen's Land, produces coal in great abundance, fossil salt, slate, lime, plumbago, potter's clay; iron; white, yellow and brilliant topazes; alum and copper. These are all the important fossil productions which have been hitherto discovered; but the epidermis of the country has hardly as yet been scratched; and it is most probable

* From a review of Mission from Cape Coast Castle to Ashantee. By T. Edward Bowdich. Ed. Rev., Oct., 1819.
† Art. "Botany Bay." Ed. Rev., July, 1819

that the immense mountains which divide the eastern and western settlements, Bathurst and Sydney, must abound with every species of mineral wealth. The harbours are admirable; and the whole world, perhaps, cannot produce two such as those of Port Jackson and Derwent. The former of these is land-locked for fourteen miles in length, and of the most irregular form; its soundings are more than sufficient for the largest ships; and all the navies of the world might ride in safety within it. In the harbour of Derwent there is a road-stead forty-eight miles in length, completely land-locked;—varying in breadth from eight to two miles—in depth from thirty to four fathoms—and affording the best anchorage the whole way.

The mean heat, during the three summer months, December, January, and February, is about 80° at noon. The heat which such a degree of the thermometer would seem to indicate, is considerably tempered by the sea-breeze, which blows with considerable force from nine in the morning till seven in the evening. The three autumn months are March, April, and May, in which the thermometer varies from 55° at night to 75° at noon. The three winter months are June, July, and August. During this interval, the mornings and evenings are very chilly, and the nights excessively cold; hoar-frosts are frequent; ice, half an inch thick, is found twenty miles from the coast; the mean temperature at daylight is from 40° to 45°, and at noon, from 55° to 60°. In the three months of spring, the thermometer varies from 60° to 70°. The climate to the westward of the mountains is colder. Heavy falls of snow take place during the winter; the frosts are more severe, and the winters of longer duration. All the seasons are much more distinctly marked, and resemble much more those of this country.

Such is the climate of Botany Bay; and, in this remote part of the earth, Nature (having made horses, oxen, ducks, geese, oaks, elms, and all regular and useful productions for the rest of the world), seems determined to have a bit of play, and to amuse herself as she pleases. Accordingly, she makes cherries with the stone on the outside; and a monstrous animal, as tall as a grenadier, with the head of a rabbit, a tail as big as a bed-post, hopping along at the rate of five hops to a mile, with three or four young kangaroos looking out of its false uterus to see what is passing.

Then comes a quadruped as big as a large cat, with the eyes, colour and skin of a mole, and the bill and web-feet of a duck—puzzling Dr. Shaw, and rendering the latter half of his life miserable, from his utter inability to determine whether it was a bird or a beast. Add to this a parrot, with the legs of a sea-gull; a skate with the head of a shark; and a bird of such monstrous dimensions, that a side bone of it will dine three real carnivorous Englishmen;—together with many other productions that agitate Sir Joseph, and fill him with mingled emotions of distress and delight.

CHIMNEY-SWEEPERS.*

An excellent and well-arranged dinner is a most pleasing occurrence, and a great triumph of civilized life. It is not only the descending morsel and the enveloping sauce—but the rank, wealth, wit and beauty, which surround the meats—the learned management of light and heat—the silent and rapid services of the attendants—the smiling and sedulous host, proffering gusts and relishes—the exotic bottles—the embossed plate—the pleasant remarks—the handsome dresses—the cunning artifices in fruit and farina! The hour of dinner, in short, includes everything of sensual and intellectual gratification which a great nation glories in producing.

In the midst of all this, who knows that the kitchen chimney caught fire half an hour before dinner!—and that a poor little wretch, of six or seven years old, was sent up in the midst of the flames to put it out? We could not, previous to reading this evidence, have formed a conception of the miseries of these poor wretches, or that there should exist, in a civilized country, a class of human beings destined to such extreme and varied distress. ......

We have been thus particular in stating the case of the chimney-sweepers, and in founding it upon the basis of facts, that we may make an answer to those profligate persons who are always ready to fling an air of ridicule upon the labours of humanity, because they are desirous that what they have not virtue to do themselves, should appear to be foolish and romantic when done by others. A still higher degree of depravity than this, is to want every sort of compassion for human misery, when it is accompanied

* Ed. Rev., Oct., 1819

by filth, poverty and ignorance—to regulate humanity by the income tax, and to deem the bodily wretchedness and the dirty tears of the poor a fit subject for pleasantry and contempt. We should have been loath to believe that such deep-seated and disgusting immorality existed in these days; but the notice of it is forced upon us. Nor must we pass over a set of marvellously weak gentlemen who discover democracy and revolution in every effort to improve the condition of the lower orders, and to take off a little of the load of misery from those points where it presses the hardest. Such are the men into whose hearts Mrs. Fry has struck the deepest terror—who abhor Mr. Bentham and his penitentiary; Mr. Bennet and his hulks; Sir James Mackintosh and his bloodless assizes; Mr. Tuke and his sweeping machines—and every other human being who is great and good enough to sacrifice his quiet to his love for his fellow-creatures. Certainly we admit that humanity is sometimes the veil of ambition or of faction; but we have no doubt that there are a great many excellent persons to whom it is misery to see misery, and pleasure to lessen it; and who, by calling the public attention to the worst cases, and by giving birth to judicious legislative enactments for their improvement, have made, and are making the world somewhat happier than they found it. Upon these principles we join hands with the friends of the chimney-sweepers, and most heartily wish for the diminution of their numbers and the limitation of their trade.

CASTLEREAGH, CANNING, AND GRATTAN.*

THERE are two eminent Irishmen now in the House of Commons, Lord Castlereagh and Mr. Canning, who will subscribe to the justness of every syllable we have said upon this subject; and who have it in their power, by making it the condition of their remaining in office, to liberate their native country and raise it to its just rank among the nations of the earth. Yet the court buys them over, year after year, by the pomp and perquisites of office, and year after year they come into the House of Commons, feeling deeply and describing powerfully, the injuries of five millions of their countrymen—and continue members of a government that inflicts those evils, under the pitiful delusion that it is not a cabinet question—as if the scratchings and quarrellings of kings and

* The conclusion of an Article on Ireland. Ed. Rev., Nov., 1820

queens could alone cement politicians together in indissoluble unity, while the fate and fortune of one third of the empire might be complimented away from one minister to another, without the smallest breach in their cabinet alliance. Politicians, at least honest politicians, should be very flexible and accommodating in little things, very rigid and inflexible in great things. And is this not a great thing? Who has painted it in finer and more commanding eloquence than Mr. Canning? Who has taken a more sensible and statesmanlike view of our miserable and cruel policy than Lord Castlereagh? You would think, to hear them, that the same planet could not contain them and the oppressors of their country—perhaps not the same solar system. Yet for money, claret and patronage, they lend their countenance, assistance, and friendship, to the ministers who are the stern and inflexible enemies to the emancipation of Ireland!

Thank God that all is not profligacy and corruption in the history of that devoted people—and that the name of Irishman does not always carry with it the idea of the oppressor or the oppressed—the plunderer or the plundered—the tyrant or the slave. Great men hallow a whole people and lift up all who live in their time. What Irishman does not feel proud that he has lived in the days of GRATTAN? who has not turned to him for comfort, from the false friends and open enemies of Ireland? who did not remember him in the days of its burnings, and wastings, and murders? No government ever dismayed him—the world could not bribe him—he thought only of Ireland—lived for no other object—dedicated to her his beautiful fancy, his elegant wit, his manly courage and all the splendour of his astonishing eloquence. He was so born and so gifted, that poetry, forensic skill, elegant literature and all the highest attainments of human genius, were within his reach; but he thought the noblest occupation of a man was to make other men happy and free; and in that straight line he went on for fifty years, without one side-look, without one yielding thought, without one motive in his heart which he might not have laid open to the view of God and man. He is gone!—but there is not a single day of his honest life of which every good Irishman would not be more proud, than of the whole political existence of his countrymen—the annual deserters and betrayers of their native land.

JOHN BULL'S CHARITY SUBSCRIPTIONS.*

The English are a calm, reflecting people; they will give time and money when they are convinced; but they love dates, names, and certificates. In the midst of the most heart-rending narratives, Bull requires the day of the month, the year of our Lord, the name of the parish and the countersign of three or four respectable householders. After these affecting circumstances, he can no longer hold out; but gives way to the kindness of his nature — puffs, blubbers, and subscribes.

WISDOM OF OUR ANCESTORS.†

Our Wise Ancestors — the Wisdom of our Ancestors — the Wisdom of Ages — Venerable Antiquity — Wisdom of Old Times. — This mischievous and absurd fallacy springs from the grossest perversion of the meaning of words. Experience is certainly the mother of wisdom, and the old have, of course, a greater experience than the young; but the question is, who are the old? and who are the young? Of *individuals* living at the same period, the oldest has, of course, the greatest experience; but among *generations* of men the reverse of this is true. Those who come first (our ancestors), are the young people, and have the least experience. We have added to their experience the experience of many centuries; and, therefore, as far as experience goes, are wiser, and more capable of forming an opinion than they were. The real feeling should be, *not* can we be so presumptuous as to put our opinions in opposition to those of our ancestors? but can such young, ignorant, inexperienced persons as our ancestors necessarily were, be expected to have understood a subject as well as those who have seen so much more, lived so much longer, and enjoyed the experience of so many centuries? All this cant, then, about our ancestors is merely an abuse of words, by transferring phrases true of contemporary men to succeeding ages. Whereas (as we have before observed) of living men the oldest has, *cæteris paribus*, the most experience; of generations, the oldest has,

---

* Prisons. Ed. Rev., Feb., 1822.
† From a Review of The Book of Fallacies: from Unfinished Papers of Jeremy Bentham. By a Friend. Ed. Rev., Aug., 1825.

cæteris paribus, the least experience. Our ancestors, up to the Conquest, were children in arms; chubby boys in the time of Edward the First; striplings under Elizabeth; men in the reign of Queen Anne; and *we* only are the white-bearded, silver-headed ancients, who have treasured up, and are prepared to profit by, all the experience which human life can supply. We are not disputing with our ancestors the palm of talent, in which they may or may not be our superiors, but the palm of experience, in which it is utterly impossible they can be our superiors. And yet, whenever the chancellor comes forward to protect some abuse, or to oppose some plan which has the increase of human happiness for its object, his first appeal is always to the wisdom of our ancestors; and he himself, and many noble lords who vote with him, are, to this hour, persuaded that all alterations and amendments on their devices are an unblushing controversy between youthful temerity and mature experience!—and so, in truth, they are—only that much-loved magistrate mistakes the young for the old and the old for the young—and is guilty of that very sin against experience which he attributes to the lovers of innovation.

We cannot, of course, be supposed to maintain that our ancestors wanted wisdom, or that they were necessarily mistaken in their institutions, because their means of information were more limited than ours. But we do confidently maintain, that when we find it expedient to change anything which our ancestors have enacted, we are the experienced persons, and not they. The quantity of talent is always varying in any great nation. To say that we are more or less able than our ancestors, is an assertion that requires to be explained. All the able men of all ages, who have ever lived in England, probably possessed, if taken altogether, more intellect than all the able men now in England can boast of. But if authority must be resorted to rather than reason, the question is, What was the wisdom of that single age which enacted the law, compared with the wisdom of the age which proposes to alter it? What are the eminent men of one and the other period? If you say that our ancestors were wiser than us, mention your date and year. If the splendour of names is equal, are the circumstances the same? If the circumstances are the same, we have a superiority of experience, of which the difference between the two periods is the measure. It is necessary to insist upon this; for upon sacks of wool, and on benches forensic, sit grave men, and agricolous persons in the Commons, crying out, "Ancestors, Ancestors! *hodie non!* Saxons, Danes, save us! Fiddlefrig, help us! Howel, Ethelwolf, protect us." Any cover for nonsense—any veil for trash—any pretext for repelling the innovations of conscience and of duty!

NOODLE'S ORATION.*

The whole of these fallacies may be gathered together in a little oration, which we will denominate the Noodle's Oration.

"What would our ancestors say to this, sir? How does this measure tally with their institutions? How does it agree with their experience? Are we to put the wisdom of yesterday in competition with the wisdom of centuries? (*Hear, hear!*) Is beardless youth to show no respect for the decisions of mature age? (*Loud cries of hear! hear!*) If this measure be right, would it have escaped the wisdom of those Saxon progenitors to whom we are indebted for so many of our best political institutions? Would the Dane have passed it over? Would the Norman have rejected it? Would such a notable discovery have been reserved for these modern and degenerate times? Besides, sir, if the measure itself is good, I ask the honourable gentleman if this is the time for carrying it into execution—whether, in fact, a more unfortunate period could have been selected than that which he has chosen? If this were an ordinary measure, I should not oppose it with so much vehemence; but, sir, it calls in question the wisdom of an irrevocable law—of a law passed at the memorable period of the Revolution. What right have we, sir, to break down this firm column, on which the great men of that age stamped a character of eternity? Are not all authorities against this measure, Pitt, Fox, Cicero, and the Attorney and Solicitor General? The proposition is new, sir; it is the first time it was ever heard in this house. I am not prepared sir—this house is not prepared—to receive it. The measure implies a distrust of his majesty's government; their disapproval is sufficient to warrant opposition. Precaution only is requisite where danger is apprehended. Here the high character of the individuals in question is a sufficient

* From the same.

guarantee against any ground of alarm. Give not, then, your sanction to this measure; for whatever be its character, if you do give your sanction to it, the same man by whom this is proposed, will propose to you others to which it will be impossible to give your consent. I care very little, sir, for the ostensible measure; but what is there behind? What are the honourable gentleman's future schemes? If we pass this bill, what fresh concessions may he not require? What further degradation is he planning for his country? Talk of evil and inconvenience, sir! look to other countries — study other aggregations and societies of men, and then see whether the laws of this country demand a remedy, or deserve a panegyric. Was the honourable gentleman (let me ask him) always of this way of thinking? Do I not remember when he was the advocate in this house of very opposite opinions? I not only quarrel with his present sentiments, sir, but I declare very frankly I do not like the party with which he acts. If his own motives were as pure as possible, they cannot but suffer contamination from those with whom he is politically associated. This measure may be a boon to the constitution, but I will accept no favour to the constitution from such hands (*Loud cries of hear! hear!*) I profess myself, sir, an honest and upright member of the British Parliament, and I am not afraid to profess myself an enemy to all change, and all innovation. I am satisfied with things as they are; and it will be my pride and pleasure to hand down this country to my children as I received it from those who preceded me. The honourable gentleman pretends to justify the severity with which he has attacked the noble lord who presides in the Court of Chancery. But I say such attacks are pregnant with mischief to government itself. Oppose ministers, you oppose government; disgrace ministers, you disgrace government; bring ministers into contempt, you bring government into contempt; and anarchy and civil war are the consequences. Besides, sir, the measure is unnecessary. Nobody complains of disorder in that shape in which it is the aim of your measure to propose a remedy to it. The business is one of the greatest importance; there is need of the greatest caution and circumspection. Do not let us be precipitate, sir; it is impossible to foresee all consequences. Everything should be gradual; the example of a neighbouring nation should fill us with alarm! The honourable gentleman has taxed me with illiberality, sir. I deny the charge. I hate innovation, but I love improvement. I am an enemy to the corruption of government, but I defend its influence. I dread reform, but I dread it only when it is intemperate. I consider the liberty of the press as the great palladium of the constitution; but at the same time, I hold the licentiousness of the press in the greatest abhorrence. Nobody is more conscious than I am of the splendid abilities of the honourable mover, but I tell him at once, his scheme is too good to be practicable. It savours of Utopia. It looks well in theory, but it won't do in practice. It will not do, I repeat, sir, in practice; and so the advocates of the measure will find, if, unfortunately, it should find its way through Parliament. (*Cheers.*) The source of that corruption to which the honourable member alludes is in the minds of the people; so rank and extensive is that corruption, that no political reform can have any effect in removing it. Instead of reforming others — instead of reforming the state, the constitution, and everything that is most excellent, let each man reform himself! let him look at home, he will find there enough to do, without looking abroad, and aiming at what is out of his power. (*Loud cheers.*) And now, sir, as it is frequently the custom in this house to end with a quotation, and as the gentleman who preceded me in the debate has anticipated me in my favourite quotation of the 'Strong pull and the long pull,' I shall end with the memorable words of the assembled Barons — *Nolumus leges Angliæ mutari.*"

MR. WATERTON AND HIS WANDERINGS.*

MR. WATERTON is a Roman Catholic gentleman of Yorkshire, of good fortune, who, instead of passing his life at balls and assemblies, has preferred living with Indians and monkeys in the forests of Guiana. He appears in early life to have been seized with an unconquerable aversion to Piccadilly, and to that train of meteorological questions and answers, which forms the great staple of po-

* Wanderings in South America, the North-West of the United States, and the Antilles, in the years 1812, 1816, 1820, and 1824; with Original Instructions for the perfect Preservation of Birds, &c., for Cabinets of Natural History. By Charles Waterton, Esq. London.. Mawman. 4to. 1825 Ed. Rev., Feb., 1826.

lite English conversation. From a dislike to the regular form of a journal, he throws his travels into detached pieces, which he rather affectedly, calls Wanderings—and of which we shall proceed to give some account.

His first Wandering was in the year 1812, through the wilds of Demerara and Essequibo, a part of *ci-devant* Dutch Guiana, in South America. The sun exhausted him by day, the musquitoes bit him by night: but on went Mr. Charles Waterton!

The first thing which strikes us in this extraordinary chronicle, is the genuine zeal and inexhaustible delight with which all the barbarous countries he visits are described. He seems to love the forests, the tigers, and the apes;—to be rejoiced that he is the only man there; that he has left his species far away; and is at last in the midst of his blessed baboons! He writes with a considerable degree of force and vigour; and contrives to infuse into his reader that admiration of the great works, and undisturbed scenes of nature, which animates his style, and has influenced his life and practice. There is something, too, to be highly respected and praised in the conduct of a country-gentleman, who, instead of exhausting life in the chase, has dedicated a considerable portion of it to the pursuit of knowledge. There are so many temptations to complete idleness in the life of a country-gentleman, so many examples of it, and so much loss to the community from it, that every exception from the practice is deserving of great praise. Some country-gentlemen must remain to do the business of their counties; but, in general, there are many more than are wanted; and, generally speaking also, they are a class who should be stimulated to greater exertions. Sir Joseph Banks, a squire of large fortune in Lincolnshire, might have given up his existence to double-barrelled guns and persecutions of poachers—and all the benefits derived from his wealth, industry, and personal exertion in the cause of science, would have been lost to the community.

Mr. Waterton complains, that the trees of Guiana are not more than six yards in circumference—a magnitude in trees which it is not easy for a Scotch imagination to reach. Among these, preeminent in height rises the mora—upon whose top branches, when naked by age, or dried by accident, is perched the toucan, too huge for the gun of the fowler;—around this are the green heart, famous for hardness; the tough hackea; the ducalabali, surpassing mahogany; the ebony and letter-wood, exceeding the most beautiful woods of the Old World; the locust-tree, yielding copal; and the hayawa and olou trees, furnishing sweet-smelling resin. Upon the top of the mora grows the fig-tree. The bush-rope joins tree and tree, so as to render the forest impervious, as, descending from on high, it takes root as soon as its extremity touches the ground, and appears like shrouds and stays supporting the mainmast of a line-of-battle ship.

Demerara yields to no country in the world in her birds. The mud is flaming with the scarlet curlew. At sunset, the pelicans return from the sea to the courada trees. Among the flowers are the humming-birds. The columbine, gallinaceous, and passerine tribes people the fruit-trees. At the close of day, the vampires, or winged bats, suck the blood of the traveller, and cool him by the flap of their wings. Nor has nature forgotten to amuse herself here in the composition of snakes:—the camoudi has been killed from thirty to forty feet long; he does not act by venom, but by size and convolution. The Spaniards affirm that he grows to the length of eighty feet, and that he will swallow a bull; but Spaniards love the superlative. There is a *whipsnake* of a beautiful green. The labarri snake of a dirty brown, who kills you in a few minutes. Every lovely colour under heaven is lavished upon the counachouchi, the most venomous of reptiles, and known by name of the *bush-master*. Man and beast, says Mr. Waterton, fly before him, and allow him to pursue an undisputed path. . . . . .

One of the strange and fanciful objects of Mr. Waterton's journey was, to obtain a better knowledge of the composition and nature of the *Wourali* poison, the ingredient with which the Indians poison their arrows. In the wilds of Essequibo, far away from any European settlements, there is a tribe of Indians known by the name of *Macoushi*. The *Wourali* poison is used by all the South American savages, betwixt the Amazon and the Oroonoque; but the Macoushi Indians manufacture it with the greatest skill, and of the greatest strength. A vine grows in the forest called Wourali; and from this vine, together with a good deal of nonsense and absurdity, the poison is prepared. When a native of Macoushia goes in quest of feathered game, he seldom carries his bow and arrows. It is the blow-pipe he then uses. The reed grows to an amazing length, as the part the Indians use is from 10 to 11

THE WOURALI POISON.

feet long, and no tapering can be perceived, one end being as thick as another; nor is there the slightest appearance of a knot or joint. The end which is applied to the mouth is tied round with a small silk grass cord. The arrow is from nine to ten inches long; it is made out of the leaf of a palm-tree, and pointed as sharp as a needle: about an inch of the pointed end is poisoned: the other end is burnt to make it still harder; and wild cotton is put round it for an inch and a half. The quiver holds from 500 to 600 arrows, is from 12 to 14 inches long, and in shape like a dice-box. With a quiver of these poisoned arrows over his shoulder, and his blow-pipe in his hand, the Indian stalks into the forest in quest of his feathered game. . . . . .

Being a *Wourali* poison fancier, Mr. Waterton has recorded several instances of the power of his favourite drug. A sloth poisoned by it went gently to sleep, and died! a large ox, weighing one thousand pounds, was shot with three arrows; the poison took effect in four minutes, and in twenty-five minutes he was dead. The death seems to be very gentle; and resembles more a quiet apoplexy, brought on by hearing a long story, than any other kind of death. If an Indian happen to be wounded with one of these arrows, he considers it as certain death. We have reason to congratulate ourselves, that our method of terminating disputes is by sword and pistol, and not by these medicated pins; which, we presume, will become the weapons of gentlemen in the new republics of South America.

The *second* journey of Mr. Waterton, in the year 1816, was to Pernambuco, in the southern hemisphere, on the coast of Brazil, and from thence he proceeds to Cayenne. His plan was to have ascended the Amazon from Para, and got into the Rio Negro, and from thence to have returned toward the source of the Essequibo, in order to examine the Crystal Mountains, and to look once more for Lake Parima, or the White Sea; but on arriving at Cayenne, he found that to beat up the Amazon would be long and tedious; he left Cayenne, therefore in an American ship for Paramaribo, went through the interior to Coryntin, stopped a few days at New Amsterdam, and proceeded to Demerara.

"Leave behind you," he says to the traveller, "your high-seasoned dishes, your wines, and your delicacies, carry nothing but what is necessary for your own comfort, and the object in view, and depend upon the skill of an

Indian, or your own, for fish and game. A sheet, about twelve feet long ten wide, painted, and with loop-holes on each side, will be of great service: in a few minutes you can suspend it betwixt two trees in the shape of a roof. Under this, in your hammock, you may defy the pelting shower, and sleep heedless of the dews of night. A hat, a shirt, and a light pair of trowsers, will be all the raiment you require. Custom will soon teach you to tread lightly and barefoot on the little inequalities of the ground and show you how to pass on, unwounded amid the mantling briars."

Snakes are certainly an annoyance; but the snake, though high-spirited, is not quarrelsome; he considers his fangs to be given for defence, and not for annoyance, and never inflicts a wound but to defend existence. If you tread upon him, he puts you to death for your clumsiness, merely because he does not understand what your clumsiness means; and certainly a snake, who feels fourteen or fifteen stone stamping upon his tail, has little time for reflection, and may be allowed to be poisonous and peevish. American tigers generally run away—from which several respectable gentlemen in Parliament inferred, in the American war, that American soldiers would run away also!

The description of the birds is very animated and interesting; but how far does the gentle reader imagine the campanero may be heard, whose size is that of a jay? Perhaps 300 yards. Poor innocent, ignorant reader! unconscious of what nature has done in the forests of Cayenne, and measuring the force of tropical intonation by the sounds of a Scotch duck! The campanero may be heard three miles!—this single little bird being more powerful than the belfry of a cathedral, ringing for a new dean—just appointed on account of shabby politics, small understanding, and good family!

"The fifth species is the celebrated campanero of the Spaniards, called dara by the Indians, and bell-bird by the English. He is about the size of the jay. His plumage is white as snow. On his forehead rises a spiral tube nearly three inches long. It is jet black, dotted all over with small white feathers. It has a communication with the palate, and when filled with air, looks like a spire; when empty, it becomes pendulous. His note is loud and clear, like the sound of a bell, and may be heard at the distance of three miles. In the midst of these extensive wilds, generally on the dried top of an aged mora, almost out of gun reach, you will see the campanero. No sound or song from any of the winged inhabitants of the forest, not even the clearly pronounced 'Whip-poor-Will,' from the goatsucker, causes such astonishment as the toll of the campanero.

"With many of the feathered race he pays the common tribute of a morning and an evening song; and even when the meridian sun has shut in silence the mouths of almost the whole of animated nature, the campanero still cheers the forest. You hear his toll, and then a pause for a minute, then another toll, and then a pause again, and then a toll, and again a pause."

It is impossible to contradict a gentleman who has been in the forests of Cayenne; but we are determined, as soon as a campanero is brought to England, to make him toll in a public place, and have the distance measured. The toucan has an enormous bill, makes a noise like a puppy-dog, and lays his eggs in hollow trees. How astonishing are the freaks and fancies of nature! To what purpose, we say, is a bird placed in the woods of Cayenne, with a bill a yard long, making a noise like a puppy-dog, and laying eggs in hollow trees? The toucans, to be sure, might retort, to what purpose were gentlemen in Bond street created? To what purpose were certain foolish, prating members of Parliament created—pestering the House of Commons with their ignorance and folly, and impeding the business of the country? There is no end of such questions. So we will not enter into the metaphysics of the toucan. The houtou ranks high in beauty; his whole body is green, his wings and tail blue; his crown is of black and blue; he makes no nest, but rears his young in the sand.

There is no end to the extraordinary noises of the forest of Cayenne. The woodpecker, in striking against the tree with his bill, makes a sound so loud, that Mr. Waterton says it reminds you more of a wood-cutter than a bird. While lying in your hammock, you hear the goatsucker lamenting like one in deep distress —a stranger would take it for a Weir murdered by Thurtell.

"Suppose yourself in hopeless sorrow, begin with a high loud note, and pronounce, 'ha, ha, ha, ha, ha, ha, ha,' each note lower and lower, till the last is scarcely heard, pausing a moment or two betwixt every note, and you will have some idea of the moaning of the largest goatsucker in Demerara."

One species of the goatsucker cries, "Who are you? who are you?" Another exclaims, "Work away, work away." A third, "Willy come go. Willy come go." A fourth, "Whip poor Will, whip poor Will." It is very flattering to us that they should all speak *English!*—though we cannot much commend the elegance of their selections. The Indians never destroy these birds, believing them to be the servants of Jumbo, the African devil.

Great travellers are very fond of triumphing over civilized life; and Mr. Waterton does not omit the opportunity of remarking, that nobody ever stopped him in the forests of Cayenne to ask him for his license, or to inquire if he had a hundred a year, or to take away his gun, or to dispute the limits of a manor, or to threaten him with a tropical justice of the peace. We hope, however, that in this point we are on the eve of improvement. Mr. Peel, who is a man of high character and principles, may depend upon it that the time is come for his interference, and that it will be a loss of reputation to him not to interfere. If any one else can and will carry an alteration through Parliament, there is no occasion that the hand of government should appear; but some hand *must* appear. The common people are becoming ferocious, and the perdricide criminals are more numerous than the violators of all the branches of the Decalogue.

"The king of the vultures is very handsome, and seems to be the only bird which claims regal honours from a surrounding tribe. It is a fact beyond all dispute, that when the scent of carrion has drawn together hundreds of the common vultures, they all retire from the carcass as soon as the king of the vultures makes his appearance. When his majesty has satisfied the cravings of his royal stomach with the choicest bits from the most stinking and corrupted parts, he generally retires to a neighbouring tree, and then the common vultures return in crowds to gobble down his leavings. The Indians, as well as the whites, have observed this; for when one of them, who has learned a little English, sees the king, and wishes you to have a proper notion of the bird, he says, 'There is the governor of the carrion crows.'

"Now, the Indians have never heard of a personage in Demerara higher than that of governor; and the colonists, through a common mistake, call the vultures carrion crows. Hence the Indian, in order to express the dominion of this bird over the common vultures, tells you he is governor of the carrion crows. The Spaniards have also observed it, for, through all the Spanish Main, he is called Rey de Zamuros, king of the vultures."

This, we think, explains satisfactorily the origin of kingly government. As men have "learnt from the dog the physic of the field," they may probably have learnt from the vulture those high lessons of policy upon which, in Europe, we suppose the whole happiness of society, and the very existence of the human race, to depend.

Just before his third journey, Mr. Waterton takes leave of Sir Joseph Banks, and speaks of him with affectionate regret. "I saw," says Mr. W., "with sorrow, that death was going to rob us of him. We talked of stuffing quadrupeds; I agreed that the lips and nose ought to be cut off, and stuffed with wax." This is the way great naturalists take an eternal farewell of each other!

THE SLOTH.

Upon stuffing animals, however, we have a word to say. Mr. Waterton has placed at the head of his book the picture of what he is pleased to consider a nondescript species of monkey. In this exhibition our author is surely abusing his stuffing talents, and laughing at the public. It is clearly the head of a master in chancery—whom we have often seen backing in the House of Commons after he has delivered his message. It is foolish thus to trifle with science and natural history. Mr. Waterton gives an interesting account of the sloth, an animal of which he appears to be fond, and whose habits he has studied with peculiar attention.

"Some years ago I kept a sloth in my room for several months. I often took him out of the house and placed him upon the ground, in order to have an opportunity of observing his motions. If the ground were rough, he would pull himself forward, by means of his fore legs, at a pretty good pace; and he invariably shaped his course toward the nearest tree. But if I put him upon a smooth and well-trodden part of the road, he appeared to be in trouble and distress: his favourite abode was the back of a chair; and after getting all his legs in a line upon the topmost part of it, he would hang there for hours together, and often, with a low and inward cry, would seem to invite me to take notice of him."

The sloth, in its wild state, spends its life in trees, and never leaves them but from force or accident. The eagle to the sky, the mole to the ground, the sloth to the tree; but what is most extraordinary, he lives not *upon* the branches, but *under* them. He moves suspended, rests suspended, sleeps suspended, and passes his life in suspense—like a young clergyman distantly related to a bishop. Strings of ants may be observed, says our good traveller, a mile long, each carrying in its mouth a green leaf the size of a sixpence! he does not say whether this is a loyal procession, like Oak-apple Day, or for what purpose these leaves are carried; but it appears, while they are carrying the leaves, that three sorts of ant-bears are busy in eating them. The habits of the largest of these three animals are curious, and to us new. We recommend the account to the attention of the reader.

"He is chiefly found in the inmost recesses of the forest, and seems partial to the low and swampy parts near creeks, where the Trooly tree grows. There he goes up and down in quest of ants, of which there is never the least scarcity; so that he soon obtains a sufficient supply of food, with very little trouble. He can not travel fast; man is superior to him in speed. Without swiftness to enable him to escape from his enemies, without teeth, the possession of which would assist him in self defence, and without the power of burrowing in the ground, by which he might conceal himself from his pursuers, he still is capable of ranging through these wilds in perfect safety nor does he fear the fatal pressure of the serpent's fold, or the teeth of the famished jaguar. Nature has formed his fore-legs wonderfully thick, and strong, and muscular, and armed his feet with three tremendous sharp and crooked claws. Whenever he seizes an animal with these formidable weapons, he hugs it close to his body and keeps it there till it dies through pressure, or through want of food. Nor does the ant-bear, in the meantime, suffer much from loss of aliment, as it is a well-known fact, that he can go longer without food than perhaps any other animal, except the land tortoise. His skin is of a texture that perfectly resists the bite of a dog; his hinder parts are protected by thick and shaggy hair, while his immense tail is large enough to cover his whole body.

"The Indians have a great dread of coming in contact with the ant-bear; and, after disabling him in the chase, never think of approaching him till he be quite dead."

The vampire measures about twenty-six inches from wing to wing. There are two species, large and small. The large suck men, and the smaller, birds. Mr. W. saw some fowls which had been sucked the night before, and they were scarcely able to walk.

"Some years ago I went to the river Paumaron with a Scotch gentleman, by name Tarbet. We hung our hammocks in the thatched loft of a planter's house. Next morning I heard this gentleman muttering in his hammock, and now and then letting fall an imprecation or two, just about the time he ought to have been saying his morning prayers. 'What is the matter, sir?' said I, softly; 'is anything amiss?'—'What's the matter?' answered he, surlily; 'why, the vampires have been sucking me to death.' As soon as there was light enough, I went to his hammock, and saw it much stained with blood. 'There,' said he, thrusting his foot out of the hammock, 'see how these infernal imps have been drawing my life's blood.' On examining his foot, I found the vampire had tapped his great toe: there was a wound somewhat less than that made by a leech; the blood was still oozing from it; I conjectured he might have lost from ten to twelve ounces of blood. Whilst examining it, I think I put him into a worse humour, by remarking, that a European surgeon would not have been so generous as to have blooded him without making a charge. He looked up in my face, but did not say a word: I saw he was of opinion that I had better have spared this piece of ill-timed levity."

The story which follows this account is vulgar, unworthy of Mr. Waterton, and should have been omitted.

Every animal has its enemies. The land-tortoise has two enemies, man and the boa-constrictor. The natural defence of the land-tortoise is to draw himself up in his shell, and to remain quiet. In this state, the tiger, however famished, can do nothing with him, for the shell is too strong for the stroke of his paw. Man, however, takes him home and roasts him—and the boa-constrictor swallows him whole, shell and all, and consumes him slowly in the interior, as the Court of Chancery does a great estate.

The danger seems to be much less with snakes and wild beasts, if you conduct yourself like a gentleman, and are not abruptly intrusive. If you will pass on gently, you may walk unhurt within a yard of the Labairi snake, who would put you to death if you rushed upon him. The taguan knocks you down with a blow of his paw, if suddenly interrupted, but will run away, if you will give him time to do so. In short, most animals look upon man as a very ugly customer; and, unless sorely pressed for food, or from fear of their own safety, are not fond of attacking him. Mr. Waterton, though much given to sentiment, made a Labairi snake bite itself, but no bad consequences ensued—nor would any bad consequences ensue, if a court-martial were to order a sinful soldier to give himself a thousand lashes. It is barely possible that the snake had some faint idea of whom and what he was biting.

Insects are the curse of tropical climates. The bête rouge lays the foundation of a tremendous ulcer. In a moment you are covered with ticks. Chigoes bury themselves in your flesh, and hatch a large colony of young chigoes in a few hours. They will not live together, but every chigoe sets up a separate ulcer, and has his own private portion of pus. Flies get entry into your mouth, into your eyes, into your nose; you eat flies, drink flies, and breathe flies. Lizards, cockroaches, and snakes, get into the bed; ants eat up the books; scorpions sting you on the foot. Everything bites, stings, or bruises; every second of your existence you are wounded by some piece of animal life that nobody has ever seen before, except Swammerdam and Meriam. An insect with eleven legs is swimming in your teacup, a nondescript with nine wings is struggling in the small beer, or a caterpillar with several dozen eyes in his belly is hastening over the bread and butter! All nature is alive, and seems to be gathering all her entomological hosts to eat you up, as you are standing, out of your coat, waistcoat, and breeches. Such are the tropics. All this reconciles us to our dews, fogs, vapours, and drizzle—to our apothecaries rushing about with gargles and tinctures—to our old, British, constitutional coughs, sore throats, and swelled faces. . . . . . .

Now, what shall we say, after all, of Mr. Waterton? That he has spent a great part of his life in wandering in the wild scenes he describes, and that he describes them with entertaining zeal and real feeling. His stories draw largely sometimes on our faith: but a man who lives in the woods of Cayenne must do many odd things, and see many odd things—things utterly unknown to the dwellers in Hackney and Highgate. We do not want to rein up Mr. Waterton too tightly—because we are convinced he goes best with his head free. But a little less of apostrophe, and some faint suspicion of his own powers of humour, would improve this gentleman's style. As it is, he has a considerable talent at describing. He abounds with good feeling; and has written a very entertaining book, which hurries the reader out of his European parlour, into the heart of tropical forests, and gives, over the rules and the cultivation of the civilized parts of the earth, a momentary superiority to the freedom of the savage, and the wild beauties of nature. We honestly recommend the book to our readers: it is well worth the perusal.

GRANBY.[*]

THERE is nothing more amusing in the spectacles of the present day, than to see the Sir Johns and Sir Thomases of the House of Commons struck aghast by the useful science and wise novelties of Mr. Huskisson and the chancellor of the exchequer. Treason, Disaffection, Atheism, Republicanism, and Socinianism—the great guns in the Noodle's park of artillery, they cannot bring to bear upon these gentlemen. Even to charge with a regiment of ancestors, is not quite so efficacious as it used to be; and all that remains, therefore, is to rail against Peter M'Culloch and Political Economy! In the meantime, day after day, down goes one piece of nonsense or another. The most approved trash, and the most trusty clamours, are found to be utterly powerless. Two-penny taunts and trumpery truisms have lost their destructive omnipotence: and the exhausted commonplace-man, and the afflicted fool, moan over the ashes of Imbecility, and strew flowers on the urn of Ignorance! General Elliot found the London tailors in a

[*] Granby. A Novel in Three Volumes. London, Colburn, 1826. Ed Rev., Feb., 182

state of mutiny, and he raised from them a regiment of light cavalry, which distinguished itself in a very striking manner at the battle of Minden. In humble imitation of this example, we shall avail ourselves of the present political disaffection and unsatisfactory idleness of many men of rank and consequence, to request their attention to the Novel of Granby—written, as we have heard, by a young gentleman of the name of Lister;* and from which we have derived a considerable deal of pleasure and entertainment.

The main question as to a novel is—did it amuse? Were you surprised at dinner coming so soon? did you mistake eleven for ten, and twelve for eleven? were you too late to dress? and did you sit up beyond the usual hour? If a novel produces these effects, it is good; if it does not—story, language, love, scandal itself, cannot save it. It is only meant to please, and it must do that, or it does nothing. Now Granby seems to us to answer this test extremely well; it produces unpunctuality, makes the reader too late for dinner, impatient of contradiction, and inattentive—even if a bishop is making an observation, or a gentleman lately from the Pyramids, or the Upper Cataracts, is let loose upon the drawing-room. The objection, indeed, to these compositions, when they are well done, is, that it is impossible to do anything, or perform any human duty, while we are engaged in them. Who can read Mr. Hallam's Middle Ages, or extract the root of an impossible quantity, or draw up a bond, when he is in the middle of Mr Trebeck and Lady Charlotte Duncan? How can the boy's lesson be heard, about the Jove-nourished Achilles, or his six miserable verses upon Dido be corrected, when Henry Granby and Mr. Courtenay are both making love to Miss Jermyn? Common life palls in the middle of these artificial scenes. All is emotion when the book is open—all dull, flat, and feeble, when it is shut.

Granby, a young man of no profession, living with an old uncle in the country, falls in love with Miss Jermyn, and Miss Jermyn with him; but Sir Thomas and Lady Jermyn, as the young gen-

* This is the gentleman who now keeps the keys of Life and Death, the Janitor of the world.—*Author's Note.* Thomas Henry Lister, 1801–1842, held the office of Registrar-General of Births, Deaths and Marriages. Besides Granby, Mr. Lister published Herbert Lacy, a Novel; Epicharis, an Historical Tragedy, performed in 1829, at Drury Lane; the Life and Administration of Edward, First Earl of Clarendon, and other writings. He was brother-in law of Lord John Russell.

tleman is not rich, having discovered by long living in the world, and patient observation of its ways, that young people are commonly Malthus-proof and have children, and that young and old must eat, very naturally do what they can to discourage the union. The young people, however, both go to town—meet at balls—flutter, blush, look and cannot speak—speak and cannot look—suspect, misinterpret, are sad and mad, peevish and jealous, fond and foolish; but the passion, after all, seems less near to its accomplishment at the end of the season than the beginning. The uncle of Granby, however, dies, and leaves to his nephew a statement, accompanied with the requisite proofs—that Mr. Tyrrel, the supposed son of Lord Malton, is illegitimate, and that he, Granby, is the heir to Lord Malton's fortune. The second volume is now far advanced, and it is time for Lord Malton to die. Accordingly Mr. Lister very judiciously despatches him; Granby inherits the estate—his virtues (for what shows off virtue like land?) are discovered by the Jermyns—and they marry in the last act.

Upon this slender story, the author has succeeded in making a very agreeable and interesting novel; and he has succeeded, we think, chiefly, by the very easy and natural picture of manners, as they really exist among the upper classes; by the description of new characters, judiciously drawn and faithfully preserved; and by the introduction of many striking and well-managed incidents; and we are particularly struck throughout the whole with the discretion and good sense of the author. He is never *nimious;* there is nothing in excess; there is a good deal of fancy and a great deal of spirit at work, but a directing and superintending judgment rarely quits him.......

Tremendous is the power of a novelist! If four or five men are in a room, and show a disposition to break the peace, no human magistrate (not even Mr. Justice Bayley) could do more than bind them over to keep the peace, and commit them if they refused. But the writer of the novel stands with a pen in his hand, and can run any of them through the body—can knock down any one individual, and keep the others upon their legs; or, like the last scene in the first tragedy written by a young man of genius, can put them all to death. Now, an author possessing such extraordinary privileges, should not have allowed Mr. Tyrrel to strike Granby. This is ill-managed; particularly as Granby does not return the blow, or turn him out of the house. Nobody should suffer his hero to have a black eye, or to be pulled by the nose. The Iliad would never have come down to these times if Agamemnon had given Achilles a box on the ear. We should have trembled for the Æneid, if any Tyrian nobleman had kicked the pious Æneas in the 4th book. Æneas may have deserved it; but he could not have founded the Roman empire after so distressing an accident.

PUBLIC-HOUSES AND DRINKING.*

What the poor shall drink—how they shall drink it—in pint cups or quart mugs—hot or cold—in the morning or the evening—whether the Three Pigeons shall be shut up, and the Shoulder of Mutton be opened—whether the Black Horse shall continue to swing in the air—or the White Horse, with animated crest and tail, no longer portend spirits within: all these great questions depend upon little clumps of squires and parsons gathered together in alehouses in the month of September—so portentous to publicans and partridges, to sots and sportsmen, to guzzling and game.

"I am by no means a friend to the multiplication of public-houses," says a plump perdricide gentleman in loose mud-coloured gaiters, bottle-green jacket and brass buttons. Perhaps not; but you are a friend to the multiplication of inns. You are well aware, that in your journeys to Buxton, Harrowgate, and Bath, the competition of inns keeps down the price of your four post-horses, and secures for you and yours the most reverential awe, from Boots upward to the crafty proprietor himself of the house of entertainment. From what other cause the sudden and overwhelming tumult at the Dragon?—Why the agonizing cry of *first inn!* Why is cake and jelly pushed in at the window? Why are four eyeless, footless, legless horses, rapidly circumscribed by breeching and bearing-reins? Why are you whisked off, amid the smiles of sallow waiters, before the landlord has had time to communicate to you the sad state of turnips in the neighbourhood? Look now a little to the right as you proceed down the main street, and you will behold the sign of the Star and Garter. Make your bow to

* From an article on the "Licensing of Ale-Houses."—Ed. Rev. Sep., 1826

the landlord, for to him you are indebted for the gratification of your wishes, and the activity of your movements. His waiters are as sallow, his vertebræ are as flexible — his first turns as prompt and decisive. Woe to the Dragon if he slumbers and sleeps! Woe to the Star if it does not glitter! Each publican keeps the other in a state of vigilant civility; and the traveller rolls along to his journey's end, lolling on the cushion of competition! Why not therefore extend the benefit of this principle to the poor villager or the needy traveller — which produces so many comforts to the landed and substantial Justice?

There are two alehouses in the village, the Red Horse and the Dun Cow. Is it common sense to suppose that these two publicans are not desirous of gaining customers from each other? — and that the means they take are not precisely the same as those of important inns — by procuring good articles, and retailing them with civility and attention? We really do not mean to accuse English magistrates of ill nature, for in general there is a good deal of kindness and consideration among them; but they do not drink ale, and are apt to forget the importance of ale to the common people. When wine-drinkers regulate the liquor and comfort of ale-drinkers, it is much as if carnivorous animals should regulate the food of graminivorous animals — as if a lion should cater for an ox, or a coach-horse order dinner for a leopard. There is no natural capacity or incitement to do the thing well — no power in the lion to distinguish between clover and cow-thistles — no disposition in the coach-horse to discriminate between the succulence of a young kid, and the distressing dryness of a superannuated cow. The want of sympathy is a source of inattention, and a cause of evil.

The immense importance of a pint of ale to a common person should never be overlooked; nor should a good-natured Justice forget that he is acting for Liliputians, whose pains and pleasures lie in a very narrow compass, and are but too apt to be treated with neglect and contempt by their superiors. About ten or eleven o'clock in the morning, perhaps, the first faint, shadowy vision of a future pint of beer dawns on the fancy of the ploughman. Far, very far is it from being fully developed. Sometimes the idea is rejected, sometimes it is fostered. At one time he is almost fixed on the Red Horse; but the blazing fire and sedulous kindness of the landlady of the Dun Cow shake him, and his soul labours! Heavy is the ploughed land—dark, dreary, and wet the day. His purpose is at last fixed for beer! Threepence is put down for the vigour of ale, one penny for the stupefaction of tobacco!—and these are the joys and holidays of millions, the greatest pleasure and relaxation which it is in the power of fortune to bestow; and these are the amusements and holidays which a wise and parental Legislature should not despise or hastily extinguish, but, on the contrary, protect with every regulation which prudence and morality would in any degree permit. We must beg leave to go into the Dun Cow with the poor man; and we beg our readers to come in for a moment with us. Hodge finds a very good fire, a very good-natured landlady, who has some obliging expressions for everybody, a clean bench, and some very good ale—and all this produced by the competition with the opposite alehouse; but for which, he must have put up with any treatment, and any refreshment the unopposed landlord might have chosen to place before him. Is Hodge not sensible that his landlady is obliging, and his ale good? How can it be supposed that the common people have not the same distinctions and niceties in their homely pleasures as the upper classes have in their luxuries? Why should they not have? Why should they not be indulged in it? Why should they be debarred from all benefit of that principle of competition, which is the only method by which such advantages are secured, or can ever be secured, to any class of mankind?—the method to which the upper classes, wherever their own pleasures are concerned, always have recourse. The licensers of public-houses are so sensible of this, that, where there is only one inn. nothing is more common than to substitute, and make exertions to set up another, and this by gentlemen who are by no means friendly to the multiplication of alehouses. . . . . . .

Public-houses are not only the inns of the travelling poor, but they are the cellars and parlours of the stationary poor. A gentleman has his own public-house, locked up in a square brick bin, *London Particular — Chalier* 1802— *Carbonell* 1803— *Sir John's present of Hock at my marriage: bought at the Duke's sale — East India Madeira — Lafitte — Noyau — Mareschino.* Such are the domestic resources of him who is to regulate the potations of the labourer. And away goes this subterraneous bacchanalian, greedy of the grape, with his feet wrapped up in flannel, to increase, on the licensing day, the difficulties of obtaining a pot of beer to the lower orders of mankind!—and believes, as all men do when they are deciding upon other persons' pleasures, that he is actuated by the highest sense of duty, and the deepest consideration for the welfare of the lower orders.* . . . . . .

In an advanced state of civilization there must be also an advanced state of misery. In the low public-houses of great cities, very wretched and very criminal persons are huddled together in great masses. But is a man to die supperless in a ditch because he is not rich, or even because he is not innocent? A pauper or a felon is not to be driven into despair, and turned into a wild beast. Such men must be; and such men must eat and sleep; and if laws are wise, and police vigilant, we do not conceive it to be any evil that the haunts of such men are known, and in some degree subject to inspection. What is meant by respectable public-houses, are houses where all the customers are rich and opulent. But who will take in the refuse of mankind, if monopoly allows him to choose better customers? There is no end to this mischievous meddling with the natural arrangements of society. It would be just as wise to set magistrates to digest for mankind, as to fix for them in what proportion any particular class of their wants shall be supplied. But there are excellent men who would place the moon under the care of magistrates, in order to improve travel-

* In an article on Botany Bay, Ed. Rev., July, 1819, Sydney Smith has this parallel passage on the Consumption of Spirits: "There has been in all governments a great deal of absurd canting about the consumption of spirits. We believe the best plan is to let people drink what they like, and wear what they like; to make no sumptuary laws either for the belly or the back. In the first place laws against rum and rum-water are made by men who change a wet coat for a dry one whenever they choose, and who do not often work up to their knees in mud and water; and, in the next place, if this stimulus did all the mischief it is thought to do by the wise men of claret, its cheapness and plenty would rather lessen than increase the avidity with which it is at present sought for. Again, human life is subject to such manifold wretchedness, that all nations have invented a something liquid and solid, to produce a brief oblivion. Poppies, barley, grasses, sugar, pepper, and a thousand other things, have been squeezed, pressed, pounded and purified to produce this temporary happiness. Noblemen and members of Parliament have large cellars full of sealed bottles, to enable them the better to endure the wretchedness of life. The poor man seeks the same end by expending three half pence in gin;—but no moralist can endure the idea of gin."

ling, and make things safe and comfortable. An enhancement of the evil is, that no reason is given for the rejection or adoption. The Magistrates have only to preserve the most impenetrable secrecy—to say only No, or Yes, and the affair is at an end. No court can interfere, no superior authority question. Hunger and thirst, or wantonness and riot, are inflicted upon a parish or a district for a whole year, without the possibility of complaint, or the hope of redress. Their Worships were in the gout, and they refused. Their Worships were mellow, and they gave leave. God bless their Worships!—and then, what would happen if small public-houses were shut? Would villany cease? Are there no other means by which the bad could congregate? Is there so foolish a person, either in or out of the Commission, as to believe that burglary and larceny would be put an end to, by the want of a place in which the plan for such deeds could be talked over and arranged?

NO-POPERY OUTCRY OF 1827.*

FEW men consider the historical view which will be taken of present events. The bubbles of last year; the fishing for half-crowns in Vigo Bay; the Milk Muffin and Crumpet Companies; the Apple, Pear and Plum Associations; the National Gooseberry and Current Company; will all be remembered as instances of that partial madness to which society is occasionally exposed. What will be said of all the intolerable trash which is issued forth at public meetings of No Popery? The follies of one century are scarcely credible in that which succeeds it. A grandmamma of 1827 is as wise as a very wise man of 1727. If the world lasts till 1927, the grandmammas of that period will be far wiser than the tip-top No-Popery men of this day. That this childish nonsense will have got out of the drawing-room, there can be no doubt. It will most probably have passed through the steward's room—and butler's pantry, into the kitchen. This is the case with ghosts. They no longer loll on couches and sip tea; but are down on their knees scrubbing with the scullion—or stand sweating, and basting with the cook. Mrs. Abigail turns up her nose at them, and the housekeeper declares for flesh and blood, and will have none of their company. . . . . .

* Article "Catholics," Ed. Rev., 1827.

We conclude with a few words of advice to the different opponents of the Catholic Question.

To the No-Popery fool.

You are made use of by men who laugh at you, and despise you for your folly and ignorance; and who, the moment it suits their purpose, will consent to emancipation of the Catholics, and leave you to roar and bellow No-Popery! to vacancy and the moon.

To the No-Popery rogue.

A shameful and scandalous game, to sport with the serious interests of the country, in order to gain some increase of public power!

To the honest No-Popery people.

We respect you very sincerely—but are astonished at your existence.

To the base.

Sweet children of turpitude, beware! the old anti-popery people are fast perishing away. Take heed that you are not surprised by an emancipating king or an emancipating administration. Leave a *locus pænitentiæ!*—prepare a place for retreat—get ready your equivocations and denials. The dreadful day may yet come when liberality may lead to place and power. We understand these matters here. It is the safest to be moderately base—to be flexible in shame, and to be always ready for what is generous, good, and just, when anything is to be gained by virtue.

To the Catholics.

Wait. Do not add to your miseries by a mad and desperate rebellion. Persevere in civil exertions, and concede all you can concede. All great alterations in human affairs are produced by compromise.

AMERICA.

CHEAPNESS OF GOVERNMENT—UNIVERSAL SUFFRAGE—CAUCUS.*

One of the great advantages of the American government is its cheapness. The American king has about five thousand pounds

---

* This and the following passages are from the article "America," Ed Rev., Dec., 1818.

sterling per annum, the vice-king one thousand pounds sterling. They hire their Lord Liverpool at about a thousand per annum, and their Lord Sidmouth (a good bargain) at the same sum. Their Mr. Crokers are inexpressibly reasonable—somewhere about the price of an English doorkeeper, or bearer of a mace. Life, however, seems to go on very well, in spite of these low salaries, and the purposes of government to be very fairly answered. Whatever may be the evils of universal suffrage in other countries, they have not yet been felt in America; and one thing at least is established by her experience, that this institution is not necessarily followed by those tumults, the dread of which excites so much apprehension in this country. In the most democratic states, where the payment of direct taxes is the only qualification of a voter, the elections are carried on with the utmost tranquillity; and the whole business, by taking votes in each parish or section, concluded all over the state in a single day. A great deal is said by Fearon* about *Caucus*, the cant word of the Americans for the committees and party meetings in which the business of the elections is prepared—the influence of which he seems to consider as prejudicial. To us, however, it appears to be nothing more than the natural, fair, and unavoidable influence which talent, popularity and activity always must have upon such occasions. What other influence can the leading characters of the democratic party in Congress possibly possess? Bribery is entirely out of the question—equally so is the influence of family and fortune. What, then, can they do, with their caucus or without it, but recommend? And what charge is it against the American government to say, that those members of whom the people have the highest opinion meet together to consult whom they shall recommend for president, and that their recommendation is successful in their different states? Could any friend to good order wish other means to be employed, or other results to follow? No statesman can wish to exclude influence, but only bad influence; not the influence of sense and character, but the influence of money and punch.

* Henry Bradshaw Fearon, who came to America in 1817, to report on the prospect for emigrants from England. He published "A Narrative of a Journey of Five Thousand Miles through the Eastern and Western States of America."

THE JUDGE, THE TAILOR, AND THE BARBER.

The Americans, we believe, are the first persons who have discarded the tailor in the administration of justice, and his auxiliary the barber — two persons of endless importance in the codes and pandects of Europe. A judge administers justice, without a calorific wig and particoloured gown, in a coat and pantaloons. He is obeyed, however; and life and property are not badly protected in the United States. We shall be denounced by the laureate as atheists and jacobins; but we must say, that we have doubts whether one atom of useful influence is added to men in important situations by any colour, quantity, or configuration of cloth and hair. The true progress of refinement, we conceive, is to discard all the mountebank drapery of barbarous ages. One row of gold and fur falls off after another from the robe of power, and is picked up and worn by the parish beadle and the exhibitor of wild beasts. Meantime, the afflicted wiseacre mourns over equality of garment; and wotteth not of two men, whose doublets have cost alike, how one shall command and the other obey.

CHEAPNESS OF LAW.

The dress of lawyers, however, is, at all events, of less importance than their charges. Law is cheap in America: in England, it is better, in a mere pecuniary point of view, to give up forty pounds than to contend for it in a court of common law. It costs that sum in England to win a cause; and, in the court of equity, it is better to abandon five hundred or a thousand pounds, than to contend for it. We mean to say nothing disrespectful of the Chancellor — who is an upright judge, a very great lawyer, and zealous to do all he can; but we believe the Court of Chancery to be in a state which imperiously requires legislative correction. We do not accuse it of any malversation, but of a complication, formality, entanglement, and delay, which the life, the wealth, and the patience of man cannot endure. How such a subject comes not to have been taken up in the House of Commons, we are wholly at a loss to conceive. We feel for climbing boys as much as anybody can do; but what is a climbing boy in a chimney to a full-grown suitor in the Master's office. And whence comes it, in the midst of ten thousand compassions and charities, that no Wilberforce, or Sister

Fry, has started up for the suitors in Chancery? and why, in the name of these afflicted and attorney-worn people, are there united in their judge three or four offices, any one of which is sufficient to occupy the whole time of a very able and active man.

LITERATURE.

LITERATURE the Americans have none—no native literature, we mean. It is all imported. They had a Franklin, indeed; and may afford to live for half a century on his fame. There is, or was, a Mr. Dwight, who wrote some poems; and his baptismal name was Timothy. There is also a small account of Virginia, by Jefferson, and an epic by Joel Barlow; and some pieces of pleasantry by Mr. Irving. But why should the Americans write books, when a six weeks' passage brings them, in their own tongue, our sense, science, and genius, in bales and hogsheads? Prairies, steamboats, grist-mills, are their natural objects for centuries to come. Then, when they have got to the Pacific Ocean—epic poems, plays, pleasures of memory, and all the elegant gratifications of an ancient people, who have tamed the wild earth, and set down to amuse themselves.—This is the natural march of human affairs.

MILITARY GLORY AND TAXES.*

DAVID Porter and Stephen Decatur are very brave men; but they will prove an unspeakable misfortune to their country, if they inflame Jonathan into a love of naval glory, and inspire him with any other love of war than that which is founded upon a determination not to submit to serious insult and injury.

We can inform Jonathan what are the inevitable consequences of being too fond of glory:—TAXES *upon every article which enters into the mouth, or covers the back, or is placed under the foot—taxes upon everything which it is pleasant to see, hear, feel, smell, or taste—taxes upon warmth, light, and locomotion—taxes on everything on earth, and the waters under the earth—on everything that comes from abroad, or is grown at home—taxes on the raw material—taxes on every fresh value that is added to it by the in-*

* This and the following passages are from the article "America," Ed. Rev., Jan., 1820.

dustry of man—taxes on the sauce which pampers man's appetite, and the drug that restores him to health—on the ermine which decorates the judge, and the rope which hangs the criminal—on the poor man's salt, and the rich man's spice—on the brass nails of the coffin, and the ribbons of the bride—at bed or board, couchant or levant, we must pay.—*The school-boy whips his taxed top—the beardless youth manages his taxed horse, with a taxed bridle, on a taxed road:—and the dying Englishman, pouring his medicine, which has paid 7 per cent., into a spoon that has paid 15 per cent., flings himself back upon his chintz bed, which has paid 22 per cent., and expires in the arms of an apothecary, who has paid a license of a hundred pounds for the privilege of putting him to death. His whole property is then immediately taxed from 2 to 10 per cent. Besides the probate, large fees are demanded for burying him in the chancel; his virtues are handed down to posterity on taxed marble; and he is then gathered to his fathers, to be taxed no more.* In addition to all this, the habit of dealing with large sums will make the government avaricious and profuse; and the system itself will infallibly generate the base vermin of spies and informers, and a still more pestilent race of political tools and retainers of the meanest and most odious description;—while the prodigious patronage which the collecting of this splendid revenue will throw into the hands of government, will invest it with so vast an influence, and hold out such means and temptations to corruption, as all the virtue and public spirit, even of republicans, will be unable to resist.

WHO READS AN AMERICAN BOOK?*

SUCH is the land of Jonathan —and thus has it been governed. In his honest endeavours to better his situation, and in his manly purpose of resisting injury and insult we most cordially sympathize. We hope he will always continue to watch and suspect his government as he now does—remembering that it is the constant

* This is the famous passage which has been the peg to hang many wearisome dissertations upon. Not needed to excite rapid American invention, it has become simply an historical landmark, from which to date extensive national achievements. Its questions in politics, art, science, literature, are an index to American triumphs.

tendency of those intrusted with power, to conceive that they enjoy it by their own merits, and for their own use, and not by delegation, and for the benefit of others. Thus far we are the friends and admirers of Jonathan. But he must not grow vain and ambitious; or allow himself to be dazzled by that galaxy of epithets by which his orators and newspaper scribblers endeavour to persuade their supporters that they are the greatest, the most refined, the most enlightened and most moral people upon earth. The effect of this is unspeakably ludicrous on this side of the Atlantic —and, even on the other, we shall imagine, must be rather humiliating to the reasonable part of the population. The Americans are a brave, industrious, and acute people; but they have, hitherto, given no indications of genius, and made no approaches to the heroic, either in their morality or character. They are but a recent offset, indeed, from England; and should make it their chief boast, for many generations to come, that they are sprung from the same race with Bacon and Shakespeare and Newton. Considering their numbers, indeed, and the favourable circumstances in which they have been placed, they have yet done marvellously little to assert the honour of such a descent, or to show that their English blood has been exalted or refined by their republican training and institutions. Their Franklins and Washingtons, and all the other sages and heroes of their Revolution, were born and bred subjects of the King of England—and not among the freest or most valued of his subjects. And since the period of their separation, a far greater proportion of their statesmen and artists and political writers have been foreigners than ever occurred before in the history of any civilized and educated people. During the thirty or forty years of their independence, they have done absolutely nothing for the Sciences, for the Arts, for Literature, or even for the statesman-like studies of Politics or Political Economy. Confining ourselves to our own country, and to the period that has elapsed since *they* had an independent existence, we would ask, where are their Foxes, their Burkes, their Sheridans, their Windhams, their Horners, their Wilberforces?—Where their Arkwrights, their Watts, their Davys?—their Robertsons, Blairs, Smiths, Stewarts, Paleys, and Malthuses?—their Porsons, Parrs, Burneys, or Blomfields? —their Scotts, Rogerses, Campbells, Byrons, Moores, or Crabbes? —their Siddonses, Kembles, Keans, or O'Neils?—their Wilkies.

Lawrences, Chantrys?—or their parallels to the hundred other names that have spread themselves over the world from our little island in the course of the last thirty years, and blest or delighted mankind by their works, inventions, or examples? In so far as we know, there is no such parallel to be produced from the whole annals of this self-adulating race. In the four quarters of the globe, who reads an American book? or goes to an American play? or looks at an American picture or statue? What does the world yet owe to American physicians or surgeons? What new substances have their chemists discovered? or what old ones have they analyzed? What new constellations have been discovered by the telescopes of Americans? What have they done in the mathematics? Who drinks out of American glasses? or eats from American plates? or wears American coats or gowns? or sleeps in American blankets? Finally, under which of the old tyrannical governments of Europe is every sixth man a slave, whom his fellow-creatures may buy and sell and torture?

When these questions are fairly and favourably answered, their laudatory epithets may be allowed: but till that can be done, we would seriously advise them to keep clear of superlatives.

RELIGIOUS LIBERTY.*

THERE is a set of miserable persons in England, who are dreadfully afraid of America and everything American—whose great delight is to see that country ridiculed and vilified—and who appear to imagine that all the abuses which exist in this country acquire additional vigour and chance of duration from every book of travels which pours forth its venom and falsehood on the United States. We shall from time to time call the attention of the public to this subject, not from any party spirit, but because we love truth, and praise excellence wherever we find it; and because we think the example of America will in many instances tend to open the eyes of Englishmen to their true interests.

The *economy* of America is a great and important object for our imitation. The salary of Mr. Bagot, our late embassador, was, we believe, rather higher than that of the President of the United

* This and the following passages are from the article "America."–Ed. Rev. July 1824.

States. The vice-president receives rather less than the second clerk of the House of Commons; and all salaries, civil and military, are upon the same scale; and yet no country is better served than America! Mr. Hume has at last persuaded the English people to look a little into their accounts, and to see how sadly they are plundered. But we ought to suspend our contempt for America, and consider whether we have not a very momentous lesson to learn from this wise and cautious people on the subject of economy.

A lesson upon the importance of religious toleration, we are determined, it would seem, *not* to learn—either from America, or from any other quarter of the globe. The High Sheriff of New York, last year, was a Jew.* It was with the utmost difficulty that a bill was carried this year to allow the first Duke of England to carry a gold stick before the king—because he was a Catholic! —and yet we think ourselves entitled to indulge in impertinent sneers at America—as if civilization did not depend more upon making wise laws for the promotion of human happiness, than in having good inns, and post-horses, and civil waiters. The circumstances of the Dissenters' marriage bill are such as would excite the contempt of a Choctaw or Cherokee, if he could be brought to understand them. A certain class of Dissenters beg they may not be compelled to say that they marry in the name of the Trinity, because they do not believe in the Trinity. Never mind, say the corruptionists, you must go on saying you marry in the name of the Trinity, whether you believe in it or not. We know that such a protestation from you will be false: but, unless you make it, your wives shall be concubines, and your children illegitimate. Is it possible to conceive a greater or more useless tyranny than this?

In fact, it is hardly possible for any nation to show a greater superiority over another than the Americans, in this particular, have done over this country. They have fairly and completely, and probably for ever, extinguished that spirit of religious persecution which has been the employment and the curse of mankind for four or five centuries; not only that persecution which imprisons and scourges for religious opinions, but the tyranny of incapacitation, which, by disqualifying from civil offices, and cutting

---

* The late M. M. Noah. It was objected to his election that a Jew would thus come to have the hanging of Christians. "Pretty Christians," replied Noah, "to need hanging!"

a man off from the lawful objects of ambition, endeavours to strangle religious freedom in silence, and to enjoy all the advantages, without the blood, and noise, and fire of persecution. What passes in the mind of one mean blockhead is the general history of all persecution. "This man pretends to know better than me—I cannot subdue him by argument: but I will take care he shall never be mayor or alderman of the town in which he lives; I will never consent to the repeal of the test act or to Catholic emancipation; I will teach the fellow to differ from me in religious opinions!" So says the Episcopalian to the Catholic—and so the Catholic says to the Protestant. But the wisdom of America keeps them all down—secures to them all their just rights—gives to each of them their separate pews, and bells, and steeples—makes them all aldermen in their turns—and quietly extinguishes the fagots which each is preparing for the combustion of the other. Nor is this indifference to religious subjects in the American people, but pure civilization — a thorough comprehension of what is best calculated to secure the public happiness and peace —and a determination that this happiness and peace shall not be violated by the insolence of any human being, in the garb, and under the sanction, of religion. In this particular, the Americans are at the head of all the nations of the world: and at the same time they are, especially in the Eastern and Midland States, so far from being indifferent on subjects of religion, that they may be most justly characterized as a very religious people: but they are devout without being unjust (the great problem in religion); a higher proof of civilization than painted tea-cups, water-proof leather, or broadcloth at two guineas a yard.

AMERICAN UNION.

Though America is a confederation of republics, they are in many cases much more amalgamated than the various parts of Great Britain. If a citizen of the United States can make a shoe, he is at liberty to make a shoe anywhere between Lake Ontario and New Orleans—he may sole on the Mississippi—heel on the Missouri—measure Mr. Birkbeck on the little Wabash, or take (which our best politicians do not find an easy matter) the length of Mr. Monroe's foot on the banks of the Potomac. But wo to the cobbler, who, having made Hessian boots for the Alderman of Newcastle, should venture to invest with these coriaceous integuments the leg of a liege subject at York. A yellow ant in a nest of red ants—a butcher's dog in a fox-kennel—a mouse in a bee-hive—all feel the effects of untimely intrusion;—but far preferable their fate to that of the misguided artisan, who, misled by six-penny histories of England, and conceiving his country to have been united at the Heptarchy, goes forth from his native town to stitch freely within the sea-girt limits of Albion. Him the mayor, him the alderman, him the recorder, him the quarter sessions would worry. Him the justices before trial would long to get into the treadmill; and would much lament that, by a recent act, they could not do so, even with the intruding tradesman's consent; but the moment he was tried, they would push him in with redoubled energy, and leave him to tread himself into a conviction of the barbarous institutions of his corporation-divided country.

JUDGE LYNCH.

In all new and distant settlements the forms of law must, of course, be very limited. No justice's warrant is current in the Dismal Swamp; constables are exceedingly puzzled in the neighbourhood of the Mississippi; and there is no treadmill, either before or after trial, on the Little Wabash. The consequence of this is, that the settlers take the law into their own hands, and give notice to a justice-proof delinquent to quit the territory—if this notice is disobeyed, they assemble and whip the culprit, and this failing, on the second visit they cut off his ears. In short, Captain Rock has his descendants in America. Mankind cannot live together without some approximation to justice; and if the actual government will not govern well, or cannot govern well, is too wicked or too weak to do so—then men prefer Rock to anarchy.

SUMMARY.

America seems, on the whole, to be a country possessing vast advantages, and little inconveniences; they have a cheap government, and bad roads; they pay no tithes, and have stage-coaches without springs. They have no poor laws and no monopolies—

but their inns are inconvenient, and travellers are teased with questions. They have no collections in the fine arts; but they have no lord-chancellor, and they can go to law without absolute ruin. They cannot make Latin verses, but they expend immense sums in the education of the poor. In all this the balance is prodigiously in their favour: but then comes the great disgrace and danger of America—the existence of slavery, which if not timously corrected, will one day entail (and ought to entail) a bloody servile war upon the Americans—which will separate America into slave states and states disclaiming slavery, and which remains at present as the foulest blot in the moral character of that people. A high-spirited nation, who cannot endure the slightest act of foreign aggression and who revolt at the very shadow of domestic tyranny—beat with cart-whips and bind with chains, and murder for the merest trifles, wretched human beings who are of a more dusky colour than themselves; and have recently admitted into their Union a new State, with the express permission of ingrafting this atrocious wickedness into their constitution! No one can admire the simple wisdom and manly firmness of the Americans more than we do, or more despise the pitiful propensity which exists among government-runners to vent their small spite at their character; but on the subject of slavery, the conduct of America is, and has been, most reprehensible. It is impossible to speak of it with too much indignation and contempt; but for it, we should look forward with unqualified pleasure to such a land of freedom, and such a magnificent spectacle of human happiness.*

* Smith previously expressed this sentiment in a letter to Jeffrey (Foston Nov. 23, 1818), who appears to have been suspicious of his friend's levity and satire in handling the Americans in the Review:—"My dear Jeffrey, I entirely agree with you respecting the Americans, and believe that I am to the full as much a Philo-Yankeeist as you are. I doubt if there ever was an instance of a new people conducting their affairs with so much wisdom, or if there ever was such an extensive scene of human happiness and prosperity. However, you could not know that such were my opinions; or if you did, you might imagine I should sacrifice them to effect; and in either case your caution was proper."

SKETCHES OF MORAL PHILOSOPHY.

SUPPLIES FOR THE MIND.*

The first thing to be done in conducting the understanding is precisely the same as in conducting the body—to give it regular and copious supplies of food, to prevent that atrophy and marasmus of mind, which comes on from giving it no new ideas. It is a mistake equally fatal to the memory, the imagination, the powers of reasoning, and to every faculty of the mind, to think too early that we can live upon our stock of understanding—that it is time to leave off business, and make use of the acquisitions we have already made, without troubling ourselves any further to add to them. It is no more possible for an idle man to keep together a certain stock of knowledge, than it is possible to keep together a stock of ice exposed to the meridian sun. Every day destroys a fact, a relation, or an inference; and the only method of preserving the bulk and value of the pile is by constantly adding to it.

LABOUR AND GENIUS.

The prevailing idea with young people has been, the incompatibility of labour and genius; and, therefore, from the fear of

---

* From the Lecture on the Conduct of the Understanding, Part I. This and the following selections embrace nearly the whole of the author's two lectures on the subject. They are here presented in paragraphs for convenience and for better effect; the passages being, in fact, short essays on the separate topics. The sequence has been preserved, though little importance was attached to that by the lecturer who commences with the remark: "As the general object of my lecture will be to guard against the most ordinary and flagrant errors committed in the conduct of the understanding, and as I see no use in preserving any order in their enumeration, I shall put them down only in the order in which they happen to occur to me."

being thought dull, they have thought it necessary to remain ignorant. I have seen, at school and at college, a great many young men completely destroyed by having been so *un*fortunate as to produce an excellent copy of verses. Their genius being now established, all that remained for them to do was, to act up to the dignity of the character; and, as this dignity consisted in reading nothing new, in forgetting what they had already read, and in pretending to be acquainted with all subjects, by a sort of off-hand exertion of talents, they soon collapsed into the most frivolous and insignificant of men. "When we have had continually before us," says Sir Joshua Reynolds, "the great works of art, to impregnate our minds with kindred ideas, we are then, and not till then, fit to produce something of the same species. We behold all about us with the eyes of those penetrating observers whose works we contemplate; and our minds, accustomed to *think* the thoughts of the noblest and brightest intellects, are prepared for the discovery and selection of all that is great and noble in nature. The greatest natural genius cannot subsist on its own stock: he who resolves never to ransack any mind but his own, will be soon reduced from mere barrenness to the poorest of all imitations; he will be obliged to imitate himself, and to repeat what he has before repeated. When we know the subject designed by such men, it will never be difficult to guess what kind of work is to be produced." There is but one method, and that is hard labour; and a man who will not pay that price for distinction, had better at once dedicate himself to the pursuits of the fox—or sport with the tangles of Neæra's hair—or talk of bullocks, and glory in the goad! There are many modes of being frivolous, and not a few of being useful; there is but one mode of being intellectually great.

It would be an extremely profitable thing to draw up a short and well-authenticated account of the habits of study of the most celebrated writers with whose style of literary industry we happen to be most acquainted. It would go very far to destroy the absurd and pernicious association of genius and idleness, by showing them that the greatest poets, orators, statesmen, and historians—men of the most brilliant and imposing talents—have actually laboured as hard as the makers of dictionaries and the arrangers of indexes; and that the most obvious reason why they have been superior to other men is, that they have taken more pains than other men.

Gibbon was in his study every morning, winter and summer, at six o'clock; Mr. Burke was the most laborious and indefatigable of human beings; Leibnitz was never out of his library; Pascal killed himself by study; Cicero narrowly escaped death by the same cause; Milton was at his books with as much regularity as a merchant or an attorney—he had mastered all the knowledge of his time; so had Homer. Raffaelle lived but thirty-seven years; and in that short space carried the art so far beyond what it had before reached, that he appears to stand alone as a model to his successors. There are instances to the contrary; but, generally speaking, the life of all truly great men has been a life of intense and incessant labour. They have commonly passed the first half of life in the gross darkness of indigent humility—overlooked, mistaken, contemned, by weaker men—thinking while others slept, reading while others rioted, feeling something within them that told them they should not always be kept down among the dregs of the world; and then, when their time was come, and some little accident has given them their first occasion, they have burst out into the light and glory of public life, rich with the spoils of time, and mighty in all the labours and struggles of the mind. Then do the multitude cry out "a miracle of genius!" Yes, he *is* a miracle of genius, because he is a miracle of labour; because, instead of trusting to the resources of his own single mind, he has ransacked a thousand minds; because he makes use of the accumulated wisdom of ages, and takes as his point of departure the very last line and boundary to which science has advanced; because it has ever been the object of his life to assist every intellectual gift of nature, however munificent, and however splendid, with every resource that art could suggest, and every attention diligence could bestow.

AFFECTATIONS OF KNOWLEDGE.

If we are to read, it is a very important rule in the conduct of the understanding, that we should accustom the mind to keep the best company, by introducing it only to the best books. But there is a sort of vanity some men have, of talking of, and reading, obscure half-forgotten authors, because it passes as a matter of course, that he who quotes authors which are so little read, must be completely and thoroughly acquainted with those authors which are in every man's mouth. For instance, it is very common to quote Shakespeare; but it makes a sort of stare to quote Massinger. I have very little credit for being well acquainted with Virgil; but if I quote Silius Italicus, I may stand some chance of being reckoned a great scholar. In short, whoever wishes to strike out of the great road, and to make a short cut to fame, let him neglect Homer, and Virgil, and Horace, and Ariosto, and Milton, and, instead of these, read and talk of Fracastorius, Sannazarius, Lorenzini, Pastorini, and the thirty-six primary sonneteers of Bettinelli; let him neglect everything which the suffrage of ages has made venerable and grand, and dig out of their graves a set of decayed scribblers, whom the silent verdict of the public has fairly condemned to everlasting oblivion. If he complain of the injustice with which they have been treated, and call for a new trial with loud and importunate clamour, though I am afraid he will not make much progress in the estimation of men of sense, he will be sure to make some noise in the crowd, and to be dubbed a man of very curious and extraordinary erudition.

Then there is another piece of foppery which is to be cautiously guarded against—the foppery of *universality*—of knowing all sciences and excelling in all arts—chemistry, mathematics, algebra, dancing, history, reasoning, riding, fencing, Low Dutch, High Dutch, natural philosophy, and enough Spanish to talk about Lope de Vega: in short, the modern precept of education very often is, "Take the Admirable Crichton for your model; I would have you ignorant of nothing!" Now *my* advice, on the contrary, is, to have the *courage* to be ignorant of a great number of things, in order to avoid the calamity of being ignorant of everything. I would exact of a young man a pledge that he would never read Lope de Vega; he should pawn to me his honour to abstain from Bettinelli, and his thirty-five original sonneteers; and I would exact from him the most rigid securities that I was never to hear anything about that race of penny poets who lived in the reigns of Cosmo and Lorenzo di Medici.

I know a gentleman of the law who has a thorough knowledge of fortifications, and whose acquaintance with bastions, and counterscarps, and parallels, is perfectly astonishing. How impossible it is for any man not professionally engaged in such pursuits to evince a thorough acquaintance with them, without lowering himself in the estimation of every man of understanding who hears him! How thoroughly aware must all such men be, that the time dedicated to such idle knowledge has been lost to the perfection of those mental habits, any one of which is better than the most enormous load of ill-arranged facts! . . . . . .

We do not want readers, for the number of readers seems to be very much upon the increase, and mere readers are very often the most idle of human beings. There is a sort of feeling of getting through a book—of getting enough out of it, perhaps, for the purpose of conversation—which is the great cause of this imperfect reading, and the forgetfulness which is the consequence of it: whereas the ambition of a man of parts should be, not to know *books*, but *things;* not to show other men that he has read Locke, and Montesquieu, and Beccaria, and Dumont, but to show them that he knows the subjects on which Locke and Beccaria and Dumont have written. It is no more necessary that a man should remember the different dinners and suppers which have made him healthy, than the different books which have made him wise. Let us see the result of good food in a strong body, and the result of great reading in a full and powerful mind.

ATTACHMENT TO TRUTH.

A SINCERE attachment to truth, moral and scientific, is a habit which cures a thousand little infirmities of mind, and is as honourable to a man who possesses it, in point of character, as it is profitable in point of improvement. There is nothing more beautiful in science than to hear any man candidly owning his ignorance. It is *so* little the habit of men who cultivate knowledge to do so—they so often have recourse to subterfuge, nonsense, or hypothesis, rather than to a plain, manly declaration, either that they themselves do not understand the subject, or that the subject is not understood—that it is really quite refreshing to witness such instances of philosophical candour, and it creates an *immediate* prepossession in favour of the person in whom it is observed.

ABUSE OF WORDS.

NEXT to this we have the abuse of words, and the fallacy of associations: compared with which all other modes of misconducting the understanding are insignificant and trivial. What do you *mean* by what you say? Are you prepared to give a clear account of words which you use so positively, and by the help of which you form opinions that you seem resolved to maintain at all hazards? Perhaps I should astonish many persons by putting to them such sort of questions:— Do you know what is meant by the word *nature?* Have you definite notions of justice? How do you explain the word chance? What is virtue? Men are every day framing the rashest propositions on such sort of subjects, and prepared to kill and to die in their defence. They never, for a single instant, doubt of the meaning of that, which was embarrassing to Locke, and in which Leibnitz and Descartes were never able to agree. Ten thousand people have been burned before now, or hanged, for one proposition. The proposition had no meaning. Looked into and examined in these days, it is absolute nonsense. A man quits his country in disgust at some supposed violation of its liberties, sells his estates, and settles in America. Twenty years afterward, it occurs to him, that he had never reflected upon the meaning of the word; that he has packed up his goods and changed his country for a sound.

Fortitude, justice, and candour, are very necessary instruments of happiness; but they require time and exertion. The instruments I am now proposing to you you must not despise — *grammar, definition,* and *interpretation* — instruments which overturn the horrible tyranny of adjectives and substantives, and free the mind from the chains of that *logocracy* in which it is so frequently enslaved. Now have the goodness to observe what I mean. If you choose to quarrel with your eldest son, do it; if you are determined to be disgusted with the world, and to go and live in Westmoreland, do so; if you are resolved to quit your country, and settle in America, go!— only, when you have settled the reasons upon which you take one or the other of these steps, have the goodness to examine whether the *words* in which those reasons are contained have really any distinct meaning; and if you find they have not, embrace your first-born, forget America, unloose your packages, and remain where you are!

There are men who suffer certain barren generalities to get the better of their understandings, by which they try all their opinions, and make them their perpetual standards of right and wrong: as thus—Let us beware of *novelty;* The excesses of the people are *always* to be feared: or these contrary maxims—that there is a natural tendency in all governments to encroach upon the liberties of the people; or that everything modern is probably an improvement of antiquity. Now what can the use be of sawing about a set of maxims to which there are a complete set of antagonist maxims? For of what use is it to tell me that governors have a tendency to encroach upon the liberties of the people? and is that a reason why you should throw yourself systematically in opposition to the government? What you *say* is very true; what you *do* is very foolish. For is there not another maxim quite as true, that the excesses of the people are to be guarded against? and does not one evil *à priori* require your attention as well as another? The business is, to determine, at any one particular period of affairs, which is in danger of being weakened, and to act accordingly, like an honest and courageous man; not to lie like a dead weight at one end of the beam, without the smallest recollection there is any other, and that the equilibrium will be violated alike whichever extreme shall preponderate. In the same manner, a thing is not good because it is new, or good because it is old;— there is no end of retorting such equally true principles: but it is good because it is fit for the purpose for which it was intended, and bad because it is not.

COURAGE IN THE USE OF TALENT.

A GREAT deal of talent is lost to the world for the want of a little courage. Every day sends to their graves a number of obscure men who have only remained obscure because their timidity has prevented them from making a first effort; and who, if they could only have been induced to begin, would in all probability have gone great lengths in the career of fame. The fact is, that in order to do anything in this world worth doing, we must not stand shivering on the bank, and thinking of the cold and the danger, but jump in and scramble through as well as we can. It will not do to be perpetually calculating risks, and adjusting nice chances: it did all very well before the Flood, when a man could consult his friends upon an intended publication for a hundred and fifty years, and then live to see its success for six or seven centuries afterward; but at present a man waits, and doubts, and hesitates, and consults his brother, and his uncle, and his first cousins, and his particular friends, till one fine day he finds that he is sixty-five years of age—that he has lost so much time in consulting first cousins and particular friends, that he has no more time left to follow their advice. There is such little time for over-squeamishness at present, the opportunity so easily slips away, the very period of life at which a man chooses to venture, *if ever,* is so confined, that it is no bad rule to preach up the necessity, in such instances, of a little violence done to the feelings, and of efforts made in defiance of strict and sober calculation.

With respect to that fastidiousness which disturbs the right conduct of the understanding, it must be observed that there are two modes of judging of anything: one, by the test of what has actually been done in the same way before; the other, by what we can conceive *may* be done in that way. Now this latter method of mere imaginary excellence can hardly be a just criterion, because it may be in fact impossible to reduce to practice what it is perfectly easy to conceive: no man, before he has tried, can tell how difficult it is to manage prejudice, jealousy, and delicacy, and to overcome all that friction which the world opposes to speculation. Therefore, the fair practical rule seems to be, to compare any exertion, by all similar exertions which have preceded it, and to allow merit to any one who has improved, or, at least, who has not deteriorated the standard of excellence, in his own department of knowledge. Fastidious men are always judging by the other standard; and, as the rest of the understanding cannot fill up in a century what the imagination can sketch out in a moment, they are always in a state of perpetual disappointment, and their conversation one uniform tenor of blame. At the same time that I say this, I beg leave to lift up both my hands against that pernicious facility of temper, in the estimation of which everything is charming and delightful. Among the smaller duties of life I hardly know any one more important than that of not praising where praise is not due. Reputation is one of the prizes for which men contend: "it is," as Mr. Burke calls it, "the cheap defence and ornament of nations, and the nurse of manly exertions;" it produces more labour and more talent than twice the wealth of a country could ever rear up. It is the coin of genius; and it is the imperious duty of every man to bestow it with the most scrupulous justice and the wisest economy.

HABIT OF DISCUSSION.

I AM about to recommend a practice in the conduct of the understanding which I dare say will be strongly objected to, by many men of the world who may overhear it, and that is, the practice of arguing, or, if that be a word in bad repute, of *discussing*. But then I have many limitations to add to such recommendation. It is as unfair to compel a man to discuss with you, who can not play the game, or does not like it, as it would be to compel a person to play at chess with you under similar circumstances: neither is such a sort of exercise of the mind suitable to the rapidity and equal division of general conversation. Such sort of practices are, of course, as ill-bred and as absurd as it would be to pull out a grammar and dictionary in a general society, and to prosecute the study of a language. But when two men meet together who love truth, and discuss any difficult point with good nature and a respect for each other's understandings, it always imparts a high degree of steadiness and certainty to our knowledge; or, what is nearly of equal value, and certainly of greater difficulty, it convinces us of our ignorance. It is an exercise grossly abused by those who have recourse to it, and is very apt to degenerate into a habit of perpetual contradiction, which is the most tiresome and most *disgusting* in all the catalogue of imbecilities. It is an exercise which timid men dread—from which irritable men ought to abstain; but which, in my humble opinion, advances a man, who is calm enough for it, and strong enough for it, far beyond any other method of employing the mind. Indeed, a promptitude to discuss, is so far a proof of a sound mind, that, whenever we feel pain and alarm at our opinions being called in question, it is almost a certain sign, that they have been taken up without examination, or that the reasons which once determined our judgment have vanished away.

I direct these observations only to those who are capable of discussing; for there are many who have not the quickness and the presence of mind necessary for it, and who, in consequence, must be compelled to yield their opinions to the last speaker

And there is no question, that it is far preferable to remain under the influence of moderate errors, than to be bandied about for the whole of life from one opinion to another, at the pleasure, and for the sport of superior intelligence.

But other men's understandings are to be made use of, in the conduct of your own, in many other methods than in that of discussion. Lord Bacon says, that to enter into the kingdom of knowledge, we must put on the spirit of little children; and if he means that we are to submit to be taught by whoever can, or will teach us, it is a habit of mind which leads to very rapid improvement; because a person who possesses it is always putting himself in a train to correct his prejudices, and dissolve his unphilosophical associations. The truth is, that most men want knowledge, not for itself, but for the superiority which knowledge confers; and the means they employ to secure this superiority, are as wrong as the ultimate object, for no man can ever end with being superior, who will not begin with being inferior. The readiest way of founding that empire of talent and knowledge which is the mistaken end such men propose to themselves of knowledge, is, patiently to gather from every understanding that will impart them, the materials of your future power and importance. There are some sayings in our language about merit being always united with modesty, &c. (I suppose because they both begin with an *m*, for alliteration has a great power over proverbs, and proverbs over public opinion); but I fancy that in the majority of instances, the fact is directly the reverse — that talents and arrogance are commonly united, and that most clever young men of eighteen or nineteen believe themselves to be about the level of Demosthenes, or Virgil, or the Admirable Crichton, or John Duke of Marlborough: but whatever the fact be with respect to modesty, and omitting all the popularity and policy of modesty, I am sure modesty *is* a part of talent; that a certain tendency to hear what others have to say, and to give it its due weight and importance, is quite as valuable as it is amiable; that it is a vast promoter of knowledge; and that the contrary habit of general contempt, is a very dangerous practice in the conduct of the understanding. It exists, I am afraid, commonly in the minds of able men, but they would be much better without it.

SKEPTICISM.

As for general skepticism, the only way to avoid it is, to seize on some first principles arbitrarily, and not to quit them. Take as few as you can help—about a tenth part of what Dr. Reid has taken will suffice—but take some, and proceed to build upon them. As I have before mentioned, the leading principle of Descartes' philosophy was, *Cogito, ergo sum*—" I think, therefore I exist;" and having laid this foundation-stone, he built an enormous building, the ruins of which lie scattered up and down among the sciences in disordered glory and venerable confusion. Some of his disciples, however, could never get a single step farther;—they admitted their own existence, but could never deduce any one single truth from it. One might almost wish that these gentlemen had disencumbered themselves of this their only idea, by running down steep places, or walking very far into profound ponds, rather than that they should exhibit such a spectacle of stupidity and perversion.

Such sort of questions as the credibility of memory, and personal identity, are not merely innocent subtilties. I admit it is quite impossible in practice to disbelieve either the one or the other: but they excite a suspicion of the perfect uncertainty of all knowledge; and they often keep young men hesitating and quibbling about the rudiments of all knowledge, instead of pushing on their inquiries with cheerfulness and vigour. I am sure I am not stating an ideal evil; but I know from actual experience, that many understandings have been retarded for years in their prosecution of solid and valuable knowledge, because they could see no evidence for first principles, and were unable to prove that which, by the very meaning of the expression must be incapable of *all* proof. They considered the whole as an unstable and unphilosophical fabric, and contracted either an indifference to, or contempt for truth. And if you choose to call all knowledge hypothetical, because first principles are arbitrarily assumed, you certainly *may* call it so, if you please; but then I only contend that it does quite as well as if it were not hypothetical, because all the various errors agree perfectly well together, and produce that happiness which is the end of knowledge.

THE ROUND MAN IN THE ROUND HOLE.

THE RIGHT MAN IN THE RIGHT PLACE.

It is a very wise rule in the conduct of the understanding, to acquire early a correct notion of your own peculiar constitution of mind, and to become well acquainted, as a physician would say, with your *idiosyncrasy*. Are you an acute man, and see sharply for small distances? or are you a comprehensive man, and able to take in wide and extensive views into your mind? Does your mind turn its ideas into wit? or are you apt to take a common-sense view of the objects presented to you? Have you an exuberant imagination, or a correct judgment? Are you quick, or slow? accurate, or hasty? a great reader, or a great thinker? It is a prodigious point gained if any man can find out where his powers lie, and what are his deficiencies—if he can contrive to ascertain what Nature intended him for: and such are the changes and chances of the world, and so difficult is it to ascertain our own understandings, or those of others, that most things are done by persons who could have done something else better. If you choose to represent the various parts in life by holes upon a table, of different shapes—some circular, some triangular, some square, some oblong—and the persons acting these parts by bits of wood of similar shapes, we shall generally find that the triangular person has got into the square hole, the oblong into the triangular, and a square person has squeezed himself into the round hole. The officer and the office, the doer and the thing done, seldom fit so exactly, that we can say they were almost made for each other.

REWARDS OF KNOWLEDGE.

But while I am descanting so minutely upon the conduct of the understanding, and the best modes of acquiring knowledge, some men may be disposed to ask, "Why conduct my understanding with such endless care? and what is the use of so much knowledge?" What is the use of so much knowledge?—what is the use of so much life?—what are we to do with the seventy years of existence allotted to us?—and how are we to live them out to the last? I solemnly declare that, but for the love of knowledge, I should consider the life of the meanest hedger and ditcher, as preferable to that of the greatest and richest man here present: for the fire of our minds is like the fire which the Persians burn in the mountains—it flames night and day, and is immortal, and not to be quenched! Upon something it *must* act and feed—upon the pure spirit of knowledge, or upon the foul dregs of polluting passions. Therefore, when I say, in conducting your understanding, love knowledge with a great love, with a vehement love, with a love coeval with life, what do I say, but love innocence—love virtue—love purity of conduct—love that which, if you are rich and great, will sanctify the blind fortune which has made you so, and make men call it justice—love that which, if you are poor, will render your poverty respectable, and make the proudest feel it unjust to laugh at the meanness of your fortunes—love that which will comfort you, adorn you, and never quit you—which will open to you the kingdom of thought, and all the boundless regions of conception, as an asylum against the cruelty, the injustice, and the pain, that may be your lot in the outer world—that which will make your motives habitually great and honourable, and light up in an instant a thousand noble disdains at the very thought of meanness and of fraud! Therefore, if any young man here have embarked his life in pursuit of Knowledge, let him go on without doubting or fearing the event;—let him not be intimidated by the cheerless beginnings of knowledge, by the darkness from which she springs, by the difficulties which hover around her, by the wretched habitations in which she dwells, by the want and sorrow which sometimes journey in her train; but let him ever follow her as the Angel that guards him, and as the Genius of his life. She will bring him out at last into the light of day, and exhibit him to the world comprehensive in acquirements, fertile in resources, rich in imagination, strong in reasoning, prudent and powerful above his fellows, in all the relations and in all the offices of life.

EMULATION.*

One of the best methods of rendering study agreeable is to live with able men, and to suffer all those pangs of inferiority, which the want of knowledge always inflicts. Nothing short of some

* This passage and the following, are from the second Lecture on the Conduct of the Understanding.

such powerful motive, can drive a young person in the full possession of health and bodily activity, to such an unnatural and such an unobvious mode of passing his life as study. But this is the way that intellectual greatness often begins. The trophies of Miltiades drive away sleep. A young man sees the honour in which knowledge is held by his fellow-creatures; and he surrenders every present gratification, that he may gain them. The honour in which living genius is held, the trophies by which it is adorned after life, it receives and enjoys from the feelings of men — not from their sense of duty: but men never obey this feeling without discharging the first of all duties, without securing the rise and growth of genius, and increasing the dignity of our nature, by enlarging the dominion of mind. No eminent man was ever yet rewarded in vain; no breath of praise was ever idly lavished upon him; it has never yet been idle and foolish to rear up splendid monuments to his name: the rumour of these things impels young minds to the noblest exertions, creates in them an empire over present passions, inures them to the severest toils, determines them to live only for the use of others, and to leave a great and lasting memorial behind them.

HEARTY READING.

BESIDE the shame of inferiority, and the love of reputation, curiosity is a passion very favourable to the love of study and a passion very susceptible of increase by cultivation. Sound travels so many feet in a second; and light travels so many feet in a second. Nothing more probable: but you do not care *how* light and sound travel. Very likely: but *make* yourself care; get up, shake yourself well, *pretend* to care, make believe to care, and very soon you *will* care, and care so much, that you will sit for hours thinking about light and sound, and be extremely angry with any one who interrupts you in your pursuits; and tolerate no other conversation but about light and sound; and catch yourself plaguing everybody to death who approaches you, with the discussion of these subjects. I am sure that a man ought to read as he would grasp a nettle:—do it lightly, and you get molested; grasp it with all your strength, and you feel none of its asperities. There is nothing so horrible as languid study; when you sit looking at the clock, wishing the time was over, or that somebody would call on you and put you out of your misery. The only way to read with any efficacy, is to read so heartily, that dinner-time comes two hours before you expected it. To sit with your Livy before you, and hear the geese cackling that saved the capitol; and to see with your own eyes the Carthaginian sutlers gathering up the rings of the Roman knights after the battle of Cannæ, and heaping them into bushels; and to be so intimately present at the actions you are reading of, that when anybody knocks at the door, it will take you two or three seconds to determine whether you are in your own study, or in the plains of Lombardy, looking at Hannibal's weather-beaten face, and admiring the splendour of his single eye ;— this is the only kind of study which is not tiresome; and almost the only kind which is not useless: this is the knowledge which gets into the system, and which a man carries about and uses like his limbs, without perceiving that is it extraneous, weighty, or inconvenient.

HABITS OF STUDY.

To study successfully, the body must be healthy, the mind at ease, and time managed with great economy. Persons who study many hours in the day, should perhaps, have two separate pursuits going on at the same time — one for one part of the day, and the other for the other; and these of as opposite a nature as possible, —as Euclid and Ariosto; Locke and Homer; Hartley on Man, and Voyages round the Globe; that the mind may be refreshed by change, and all the bad effects of lassitude avoided. There is one piece of advice, in a life of study, which I think no one will object to; and that is, every now and then to be completely idle — to do nothing at all: indeed, this part of a life of study is commonly considered as so decidedly superior to the rest, that it has almost obtained an exclusive preference over those other parts of the system, with which I wish to see it connected.

It has been often asked whether a man should study at stated intervals, or as the fit seizes him, and as he finds himself disposed to study. To this I answer, that where a man can trust himself, rules are superfluous. If his inclinations lead him to a fair share of exertion, he had much better trust to his inclinations alone;

where they do not, they must be controlled by rules. It is just the same with sleep; and with everything else. Sleep as much as you please, if your inclination lead you only to sleep as much as is convenient; if not, make rules. The system in everything ought to be — do as you please — so long as you please to do what is right. Upon these principles, every man must see how far he may trust to his inclinations, before he takes away their natural liberty. I confess, however, it has never fallen to my lot to see many persons who *could* be trusted; and the method, I believe, in which most great men have gone to work, is by regular and systematic industry.

A little hard thinking will supply the place of a great deal of reading; and an hour or two spent in this manner sometimes lead you to conclusions which it would require a volume to establish. The mind advances in its train of thought, as a restiff colt proceeds on the road in which you wish to guide him; he is always running to one side or the other, and deviating from the proper path, to which it is your affair to bring him back. I have asked several men what passes in their minds when they are thinking; and I never could find any man who could think for two minutes together. Everybody has seemed to admit that it was a perpetual deviation from a particular path, and a perpetual return to it; which, imperfect as the operation is, is the only method in which we can operate with our minds to carry on any process of thought. It takes some time to throw the mind into an attitude of thought, or into any attitude; though the power of doing this, and, in general, of thinking, is amazingly increased by habit. We acquire, at length, a greater command over our associations, and are better enabled to pursue one object, unmoved by all the other thoughts which cross it in every direction.

One of the best modes of improving in the art of thinking, is, to think over some subject, before you read upon it; and then to observe after what manner it has occurred to the mind of some great master. You will then observe whether you have been too rash or too timid; what you have omitted, and in what you have exceeded; and by this process you will insensibly catch a great manner of viewing a question. It is right in study, not only to think when any extraordinary incident provokes you to think, but from time to time to review what has passed; to dwell upon it, and to see what trains of thought voluntarily present themselves to your mind. It is a most superior habit of some minds, to refer all the particular truths which strike them, to other truths more general: so that their knowledge is beautifully methodized: and the general truth at any time suggests all the particular exemplifications; or any particular exemplification, at once leads to the general truth. This kind of understanding has an immense and decided superiority over those confused heads in which one fact is piled upon another, without the least attempt at classification and arrangement. Some men always read with a pen in their hand, and commit to paper any new thought which strikes them; others trust to chance for its reappearance. Which of these is the best method in the conduct of the understanding, must, I should suppose, depend a great deal upon the particular understanding in question. Some men can do nothing without preparation; others, little with it: some are fountains, some reservoirs. My very humble and limited experience goes to convince me, that it is a very useless practice; that men seldom read again what they have committed to paper, nor remember what they have so committed one iota the better for their additional trouble: on the contrary, I believe it has a direct tendency to destroy the promptitude and tenacity of memory, by diminishing the vigour of present attention, and seducing the mind to depend upon future reference: at least, such is the effect I hav uniformly found it to produce upon myself; and the same remark has been frequently made to me by other persons, of their own habits of study. I am by no means contending against the utility and expediency of writing; on the contrary, I am convinced there can be no very great accuracy of mind without it. I am only animadverting upon that *exaggerated* use of it, which disunites the mind from the body: renders the understanding no longer portable, but leaves a man's wit and talents neatly written out in his commonplace book, and safely locked up in the bottom drawer of his bureau. This is the abuse of writing. The use of it, I presume, is, to give perspicuity and accuracy; to fix a habitation for, and to confer a name upon, our ideas, so that they may be considered and reconsidered themselves, and in their arrangement. Every man is extremely liable to be deceived in his reflections, till he has habituated himself to putting his thoughts upon paper, and perceived, from such a process, how often propositions that appeared, before such development, to be almost demonstrable, have vanished into nonsense when a clearer light has been thrown upon them. I should presume, also, that much writing must teach a good order and method in the disposition of our reasonings; because the connection of any one part with the whole, will be made so much more evident than it can be before it is put into visible signs. Writing, also, must teach a much more accurate use of language. In conversation, any language almost will do; that is, great indulgence is extended to the language of talkers, because a talker is at hand to explain himself, and his looks and gestures are a sort of comment upon his words, and help to interpret them: but as a writer has no such auxiliary language to communicate his ideas, and no power of re-explaining them when once clothed in language, he has nothing to depend upon but a steady and careful use of terms.

CONVERSATION.

The advantage conversation has over all the other modes of improving the mind, is, that it is more natural and more interesting. A book has no eyes, and ears, and feelings; the best are apt every now and then to become a little languid; whereas, a living book walks about, and varies his conversation and manner, and prevents you from going to sleep. There is certainly a great evil in this, as well as a good; for the interest between a man and his living folio, becomes sometimes a little too keen, and in the competition for victory they become a little too animated toward, and sometimes exasperated against, each other; whereas, a man and his book generally keep the peace with tolerable success; and if they disagree, the man shuts his book, and tosses it into a corner of the room, which it might not be quite so safe or easy to do with a living folio. It is an inconvenience in a book, that you can not ask questions; there is no explanation; and a man is less guarded in conversation than in a book, and tells you with more honesty the little niceties and exceptions of his opinions; whereas, in a book, as his opinions are canvassed where they cannot be explained and defended, he often overstates a point for fear of being misunderstood; but then, on the contrary, almost every man talks a great deal better in his books, with more sense, more information, and more reflection than he can possibly do in his conversation, because he has more time.

ALLOWANCE FOR INDIVIDUAL PECULIARITIES.

It is a great thing toward making right judgments, if a man know what allowance to make for himself; and what discount should habitually be given to his opinions, according as he is old or young, French or English, clergyman or layman, rich or poor, torpid or fiery, healthy or ill, sorrowful or gay. All these various circumstances are perpetually communicating to the objects about them a colour which is not their true colour! whereas wisdom is of no age, nation, profession, or temperament; and is neither sorrowful nor sad. A man must have some particular qualities, and be affected by some particular circumstances; but the object is, to discover what they are, and habitually to allow for them.

STICK TO YOUR GENIUS.

There is one circumstance I would preach up, morning, noon, and night, to young persons for the management of their understanding. Whatever you are from nature, keep to it; never desert your own line of talent. If Providence only intended you to write posies for rings, or mottoes for twelfth-cakes, keep to posies and mottoes; a good motto for a twelfth-cake is more respectable than a villanous epic poem in twelve books. Be what nature intended you for, and you will succeed; be anything else, and you will be ten thousand times worse than nothing.

USES OF WIT.

If black and white men live together, the consequence is, that, unless great care be taken, they quarrel and fight. There is nearly as strong a disposition in men of opposite *minds* to despise each other. A grave man cannot conceive what is the use of wit in society; a person who takes a strong common-sense view of a subject, is for pushing out by the head and shoulders an ingenious theorist, who catches at the lightest and faintest analogies; and another man, who scents the ridiculous from afar, will hold no commerce with him who tastes exquisitely the fine feelings of the heart, and is alive to nothing else; whereas talent is talent, and mind is mind, in all its branches! Wit gives to life one of its best flavours; common sense leads to immediate action, and gives society its daily motion; large and comprehensive views, its annual rotation; ridicule chastises folly and impudence, and keeps men in their proper sphere; subtlety seizes hold of the fine threads of truth; analogy darts away to the most sublime discoveries; feeling paints all the exquisite passions of man's soul, and rewards him by a thousand inward visitations for the sorrows that come from without. God made it all! It is all good! We must despise no sort of talent; they all have their separate duties and uses; all, the happiness of man for their object; they all improve, exalt, and gladden life.

CAUTION.

Caution, though it must be considered as something very different from talent, is no mean aid to every species of talent. As some men are so skilful in economy, that they will do as much with a hundred pounds as another will do with two, so there are a species of men, who have a wonderful management of their understandings, and will make as great a show, and enjoy as much consideration, with a certain quantity of understanding, as others will do with the double of their portion; and this by watching times and persons; by taking strong positions, and never fighting but from the vantage ground, and with great disparity of numbers; in short, by risking nothing, and by a perpetual and systematic attention to the security of reputation. Such rigid economy—by laying out every shilling at compound interest—very often accumulates a large stock of fame, where the original capital has been very inconsiderable; and, of course, may command any degree of opulence, where it sets out from great beginnings, and is united with real genius. For the want of this caution, there is an habitual levity sometimes fixes itself upon the minds of able men, and a certain manner of viewing and discussing all questions in a frivolous mocking manner, as if they had looked through all human knowledge, and found in it nothing but what they could easily master, and were entitled to despise. Of all mistakes the greatest, to live and to think life of no consequence; to fritter away the powers of the understanding, merely to make others believe that you possess them in a more eminent degree; and gradually to diminish your interest in human affairs, from an affected air of superiority, to which neither yourself nor any human being can possibly be entitled. It is a beautiful mark of a healthy and right understanding, when a man is serious and attentive to all great questions; when you observe him, with modesty and attention, adding gradually to his conviction and knowledge on such topics; not repulsed by his own previous mistakes, not disgusted by the mistakes of others, but in spite of violence and error, believing that there is, somewhere or other, moderation and truth—and that to seek that truth with diligence, with seriousness, and with constancy, is one of the highest and best objects for which a man can live.

Some men get early disgusted with the task of improvement, and the cultivation of the mind, from some excesses which they have committed, and mistakes into which they have been betrayed, at the beginning of life. They abuse the whole art of navigation, because they have stuck upon a shoal; whereas, the business is, to refit, careen, and set out a second time. The navigation is very difficult; few of us get through it at first, without some rubs and losses—which the world are always ready enough to forgive, where they are honestly confessed, and diligently repaired. It would, indeed, be a piteous case, if a young man were pinioned down through life to the first nonsense he happens to write or talk; and the world are, to do them justice, sufficiently ready to release them from such obligation; but what they do *not* forgive is, that juvenile enthusiasm and error, which ends in mature profligacy; which begins with mistaking what is right, and ends with denying that there is any right at all; which leaps from partial confidence to universal skepticism; which says, "There is no such thing as true religion and rational liberty, because I have been a furious zealot, or a seditious demagogue." Such men should be taught that wickedness is never an atonement for mistake; and they should be held out as a lesson to the young, that unless they are contented to form their opinions modestly, they will too often be induced to abandon them entirely.

There is something extremely fascinating in quickness; and most men are desirous of appearing quick. The great rule for becoming so, is, *by not attempting to appear quicker than you really are;* by resolving to understand yourself and others, and to know what *you* mean, and what *they* mean, before you speak or answer. Every man must submit to be slow before he is quick; and insignificant before he is important.

PLEASURES OF KNOWLEDGE.

The too early struggle against the pain of obscurity, corrupts no small share of understandings. Well and happily has that man conducted his understanding, who has learned to derive from the exercise of it, regular occupation and rational delight; who, after having overcome the first pain of application, and acquired a habit of looking inwardly upon his own mind, perceives that every day is multiplying the relations, confirming the accuracy, and augmenting the number of his ideas; who feels that he is rising in the scale of intellectual beings, gathering new strength with every difficulty which he subdues, and enjoying to-day as his pleasure, that which yesterday he laboured at as his toil. There are many consolations in the mind of such a man, which no common life can ever afford; and many enjoyments which it has not to give! It is not the mere cry of moralists, and the flourish of rhetoricians; but it is *noble* to seek truth, and it is *beautiful* to find it. It is the ancient feeling of the human heart, that knowledge is better than riches; and it is deeply and *sacredly true!* To mark the course of human passions as they have flowed on in the ages that are past; to see why nations have risen, and why they have fallen; to speak of heat, and light, and the winds; to know what man has discovered in the heavens above, and in the earth beneath; to hear the chemist unfold the marvellous properties that the Creator has locked up in a speck of earth; to be told that there are worlds so distant from our sun, that the quickness of light travelling from the world's creation, has never yet reached us, to wander in the creations of poetry, and grow warm again, with that eloquence which swayed the democracies of the old world; to go up with great reasoners to the First Cause of all, and to perceive in the midst of all this dissolution and decay, and cruel separation, that there *is* one thing unchangeable, indestructible, and everlasting;—it is **worth while in the days of our youth to strive hard for this great** discipline; to pass sleepless nights for it, to give up to it laborious days; to spurn for it present pleasures; to endure for it afflicting poverty; to wade for it through darkness, and sorrow, and contempt, as the great spirits of the world have done in all ages and all times.

I appeal to the experience of any man who is in the habit of exercising his mind vigorously and well, whether there is not a satisfaction in it, which tells him he has been acting up to one of the great objects of his existence? The end of nature has been answered: his faculties have done that which they were created to do — not languidly occupied upon trifles — not enervated by sensual gratification, but exercised in that toil which is so congenial to their nature, and so worthy of their strength. A life of knowledge is not often a life of injury and crime. Whom does such a man oppress? with whose happiness does he interfere? whom does his ambition destroy, and whom does his fraud deceive? In the pursuit of science he injures no man, and in the acquisition he does good to all. A man who dedicates his life to knowledge, becomes habituated to pleasure which carries with it no reproach: and there is one security that he will never love that pleasure which is paid for by anguish of heart — his pleasures are all cheap, all dignified, and all innocent; and, as far as any human being can expect permanence in this changing scene, he has secured a happiness which no malignity of fortune can ever take away, but which must cleave to him while he lives — ameliorating every good and diminishing every evil of his existence.

ESSENTIALS OF WIT.*

To begin at the beginning of this discussion, it is plain that wit concerns itself with the relations which subsist between our ideas: and the first observation which occurs to any man turning his attention to this subject is, that it cannot, of course, concern itself with *all* the relations which subsist between all our ideas; for then every proposition would be witty; — The rain wets me through — Butter is spread upon bread — would be propositions replete with

* This and the following passages are from Lectures on Wit and Humour, Part I.

irth; and the moment the mind observed the plastic and diffusible nature of butter, and the excellence of bread as a substratum, it would become enchanted with this flash of facetiousness. Therefore, the first limit to be affixed to that observation of relations, which produces the feeling of wit, is, that they must be relations which excite *surprise*. If you tell me that all men must die, I am very little struck with what you say, because it is not an assertion very remarkable for its novelty; but if you were to say that man was like a time-glass—that both must run out, and both render up their dust, I should listen to you with more attention, because I should feel something like surprise at the sudden relation you had struck out between two such apparently dissimilar ideas as a man and a time-glass.

Surprise is so essential an ingredient of wit, that no wit will bear repetition—at least the original electrical feeling produced by any piece of wit can never be renewed. There is a sober sort of approbation succeeds at hearing it the second time, which is as different from its original rapid, pungent volatility, as a bottle of champagne that has been open three days is, from one that has at that very instant emerged from the darkness of the cellar. To hear that the top of Mont Blanc is like an umbrella, though the relation be new to me, is not sufficient to excite surprise; the idea is so very obvious, it is so much within the reach of the most ordinary understandings, that I can derive no sort of pleasure from the comparison. The relation discovered, must be something remote from all the common tracks and sheep-walks made in the mind; it must not be a comparison of colour with colour, and figure with figure, or any comparison which, though individually new, is specifically stale, and to which the mind has been in the habit of making many similar; but it must be something removed from common apprehension, distant from the ordinary haunts of thought—things which are never brought together in the common events of life, and in which the mind has discovered relations by its own subtilty and quickness.

Now, then, the point we have arrived at, at present, in building up our definition of wit, is, that it is the discovery of those relations in ideas which are calculated to excite surprise. But a great deal must be taken away from this account of wit before it is sufficiently accurate; for, in the first place, there must be no feeling or conviction of the *utility* of the relation so discovered. If you go to see a large cotton-mill, the manner in which the large water-wheel below works the little parts of the machinery seven stories high, the relation which one bears to another, is extremely surprising to a person unaccustomed to mechanics; but, instead of feeling as you feel at a piece of wit, you are absorbed in the contemplation of the *utility* and *importance* of such relations—there is a sort of rational approbation mingled with your surprise, which makes the *whole* feeling very different from that of wit. At the same time, if we attend very accurately to our feelings, we shall perceive that the discovery of any surprising relation whatever, produces some slight sensation of wit. When first the manner in which a steam-engine opens and shuts its own valves is explained to me, or when I at first perceive the ingenious and complicated contrivances of any piece of machinery, the surprise that I feel at the discovery of these connections has always something in it which resembles the feeling of wit, though that is very soon extinguished by others of a very different nature. Children, who view the different parts of a machine not so much with any notions of its utility, feel something still more like the sensation of wit when first they perceive the effect which one part produces upon another. Show a child of six years old, that, by moving the treadle of a knife-grinder's machine, you make the large wheel turn round, or that by pressing the spring of a repeating-watch you make the watch strike, and you probably raise up a feeling in the child's mind precisely similar to that of wit. There is a mode of teaching children geography by disjointed parts of a wooden map, which they fit together. I have no doubt that the child, in finding the kingdom or republic which fits into a great hole in the wooden sea, feels exactly the sensation of wit. Every one must remember that fitting the inviting projection of Crim Tartary into the Black Sea was one of the greatest delights of their childhood; and almost all children are sure to scream with pleasure at the discovery.

The relation between ideas which excite surprise, in order to be witty, must not excite any feeling of the beautiful. "The good man," says a Hindoo epigram, "goes not upon enmity, but rewards with kindness the very being who injures him. So the sandalwood, while it is felling, imparts to the edge of the axe its aromatic flavour." Now here is a relation which would be witty if it were not beautiful: the relation discovered betwixt the falling sandal-wood, and the returning good for evil, is a new relation which excites surprise; but the *mere* surprise at the relation, is swallowed up by the contemplation of the moral beauty of the thought, which throws the mind into a more solemn and elevated mood than is compatible with the feeling of wit.

It would not be a difficult thing to do (and if the limits of my lecture allowed I would do it), to select from Cowley and Waller a suite of passages, in order to show the effect of the beautiful in destroying the feeling of wit, and *vice versâ*. First, I would take a passage purely witty, in which the mind merely contemplated the singular and surprising relation of the ideas: next, a passage where the admixture of some beautiful sentiment—the excitation of some slight moral feeling—arrested the mind from the contemplation of the relation between the ideas; then, a passage in which the beautiful overpowered still more the facetious, till, at last, it was totally destroyed.

If the relation between the ideas, to produce wit, must not be mingled with the beautiful, still less must they be so with the sublime. In that beautiful passage in Mr. Campbell's poem of "Lochiel," the wizard repeats these verses—which were in every one's mouth when first the poem was written:—

> "Lochiel! Lochiel! though my eyes I should seal,
> Man can not keep secret what God would reveal
> 'Tis the sunset of life gives *me* mystical lore,
> And *coming events cast their shadows before.*"

Now this comparison of the dark uncertain sort of prescience of future events implied by the gift of second sight, and the notice of an approaching solid body by the previous approach of its shadow, contains a new and striking relation; but it is not *witty*, nor would it ever have been considered as witty, if expressed in a more concise manner, and with the rapidity of conversation, because it inspires feelings of a much higher cast than those of wit, and, instead of suffering the mind to dwell upon the mere relation of ideas, fills it with a sort of mysterious awe, and gives an air of sublimity to the fabulous power of prediction. Every one knows the Latin line on the miracle at the marriage-supper in Cana of Galilee—on the conversion of water into wine. The poet says.

"The modest wate saw its God, and blushed!"*

Now, in my mind, that sublimity which some persons discover in this passage is destroyed by its wit; it appears to me witty, and *not* sublime. I have no *great* feelings excited by it, and can perfectly well stop to consider the mere relation of ideas. I hope I need not add, that the line, *if it produce the effect of a witty conceit, and not of a sublime image*, is *perfectly misplaced* and *irreverent:* the *intent*, however, of the poet, was *undoubtedly* to be *serious.* In the same manner, whenever the mind is not left to the mere surprise excited by the relation of ideas, but when that relation excites any powerful emotion—as those of the sublime and beautiful, or any high passion—as anger or pity, or any train of reflections upon the *utility* of the relations, the feeling of wit is always diminished or destroyed. It seems to be occasioned by those relations of ideas which excite surprise, and surprise *alone.* Whenever relations excite any other strong feeling as well as surprise, the wit is either destroyed, diminished, or the two co-existent feelings of wit and the other emotion may, by careful reflection, be distinguished from each other. I may be very wrong (for these subjects are extremely difficult), but I know no single passage in any author which is at once beautiful and witty, or sublime and witty. I know innumerable passages which are intended to be beautiful or sublime, and which are merely witty; and I know many passages in which the relation of ideas is very new and surprising, and which are *not* witty because they are beautiful and sublime. Lastly, when the effect of wit is heightened by strong sense and useful truth, we may perceive in the mind what part of the pleasure arises from the mere relation of ideas, what from the utility of the precept; and many instances might be produced, where the importance and utility of the thing said, prevent the mind from contemplating the mere relation, and considering it as wit. For example: in that apophthegm of Rochefoucault, that hypocrisy is a homage which vice renders to virtue, the image is witty, but all attention to the *mere wit* is swallowed

* Campbell (Specimens of British Poets) assigns the Latin line to Crashaw:—

"Lympha pudica Deum vidit et erubuit."

The conceit had been previously employed by Vida. It is traced by a writer in Notes and Queries. Oct. 16, 1852.

up in the justness and value of the observation. So that I think I have some colour for saying, that wit is produced by those relations between ideas which excite surprise, and surprise only. Observe, I am only defining the *causes* of a certain feeling in the mind called wit; I can no more define the feeling itself, than I can define the flavour of venison. We all seem to partake of one and the other, with a very great degree of satisfaction; but why each feeling *is* what it is, and nothing else, I am sure I cannot pretend to determine.

Louis XIV. was exceedingly molested by the solicitations of a general officer at the levée, and cried out, loud enough to be overheard, "That gentleman is the most troublesome officer in the whole army." "Your Majesty's enemies have said the same thing more than once," was the answer. The wit of this answer consists in the sudden relation discovered in his assent to the King's invective and his own defence. By admitting the King's observation, he seems, at first sight, to be subscribing to the imputation against him; whereas, in reality, he effaces it by this very means. A sudden relation is discovered where none was suspected. Voltaire, in speaking of the effect of epithets in weakening style, said, that the adjectives were the greatest enemies of the substantives, though they agreed in gender, number, and in cases. Here, again, it is very obvious that a relation is discovered which, upon first observation, does not appear to exist. These instances may be multiplied to any extent. A gentleman at Paris, who lived very unhappily with his wife, used, for twenty years together, to pass his evenings at the house of another lady, who was very agreeable, and drew together a pleasant society. His wife died; and his friends all advised him to marry the lady in whose society he had found so much pleasure. He said, no, he certainly should not, for that, if he married her, he should not know where to spend his evenings. Here we are suddenly surprised with the idea that the method proposed of securing his comfort may possibly prove the most effectual method of destroying it. At least, to enjoy the pleasantry of the reply, we view it through *his* mode of thinking, who had not been very fortunate in the connection established by his first marriage. I have, in consequence of the definition I have printed of wit in the cards of the Institution, passed one of the most polemical weeks that ever I remember to have spent in my life. I think, however, that if my words are understood in their fair sense, I am not wrong. I have said, surprising relations between *ideas*—not between *facts*. The difference is very great. A man may tell me he sees a fiery meteor on the surface of the sea: he has no merit in the discovery—it is no extraordinary act of mind in him—any one who has eyes can ascertain this relation of facts as well, if it really exist; but to discover a surprising relation in *ideas*, is an act of power in the discoverer, in which, if his wit be good, he exceeds the greater part of mankind: so that the very terms I have adopted, imply comparison and superiority of mind. The discovery of any relation of ideas exciting pure surprise involves the notion of such superiority, and enhances the surprise. To discover relations between facts exciting pure surprise, involves the notion of no such superiority; for any man could ascertain that a calf had two heads if it had two heads: therefore, I again repeat, let any man show me that which is an acknowledged proof of wit, and I believe I could analyze the pleasure experienced from it into surprise, partly occasioned by the unexpected relation established, partly by the display of talent in discovering it; and, putting this position synthetically, I would say, whenever there is a superior act of intelligence in discovering a relation between ideas, which relation excites surprise, and no other high emotion, the mind will have the feeling of wit. Why is it not witty to find a gold watch and seals hanging upon a hedge? Because it is a mere relation of facts discovered without any effort of mind, and not (as I have said in my definition), a relation of ideas. Why is it not witty to discover the relation between the moon and the tides? Because it raises other notions than those of mere surprise. Why are not all the extravagant relations in Garagantua witty? Because they are merely odd and extravagant; and mere oddity and extravagance is too easy to excite surprise. Why is it witty, in one of Addison's plays,[*] where the undertaker reproves one of his mourners for laughing at a funeral, and says to him, "You rascal, you! I have been raising your wages for these two years past, upon condition that you should

---

[*] Not Addison, but Steele, in the comedy of "The Funeral: or, Grief A-La-Mode," where Sable addresses one of his men: "Did not I give you ten, then fifteen, now twenty shillings a week, to be sorrowful? and the more I give you, I think, the gladder you are."

appear more sorrowful, and the higher wages you receive the happier you look!" Here is a relation between ideas, the discovery of which implies superior intelligence, and excites no other emotion than surprise.

WIT A CULTIVABLE FACULTY.

It is imagined that wit is a sort of inexplicable visitation, that it comes and goes with the rapidity of lightning, and that it is quite as unattainable as beauty or just proportion. I am so much of a contrary way of thinking, that I am convinced a man might sit down as systematically, and as successfully to the study of wit, as he might to the study of mathematics: and I would answer for it, that, by giving up only six hours a day to being witty, he should come on prodigiously before midsummer, so that his friends should hardly know him again. For what is there to hinder the mind from gradually acquiring a habit of attending to the lighter relations of ideas in which wit consists? Punning grows upon everybody, and punning is the wit of words. I do not mean to say that it is so easy to acquire a habit of discovering new relations in *ideas* as in *words*, but the difficulty is not so much greater as to render it insuperable to habit. One man is unquestionably much better calculated for it by nature than another: but association, which gradually makes a bad speaker a good one, might give a man wit who had it not, if any man chose to be so absurd as to sit down to acquire it.

PUNS.

I have mentioned puns. They are, I believe, what I have denominated them—the wit of words. They are exactly the same to words which wit is to ideas, and consist in the sudden discovery of relations in language. A pun, to be perfect in its kind, should contain two distinct meanings; the one common and obvious; the other, more remote: and in the notice which the mind takes of the relation between these two sets of words, and in the surprise which that relation excites, the pleasure of a pun consists. Miss Hamilton, in her book on Education, mentions the instance of a boy so very neglectful, that he could never be brought to read the word *patriarchs;* but whenever he met with it he always pronounced it *partridges.* A friend of the writer observed to her, that it could hardly be considered as a mere piece of negligence, for it appeared to him that the boy, in calling them partridges, was *making game* of the patriarchs. Now here are two distinct meanings contained in the same phrase: for to make game of the patriarchs is to laugh at them; or to make game of them is, by a very extravagant and laughable sort of ignorance of words, to rank them among pheasants, partridges, and other such delicacies, which the law takes under its protection and calls *game:* and the whole pleasure derived from this pun consists in the sudden discovery that two such different meanings are referable to one form of expression. I have very little to say about puns; they are in very bad repute and so they *ought* to be. The wit of language is so miserably inferior to the wit of ideas, that it is very deservedly driven out of good company. Sometimes, indeed, a pun makes its appearance which seems for a moment to redeem its species; but we must not be deceived by them; it is a radically bad race of wit. By unremitting persecution, it has been at last got under, and driven into cloisters, — from whence it must never again be suffered to emerge into the light of the world. One invaluable blessing produced by the banishment of punning is, an immediate reduction of the number of wits. It is a wit of so low an order, and in which some sort of progress is so easily made, that the number of those endowed with the gift of wit would be nearly equal to those endowed with the gift of speech. The condition of putting together ideas in order to be witty operates much in the same salutary manner as the condition of finding rhymes in poetry;— it reduces the number of performers to those who have vigour enough to overcome incipient difficulties, and makes a sort of provision that that which need not be done at all, should be done *well* whenever it *is* done. For we may observe, that mankind are always more fastidious about that which is pleasing, than they are about that which is useful. A commonplace piece of morality is much more easily pardoned than a commonplace piece of poetry or of wit; because it is absolutely necessary for the well-being of society that the rules of morality should be frequently repeated and enforced; and though in any individual instance the thing may be badly done, the sacred necessity of the practice itself, atones in some degree for the individual failure; but as there is no absolute necessity that men should be either wits or poets, we are less inclined to tolerate their mediocrity in superfluities. If a man have ordinary chairs and tables, no one notices it; but if he stick vulgar gaudy pictures on his walls, which he need not have at all, every one laughs at him for his folly.

A SARCASM.

A SARCASM (which is another species of wit) generally consists in the obliquity of the invective. It must not be direct assertion, but something established by inference and analogy;— something which the mind does not at first perceive, but in the discovery of which it experiences the pleasure of surprise. A true sarcasm is like a sword-stick — it appears, at first sight, to be much more innocent than it really is, till, all of a sudden, there leaps something out of it — sharp, and deadly, and incisive — which makes you tremble and recoil.

SUPERIORITY TO RIDICULE.

I KNOW of no principle which it is of more importance to fix in the minds of young people than that of the most determined resistance to the encroachments of ridicule. Give up to the world, and to the ridicule with which the world enforces its dominion, every trifling question of manner and appearance: it is to toss courage and firmness to the winds, to combat with the mass upon such subjects as these. But learn from the earliest days to inure your principles against the perils of ridicule: you can no more exercise your reason, if you live in the constant dread of laughter, than you can enjoy your life, if you are in the constant terror of death. If you think it right to differ from the times, and to make a stand for any valuable point of morals, do it, however rustic, however antiquated, however pedantic, it may appear; — do it, not for insolence, but *seriously* and *grandly* — as a man who wore a soul of his own in his bosom, and did not wait till it was breathed into him by the breath of fashion. Let men call you mean, if you know you are just; hypocritical, if you are honestly religious; pusillanimous, if you feel that you are firm: resistance soon converts unprincipled wit into sincere respect; and no after time can tear from you those feelings which every man carries within him who has made a noble and successful exertion in a virtuous cause.

NATURE OF HUMOUR.*

HOBBES defines laughter to be "a sudden glory, arising from a sudden conception of some eminency in ourselves, by comparison with infirmity of others, or our own former infirmity." By *infirmity* he must mean, I presume, marked and decided inferiority, whether accidental and momentary, or natural and permanent. He cannot, of course, mean by it, what we usually denominate infirmity of body or mind; for it must be obvious, at the first moment, that humour has a much wider range than this. If we were to see a little man walking in the streets with a hat half as big as an umbrella, we should laugh; and that laughter certainly could not be ascribed to the infirmities either of his body or mind: for his diminutive figure, without his disproportionate hat, I shall suppose by hypothesis, to be such as would excite no laughter at all; —and, indeed, an extraordinary large man, with a hat such as is worn by boys of twelve years old, would be an object quite as ludicrous.

Taking, therefore, the language of Hobbes to mean the sudden discovery of any inferiority, it will be very easy to show that such is *not* the explanation of that laughter excited by humour: for I may discover suddenly that a person has lost half-a-crown — or, that his tooth aches — or, that his house is not so well built, or his coat not so well made, as mine; and yet none of these discoveries give me the slightest sensation of the humourous. If it be suggested that these proofs of inferiority are very slight, the theory of Hobbes is still more weakened, by recurring to greater instances of inferiority: for the sudden information that any one of my acquaintance has broken his leg, or is completely ruined in his fortunes, has decidedly very little of humour in it;—at least it is not very customary to be thrown into paroxysms of laughter by such sort of intelligence. It is clear, then, that there are many instances of the sudden discovery of inferiorities and infirm-

* This passage and the following are from the Lecture on Wit and Humour, Part II

ities in others, which excite no laughter; and, therefore, pride is not the explanation of laughter excited by the humourous. It is true, the object of laughter is always inferior to us; but then the converse is *not* true—that every one who is inferior to us is an object of laughter: therefore, as some inferiority is ridiculous, and other inferiority *not* ridiculous, we must, in order to explain the nature of the humourous, endeavour to discover the discriminating cause.

This discriminating cause is *incongruity,* or the conjunction of objects and circumstances not usually combined—and the conjunction of which is either useless, or what in the common estimation of men would be considered as rather troublesome, and not to be desired. To see a young officer of eighteen years of age come into company in full uniform, and with such a wig as is worn by grave and respectable clergymen advanced in years, would make every body laugh, because it certainly is a very unusual combination of objects, and such as would not atone for its novelty by any particular purpose of utility to which it was subservient. It is a complete instance of incongruity. Add ten years to the age of this incongruous officer, the incongruity would be very faintly diminished;—make him eighty years of age, and a celebrated military character of the last reign, and the incongruity almost entirely vanishes: I am not sure that we should not be rather more disposed to *respect* the peculiarity than to laugh at it. As you increase the incongruity, you increase the humour; as you diminish it, you diminish the humour. If a tradesman of a corpulent and respectable appearance, with habiliments somewhat ostentatious, were to slide down gently into the mud, and decorate a pea-green coat, I am afraid we should all have the barbarity to laugh. If his hat and wig, like treacherous servants, were to desert their falling master, it certainly would not diminish our propensity to laugh; but if he were to fall into a violent passion, and abuse everybody about him, nobody could possibly resist the incongruity of a pea-green tradesman, very respectable, sitting in the mud, and threatening all the passers-by with the effects of his wrath. Here, every incident heightens the humour of the scene: —the gayety of his tunic, the general respectability of his appearance, the rills of muddy water which trickle down his cheeks, and the harmless violence of his rage! But if, instead of this, we were to observe a dustman falling into tne mud, it would hardly attract any attention, because the opposition of ideas is so trifling, and the incongruity so slight.

Surprise is as essential to humour as it is to wit. In going into a foreign country for the first time, we are exceedingly struck with the absurd appearance of some of the ordinary characters we meet with: a very short time, however, completely reconciles us to the phenomena of French abbés and French postilions, and all the variety of figures so remote from those we are accustomed to, and which surprise us so much at our first acquaintance with that country. I do not mean to say, either of one class of the ridiculous or of the other, that perfect novelty is *absolutely* a necessary ingredient to the production of any degree of pleasure, but that the pleasure arising from humour diminishes, as the surprise diminishes; it is less at the second exhibition of any piece of humour than at the first, less at the third than the second, till at last it becomes trite and disgusting. A piece of humour will, however, always bear repetition much better than a piece of wit; because, as humour depends in some degree on manner, there will probably always be in that manner, something sufficiently different from what it was before, to prevent the disagreeable effects of complete sameness. If I say a good thing to-day, and repeat it again to-morrow in another company, the flash of to-day is as much like the flash of to-morrow as the flash of one musket is like the flash of another; but if I tell a humourous story, there are a thousand little diversities in my voice, manner, language, and gestures, which make it rather a different thing from what it was before, and infuse a tinge of novelty into the repeated narrative.

It is by no means, however, sufficient, to say of humour, that it is incongruity which excites surprise; the same limits are necessary here which I have before affixed to wit—it must excite surprise, and nothing *but* surprise; for the moment it calls into action any other high and impetuous emotion, all sense of the humourous is immediately at an end. For, to return again to our friend dressed in green, whom we left in the mud—suppose, instead of a common, innocent tumble, he had experienced a very severe fall, and we discovered that he had broken a limb; our laughter is immediately extinguished, and converted into a lively feeling of compassion. The *incongruity* is precisely as great as it was before; but as it has excited another feeling not compatible with the ridiculous, all mixture of the humourous is at end.

The sense of the humourous is as incompatible with tenderness and respect as with compassion. No man would laugh to see a little child fall; and he would be shocked to see such an accident happen to an old man, or a woman, or to his father! It is an odd case to put, but I should like to know if any man living could have laughed if he had seen Sir Isaac Newton rolling in the mud? I believe that not only Senior Wranglers and Senior Optimi would have run to his assistance, but that dustmen, and carmen, and coal-heavers would have run and picked him up, and set him to rights. It is a beautiful thing to observe the boundaries which nature has affixed to the ridiculous, and to notice how soon it is swallowed up by the more illustrious feelings of our minds. Where is the heart so hard that could bear to see the awkward resources and contrivances of the poor turned into ridicule? Who could laugh at the fractured, ruined body of a soldier? Who is so *wicked* as to amuse himself with the infirmities of extreme old age? or to find subject for humour in the weakness of a perishing, dissolving body? Who is there that does not feel himself disposed to overlook the little peculiarities of the truly great and wise, and to throw a veil over that ridicule which they have redeemed by the magnitude of their talents, and the splendour of their virtues? Who ever thinks of turning into ridicule our great and ardent hope of a world to come? Whenever the man of humour meddles with these things, he is astonished to find, that in all the great feelings of their nature the mass of mankind always think and act aright;—that they are ready enough to laugh —but that they are quite as ready to drive away with indignation and contempt, the light fool who comes with the feather of wit to crumble the bulwarks of truth, and to beat down the Temples of God!

So, then, this turns out to be the nature of humour; that it is incongruity which creates surprise, and *only* surprise. Try the most notorious and classical instances of humour by this rule, and you will find it succeed. If you find incongruities which create surprise and are not humourous, it is always, I believe, because they are accompanied with some *other* feeling—emotion, or an interesting train of thought, beside surprise. Find an incongruity which creates surprise, and surprise *only*, and, if it be not humourous, I am, what I very often am, completely wrong; and this theory is what theories very often are, unfounded in fact.

Most men, I observe, are of opinion that humour is entirely confined to character;—and if you choose to confine the word humour to those instances of the ridiculous which are excited by character, you may do so if you please—this is not worth contending. All that I wish to show is, that this species of feeling is produced by something beside character; and if you allow it to be the same feeling, I am satisfied, and you may call it by what name you please. One of the most laughable scenes I ever saw in my life was, the complete overturning of a very large table, with all the dinner upon it—which I believe one or two gentlemen in this room remember as well as myself. What of character is there in seeing a roasted turkey sprawling on the floor? or ducks lying in different parts of the room, covered with trembling fragments of jelly? It is impossible to avoid laughing at such absurdities, because the incongruities they involve are so very great; though they have no more to do with character than they have with chemistry. A thousand little circumstances happen every day which excite violent laughter, but have no sort of reference to character. The laughter is excited by throwing inanimate objects into strange and incongruous positions. Now, I am quite unable, by attending to what passes in my own mind, to say, that these classes of sensations are not alike: they may differ in degree, for the incongruous observed of things living, is always more striking than the incongruous observed in things inanimate; but there *is* an incongruous not observable in character, which produces the feeling of humour.

BUFFOONERY AND ITS ASSOCIATES.

Buffoonery is voluntary incongruity. To play the buffoon, is to counterfeit some peculiarity incongruous enough to excite laughter: not incongruities of *mind*, for this is a humour of a higher class, and constitutes comic acting; but incongruities of body—imitating a drunken man, or a clown, or a person with a hunched back, or puffing out the cheeks as the lower sort of comic actors do upon the stage. Buffoonery is general in its imitations; mimicry is particular, and seizes on the incongruous in *individual* characters. I think we must say, that mimicry is always employed upon defects: a good voice, a gentleman-like appearance, and rational, agreeable manners, can never be the subject of mimicry;—they may be exactly represented and imitated, but nobody would call this mimicry, as the word always means the representation of defects. Parody is the adaptation of the same thoughts to other subjects. Burlesque is that species of parody, or adaptation of thoughts to other subjects, which is intended to make the original ridiculous. Pope has parodied several Odes of Horace; Johnson has parodied Juvenal; Cervantes has burlesqued the old romances.

BULLS.

A BULL—which must by no means be passed over in this recapitulation of the family of wit and humour—a bull is exactly the counterpart of a witticism: for as wit discovers real relations that are not apparent, bulls admit apparent relations that are not real. The pleasure arising from bulls, proceeds from our surprise at suddenly discovering two things to be dissimilar in which a resemblance might have been suspected. The same doctrine will apply to wit and bulls in action. Practical wit discovers connection or relation between actions, in which duller understandings discover none; and practical bulls originate from an apparent relation between two actions which more correct understandings immediately perceive to have none at all. In the late rebellion in Ireland, the rebels, who had conceived a high degree of indignation against some great banker, passed a resolution that they would burn his notes;—which they accordingly did, with great assiduity; forgetting, that in burning his notes they were destroying his debts, and that for every note which went into the flames, a correspondent value went into the banker's pocket. A gentleman, in speaking of a nobleman's wife, of great rank and fortune, lamented very much that she had no children. A medical gentleman who was present observed, that to have no children was a great misfortune, but he thought he had remarked it was *hereditary* in some families. Take any instances of this branch of the ridiculous, and you will always find an apparent relation of ideas leading to a complete inconsistency.

CHARADES.

I SHALL say nothing of charades, and such sorts of unpardonable trumpery: if charades are made at all, they should be made without benefit of clergy, the offender should instantly be hurried off to execution, and be cut off in the middle of his dullness, without being allowed to explain to the executioner why his first is like his second, or what is the resemblance between his fourth and his ninth.

DANGERS AND ADVANTAGES OF WIT.

I WISH, after all I have said about wit and humour, I could satsify myself of their good effects upon the character and disposition; but I am convinced the probable tendency of both is, to corrupt the understanding and the heart. I am not speaking of wit where it is kept down by more serious qualities of mind, and thrown into the background of the picture; but where it stands out boldly and emphatically, and is evidently the master quality in any particular mind. Professed wits, though they are generally courted for the amusement they afford, are seldom respected for the qualities they possess. The habit of seeing things in a witty point of view, increases and makes incursions from its own proper regions, upon principles and opinions which are ever held sacred by the wise and good. A witty man is a dramatic performer; in process of time, he can no more exist without applause, than he can exist without air; if his audience be small, or if they are inattentive, or if a new wit defrauds him of any portion of his admiration, it is all over with him — he sickens, and is extinguished. The applauses of the theatre on which he performs are so essential to him that he must obtain them at the expense of decency, friendship, and good feeling. It must always be *probable*, too, that a *mere* wit is a person of light and frivolous understanding. His business is not to discover relations of ideas that are *useful*, and have a real influence upon life, but to discover the more trifling relations which are only amusing; he never looks at things with the naked eye of common sense, but is always gazing at the world through a Claude Lorraine glass — discovering a thousand appearances which are created only by the instrument of inspection, and covering every object with factitious and unnatural colours. In short, the character of a *mere* wit it is impossible to consider as very amiable, very respectable, or very safe. So far the world, in judging of wit where it has swallowed up all other qualities, judge aright; but I doubt if they are sufficiently indulgent to this faculty where it exists in a lesser degree, and as one out of many other ingredients of the understanding. There is an association in men's minds between dullness and wisdom, amusement and folly, which has a very powerful influence in decision upon character, and is not overcome without considerable difficulty. The reason is, that the *outward* signs of a dull man and a wise man are the same, and so are the outward signs of a frivolous man and a witty man; and we are not to expect that the majority will be disposed to look to much *more* than the outward sign. I believe the fact to be, that wit is very seldom the *only* eminent quality which resides in the mind of any man; it is commonly accompanied by many other talents of every description, and ought to be considered as a strong evidence of a fertile and superior understanding. Almost all the great poets, orators, and statesmen of all times have been witty. Cæsar, Alexander, Aristotle, Descartes, and Lord Bacon, were witty men; so were Cicero, Shakespeare, Demosthenes, Boileau, Pope, Dryden, Fontenelle, Jonson, Waller, Cowley, Solon, Socrates, Dr. Johnson, and almost every man who has made a distinguished figure in the House of Commons. I have talked of the *danger* of wit; I do not mean by that to enter into commonplace declamation against faculties because they *are* dangerous; — wit is dangerous, eloquence is dangerous, a talent for observation is dangerous, *every* thing is dangerous that has efficacy and vigour for its characteristics; nothing is safe but mediocrity. The business is, in conducting the understanding well, to risk something; to aim at uniting things that are commonly incompatible. The meaning of an extraordinary man is, that he is *eight* men, not one man; that he has as much wit as if he had no sense, and as much sense as if he had no wit; that his conduct is as judicious as if he were the dullest of human beings, and his imagination as brilliant as if he were irretrievably ruined. But when wit is combined with sense and information when it is softened by benevolence, and restrained by strong principle; when it is in the hands of a man who can use it and despise it, who can be witty and something much *better* than witty, who loves honour, justice, decency, good nature, morality, and religion, ten thousand times better than wit;—wit is *then* a beautiful and delightful part of our nature. There is no more interesting spectacle than to see the effects of wit upon the different characters of men; than to observe it expanding caution, relaxing dignity, unfreezing coldness—teaching age, and care, and pain, to smile—extorting reluctant gleams of pleasure from melancholy, and charming even the pangs of grief. It is pleasant to observe how it penetrates through the coldness and awkwardness of society, gradually bringing men nearer together, and, like the combined force of wine and oil, giving every man a glad heart and a shining countenance. Genuine and innocent wit like this, is surely the *flavour of the mind!* Man could direct his ways by plain reason, and support his life by tasteless food; but God has given us wit, and flavour, and brightness, and laughter, and perfumes, to enliven the days of man's pilgrimage, and to "charm his pained steps over the burning marle."

INHERENT SUBLIMITY.*

It is very true what Mr. Alison says, that "there are many sensations universally called sublime, which association may make otherwise." I admit readily, that a fortuitous connection of thought can make it otherwise than sublime; but the question is, Did it receive from nature the character of sublime? does *any* thing receive from nature the character of sublime, or the character of beautiful? and would anything perpetually display, and constantly preserve such a character, if no accident intervened to raise up a contrary association? Certainty on such subjects can not be attained; but I, for one, strongly believe in the affirmative of the question—that Nature speaks to the mind of man *immediately* in beautiful and sublime language; that she astonishes him with magnitude, appals him with darkness, cheers him with splendour, soothes him with harmony, captivates him with emotion, enchants him with fame; she never intended man should walk among

* From the Essay on Taste.

her flowers, and her fields, and her streams, unmoved; nor did she rear the strength of the hills in vain, or mean that we should look with a stupid heart on the wild glory of the torrent, bursting from the darkness of the forest, and dashing over the crumbling rock. I would as soon deny hardness, or softness, or figure, to be qualities of matter, as I would deny beauty or sublimity to belong to its qualities.

Every man is as good a judge of a question like this, as the ablest metaphysician. Walk in the fields in one of the mornings of May, and if you carry with you a mind unpolluted with harm, watch how it is impressed. You are delighted with the beauty of colours; are not those colours beautiful? You breathe vegetable fragrance; is not that fragrance grateful? You see the sun rising from behind a mountain, and the heavens painted with light; is not that renewal of the light of the morning sublime? You reject all obvious reasons, and say that these things are beautiful and sublime because the accidents of life have made them so;—I say they are beautiful and sublime, BECAUSE GOD HAS MADE THEM SO! that it is the original, indelible character impressed upon them by Him, who has opened these sources of simple pleasure, to calm, perhaps, the perturbations of sense, and to make us love that joy which is purchased without giving pain to another man's heart, and without entailing reproach upon our own.

CERTAINTY OF TASTE.*

THE progress of good taste, however, though it is certain and irresistible, is slow. Mistaken pleasantry, false ornament, and affected conceit, perish by the discriminating hand of time, that lifts up from the dust of oblivion, the grand and simple efforts of genius. Title, rank, prejudice, party, artifice, and a thousand disturbing forces, are always at work to confer unmerited fame; but every recurring year contributes its remedy to these infringements on justice and good sense. The breath of living acclamation can not reach the ages which are to come: the judges and the judged are no more; passion is extinguished; party is forgotten; and the mild yet inflexible decisions of taste, will receive nothing, as the price of praise, but the solid exertions of superior talent. Justice

* From the same.

is pleasant, even when she destroys. It is a grateful homage to common sense, to see those productions hastening to that oblivion, in their progress to which they should never have been retarded. But it is much *more* pleasant to witness the power of taste in the work of preservation and lasting praise;—to think that, in these fleeting and evanescent feelings of the beautiful and the sublime, men have discovered something as fixed and as positive, as if they were measuring the flow of the tides, or weighing the stones on which they tread;—to think that there lives not, in the civilized world, a being who knows he has a mind, and who knows not that Virgil and Homer have written, that Raffaelle has painted, and that Tully has spoken. Intrenched in these everlasting bulwarks against barbarism, Taste points out to the races of men, as they spring up in the order of time, on what path they shall guide the labours of the human spirit. Here she is safe; hence she never *can* be driven, while one atom of matter clings to another, and till man, with all his wonderful system of feeling and thought, is called away to Him who is the great Author of all that is beautiful, and all that is sublime, and all that is good!

INCENTIVES OF THE BEAUTIFUL.*

WHAT are half the crimes in the world committed for? What brings into action the best virtues? The desire of possessing. Of possessing what?—not mere money, but every species of the beautiful which money can purchase. A man lies hid in a little, dirty, smoky room for twenty years of his life, and sums up as many columns of figures as would reach round half the earth, if they were laid at length; he gets rich; what does he do with his riches? He buys a large, well-proportioned house: in the arrangement of his furniture, he gratifies himself with all the beauty which splendid colours, regular figures, and smooth surfaces, can convey; he has the beauties of variety and association in his grounds: the cup out of which he drinks his tea is adorned with beautiful figures; the chair in which he sits is covered with smooth, shining leather; his table-cloth is of the most beautiful damask; mirrors reflect the lights from every quarter of the room; pictures

* From the Lectures on the Beautiful.—Part II.

of the best masters feed his eye with all the beauties of imitation. A million of human creatures are employed in this country in ministering to this feeling of the beautiful. It is only a barbarous, ignorant people that can ever be occupied by the necessaries of life *alone*. If to eat, and to drink, and to be warm, were the only passions of our minds, we should all be what the lowest of us all are at this day. The love of the beautiful calls man to fresh exertions, and awakens him to a more noble life; and the glory of it is, that as painters imitate, and poets sing, and statuaries carve, and architects rear up the gorgeous trophies of their skill — as everything becomes beautiful, and orderly, and magnificent — the activity of the mind rises to still greater, and to better objects. The principles of justice are sought out; the powers of the ruler, and the rights of the subject, are fixed; man advances to the enjoyment of rational liberty, and to the establishment of those great moral laws, which God has written in our hearts, to regulate the destinies of the world.

SONNET ON THE SABBATH.[*]

The first reason, then, why poetry is beautiful, is, because it describes natural objects, or moral feelings, which are themselves beautiful. For an example, I will read to you a beautiful sonnet of Dr. Leyden's upon the Sabbath morning, which has never been printed:—

> "With silent awe I hail the sacred morn,
>   Which slowly wakes while all the fields are still;
> A soothing calm on every breeze is borne,
> A graver murmur gurgles from the rill,
> And Echo answers softer from the hill,
> And softer sings the linnet from the thorn,
>   The skylark warbles in a tone less shrill.
> Hail, light serene! hail, sacred Sabbath morn!
> The rooks float silent by, in airy drove;
> The sun, a placid yellow lustre shows;
> The gales, that lately sighed along the grove,
>   Have hushed their downy wings in dead repose
> The hov'ring rack of clouds forget to move:—
>   So smiled the day when the first morn arose!"

---

[*] This and the following passage is from the Lecture on the Beautiful.— Part III.

Now, there is not a single image introduced into this very beautiful sonnet, which is not of itself beautiful; the soothing calm of the breeze, the noise of the rill, the song of the linnet, the hovering rack of clouds, and the airy drove of rooks floating by, are all objects that would be beautiful in nature, and, of course, are so in poetry. The notion that the whole appearance of the world is more calm and composed on the Sabbath, and that its sanctity is felt in the whole creation, is *unusually* beautiful and poetical. There is a pleasure in imitation—this is exactly a picture of what a beautiful placid morning is, and we are delighted to see it so well represented.

A BEAUTIFUL ACTION.

A LONDON merchant, who, I believe, is still alive, while he was staying in the country with a friend, happened to mention that he intended, the next year, to buy a ticket in the lottery; his friend desired he would buy one for him at the same time, which, of course, was very willingly agreed to. The conversation dropped, the ticket never arrived, and the whole affair was entirely forgotten, when the country gentleman received information that the ticket purchased for him by his friend, had come up a prize of twenty thousand pounds. Upon his arrival in London, he inquired of his friend where he had put the ticket, and why he had not informed him that it was purchased. "I bought them both the same day, mine and your ticket, and I flung them both into a drawer of my bureau, and I never thought of them afterward." "But how do you distinguish one ticket from the other? and why am I the holder of the fortunate ticket, more than you?" "Why, at the time I put them into the drawer, I put a little mark in ink upon the ticket which I resolved should be yours; and upon re-opening the drawer, I found that the one so marked was the fortunate ticket." Now this action appears to me perfectly beautiful; it is *le beau ideal* in morals, and gives that calm, yet deep emotion of pleasure, which every one so easily receives from the beauty of the exterior world.

AURUNGZEBE.*

A MIXTURE of wonder and terror almost always excites the feeling of the sublime. Extraordinary power generally excites the feeling of the sublime by these means—by mixing wonder with terror. A person who has never seen anything of the kind but a little boat, would think a sloop of eighty tons a goodly and somewhat of a grand object, if all her sails were set, and she were going gallantly before the wind; but a first-rate man-of-war would sail over such a sloop, and send her to the bottom, without any person on board the man-of-war perceiving that they had encountered any obstacle. Such power is wonderful and terrible—therefore, sublime. Everybody possessed of power is an object either of awe or sublimity, from a justice of peace up to the Emperor Aurungzebe—an object quite as stupendous as the Alps. He had thirty-five millions of revenue, in a country where the products of the earth are at least six times as cheap as in England: his empire extended over twenty-five degrees of latitude, and as many of longitude: he had put to death above twenty millions of people. I should like to know the man who could have looked at Aurungzebe without feeling him to the end of his limbs, and in every hair of his head! Such emperors are more sublime than cataracts. I think any man would have shivered more at the sight of Aurungzebe, than at the sight of the two rivers which meet at the Blue Mountains in America, and, bursting through the whole breadth of the rocks, roll their victorious and united waters to the Eastern Sea.

SUBLIMITY OF ECONOMY.

I AM going to say rather an odd thing, but I can not help thinking that the severe and rigid economy of a man in distress, has something in it very sublime, especially if it be endured for any length of time serenely and in silence. I remember a very striking instance of it in a young man, since dead. He was the son of a country curate, who had got him a berth on board a man-of-war, as midshipman. The poor curate made a great effort for his son; fitted him out well with clothes, and gave him fifty pounds in money. The first week, the poor boy lost his chest, clothes,

* This and the following passage are from the Lecture on the Sublime.

money, and everything he had in the world. The ship sailed for a foreign station; and his loss was without remedy. He immediately quitted his mess, ceased to associate with the other midshipmen, who were the sons of gentlemen; and for five years, without mentioning it to his parents—who he knew could not assist him —or without borrowing a farthing from any human being, without a single murmur or complaint, did that poor lad endure the most abject and degrading poverty, at a period of life when the feelings are most alive to ridicule, and the appetites most prone to indulgence. Now, I confess I am a mighty advocate for the sublimity of such long and patient endurance. If you can make the world stare and look on, there, you have vanity, or compassion, to support you; but to bury all your wretchedness in your own mind—to resolve that you will have no man's pity, while you have one effort left to procure his respect—to harbour no mean thought in the midst of abject poverty, but, at the very time you are surrounded by circumstances of humility and depression, to found a spirit of modest independence upon the consciousness of having always acted well; this is a sublime, which, though it is found in the shade and retirement of life, ought to be held up to the praises of men, and to be looked upon as a noble model for imitation.

INSTINCT AND TALENT.*

All the wonderful instincts of animals, which, in my humble opinion, are proved beyond a doubt, and the belief in which has not decreased with the increase of science and investigation—all these instincts are given them only for the combination or preservation of their species. If they had not these instincts, they would be swept off the earth in an instant. This bee, that understands architecture so well, is as stupid as a pebblestone, out of his own particular business of making honey: and, with all his talents, he only exists that boys may eat his labours and poets sing about them. *Ut pueris placeas et declamatio fias.* A peasant-girl of ten years old puts the whole republic to death with a little smoke; their palaces are turned into candles, and every clergyman's wife makes mead-wine of the honey; and there is an end of the glory and

* This and the following passage are from the Lecture on the Faculties of Animals and of Man.

wisdom of the bees! Whereas, man has talents that have no sort of reference to his existence; and without which, his species might remain upon earth in the same safety as if they had them not. The bee works at that particular angle which saves most time and labour; and the boasted edifice he is constructing is only for his egg: but Somerset House, and Blenheim, and the Louvre, have nothing to do with breeding. Epic poems, and Apollo Belvideres, and Venus de Medicis, have nothing to do with living and eating. We might have discovered pig-nuts without the Royal Society, and gathered acorns without reasoning about curves of the ninth order. The immense superfluity of talent given to man, which has no bearing upon animal life, which has nothing to do with the mere preservation of existence, is one very distinguishing circumstance in this comparison. There is no other animal but man to whom mind appears to be given for any *other* purpose than the preservation of body.

CHANGE OF INSTINCT.

THE most curious instance of a change of instinct is mentioned by Darwin. The bees carried over to Barbadoes and the Western Isles, ceased to lay up any honey after the first year; as they found it not useful to them. They found the weather so fine and materials for making honey so plentiful, that they quitted their grave, prudent, and mercantile character, became exceedingly profligate and debauched, eat up their capital, resolved to work no more, and amused themselves by flying about the sugar-houses, and stinging the blacks. The fact is, that by putting animals in different situations, you may change, and even reverse, any of their original propensities. Spallanzani brought up an eagle upon bread and milk, and fed a dove on raw beef. The circumstances by which an animal is surrounded, impel him to do so and so, by the changes they produce in his body and mind. Alter those circumstances, and he no longer does as he did before. This, instead of disproving the existence of an instinct, only points out the *causes* on which it depends.

ANECDOTE OF AN ELEPHANT.*

The artifices of a gentleman pursued by bailiffs, and the artifices of an animal pursued for his life, are the same thing—call them by what name you please. Of all animals, the most surprising stories are told of the docility of elephants. The black people, who have the care of them, often go away, leaving them chained to a stake, and place near them their young children, as if under their care: the elephant allows the little creature to crawl as far as its trunk can reach, and then gently takes the young master up, and places him more within his own control. Every one knows the old story of the tailor and the elephant, which, if it be not true, at least shows the opinion the Orientals, who know the animal well, entertain of his sagacity. An eastern tailor to the court was making a magnificent doublet for a bashaw of nine tails, and covering it, after the manner of eastern doublets, with gold, silver, and every species of metallic magnificence. As he was busying himself on this momentous occasion, there passed by, to the pools of water, one of the royal elephants, about the size of a broad-wheeled wagon, rich in ivory teeth, and shaking, with its ponderous tread, the tailor's shop to its remotest thimble. As he passed near the window, the elephant happened to look in; the tailor lifted up his eyes, perceived the proboscis of the elephant near him, and, being seized with a fit of facetiousness, pricked the animal with his needle; the mass of matter immediately retired, stalked away to the pool, filled his trunk full of muddy water, and, returning to the shop, overwhelmed the artisan and his doublet with the dirty effects of his vengeance.

LONGEVITY AND WISDOM.*

The wisdom of a man is made up of what he observes, and what others observe for him; and of course the sum of what he can acquire must principally depend upon the time in which he can acquire it. All that we add to our knowledge is not an increase, by that exact proportion, of all we possess; because we lose some things, as we gain others; but upon the whole, while the body and mind remain healthy, an active man increases in intelligence, and

* From the Lecture on the Faculties of Beasts.

consequently in power. If we lived seven hund..:d years instead of seventy, we should write better epic poems, build better houses, and invent more complicated mechanism, than we do now. I should question very much if Mr. Milne could build a bridge so well as a gentleman who had engaged in that occupation for seven centuries : and if I had had only two hundred years' experience in lecturing on moral philosophy, I am well convinced I should do it a little better than I now do. On the contrary, how diminutive and absurd all the efforts of man would have been, if the duration of his life had only been twenty years, and if he had died of old age just at the period when every human being begins to suspect that he is the wisest and most extraordinary person that ever did exist! I think it is Helvetius who says, he is quite certain we only owe our superiority over the orang-outangs to the greater length of life conceded to us; and that, if our life had been as short as theirs, they would have totally defeated us in the competition for nuts and ripe blackberries. I can hardly agree to this extravagant statement; but I think, in a life of twenty years the efforts of the human mind would have been so considerably lowered, that we might probably have thought Helvetius a good philosopher, and admired his skeptical absurdities as some of the greatest efforts of the human understanding. Sir Richard Blackmore would have been our greatest poet; our wit would have been Dutch; our faith, French; the Hottentots would have given us the model for manners, and the Turks for government; and we might probably have been such miserable reasoners respecting the sacred truths of religion, that we should have thought they wanted the support of a puny and childish jealousy of the poor beasts that perish. His gregarious nature is another cause of man's superiority over all other animals. A lion lies under a hole in a rock; and if any other lion happen to pass by, they fight. Now, whoever gets a habit of lying under a hole in a rock, and fighting with every gentleman who passes near him, can not possibly make any progress. Every man's understanding and acquirements, how great and extensive soever they may appear, are made up from the contributions of his friends and companions. You spend your morning in learning from Hume what happened at particular periods of your own history: you dine where some man tells you what he has observed in the East Indies, and another discourses of brown sugar and Jamaica. It is from these perpetual rills of knowledge, that you refresh yourself, and become strong and healthy as you are. If lions would consort together, and growl out the observations they have made, about killing sheep and shepherds, the most likely places for catching a calf grazing, and so forth, they could not fail to improve; because they would be actuated by such a wide range of observation, and operating by the joint force of so many minds. It may be said, that the gregarious spirit in man may proceed from his wisdom; and not his wisdom from his gregarious spirit. This I should doubt. It appears to be an original principle in some animals, and not in others; and is a quality given to some to better their condition, as swiftness or strength is given to others. The tiger lives alone—bulls and cows do not; yet, a tiger is as wise an animal as a bull. A wild boar lives with the herd till he comes of age, which he does at three years, and then quits the herd and lives alone. There is a solitary species of bee, and there is a gregarious bee. Whether an animal should herd or not, seems to be as much a provision of nature, as whether it should crawl, creep, or fly.

SHYNESS.*

The most curious offspring of shame, is shyness;—a word always used, I fancy, in a bad sense, to signify misplaced shame: for a person who felt only diffident, exactly in proportion as he ought, would never be called shy. But a shy person feels more shame, than it is graceful, or proper, he should feel; generally, either from ignorance or pride. A young man, in making his first entrance into society, is so ignorant as to imagine he is the object of universal attention; and that everything he does is subject to the most rigid criticism. Of course, under such a supposition, he is shy and embarrassed: he regains his ease, as he becomes aware of his insignificance. An excessive jealousy of reputation, is the very frequent parent of shyness, and makes us all afraid of saying and doing, what we might say and do, with the utmost propriety and grace. We are afraid of hazarding anything; and the game stands still, because no man will venture any stake: whereas, the

* This and the next are from the Lecture of the Evil Affections.

object of living together, is not security only, but enjoyment. Both objects are promoted by a moderate dread of shame; both destroyed by that passion, when it amounts to shyness;—for a shy person not only *feels* pain, and *gives* pain; but, what is worse, he incurs blame, for a want of that rational and manly confidence, which is so useful to those who possess it, and so pleasant to those who witness it. I am severe against shyness, because it looks like a virtue without *being* a virtue; and because it gives us false notions of what the *real* virtue is. I admit that it is sometimes an affair of body, rather than of mind; that where a person wishes to say what he knows will be received with favour, he cannot command himself enough to do it. But this is merely the effect of habit, where the cause that created the habit has for a moment ceased. When the feelings respecting shame are disciplined by good sense, and commerce with the world, to a fair medium, the body will soon learn to obey the decisions of the understanding.

Nor let any young man imagine (however it may flatter the vanity of those who perceive it), that there can be anything worthy of a man, in faltering, and tripping, and stammering, and looking like a fool, and acting like a clown. A silly college pedant believes that this highest of all the virtues, consists in the shame of the body; in losing the ease and possession of a gentleman; in turning red; and tumbling down; in saying this thing, when you mean that; in overturning everybody within your reach, out of pure bashfulness; and in a general stupidity and ungainliness, and confusion of limb, and thought, and motion. But that dread of shame, which virtue and wisdom teach, is, to act so, from the cradle to the tomb, that no man can cast upon you the shadow of reproach; not to swerve on this side for wealth, or on that side for favour; but to go on speaking truly, and acting justly; no man's oppressor, and no man's sycophant and slave. This is the shame of the soul; and these are the blushes of the inward man; which are worth all the distortions of the body, and all the crimson of the face.

USES OF THE EVIL AFFECTIONS.

It appears, then, from this enumeration of the ungrateful passions, which lead men to act from feelings of aversion, that they are all referable to the memory of evil, the actual sensation, the future anticipation of it, or the resentment which any one of these notions is apt to excite. The remembrance of past evils, produces melancholy: the sensation of present evils, if they be referred to the body, pain; if to the mind, grief. Envy, hatred, and malice, are all modifications of resentment, differing in the causes which have excited that resentment, as well as in the degree in which it is entertained. Shame is that particular species of grief, which proceeds from losing the esteem of our fellow-creatures; fear, the anticipation of future evils. This is the catalogue of human miseries and pains; and it is plain why they have been added to our nature. By the miseries of the body, man is controlled within his proper sphere, and learns what manner of life it was intended he should lead: fear and suspicion are given to guard him from harm: resentment, to punish those who inflict it; and by punishment, to deter them. By the pain of inactivity, we are driven to exertion: by the dread of shame, to labour for esteem. But all these pregnant and productive feelings are poured into the heart of man, not with anything that has the air of human moderation—not with a measure that looks like precision and adjustment—but wildly, lavishly, and in excess. Providence only impels; it makes us start up from the earth, and do something; but whether that something shall be good or evil, is the arduous decision which that Providence has left to us. You cannot sit quietly till the torch is held up to your cottage, and the dagger to your throat: if you could, this scene of things would not long be what it now is. The solemn feeling which rises up in you at such times, is as much the work of God, as the splendour of the lightning is his work; but that feeling may degenerate into the fury of a savage, or be disciplined into the rational opposition of a wise and a good man. You *must* be affected by the distinctions of your fellow-creatures—you cannot help it; but you may envy those distinctions, or you may emulate them. The dread of shame may enervate you for every manly exertion, or be the vigilant guardian of purity and innocence. In a strong mind, fear grows up into cautious sagacity; grief, into amiable tenderness. Without the noble toil of moral education, the one is abject cowardice, the other eternal gloom; therefore, there is the good, and there is the evil! Every man's destiny is in his own hands. Nature has given us those beginnings, which are the elements of the foulest vices, and the seeds of every sweet and immortal virtue: but though Nature has given you the liberty to choose, she has terrified you by her punishments, and lured you by her rewards, to choose aright; for she has not only taken care that envy, and cowardice, and melancholy, and revenge, shall carry with them their own curse—but she has rewarded emulation, courage, patience, cheerfulness, and dignity, with that feeling of calm pleasure, which makes it the highest act of human wisdom to labour for their attainment.

PAST HAPPINESS.*

The memory of past good, and the memory of past evil, are both without a specific name in our language; though it should seem, that they require one, as much as hope or fear—to which, in point of time, they are contrasted. We all know that present happiness is very materially affected by happiness in prospect: but, perhaps, it is not enough urged as a motive for benevolence.

Mankind are always happier for having been happy; so that if you make them happy now, you make them happy twenty years hence by the memory of it. A childhood passed with a due mixture of rational indulgence, under fond and wise parents, diffuses over the whole of life, a feeling of calm pleasure; and, in extreme old age, is the very last remembrance which time can erase from the mind of man. No enjoyment, however inconsiderable, is confined to the present moment. A man is the happier for life, from having made once an agreeable tour, or lived for any length of time with pleasant people, or enjoyed any considerable interval of innocent pleasure: and it is most probably the recollection of their past pleasures, which contributes to render old men so inattentive to the scenes before them; and carries them back to a world that is past, and to scenes never to be renewed again.

THE FORCE OF HABIT.—HOBBES AND HIS PIPE.†

Habits may be divided into active and passive;—those things which we do by an act of the will, and those things which we

* From the Lecture on the Benevolent Affections.
† From the Lecture on Habit, Part I.

suffer by the agency of some external power. I begin with the active habits; and, after stating a few of the most familiar of them, I will shortly analyze the examples, in order to show that they are merely referable to association. It may be as well, perhaps to give a specimen of the life of a man whose existence was, at last, entirely dependent upon the habits he had contracted: it is a fair picture of the dominion which habit establishes over us, at the close of life. "The professed rule of Mr. Hobbes," says Dr. White Kennet in his Memoirs of the Cavendish family, "was to dedicate the morning to exercise, and the evening to study. At his first rising, he walked out, and climbed up a hill: if the weather was not dry, he made a point of fatiguing himself within doors, so as to perspire; remarking constantly, that an old man had more moisture than heat; and by such motion, heat was to be acquired, and moisture expelled. After this, the philosopher took a very comfortable breakfast, and then went round the lodgings to wait upon the earl, the countess, the children, and any considerable strangers; paying some short addresses to all of them. He kept these rounds till about twelve o'clock, when he had a little dinner provided for him, which he eat always by himself, without ceremony. Soon after dinner, he retired to his study, and had his candle, with ten or twelve pipes of tobacco, laid by him; then, shutting the door, he fell to smoking, thinking, and writing, for several hours. He could never endure to be left in an empty house; whenever the earl removed, he would go along with him, even to his last stage, from Chatsworth to Hardwick. This was the constant tenor of his life, from which he never varied, no, not a moment, nor an atom."

This is the picture of a man whose life appears to have been entirely regulated by the past; who did a thing because he *had* done it; who, so far as bodily actions were concerned, could hardly be said to have any fresh motives; but was impelled by one regular set of volitions, constantly recurring at fixed periods. Now, take any one of his habits, and examine its progress; it will afford a natural history of this law of the mind, and will show what circumstances in that law are most worthy of observation.

He smoked: how did this begin? It might have begun any how. He was staying, perhaps, at some house where smoking was in fashion, and began to smoke out of compliance with the humours of other persons. At first, he thought it unpleasant; and as all the expirations and inspirations were new and difficult, it required considerable attention; and at the close of the evening he could have distinctly recollected, if he had tried to do so, that his mind had been employed in thinking how he was to manage and manœuvre the pipe. The practice goes on; the disgust vanishes; much less attention is necessary to smoke well: in a few days the association is formed; the moment the cloth is taken away after supper, the idea of smoking occurs: if any accident happen to prevent it, a slight pain is felt in consequence; it seems as if things did not go on in their regular track, and some confusion had crept into the arrangements of the evening. As the association goes on, it gathers strength from the circumstances connected with it; from the mirth and conversation with which it is joined: at last, after a lapse of years, we see the philosopher of Malmsbury advanced from one, to one dozen of pipes; so perfect in all the tactics of a smoker, so dexterous in all the manual of his dirty recreation, that he would fill, light, and smoke out his pipe, without the slightest remembrance of what he had been doing, or the most minute interruption to any immoral, irreligious, or unmathematical track of thought, in which he happened to be engaged: but we must not forget, that though his amusement occupied him so little, and was passed over with such a small share of his attention, the *want* of it would have occupied him so much, that he could have done nothing without it; all his speculations would have been at an end, and without his twelve pipes he might have been a friend to devotion, to freedom, or anything else which, in the customary tenor of his thoughts, he certainly was not. The phenomenon observable here is, that the physical taste lost its effect; that which was nauseous ceased to be so. Next, the habit began with a considerable difficulty of bodily action, and with a full attention of the mind to what was passing. It was not easy to smoke, and the philosopher was compelled to be careful, in order to do it properly; but as the habit increased, he indulged in it with such little attention of mind or exertion of body, that he did it without knowing he did it. Lastly, any interruption of the habit would have occasioned to him the greatest uneasiness

THE ORBIT OF A HABIT.*

The period of time in which a habit renews its action, or (if I may be allowed the expression) the orbit of a habit, is of very different dimensions. We may have a habit of shrugging up the shoulders every half-hour; or, of eating three eggs every morning; or, of dining at a club once a month; or, of going down to see a relation once a year: but it is difficult to conceive any habit forming itself for a period greater than a year. I can easily conceive that a person who set off on every 1st of June, to pay a visit, might have the force of habit added to his other inducements, and go, partly because he loved the persons, partly because he had done it before; but is it easy to believe that there is a habit of doing anything every other year? or, how very ridiculous it would sound for two persons to say. "We agreed a long time ago to dine together every Bissextile, or leap-year, and it is now grown into a perfect habit!" This limitation of habits to the period of a year—which I by no means lay any great stress upon, but which has some degree of truth in it—depends somewhat upon the revolution of names and appearances. To do anything the first day of a month, or on one particular day every year, is to strengthen a habit by the recurrence of names or seasons; but if an action be performed every third or fourth year, the same name and the same appearances have occurred, without being connected with the same deed, and therefore the habit is impaired.

SUPERIORITY TO HABIT.

Men aware of the power of habit, escape its influence; and therefore, it is among the most trite principles of education to discover the particular habits to which we are exposed by situation and profession; and, when they are discovered, to resist them. Without any intentional efforts to resist professional habits, they are unconsciously resisted by the magnitude and variety of some men's minds; and by the liberal pursuits which they contrive to connect with their professions. There is an effect of custom and habit to which we are all extremely indebted, and that is, that it

* This and the following passages are from the Lectures on Habit, Part II.

regulates everything which nothing else regulates, where there is no propriety, and no duty, to be consulted. The reference is always to habit — in dress, in ceremony, in equipage, in all the circumstances of life, where almost any conduct would be virtuous, a compliance with custom is the only conduct that is wise, and a man of sense is rather pleased that the public legislate for him on points where choice would neither be easy nor useful. It is a strong mark of a good understanding, to allow custom an easy empire on these occasions. It is a much surer mark of talent, that men should rise above the influence of habit, and be better and greater than that to which the circumstances of their lives, or the character of their age, would appear to doom them. This is the reason why we admire men, who, born in poverty, and accustomed to objects of sense, have been able to conceive the dignity, the value, and the pleasure of intellectual gratification; who, deviating from every model they had seen, and guided only by their inward light, have steadily, and successfully, pursued the path of virtuous fame. By this subjugation of habitual thoughts, and escape from habitual objects, Bacon the friar, Czar Peter, Lord Verulam, and all great men, in law and in arts, have preceded the ages in which they lived, and become the beacons of future times. The mass of men, say whatever is said, do whatever is done, think whatever is thought, and can not easily conceive anything greater and better than what is already created. But, in the grossest period of monastic ignorance, Bacon saw that the whole art of war might be changed by the invention of gunpowder; the Czar pulled down a nation habitually victorious, roused and elevated a people habitually stupid and depressed: Lord Verulam looked upon his own times with the same cool estrangement from the influence of habit, as if he were contemplating a nation of the ancient world; and was so little imposed upon by the imperfect philosophy which then prevailed, that he effected that entire revolution in physical reasoning, by which we are all benefited to the present hour. Such victories over present objects — such power of reflecting, where attention is not stimulated by novelties — are generally great triumphs of the human understanding, and decisive proofs of its vigour and excellence, in every individual instance where they are found. Whoever is learned in an ignorant age; whoever is liberal in a bigoted age; whoever is temperate and respectable in a licentious age; whoever is elegant and enlarged in his views, where his profession chains him down to technical rules and narrow limits; whoever has gained any good which habit opposes, or avoided any evil which habit might induce—that man has vindicated the dignity and the power of his mind, by the fairest of all tests—by doing what the mass of mankind cannot do.

EFFECT OF HABIT.

A BEAUTIFUL effect of habit is, that it endows with preternatural strength every quality of the mind or heart which it calls into more than ordinary action. If protection is wanted, men are ready, long *habituated* to the fear of death. If gentleness and benevolence are wanted to lessen the miseries of life, women are *habitually* gentle and benevolent. If patient industry, you have it in the laborer, and the mechanic. What but the power of habit, has given to us the advantage of those fine legal understandings, that have gradually formed the system of law in this country? How are our naval victories gained, but by *habitual* character, skill, and courage? Whence the effusions of eloquence every day to be witnessed in the senate, but by that intrepidity, self-possession, and command of words and images, which habit only can confer? Fresh, youthful, untaught nature can *never* do such things as these. It is nature in its *manhood*, instructed by failure, fortified by precedent, confirmed by success, *riveted by habit*, and carried to a pitch of glory, by intense adhesion to one object, which, with all the primary efforts of its rude vigour, it never could have reached; diminishing the pleasure of vice, and strengthening the *habit* of virtue.

THE PASSIONS.

THE passions are in morals, what motion is in physics: they create, preserve, and animate; and without them, all would be silence and death. Avarice guides men across the deserts of the ocean; pride covers the earth with trophies, and mausoleums, and pyramids; love turns men from their savage rudeness; ambition shakes the very foundations of kingdoms. By the love of glory, weak nations swell into magnitude and strength. Whatever there is of terrible, whatever there is of beautiful in human events, all that shakes the soul to and fro, and is remembered while thought and flesh cling together—all these have their origin from the passions. As it is only in storms, and when their coming waters are driven up into the air, that we catch a sight of the depths of the sea, it is only in the season of perturbation that we have a glimpse of the real internal nature of man. It is then only, that the might of these eruptions shaking his frame, dissipates all the feeble coverings of opinion, and rends in pieces that cobweb veil, with which fashion hides the feelings of the heart. It is then only that Nature speaks her genuine feelings; and, as at the last night of Troy, when Venus illumined the darkness, Æneas saw the gods themselves at work—so may we, when the blaze of passion is flung upon man's nature, mark in him the signs of a celestial origin, and tremble at the invisible agents of God!

Look at great men in critical and perilous moments, when every cold and little spirit is extinguished: their passions always bring them out harmless; and at the very moment when they *seem* to perish, they emerge into greater glory. Alexander, in the midst of his mutinous soldiers; Frederick of Prussia, combating against the armies of three kingdoms; Cortes breaking in pieces the Mexican empire:—their passions led all these great men to fix their attention strongly upon the objects of their desires; they saw them under aspects unknown to, and unseen by common men, and which enabled them to conceive and execute those hardy enterprises, deemed rash and foolish, till their wisdom was established by their success. It is in fact the great passions alone which enable men to distinguish between what is difficult and what is impossible: a distinction always confounded by merely *sensible* men; who do not even *suspect* the existence of those means, which men of genius employ to effect their object. It is only passion which gives a man that high enthusiasm for his country, and makes him regard it as the only object worthy of human attention; —an enthusiasm, which to common eyes appears madness and extravagance; but which always creates fresh powers of mind, and commonly insures their ultimate success. In fact, it is only the great passions, which, tearing us away from the seductions of indolence, endow us with that continuity of attention, to which alone superiority of mind is attached. It is to their passions, alone, under the providence of God, that nations must trust, when perils gather thick about them, and their last moments seem to be at hand. The history of the world shows us that men are not to be counted by their numbers, but by the fire and vigour of their passions; by their deep sense of injury; by their memory of past glory; by their eagerness for fresh fame; by their clear and steady resolution of ceasing to live, or of achieving a particular object, which, when it is *once* formed, strikes off a load of manacles and chains, and gives free space to all heavenly and heroic feelings. All great and extraordinary actions come from the heart. There are seasons in human affairs, when qualities fit enough to conduct the common business of life, are feeble and useless; and when men must trust to emotion, for that safety which reason at such times can never give. These are the feelings which led the ten thousand over the Carduchian mountains; these are the feelings by which a handful of Greeks broke in pieces the power of Persia: they have, by turns, humbled Austria, reduced Spain; and in the fens of the Dutch, and on the mountains of the Swiss, defended the happiness, and revenged the oppressions, of man! God calls all the passions out in their keenness and vigour, for the present safety of mankind. Anger and revenge, and the heroic mind, and a readiness to suffer:—all the secret strength, all the invisible array, of the feelings—all that nature has reserved for the great scenes of the world. For the usual hopes, and the common aids of man, are all gone! Kings have perished, armies are subdued, nations mouldered away! Nothing remains, under God, but those passions which have often proved the best ministers of his vengeance, and the surest protectors of the world.

PASSAGES FROM SERMONS.

OF SERMONS.*

PREACHING has become a bye-word for long and dull conversation of any kind; and whoever wishes to imply, in any piece of writing, the absence of everything agreeable and inviting, calls it a sermon.

One reason for this is the bad choice of subjects for the pulpit The clergy are allowed about twenty-six hours every year for the instruction of their fellow-creatures; and I can not help thinking this short time had better be employed on practical subjects, in explaining and enforcing that conduct which the spirit of Christianity requires, and which mere worldly happiness commonly coincides to recommend. These are the topics nearest the heart, which make us more fit for this and a better world, and do all the good that sermons ever will do. Critical explanations of difficult passages of Scripture, dissertations on the doctrinal and mysterious points of religion, learned investigations of the meaning and accomplishment of prophecies, do well for publication, but are ungenial to the habits and taste of a general audience. Of the highest importance they are to those who can defend the faith and study it profoundly; but God forbid it should be necessary to be a scholar, or a critic, in order to be a Christian. To the multitude, whether elegant or vulgar, the result only of erudition, employed for the defence of Christianity, can be of any consequence: with the erudition itself they can not meddle, and must be fatigued if they are doomed to hear it. In every congregation there are a certain number whom principle, old age, or sickness, has rendered truly de

* From the Preface to the Collection of Sermons, at Edinburgh, 1800.

vout; but in preaching, as in everything else, the greater number of instances constitute the rule, and the lesser the exception.

A distinction is set up, with the usual inattention to the meaning of words, between moral and religious subjects of discourse; as if every moral subject must not necessarily be a Christian subject. If Christianity concern itself with our present, as well as our future happiness, how can any virtue, or the doctrine which inculcates it, be considered as foreign to our sacred religion? Has our Saviour forbidden justice—proscribed mercy, benevolence, and good faith? or, when we state the more sublime motives for their cultivation, which we derive from revelation, why are we not to display the temporal motives also, and to give solidity to elevation by fixing piety upon interest?

There is a bad taste in the language of sermons evinced by a constant repetition of the same scriptural phrases, which, perhaps, were used with great judgment two hundred years ago, but are now become so trite that they may, without any great detriment, be exchanged for others. "Putting off the old man—and putting on the new man." "The one thing needful." "The Lord hath set up his candlestick," "The armour of righteousness," etc., etc., etc., etc. The sacred Scriptures are surely abundant enough to afford us the same idea with some novelty of language: we can never be driven, from the penury of these writings, to wear and fritter their holy language into a perfect cant, which passes through the ear without leaving any impression.

To this cause of the unpopularity of sermons may be added the extremely ungraceful manner in which they are delivered. The English, generally remarkable for doing very good things in a very bad manner, seem to have reserved the maturity and plenitude of their awkwardness for the pulpit. A clergyman clings to his velvet cushion with either hand, keeps his eye riveted upon his book, speaks of the ecstasies of joy and fear with a voice and a face which indicate neither, and pinions his body and soul into the same attitude of limb and thought, for fear of being called theatrical and affected. The most intrepid veteran of us all dares no more than wipe his face with his cambric sudarium;* if, by mischance, his hand slip from its orthodox gripe of the velvet, he draws it back as from liquid brimstone, or the caustic iron of the law, and atones

* Classical Latin for a cloth to wipe away perspiration, or, a handkerchief.

for this indecorum by fresh inflexibility and more rigorous sameness. Is it wonder, then, that every semi-delirious sectary who pours forth his animated nonsense with the genuine look and voice of passion should gesticulate away the congregation of the most profound and learned divine of the Established Church, and in two Sundays preach him bare to the very sexton? Why are we natural everywhere but in the pulpit? No man expresses warm and animated feelings anywhere else, with his mouth alone, but with his whole body; he articulates with every limb, and talks from head to foot with a thousand voices. Why this holoplexia* on sacred occasions alone? Why call in the aid of paralysis to piety? Is it a rule of oratory to balance the style against the subject, and to handle the most sublime truths in the dullest language and the driest manner? Is sin to be taken from men as Eve was from Adam, by casting them into a deep slumber? Or from what possible perversion of common sense are we all to look like field-preachers in Zembla, holy lumps of ice numbed into quiescence, and stagnation, and mumbling?

It is theatrical to use action, and it is Methodistical to use action.

But we have cherished contempt for sectaries, and persevered in dignified tameness so long, that while we are freezing common sense for large salaries in stately churches, amidst whole acres and furlongs of empty pews, the crowd are feasting on ungrammatical fervour and illiterate animation in the crumbling hovels of Methodists. If influence over the imagination can produce these powerful effects; if this be the chain by which the people are dragged captive at the wheel of enthusiasm, why are we, who are rocked in the cradle of ancient genius, who hold in one hand the book of the wisdom of God, and in the other grasp that eloquence which ruled the Pagan world, why are we never to rouse, to appeal, to inflame, to break through every barrier, up to the very haunts and chambers of the soul? If the vilest interest upon earth can daily call forth all the powers of mind, are we to harangue on public order, and public happiness, to picture a reuniting world, a resurrection of souls, a rekindling of ancient affections, the dying day of heaven and of earth, and to unveil the throne of God, with a

---

* A medical term, indicating a paralysis of the whole body, as opposed to araplegia or hemiplegia, a palsy of a part.

wretched apathy which we neither feel nor show in the most trifling concerns of life? This surely can be neither decency nor piety, but ignorant shame, boyish bashfulness, luxurious indolence, or anything but propriety and sense. There is, I grant, something discouraging at present to a man of sense in the sarcastical phrase of popular preacher; but I am not entirely without hope that the time may come when energy in the pulpit will be no longer considered as a mark of superficial understanding; when animation and affectation will be separated; when churches will cease (as Swift says) to be public dormitories;* and sleep be no longer looked upon as the most convenient vehicle of good sense.

I know well that out of ten thousand orators by far the greater number must be bad, or none could be good; but by becoming sensible of the mischief we have done, and are doing, we may all advance a proportional step; the worst may become what the best are, and the best better.

There is always a want of grandeur in attributing great events to little causes; but this is in some small degree compensated for by truth. I am convinced we should do no great injury to the cause of religion if we remembered the old combination of *aræ et foci*, and kept our churches a little warmer. An experienced clergyman can pretty well estimate the number of his audience by the indications of a sensible thermometer. The same blighting wind chills piety which is fatal to vegetable life; yet our power of encountering weather varies with the object of our hardihood; we are very Scythians when pleasure is concerned, and Sybarites when the bell summons us to church.

No reflecting man can ever wish to adulterate manly piety (the parent of all that is good in the world) with mummery and parade. But we are strange, very strange creatures, and it is better, perhaps, not to place too much confidence in our reason alone. If anything, there is, perhaps, too little pomp and ceremony in our worship, instead of too much. We quarreled with the Roman Catholic church, in a great hurry and a great passion, and furious with spleen; clothed ourselves with sackcloth, because she was

---

* Fuller, in his Holy State, has said: "It is a shame when the Church itself is cœmeterium, wherein the living sleep above ground, as the dead do beneath." Swift makes the most of this subject in his witty sermon on **Sleeping in Church.**

habited in brocade; rushing, like children, from one extreme to another, and blind to all medium between complication and barrenness, formality and neglect. I am very glad to find we are calling in, more and more, the aid of music to our service. In London, where it can be commanded, good music has a prodigious effect in filling a church; organs have been put up in various churches in the country, and, as I have been informed, with the best possible effect. Of what value, it may be asked, are auditors who come there from such motives? But our first business seems to be, to bring them there from any motive which is not undignified and ridiculous, and then to keep them there from a good one: those who come for pleasure may remain for prayer.

Pious and worthy clergymen are ever apt to imagine that mankind are what they ought to be—to mistake the duty for the fact—to suppose that religion can never weary its votaries—that the same novelty and ornament which are necessary to enforce every temporal doctrine are wholly superfluous in religious admonition; and that the world at large consider religion as the most important of all concerns, merely because it is so: whereas, if we refer to facts, the very reverse appears to be the case. Every consideration influences the mind in a compound ratio of the importance of the effects which it involves, and their proximity. A man who was sure to die a death of torture in ten years would think more of the most trifling gratification or calamity of the day than of his torn flesh and twisted nerves years hence. If we were to read the gazette of a naval victory from the pulpit, we should be dazzled with the eager eyes of our audience—they would sit through an earthquake to hear us. The cry of a child, the fall of a book, the most trifling occurrence is sufficient to dissipate religious thought, and to introduce a more willing train of ideas: a sparrow fluttering about the church is an antagonist which the most profound theologian in Europe is wholly unable to overcome. A clergyman has so little previous disposition to attention in his favour, that, without the utmost efforts, he can neither excite it nor preserve it when excited. It is his business to awaken mankind by every means in his power, and to show them their true interest. If he despise energy of manner and labour of composition, from a conviction that his audience are willing, and that his subject alone will support him, he will only add lethargy to languor, and confirm the drowsiness of his hearers by becoming a great example of sleep himself.

That many greater causes are at work to undermine religion I seriously believe; but I shall probably be laughed at when I say that warm churches, solemn music, animated preaching upon practical subjects, and a service some little abridged, would be no contemptible seconds to the just, necessary, and innumerable invectives which have been levelled against Rousseau, Voltaire, D'Alembert, and the whole pandemonium of those martyrs to atheism who toiled with such laborious malice, and suffered odium with such inflexible profligacy, for the wretchedness and despair of their fellow-creatures.

I have merely expressed what appears to me to be the truth in these remarks. I hope I shall not give offence; I am sure I do not mean to do it. Some allowance should be made for the severity of censure when the provident satirist furnishes the raw material for his own art, and commits every fault which he blames.

AN ILLUSTRATION.*

THE sun is now fallen in the heavens, and the habitations of men are shaded in gross darkness. That sun is hastening onward to other climates, to carry to all tongues, and people, and nations the splendour of day. What scenes of mad ambition and of bleeding war will it witness in its course. What cruel stripes; what iron bondage of the human race; what debasing superstition; what foul passions; what thick and dismal ignorance! It will beam upon the savage and sensual Moor; it will lighten the robber of Arabia to his prey; it will glitter on the chains of the poor negro. It will waken the Indian of the ocean to eat the heart of his captive. The bigot Turk will hail it from the summit of his mosque; it will guide the Brahmin to his wooden gods; but in all its course it will witness perhaps no other spectacle of a free, rational people, gathered together under the influence of Revelation, to lighten the load of human misery, and to give of their possessions to the afflicted, and the poor.

* From a Sermon preached for the Scotch Lying-in Hospital, at Edinburgh

TREATMENT OF SERVANTS.*

UNCHRISTIANLIKE conduct to servants does not always proceed from a bad heart; many are guilty of it who have much of compassion and goodness in their nature; but it seems to proceed from a notion early imbibed, never effectually checked, and aided by our natural indolence and pride, that a sense of those injuries which are conveyed by manner and expression, is almost exclusively confined to those whose minds are refined by education, or whose condition is ennobled by birth;† but in spite of all the ills which poverty can inflict, no human being is base or abject in his own eyes. Without wealth, or beauty, or learning, or fame, nay, without one soul in all the earth that harbours a thought of him, without a place where to lay his head, loathsome from disease, and shunned by men, the poorest outcast has still something for which he cherishes and fosters himself; he has still some one pride in reserve, and you may still make his tears more bitter, and his heart more heavy; do not then take away from men who give you their labour for their bread, those feelings of self-complacency which are dear to all conditions, but doubly dear to this; do not take away that from thy poor brother, which cheers him in his toil, which gives him a light heart, and wipes the sweat from his brow; and be thou good and kind to him, and speak gentle words to him, for the strength of his youth is thine, and remember there is above a God, whom thou cannot ask to pardon thy follies, and thy crimes, if thou forgivest not also the trespasses which are done against thee.

* From a Sermon on the Treatment of Servants.

† The Rev. Charles Kingsley, in one of his practical religious discourses, a lecture on "The Country Parish," after describing the rough-shod benevolence of certain tempers in intercourse with the poor, says finely, of the opposite traits in the character of Sydney Smith: "The love and admiration which that truly brave and loving man won from every one, rich or poor, with whom he came in contact, seems to me to have arisen from the one fact, that without, perhaps having any such conscious intention, he treated rich and poor, his own servants, and the noblemen, his guests, *alike*, and alike courteously, considerately, cheerfully, affectionately—so leaving a blessing, and reaping a blessing, wheresoever he went."—Lectures to Ladies on Practical Subjects

THE BLIND.*

CONSIDER the deplorable union of indigence and blindness, and what manner of life it is from which you are rescuing these unhappy people; the blind man comes out in the morning season to cry aloud for his food; when he hears no longer the feet of men he knows that it is night, and gets him back to the silence and the famine of his cell. Active poverty becomes rich; labour and prudence are rewarded with distinction: the weak of the earth have risen up to be strong; but he is ever dismal, and ever forsaken! The man who comes back to his native city after years of absence, beholds again the same extended hand into which he cast his boyish alms; the self-same spot, the old attitude of sadness, the ancient cry of sorrow, the intolerable sight of a human being that has grown old in supplicating a miserable support for a helpless, mutilated frame—such is the life these unfortunate children would lead, had they no friend to appeal to your compassion—such are the evils we will continue to remedy, if they experience from you that compassion which their magnitude so amply deserves.

The author of the book of Ecclesiastes has told us that the light is sweet, that it is a pleasant thing for the eyes to behold the sun; the sense of sight is, indeed, the highest bodily privilege, the purest physical pleasure, which man has derived from his Creator: To see that wandering fire, after he has finished his journey through the nations, coming back to us in the eastern heavens; the mountains painted with light; the floating splendour of the sea; the earth waking from deep slumber; the day flowing down the sides of the hills, till it reaches the secret valleys; the little insect recalled to life; the bird trying her wings; man going forth to his labour; each created being moving, thinking, acting, contriving according to the scheme and compass of its nature; by force, by cunning, by reason, by necessity—is it possible to joy in this animated scene and feel no pity for the sons of darkness? for the eyes that will never taste the sweet light? for the poor, clouded in everlasting gloom? If you ask me why they are miserable and dejected, I turn you to the plentiful valleys; to the fields now bringing forth their increase; to the freshness and the flowers of

* From a Charity Sermon for the Blind, at Edinburgh

the earth; to the endless variety of its colours; to the grace, the symmetry, the shape of all it cherishes, and all it bears; these you have forgotten because you have always enjoyed them; but these are the means by which God Almighty makes man what he is cheerful, lively, erect; full of enterprise, mutable, glancing from Heaven to earth; prone to labour and to act. Why was not the earth left without form and void? Why was not darkness suffered to remain on the face of the deep? Why did God place lights in the firmament for days, for seasons, for signs, and for years? that he might make man the happiest of beings, that he might give to this his favourite creation a wider scope, a more permanent duration; a richer diversity of joy: this is the reason why the blind are miserable and dejected, because their soul is mutilated and dismembered of its best sense; because they are a laughter and a ruin, and the boys of the streets mock at their stumbling feet; therefore I implore you, by the Son of David, have mercy on the blind: if there is not pity for all sorrows, turn the full and perfect man to meet the inclemency of fate: let not those who have never tasted the pleasures of existence, be assailed by any of its sorrows; the eyes which are never gladdened by light should never stream with tears.*

ON TRUTH.

Upon truth rests all human knowledge: to truth man is indebted for the hourly preservation of his life, and for a perpetual guide to his actions; without truth the affairs of the world could no longer exist, as they now are, than they could if any of the great physical laws of the universe were suspended. As truth is of indispensable necessity in the great concerns of the world, it is also of immense importance as it relates to the common and daily intercourse of life. Falsehood must have a direct and powerful tendency to disturb the order of human affairs, and to introduce into the bosom of society every gradation and variety of mischief.

There is a natural tendency in all men to speak the truth, because it is absolutely necessary we should inform ourselves of the truth for the common purposes of existence, and we do not say one

* "This passage," Lady Holland remarks, "was greatly admired by Dugald Stewart."

thing while we know another, but for the intervention of causes which are comparatively infrequent and extraordinary; the first of these which I shall mention is vanity. The vanity of being interesting, of exciting curiosity, and escaping from the pain of obscurity:—Great part of the mischief done to character, and of those calumnies which ruffle the quiet of life, have their origin in this source. . . . . . .

There is a liar, who is not so much a liar from vanity as from warmth of imagination, and levity of understanding; such a man has so thoroughly accustomed his mind to extraordinary combinations of circumstances, that he is disgusted with the insipidity of any probable event; the power of changing the whole course of nature is too fascinating for resistance; every moment must produce rare emotions, and stimulate high passions; life must be a series of zests, and relishes, and provocations, and languishing existence be refreshed by daily miracles: In the meantime, the dignity of man passes away, the bloom of Heaven is effaced, friends vanish from this degraded liar; he can no longer raise the look of wonder, but is heard in deep, dismal, contemptuous silence; he is shrunk from and abhorred, and lives to witness a gradual conspiracy against him of all that is good and honourable, and wise and great.

Fancy and vanity are not the only parents of falsehood—the worst, and the blackest species of it, has its origin in fraud—and, for its object, to obtain some advantage in the common intercourse of life. Though this kind of falsehood is the most pernicious, in its consequences, to the religious character of him who is infected by it; and the most detrimental to the general happiness of society, it requires (from the universal detestation in which it is held), less notice in an investigation of the nature of truth, intended for practical purposes. He whom the dread of universal infamy, the horror of being degraded from his rank in society, the thought of an hereafter will not inspire with the love of truth—who prefers any temporary convenience of a lie, to a broad, safe, and refulgent veracity—that man is too far sunk in the depths of depravity for any religious instruction he can receive in this place—the canker of disease is gone down to the fountains of his blood, and the days of his life are told.

Truth is sacrificed to a greater variety of causes than the narrow limits of a discourse from the pulpit will allow me to state—it is sacrificed to boasting, to malice, and to all the varieties of hatred—it is sacrificed, also, to that verbal benevolence which delights in the pleasure of promising, as much as it shrinks from the pain of performing, which abounds in gratuitous sympathy, and has words, and words only, for every human misfortune.

I have hitherto considered the love of truth on the negative side only, as it indicates what we are not to do—the vices from which we are to abstain; but there is an heroic faith—a courageous love of truth, the truth of the Christian warrior—an unconquerable love of justice, that would burst the heart in twain, if it had not vent—which makes women men—and men saints—and saints angels. Often it has published its creed from amid the flames—often it has reasoned under the axe, and gathered firmness from a mangled body—often it has rebuked the madness of the people—often it has burst into the chambers of princes, to tear down the veil of falsehood, and to speak of guilt, of sorrow, and of death. Such was the truth which went down with Shadrach to the fiery furnace, and descended with Daniel to the lion's den. Such was the truth which made the potent Felix tremble at his eloquent captive. Such was the truth which roused the timid Peter to preach Christ crucified before the Sanhedrim of the Jews—and such was the truth which enabled that Christ, whom he did preach, to die the death upon the cross.......

We shall love truth better if we believe that falsehood is useless; and we shall believe falsehood to be useless if we entertain the notion that it is difficult to deceive; the fact is (and there can be no greater security for well doing than such an opinion), that it is almost impossible to deceive the great variety of talent, information, and opinion, of which the world is composed. Truth prevails, by the universal combination of all things animate, or inanimate, against falsehood; for ignorance makes a gross and clumsy fiction; carelessness omits some feature of a fiction that is ingenious; bad fellowship in fraud betrays the secret; conscience bursts it into atoms; the subtlety of angry revenge unravels it; mere brute, unconspiring matter reveals it; death lets in the light of truth; all things teach a wise man the difficulty and bad success of falsehood; and truth is inculcated by human policy, as well as by Divine command.

The highest motive to the cultivation of truth, is, that God requires it of us; he requires it of us, because falsehood is contrary to his nature—because the spirit of man, before it can do homage to its Creator, must be purified in the furnace of truth. There is no more noble trial for him who seeks the kingdom of heaven, than to speak the truth; often the truth brings upon him much sorrow; often it threatens him with poverty, with banishment, with hatred, with loss of friends, with miserable old age; but, as one friend loveth another friend the more if they had suffered together in a long sorrow, so the soul of a just man, for all he endures, clings nearer to the truth; he mocks the fury of the people, and laughs at the oppressor's rod; and if needs be, he sitteth down like Job in the ashes, and God makes his morsel of bread sweeter than the feasts of the liar, and all the banquets of sin.

ON RICHES.

It is difficult for a rich man to enter into the kingdom of God. The first cause to be alleged for this difficulty is, that he wants that important test of his own conduct, which is to be gained from the conduct of his fellow-creatures toward him; he may be going far from the kingdom of God, on the feet of pride, and over the spoils of injustice, without learning, from the averted looks, and the alienated hearts of men, that his ways are the ways of death. Wealth is apt to inspire a kind of awe, which fashions every look, modulates every word, and influences every action; and this, not so much from any view to interest, as from that imposing superiority, exercised upon the imagination by prosperous fortune, from which it is extremely difficult for any man to emancipate himself, who has not steadily accustomed his judgment to measure his fellow-creatures by real, rather than artificial distinctions, and to appeal from the capricious judgments of the world to his own reflections, and to the clear and indisputable precepts of the Gospel.

The general presumption, indeed, which we are apt to form, is, that the mischief is already done; that the rich man has been accustomed to such flattering reception, such gracious falsehoods, and such ingenious deceit, that to treat him justly, is to treat him harshly; and, to defer to him only in the proportion of his merit, is a violation of established forms. No man feels it to be his duty to combat with the gigantic errors of the world, and to exalt himself into a champion of righteousness; he leaves the state of society just as he found it, and indolently contributes his quota of deceit, to make the life of a human being a huge falsehood from the cradle to the tomb. It is this which speaks to Dives the false history of his shameless and pampered life;—here it is, in the deceitful mirror of the human face, that he sees the high gifts with which God has endowed him; and here it is, in that mirror, so dreadfully just to guilty poverty, he may come back, after he has trampled on every principle of honour and justice, and see joy, and delight, and unbounded hospitality, and unnumbered friends. Therefore, I say to you, when you enter in among your fellows, in the pomp, and plenitude of wealth—when the meek eye of poverty falls before you—when all men listen to your speech, and the approving smile is ready to break forth on every brow—then keep down your rising heart, and humble yourself before your father who seeth in secret; then fear very greatly for your salvation; then tremble more than Felix trembled; then remember that it is easier for a camel to go through the eye of a needle, than for a rich man to enter into the kingdom of heaven.

The second reason why it so difficult for a rich man to enter into the kingdom of God is, that he loves the kingdom of the world too well. Death is very terrible, says the son of Sirach, to him who lives at ease in his possessions; and in truth the pleasure of life does, in a great measure, depend upon the lot which we draw, and the heritage which we enjoy; it may be urged, that a person who knows no other situation, wishes no other; and that the boundary of his experience is the boundary of his desire. This would be true enough if we did not derive our notions of happiness and misery from a wider range of observation than our own destiny can afford; I will not speak of great misfortunes, for such instances prove put too clearly, how much the love of life depends on the enjoyment it affords;—but a man who is the eternal prey of solicitude, wishes for the closing of the scene; a constant, cheerless struggle with little miseries, will dim the sun, and wither the green herb, and taint the fresh wind;—he will cry out, let me depart—he will count his gray hairs with joy, and one day will seem unto him as many. Those who are not reminded of the wretchedness of human existence by such reflections as these, who are born to luxury and respect, and sheltered from the various perils of poverty, begin to forget the precarious tenure of worldly enjoyments, and to build sumptuously on the sand; they put their trust (as the Psalmist says) in chariots and horses, and dream they shall live for ever in those palaces which are but the outhouses of the grave. There are very few men, in fact, who are capable of withstanding the constant effect of artificial distinctions; it is difficult to live upon a throne, and to think of a tomb; it is difficult to be clothed in splendour, and to remember we are dust; it is difficult for the rich and the prosperous to keep their hearts as a burning coal upon the altar, and to humble themselves before God as they rise before men. In the meantime, while pride gathers in the heart, the angel is ever writing in the book, and wrath is ever mantling in the cup; complain not in the season of wo, that you are parched with thirst; ask not for water, as Dives asked, you have a warning which he never had. There stand the ever-memorable words of the text, which break down the stateliness of man, and dissipate the pageantry of the earth;—thus it is that the few words of a God can make the purple of the world appear less beautiful than the mean garments of a beggar, and striking terror into the hearts of rulers and of exarchs, turn the banners of dominion to the ensigns of death, and make them shudder at the sceptre which they wield. To-day, you are clothed in fine linen, and fare sumptuously; in a few and evil years, they shall hew you out a tomb of marble, whiter than snow, and the cunning artifice of the workman shall grave on it weeping angels, and make a delicate image of one fleeing up to heaven, as if it were thee, and shall relate in golden letters, the long story of your honours and your birth — thou fool!! He that dieth by the roadside for the lack of a morsel of bread, God loveth him as well as he loveth thee; and at the gates of heaven, and from the blessed angels, thou shalt learn, that it is easier for a camel to go through the eye of a needle, than for a rich man to enter into the kingdom of heaven.

Another fatal effect of great wealth is, that it is apt to harden the heart; wealth gives power; power produces immediate gratification; the long habit of immediate gratification, an impatience of unpleasant feelings; a claim to be exempted from the contemplation of human misery, of everything calculated to inspire gloom, to pollute enjoyment, and protrude a sense of painful duties; the compassion with which prosperous men are born in common with us all, is never cherished by a participation in the common suffering, a share in the general struggle; it wants that sense of the difficulty and wretchedness of existence, by which we obtain the best measure of the sufferings of our fellow-creatures. We talk of human life as a journey, but how variously is that journey performed? there are some who come forth girt, and shod, and mantled, to walk on velvet lawns, and smooth terraces, where every gale is arrested, and every beam is tempered; there are others who walk on the alpine paths of life, against driving misery, and through stormy sorrows; and over sharp afflictions, walk with bare feet and naked breast, jaded, mangled, and chilled It is easy enough to talk of misfortunes; that they exist, no man can be ignorant; it is not the bare knowledge of them that is wanting, but that pungent, vital commiseration, under the influence of which a man springs up from the comforts of his home, deserts his favourite occupations, toils, invents, investigates, struggles, wades through perplexity, disappointment, and disgust, to save a human being from shame, poverty, and destruction: here then is the jet, and object of our blessed Saviour's menace; and reasonable enough it is that he who practically withdraws himself from the great Christian community of benevolence, should be cut off from the blessings of Christian reward. If we suffer ourselves to be so infatuated by the enjoyments of this world, as to forget the imperious claims of affliction, and to render our minds, from the long habit of selfish gratification, incapable of fulfilling the duties we owe to mankind, then let us not repine, that our lot ceases in this world, or that the rich man shall never inherit immortal life.

As to that confidence and pride of which riches are too often the source, what can the constitution of that mind be, which has formed these notions of Divine wisdom and justice? Was this inequality of possessions contrived for the more solid establishment of human happiness, that there might be gradation and subordination among men? or was it instituted to give an arbitrary and useless superiority of one human being over another? Are any

USES OF WEALTH. 271

duties exacted for the good conferred? or was a rich man only born to sleep quietly, to fare sumptuously, and to be clothed in brave apparel? Has He, who does not create a particle of dust but it has its use, has He, do you imagine, formed one human being merely as a receptable of choice fruits and delicate viands; and has He stationed a thousand others about him, of the same flesh and blood, that they might pick up the crumbs of his table, and gratify the wishes of his heart? No man is mad enough to acknowledge such an opinion; but many enjoy wealth as if they had no other notion respecting it than that they were to extract from it the greatest enjoyment possible, to eat and drink to-day, and to mock at the threatened death of to-morrow.

The command of our Saviour to the rich man, was, "Go thy way quickly, sell all thou hast, divide it among the poor, and take up thy cross and follow me;" but this precept of our blessed Lord, as it was intended only for the interests of the Gospel, and the state of the world at that period, cannot be considered as applicable to the present condition of mankind; to preach such exalted doctrine in these latter days, would, I am afraid, at best be useless; our object is to seek for some fair medium between selfishness and enthusiasm. If something of great possessions be dedicated to inspire respect, and preserve the gradations of society, a part to the real wants, a little to the ornaments and superfluities of life, a little even to the infirmities of the possessor, how much will remain for the unhappy, who ask only a preference over vicious pleasure, disgraceful excess, and idle ostentation.

Neither is it to objects only of individual misery, that the application of wealth is to be confined; whatever has for its object to enlarge human knowledge, or to propagate moral and religious principle; whatever may effect, immediately or remotely, directly or indirectly, the public happiness, may add to the comforts, repress the crimes, or animate the virtues of social life; to every sacred claim of this nature, the appetite for frivolous pleasure, and the passion for frivolous display, must implicitly yield: if the minutiæ of individual charity present an object too inconsiderable for a capacious mind, there are vast asylums for sickness and want, which invite your aid; breathe among their sad inhabitants the spirit of consolation and order, give to them wiser arrangements and wider limits, prepare shelter for unborn wretchedness, and medicine for future disease; give opportunity to talents, and scope to goodness; go among the multitude, and see if you can drag from the oblivious heap some child of God, some gift of heaven, whose mind can burst through the secrets of nature, and influence the destiny of man. This is the dignified and religious use of riches, which, when they cherish boyish pride, to minister to selfish pleasure, shall verily doom their possessor to the flames of hell. — But he who knows wherefore God has given him great possessions, he shall die the death of Lazarus, without leading his life, and rest in the bosom of Abraham, though he never stretched forth his wounds to the dogs, nor gathered up the crumbs of the table for his food.

The best mode of guarding against that indirect flattery, which is always paid to wealth, is to impress the mind with a thorough belief of the fact; and to guard, by increased inward humility, against the danger of corruption from without. The wealthy man who attributes to himself great or good qualities, from what he conceives to be the opinion of the world, exposes himself to dangerous errors; on the most important of all subjects, this source of self-judgment is for him most effectually poisoned; he must receive such evidence with the utmost distrust, weigh every circumstance with caution, court animadversion and friendly candour, and cherish the man by whose polished justice his feelings are consulted, while his follies are repressed.

For the pride which is contracted by the contemplation of little things, there is no better cure than the contemplation of great things. Let a rich man turn from his own pompous littleness, and think of heaven, of eternity, and of salvation; let him think of all the nations that lie dead in the dust, waiting for the trumpet of God; he will smile at his own brief authority, and be as one lifted up to a high eminence, to whom the gorgeous palaces of the world are the specks and atoms of the eye; the great laws of nature pursue their eternal course, and heed not the frail distinctions of this life; the fever spares not the rich and the great; the tempest does not pass by them; they are racked by pain, they are weakened by disease, they are broken by old age, they are agonized in death like other men, they moulder in the tomb, they differ only from other men in this, that God will call them to a more severe account, that they must come before him with deeds of Christian charity and acts of righteousness, equal to all the opportunities and blessings which they have enjoyed.

Let the rich man, then, remember, in the midst of his enjoyments, by what slight tenure those enjoyments are held. In addition to the common doubt which hangs over the life of all men, fresh perils lie hid in his pleasures, and the very object for which he lives may be the first to terminate his existence. "Remember thou art mortal," was said every day to a great king. So, after the same fashion, I would that a man of great possessions should frequently remember the end of all things, and the long home, and the sleeping-place of a span in breadth; I would have him go from under the gilded dome down to the place where they will gather him to the bones of his fathers; he should tread in the dust of the noble, and trample on the ashes of the proud; I would heap before him sights of woe and images of death and terror; I would break down his stateliness, and humble him before his Redeemer and his Judge. My voice should ever sound in his ears, that it is easier for a camel to go through the eye of a needle, than for a rich man to enter into the kingdom of heaven.

TRIBUTE TO SIR SAMUEL ROMILLY.*

And let me ask you, my brethren, we who see the good and great daily perishing before our eyes, what comfort have we but this hope in Christ that we shall meet again? Remember the eminent men who, within the few years last past, have paid the great debt of nature. The earth stripped of its moral grandeur, sunk in its spiritual pride. The melancholy wreck of talents and of wisdom gone, my brethren, when we feel how dear, how valuable they were to us, when we would have asked of God, on our bended knees, their preservation and their life. Can we live with all that is excellent in human nature, can we study it, can we contemplate it, and then lose it, and never hope to see it again?

Can we say of any human being, as we may say of that great man who was torn from us in the beginning of this winter, that he acted with vast capacity upon all the great calamities of life; that he came with unblemished purity to restrain iniquity; that, con-

---

* From a sermon on Meditation on Death. Romilly, in a fit of temporary insanity, brought on by grief for the death of his wife, committed suicide, November 2, 1818.

demning injustice, he was just; that, restraining corruption, he was pure; that those who were provoked to look into the life of a great statesman, found him a good man also, and acknowledged he was sincere, even when they did not believe he was right? Can we say of such a man, with all the career of worldly ambition before him, that he was the friend of the wretched and the poor; that in the midst of vast occupation, he remembered the debtor's cell, the prisoner's dungeon, the last hour of the law's victim; that he meditated day and night on wretchedness, weakness, and want? Can we say all this of any human being, and then have him no more in remembrance? When you "die daily," my brethren; when you remember my text, paint to yourselves the gathering together again of the good and the just.

Remember that God is to be worshipped, that death is to be met, by such a life as this; remember, in the last hour, that rank, that birth, that wealth, that all earthly things will vanish away, that you will then think only of the wretchedness you have lessened and the good you have done.

POPULAR EDUCATION.*

FIRST and foremost, I think the new Queen should bend her mind to the very serious consideration of educating the people. Of the importance of this, I think no reasonable doubt can exist; it does not, in its effects, keep pace with the exaggerated expectations of its injudicious advocates, but it presents the best chance of national improvement.

Reading and writing are mere increase of power. They may be turned, I admit, to a good or a bad purpose; but for several years of his life the child is in your hands, and you may give to that power what bias you please: thou shalt not kill—thou shalt not steal—thou shalt not bear false witness;—by how many fables, by how much poetry, by how many beautiful aids of imagination, may not the fine morality of the sacred Scriptures be engraven on the minds of the young? I believe the arm of the assassin may be often stayed by the lessons of his early life. When I see the

* This and the succeeding passage are from a sermon, preached at St. Paul's on the accession of Victoria, on the Duties of the Queen—from the text, Dan. iv. 31 · "Oh king, thy kingdom is departed from thee."

village-school, and the tattered scholars, and the aged master or mistress teaching the mechanical art of reading or writing, and thinking that they are teaching that alone, I feel that the aged instructor is protecting life, insuring property, fencing the altar, guarding the throne, giving space and liberty to all the fine powers of man, and lifting him up to his own place in the order of creation.

There are, I am sorry to say, many countries in Europe, which have taken the lead of England in the great business of education, and it is a thoroughly commendable and legitimate object of ambition in a sovereign to overtake them. The names, too, of malefactors, and the nature of their crimes, are subjected to the sovereign;—how is it possible that a sovereign, with the fine feelings of youth, and with all the gentleness of her sex, should not ask herself, whether the human being whom she dooms to death, or at least does not rescue from death, has been properly warned in early youth, of the horrors of that crime for which his life is forfeited? "Did he ever receive any education at all?—did a father and mother watch over him?—was he brought to places of worship?—was the Word of God explained to him?—was the book of knowledge opened to him?—Or am I, the fountain of mercy, the nursing-mother of my people, to send a forsaken wretch from the streets to the scaffold, and to prevent, by unprincipled cruelty, the evils of unprincipled neglect?"

Many of the objections found against the general education of the people are utterly untenable; where all are educated, education cannot be a source of distinction and a subject for pride. The great source of labour is want; and as long as the necessities of life call for labour—labour is sure to be supplied. All these fears are foolish and imaginary; the great use and the great importance of education properly conducted, are, that it creates a great bias in favour of virtue and religion, at a period of life when the mind is open to all the impressions which superior wisdom may choose to affix upon it; the sum and mass of these tendencies and inclinations make a good and virtuous people, and draw down upon us the blessing and protection of Almighty God.

WAR.

A SECOND great object which I hope will be impressed upon the mind of this royal lady is, a rooted horror of war—an earnest and passionate desire to keep her people in a state of profound peace. The greatest curse which can be entailed upon mankind is a state of war. All the atrocious crimes committed in years of peace—all that is spent in peace by the secret corruptions, or by the thoughtless extravagance of nations, are mere trifles compared with the gigantic evils which stalk over the world in a state of war; God is forgotten in war—every principle of Christian charity trampled upon—human labour destroyed—human industry extinguished;—you see the son, and the husband, and the brother, dying miserably in distant lands—you see the waste of human affections—you see the breaking of human hearts—you hear the shrieks of widows and children after the battle—and you walk over the mangled bodies of the wounded calling for death. I would say to that royal child, worship God, by loving peace—it is not *your* humanity to pity a beggar by giving him food and raiment—*I* can do that; that is the charity of the humble, and the unknown—widen you your heart for the more expanded miseries of mankind—pity the mothers of the peasantry, who see their sons torn away from their families—pity your poor subjects crowded into hospitals, and calling in their last breath, upon their distant country and their young queen—pity the stupid, frantic folly of human beings, who are always ready to tear each other to pieces, and to deluge the earth with each other's blood; this is your extended humanity—and this the great field of your compassion. Extinguish in your heart the fiendish love of military glory, from which your sex does not necessarily exempt you, and to which the wickedness of flatterers may urge you. Say upon your death-bed, " I have made few orphans in my reign—I have made few widows—my object has been peace. I have used all the weight of my character, and all the power of my situation, to check the irascible passions of mankind, and to turn them to the arts of honest industry: this has been the Christianity of my throne, and this the Gospel of my sceptre; in this way I have striven to worship my Redeemer and my Judge."

I would add (if any addition were wanted as a part of the lesson to youthful royalty), the utter folly of all wars of ambition, where the object sought for—if attained at all—is commonly attained at manifold its real value, and often wrested, after short enjoyment, from its possessor, by the combined indignation and just vengeance of the other nations of the world. It is all misery, and folly, and impiety, and cruelty. The atrocities, and horrors, and disgusts of war, have never been half enough insisted upon by the teachers of the people; but the worst of evils and the greatest of follies, have been varnished over with specious names, and the gigantic robbers and murderers of the world have been holden up, for their imitation, to the weak eyes of youth. May honest counsellors keep this poison from the mind of the young queen. May she love what God bids, and do what makes men happy!

ESSAYS AND SKETCHES.

PRACTICAL ESSAYS.*

OF THE BODY.

Happiness is not impossible without health, but it is of very difficult attainment. I do not mean by health merely an absence of dangerous complaints, but that the body should be in perfect tune — full of vigor and alacrity.

The longer I live, the more I am convinced that the apothecary is of more importance than Seneca; and that half the unhappiness in the world proceeds from little stoppages, from a duct choked up, from food pressing in the wrong place, from a vexed duodenum, or an agitated pylorus.

The deception, as practised upon human creatures, is curious and entertaining. My friend sups late; he eats some strong soup, then a lobster, then some tart, and he dilutes these esculent varieties with wine. The next day I call upon him. He is going to sell his house in London, and to retire into the country. He is alarmed for his eldest daughter's health. His expenses are hourly increasing, and nothing but a timely retreat can save him from ruin. All this is the lobster; and when over-excited nature has had time to manage this testaceous encumbrance, the daughter recovers, the finances are in good order, and every rural idea effectually excluded from the mind.

In the same manner old friendships are destroyed by toasted cheese, and hard salted meat has led to suicide. Unpleasant

* Published in Lady Holland's Memoir as, "A few Unfinished Sketches from a Projected Series of 'Practical Essays.'"

feelings of the body produce correspondent sensations in the mind, and a great scene of wretchedness is sketched out by a morsel of indigestible and misguided food. Of such infinite consequence to happiness is it to study the body!

I have nothing new to say upon the management which the body requires. The common rules are the best: exercise without fatigue; generous living without excess; early rising, and moderation in sleeping. These are the apothegms of old women; but if they are not attended to, happiness becomes so extremely difficult that very few persons can attain to it. In this point of view, the care of the body becomes a subject of elevation and importance. A walk in the fields, an hour's less sleep, may remove all those bodily vexations and disquietudes which are such formidable enemies to virtue; and may enable the mind to pursue its own resolves without that constant train of temptations to resist, and obstacles to overcome, which it always experiences from the bad organization of its companion. Johnson says, every man is a rascal, when he is sick; meaning, I suppose, that he has no benevolent dispositions at that period toward his fellow-creatures, but that his notions assume a character of greater affinity to his bodily feelings, and that, *feeling* pain, he becomes malevolent; and if this be true of great diseases, it is true in a less degree of the smaller ailments of the body.

Get up in a morning, walk before breakfast, pass four or five hours of the day in some active employment; then eat and drink overnight, lie in bed till one or two o'clock, saunter away the rest of the day in doing nothing!—can any two human beings be more perfectly dissimilar than the same individual under these two different systems of corporeal management? and is it not of as great importance toward happiness to pay a minute attention to the body, as it is to study the wisdom of Chrysippus and Crantor?

OF OCCUPATION.

A GOOD stout bodily machine being provided, we must be actively occupied, or there can be little happiness.

If a good useful occupation be *not* provided, it is so ungenial to the human mind to do nothing, that men occupy themselves *perilously*, as with gaming or *frivolously*, as with walking up and down a street at a watering-place, and looking at the passers-by; or *malevolently*, as by teazing their wives and children. It is impossible to support, for any length of time, a state of perfect *ennui*; and if you were to shut a man up for any length of time within four walls, without occupation, he would go mad. If idleness do not produce vice or malevolence, it commonly produces melancholy.

A stockbroker or a farmer has no leisure for imaginary wretchedness; their minds are usually hurried away by the necessity of noticing external objects, and they are guaranteed from that curse of idleness, the eternal disposition to think of themselves.

If we have no necessary occupation, it becomes extremely difficult to make to ourselves occupations as entirely absorbing as those which necessity imposes.

The profession which a man makes for himself is seldom more than a half profession, and often leaves the mind in a state of vacancy and inoccupation. We must lash ourselves up, however, as well as we can, to a notion of its great importance; and as the dispensing power is in our own hands, we must be very jealous of remission and of idleness.

It may seem absurd that a gentleman who does not live by the profits of farming should rise at six o'clock in the morning to look after his farm; or, if botany be his object, that he should voyage to Iceland in pursuit of it. He is the happier however for his eagerness; his mind is more fully employed, and he is much more effectually guaranteed from all the miseries of *ennui*.

It is asked, if the object *can* be of such great importance. Perhaps not; but the pursuit *is*. The fox, when caught, is worth nothing: he is followed for the pleasure of the following.

What is a man to do with his life who has nothing which he *must* do? It is admitted he must find some employment, but does it signify what that employment is? Is he employed as much for his own happiness in cultivating a flower-garden as in philosophy, literature, or politics? This must depend upon the individual himself, and the circumstances in which he is placed. As far as the mere occupation or exclusion of *ennui* goes, this can be settled only by the feelings of the person employed; and if the attention be equally absorbed, in this point of view one occupation is as good as another; but a man who is conscious he was capable of doing great things, and has occupied himself with trifles beneath the level of his understanding, is apt to feel envy at the lot of those who have excelled him, and remorse at the misapplication of his own powers; he has not added to the pleasures of occupation the pleasures of benevolence, and so has not made his occupation as agreeable as he might have done, and he has probably not gained as much fame and wealth as he might have done if his pursuits had been of a higher nature. For these reasons it seems right that a man should attend to the highest pursuits in which he has any fair chance of excelling; he is as much occupied, gains more of what is worth gaining, and excludes remorse more effectually, even if he fail, because he is conscious of having made the effort.

When a very clever man, or a very great man, takes to cultivating turnips and retiring, it is generally an imposture. The moment men cease to talk of their turnips, they are wretched and full of self-reproach. Let every man be *occupied*, and occupied in the highest employment of which his nature is capable, and die with the consciousness that *he has done his best!*"

OF FRIENDSHIP.

LIFE is to be fortified by many friendships. To love, and to be loved, is the greatest happiness of existence. If I lived under the burning sun of the equator, it would be a pleasure to me to think that there were many human beings on the other side of the world who regarded and respected me; I could and would not live if I were alone upon the earth, and cut off from the remembrance of my fellow-creatures. It is not that a man has occasion often to fall back upon the kindness of his friends; perhaps he may never experience the necessity of doing so; but we are governed by our imaginations, and they stand there as a solid and impregnable bulwark against all the evils of life.

Friendships should be formed with persons of all ages and conditions, and with both sexes. I have a friend who is a bookseller, to whom I have been very civil, and who would do anything to serve me; and I have two or three small friendships among persons in much humbler walks of life, who, I verily believe, would do me a considerable kindness according to their means. It is a great happiness to form a sincere friendship with a woman; but a friendship among persons of different sexes rarely or ever takes place in this country. The austerity of our manners hardly admits of such a connection — compatible with the most perfect innocence, and a source of the highest possible delight to those who are fortunate enough to form it.

Very few friends will bear to be told of their faults; and if done at all, it must be done with infinite management and delicacy; for if you indulge often in this practice, men think you hate, and avoid you. If the evil is not very alarming, it is better, indeed, to let it alone, and not to turn friendship into a system of lawful and unpunishable impertinence. I am for frank explanations with friends in cases of affronts. They sometimes save a perishing friendship, and even place it on a firmer basis than at first; but secret discontent must always end badly.

OF CHEERFULNESS.

CHEERFULNESS and good spirits depend, in a great degree, upon bodily causes, but much may be done for the promotion of this turn of mind. Persons subject to low spirits should make the rooms in which they live as cheerful as possible; taking care that the paper with which the wall is covered should be of a brilliant, lively colour, hanging up pictures or prints, and covering the chimney-piece with beautiful china. A bay-window looking upon pleasant objects, and, above all, a large fire whenever the weather will permit, are favourable to good spirits, and the tables near should be strewed with books and pamphlets. To this must be added as much eating and drinking as is consistent with health; and some manual employment for men — as gardening, a carpenter's shop, the turning-lathe, etc. Women have always manual employment enough, and it is a great source of cheerfulness. Fresh air, exercise, occupation, society, and travelling, are powerful remedies.

Melancholy commonly flies to the future for its aliment, and must be encountered in this sort of artifice, by diminishing the range of our views. I have a large family coming on, my income is diminishing, and I shall fall into pecuniary difficulties. Well! but you are not *now* in pecuniary difficulties. Your eldest child is only seven years old; it must be two or three years before your family make any additional demands upon your purse. Wait till he time comes. Much may happen in the interval to better your situation; and if nothing does happen, at least enjoy the two or three years of ease and uninterruption which are before you. You are uneasy about your eldest son in India; but it is now June, and, at the earliest, the fleet will not come in till September; it may bring accounts of his health and prosperity, but at all events there are eight or nine weeks before you can hear news. Why are they to be spent as if you had heard the worst? The habit of taking very short views of human life may be acquired by degrees, and a great sum of happiness is gained by it. It becomes as customary at last to view things on the good side of the question as it was before to despond, and to extract misery from every passing event.

A firm confidence in an overruling Providence—a remembrance of the shortness of human life, that it will soon be over and finished—that we scarcely know, unless we could trace the remote consequences of every event, what would be good and what an evil; these are very important topics in that melancholy which proceeds from grief.

It is wise to state to friends that our spirits are low, to state the cause of the depression, and to hear all that argument or ridicule can suggest for the cure. Melancholy is always the worse for concealment, and many causes of depression are so frivolous, that we are shamed out of them by the mere statement of their existence.

FALLACIES.*

Fallacy I.—" *Because I have gone through it, my son shall go through it also.*"

A MAN gets well pommelled at a public school; is subject to every misery and every indignity which seventeen years of age can inflict upon nine and ten; has his eye nearly knocked out, and his clothes stolen and cut to pieces; and twenty years afterward, when he is a chrysalis, and has forgotten the miseries of his grub state,

* Lady Holland introduces the "Fallacies" in her Memoir with the remark of Sydney Smith: "It is astonishing the influence foolish apothegms have upon the mass of mankind, though they are not unfrequently fallacies. Here are a few I amused myself with writing long before Bentham's book on Fallacies."

is determined to act a manly part in life, and says, "I passed through all that myself, and I am determined my son shall pass through it as I have done;" and away goes his bleating progeny to the tyranny and servitude of the long chamber or the large dormitory. It would surely be much more rational to say, "Because I have passed through it, I am determined my son shall not pass through it; because I was kicked for nothing, and cuffed for nothing, and fagged for everything, I will spare all these miseries to my child." It is not for any good which may be derived from this rough usage; that has not been weighed and considered; few persons are capable of weighing its effects upon character; but there is a sort of compensatory and consolatory notion, that the present generation (whether useful or not, no matter) are not to come off scot-free, but are to have their share of ill-usage; as if the black eye and bloody nose which Master John Jackson received in 1800, are less black and bloody by the application of similar violence to similar parts of Master Thomas Jackson, the son, in 1830. This is not only sad nonsense, but cruel nonsense. The only use to be derived from the recollection of what we have suffered in youth, is a fixed determination to screen those we educate from every evil and inconvenience, from subjection to which there are not cogent reasons for submitting. Can anything be more stupid and preposterous than this concealed revenge upon the rising generation, and latent envy lest they should avail themselves of the improvements time has made, and pass a happier youth than their fathers have done?

Fallacy II.—"*I have said I will do it, and I will do it; I will stick to my word.*"

This fallacy proceeds from confounding resolutions with promises. If you have promised to give a man a guinea for a reward, or to sell him a horse or a field, you must do it; you are dishonest if you do not. But if you have made a resolution to eat no meat for a year, and everybody about you sees that you are doing mischief to your constitution, is it any answer to say, you have said so, and you will stick to your word? With whom have you made the contract but with yourself? and if you and yourself, the two contracting parties, agree to break the contract, where is the evil, or who is injured?

Fallacy III.—" *I object to half-measures—it is neither one thing nor the other.*"

But why *should* it be either one thing or the other? why not something between both? Why are half-measures necessarily or probably unwise measures? I am embarrassed in my circumstances; one of my plans is, to persevere boldly in the same line of expense, and to trust to the chapter of accidents for some increase of fortune; the other is, to retire entirely from the world, and to hide myself in a cottage; but I end with doing neither, and take a middle course of diminished expenditure. I do neither one thing nor the other, but possibly act wiser than if I had done either. I am highly offended by the conduct of an acquaintance; I neither overlook it entirely nor do I proceed to call him out; I do neither, but show him, by a serious change of manner, that I consider myself to have been ill-treated. I effect my object by half-measures. I cannot agree entirely with the Opposition or the Ministry; it may very easily happen that my half-measures are wiser than the extremes to which they are opposed. But it is a sort of metaphor which debauches the understanding of *foolish* people; and when half-measures are mentioned, they have much the same feeling as if they were cheated—as if they had bargained for a whole bushel and received but half. To act in extremes is sometimes wisdom; to *avoid* them is sometimes wisdom; every measure must be judged of by its own particular circumstances.

A NICE PERSON.*

A NICE person is neither too tall nor too short, looks clean and cheerful, has no prominent feature, makes no difficulties, is never misplaced, sits bodkin, is never foolishly affronted, and is void of affectations.

* Lady Holland gives the following account of this little sketch:—" In the course of the summer [1823] a young friend came to spend a month with us, at Foston, the freshness and originality of whose character both interested and amused my father; he chanced on one occasion to call her 'a nice person.' 'Oh, don't call me "*nice*," Mr. Sydney; people only say that where they can say nothing else.' 'Why? have you ever reflected what "a *nice* person" means?' 'No, Mr. Sydney,' said she, laughing, 'but I don't like it.' 'Well, give me pen and ink; I will show you,' said my father, 'a definition of a nice person.'"

A nice person helps you well at dinner, understands you, is always gratefully received by young and old, whig and tory, grave and gay.

There is something in the very air of a nice person which inspires you with confidence, makes you talk, and talk without fear of malicious misrepresentation; you feel that you are reposing upon a nature which God has made kind, and created for the benefit and happiness of society. It has the effect upon the mind which soft air and a fine climate have upon the body.

A nice person is clear of little, trumpery passions, acknowledges superiority, delights in talent, shelters humility, pardons adversity, forgives deficiency, respects all men's rights, never stops the bottle, is never long and never wrong, always knows the day of the month, the name of everybody at table, and never gives pain to any human being.

If anybody is wanted for a party, a nice person is the first thought of; when the child is christened, when the daughter is married—all the joys of life are communicated to nice people; the hand of the dying man is always held out to a nice person.

A nice person never knocks over wine or melted butter, does not tread upon the dog's foot, or molest the family cat, eats soup without noise, laughs in the right place, and has a watchful and attentive eye.

DEFINITION OF HARDNESS OF CHARACTER.[*]

HARDNESS is a want of minute attention to the feelings of others. It does not proceed from malignity or a carelessness of inflicting pain, but from a want of delicate perception of those little things by which pleasure is conferred or pain excited.

A hard person thinks he has done enough if he does not speak ill of your relations, your children, or your country; and then, with the greatest good-humour and volubility, and with a total inattention to your individual state and position, gallops over a

---

[*] This was written in 1843, when, in the month of July, "he spent a few days at Nuneham, on a visit to his former diocesan, the Archbishop of York. He met there a large and agreeable party; and a discussion arising on hardness of character, my father, at the request of Miss Georgiana Harcourt wrote this definition of it."— *Lady Holland's Memoir,* p. 262.

thousand fine feelings, and leaves in every step the mark of his hoofs upon your heart. Analyze the conversation of a well-bred man who is clear of the besetting sin of hardness; it is a perpetual homage of polite good-nature. He remembers that you are connected with the Church, and he avoids (whatever his opinions may be) the most distant reflections on the Establishment. He knows that you are admired, and he admires you as far as is compatible with good-breeding. He sees that, though young, you are at the head of a great establishment, and he infuses into his manner and conversation that respect which is so pleasing to all who exercise authority. He leaves you in perfect good-humour with yourself, because you perceive how much and how successfully you have been studied.

In the meantime, the gentleman on the other side of you (a highly moral and respectable man) has been crushing little sensibilities, and violating little proprieties, and overlooking little discriminations; and, without violating anything which can be called a *rule*, or committing what can be denominated a *fault*, has displeased and dispirited you, from wanting that fine vision which sees little things, and that delicate touch which handles them, and that fine sympathy which this superior moral organization always bestows.

So great an evil in society is *hardness*, and that want of perception of the minute circumstances which occasion pleasure or pain!

ADVICE TO PARISHIONERS.[*]

IF you begin stealing a little, you will go on from little to much, and soon become a regular thief; and then you will be hanged, or sent over seas to Botany Bay. And give me leave to tell you, transportation is no joke. Up at five in the morning, dressed in

[*] Lady Holland, in her sketches of "Life and Conversation at Combe Florey," introduces this with the following prefatory explanation by Sydney Smith himself: "It is lamentable to see how ignorant the poor are. I do not mean of reading and writing, but about the common affairs of life. They are as helpless as children in all difficulties. Nothing would be so useful as some short and cheap book, to instruct them what to do, to whom to go, and to give them a little advice; I mean mere practical advice. I have begun something of this sort for my parishioners; here it is."

a jacket half blue half yellow, chained on to another person like two dogs, a man standing over you with a great stick, weak porridge for breakfast, bread and water for dinner, boiled beans for supper, straw to lie upon; and all this for thirty years; and then you are hanged there by order of the governor, without judge or jury. All this is very disagreeable, and you had far better avoid it by making a solemn resolution to take nothing which does not belong to you.

Never sit in wet clothes. Off with them as soon as you can: no constitution can stand it. Look at Jackson, who lives next door to the blacksmith; he was the strongest man in the parish. Twenty different times I warned him of his folly in wearing wet clothes. He pulled off his hat and smiled, and was very civil, but clearly seemed to think it all old woman's nonsense. He is now, as you see, bent double with rheumatism, is living upon parish allowance, and scarcely able to crawl from pillar to post.

Off with your hat when you meet a gentleman. What does it cost? Gentlemen notice these things, are offended if the civility is not paid, and pleased if it is; and what harm does it do you? When first I came to this parish, Squire Tempest wanted a postilion. John Barton was a good, civil fellow; and in thinking over the names of the village, the Squire thought of Barton, remembered his constant civility, sent for one of his sons, made him postilion, then coachman, then bailiff, and he now holds a farm under the Squire of £500 per annum. Such things are constantly happening.

I will have no swearing. There is pleasure in a pint of ale, but what pleasure is there in an oath? A swearer is a low, vulgar person. Swearing is fit for a tinker or a razor-grinder, not for an honest labourer in my parish.

I must positively forbid all poaching; it is absolute ruin to yourself and your family. In the end you are sure to be detected —a hare in one pocket and a pheasant in the other. How are you to pay ten pounds? You have not tenpence beforehand in the world. Daniel's breeches are unpaid for; you have a hole in your hat, and want a new one; your wife, an excellent woman, is about to lie in—and you are, all of a sudden, called upon by the justice to pay ten pounds. I shall never forget the sight of poor Cranford, hurried to Taunton jail; a wife and three daughters on their knees to the justice, who was compelled to do his duty, and commit him. The next day, beds, chairs, and clothes, sold, to get the father out of jail. Out of jail he came; but the poor fellow could not bear the sight of his naked cottage, and to see his family pinched with hunger. You know how he ended his days. Was there a dry eye in the churchyard when he was buried? It was a lesson to poachers. It is indeed a desperate and foolish trade. Observe, I am not defending the game-laws, but I am advising you, as long as the game-laws exist, to fear them, and to take care that you and your family are not crushed by them. And then, smart, stout young men hate the gamekeeper, and make it a point of courage and spirit to oppose him. Why? The gamekeeper is paid to protect the game, and he would be a very dishonest man if he did not do his duty. What right have you to bear malice against him for this? After all, the game in justice belongs to the land-owners, who feed it; and not to you, who have no land at all, and can feed nothing.

I don't like that red nose, and those blear eyes, and that stupid, downcast look. You are a drunkard. Another pint, and one pint more; a glass of gin and water, rum and milk, cider and pepper, a glass of peppermint, and all the beastly fluids which drunkards pour down their throats. It is very possible to conquer it, if you will but be resolute. I remember a man in Staffordshire who was drunk every day of his life. Every farthing he earned went to the ale-house. One evening he staggered home, and found at a late hour his wife sitting alone, and drowned in tears. He was a man not deficient in natural affections; he appeared to be struck with the wretchedness of the woman, and with some eagerness asked her why she was crying. "I don't like to tell you, James," she said, "but if I must, I must; and truth is, my children have not touched a morsel of anything this blessed day. As for me, never mind me; I must leave *you* to guess how it has fared with me. But not one morsel of food could I beg or buy for those children that lie on that bed before you; and I am sure, James, it is better for us all we should die, and to my soul I wish we were dead." "Dead!" said James, starting up as if a flash of lightning had darted upon him; "dead, Sally! You and Mary and the two young ones dead? Look ye, my lass, you see what I am now — like a brute. I have wasted your substance — the curse of God is upon me — I am drawing near to the pit of destruction — but there's an end; I feel there's an end. Give me that glass, wife." She gave it him with astonishment and fear. He turned it topsy-turvy; and, striking the table with great violence, and flinging himself on his knees, made a most solemn and affecting vow to God of repentance and sobriety. From that moment to the day of his death he drank no fermented liquor, but confined himself entirely to tea and water.* I never saw so sudden and astonishing a change. His looks became healthy, his cottage neat, his children were clad, his wife was happy; and twenty times the poor man and his wife, with tears in their eyes, have told me the story, and blessed the evening of the fourteenth of March, the day of James's restoration, and have shown me the glass he held in his hand when he made the vow of sobriety. It is all nonsense about not being able to work without ale, and gin, and cider, and fermented liquors. Do lions and cart-horses drink ale? It is mere habit. If you have good nourishing food, you can do very well without ale. Nobody works harder than the Yorkshire people, and for years together there are many Yorkshire labourers who never taste ale. I have no objection, you will observe, to a moderate use of ale, or any other liquor you can *afford* to purchase. My objection is, that you cannot afford it; that every penny you spend at the ale-house comes out of the stomachs of the poor children, and strips off the clothes of the wife.

My dear little Nanny, don't believe a word he says. He merely means to ruin and deceive you. You have a plain answer to give: "When I am axed in the church, and the parson has read the service, and all about it is written down in the book, then I will listen to your nonsense, and not before." Am not I a Justice of the Peace? and have not I had a hundred foolish girls brought before me, who have all come with the same story? "Please, your worship, he is a false man; he promised me marriage over and over again." I confess I have often wished for the power of hanging these rural lovers. But what use is my wishing? All that can be done with the villain is to make him pay half a crown a week, and you are handed over to the poor-house, and to infamy. Will no example teach you? Look to Mary Willet — three years ago the handsomest and best girl in the village, now a slattern in

* A fact. — *Author's Note.*

the poor-house! Look at Harriet Dobson, who trusted in the promises of James Harefield's son, and, after being abandoned by him, went away in despair with a party of soldiers. How can you be such a fool as to surrender your character to the stupid flattery of a ploughboy? If the evening is pleasant, and birds sing, and flowers bloom, is that any reason why you are to forget God's Word, the happiness of your family, and your own character? What is a woman worth without character? A profligate carpenter or a debauched watchmaker may gain business from his skill; but how is a profligate woman to gain her bread? Who will receive *her*?

But this is enough of my parish advice.

LETTER TO MR. SWING.*

THE wool your coat is made of is spun by machinery, and this machinery makes your coat two or three shillings cheaper— perhaps six or seven. Your white hat is made by machinery at half price. The coals you burn are pulled out of the pit by machinery, and are sold to you much cheaper than they could be if they were pulled out by hand. You do not complain of *these* machines, because they d. you good, though they throw many artisans out of work. But what right have you to object to fanning machines, which make bread cheaper to the artisans, and to avail yourselves of *other* machines which make manufactures cheaper to you?

If all machinery were abolished, everything would be so dear that you would be ten times worse off than you now are. Poor people's cloth would get up to a guinea a yard. Hats could not be sold for less than eighteen shillings. Coals would be three shillings per hundred. It would be quite impossible for a poor man to obtain any comfort.

If you begin to object to machinery in farming, you may as well

* Lady Holland, in Memoir, p. 212, says: "There were at this time so many mischievous publications circulating among the people, and threatening letters so frequently sent to my father and other gentlemen in the neighbourhood, that he thought it right to endeavour to counteract them, and published some cheap letters for circulation among the poor, called 'Letters to Swing,' of which this from the 'Taunton Courier' of Wednesday, Dec. 8th, 1830, has been accidentally preserved."

object to a plough, because it employs fewer men than a spade. You may object to a harrow, because it employs fewer men than a rake. You may object even to a spade, because it employs fewer men than fingers and sticks, with which savages scratch the ground in Otaheite. If you expect manufacturers to turn against machinery, look at the consequence. They may succeed, perhaps, in driving machinery out of the town they live in, but they often drive the manufacturer *out* of the town also. He sets up his trade in some distant part of the country, gets new men, and the disciples of Swing are left to starve in the scene of their violence and folly. In this way the lace manufacture travelled in the time of Ludd, Swing's grandfather, from Nottingham to Tiverton. Suppose a free importation of corn to be allowed, as it ought to be, and will be. If you will not allow farmers to grow corn here as cheap as they can, more corn will come from America; for every thrashing-machine that is destroyed, more *Americans* will be employed, *not* more Englishmen.

Swing! Swing! you are a stout fellow, but you are a bad adviser. The law is up, and the Judge is coming. Fifty persons in Kent are already transported, and will see their wives and children no more. Sixty persons will be hanged in Hampshire. There are two hundred for trial in Wiltshire — all scholars of Swing! I am no farmer: I have not a machine bigger than a peppermill. I am a sincere friend to the poor, and I think every man should live by his labour: but it cuts me to the very heart to see honest husbandmen perishing by that worst of all machines, the gallows — under the guidance of that most fatal of all leaders — Swing!"

MAXIMS AND RULES OF LIFE.*

REMEMBER that every person, however low, has *rights* and *feelings*. In all contentions, let peace be rather your object, than triumph: value triumph only as the means of peace.

* "These are extracts from such few portions of his diary as have been preserved, written at various times. These slight, unfinished fragments are not, of course, given as specimens of composition; but they are, I think, of great value, as indicating the occupation and direction of his thoughts, and the wholesome training of his mind, in his leisure hours, and in solitude, of

Remember that your children, your wife, and your servants, have rights and feelings; treat them as you would treat persons who could turn again. Apply these doctrines to the administration of justice as a magistrate. Rank poisons make good medicines; error and misfortune may be turned into wisdom and improvement.

Do not attempt to frighten children and inferiors by passion; it does more harm to your own character than it does good to them; the same thing is better done by firmness and persuasion.

If you desire the common people to treat you as a gentleman, you must conduct yourself as a gentleman should do to them.

When you meet with neglect, let it rouse you to exertion, instead of mortifying your pride. Set about lessening those defects which expose you to neglect, and improve those excellences which command attention and respect.

Against general fears, remember how very precarious life is, take what care you will; how short it is, last as long as it ever does.

Rise early in the morning, not only to avoid self-reproach, but to make the most of the little life that remains; not only to save the hours lost in sleep, but to avoid that languor which is spread over mind and body for the whole of that day in which you have lain late in bed.

Passion gets less and less powerful after every defeat. Husband energy for the real demand which the dangers of life make upon it.

Find fault, when you must find fault, in private, if possible; and some time after the offence, rather than at the time. The blamed are less inclined to resist, when they are blamed without witnesses; both parties are calmer, and the accused party is struck with the forbearance of the accuser, who has seen the fault, and watched for a private and proper time for mentioning it.

My son writes me word he is unhappy at school. This makes

which he seems to have felt the full value for the improvement of his character. In one of his letters to Jeffrey about this period, he says: 'Living a great deal alone (as I now do) will, I believe, correct me of my faults, for a man can do without his own approbation in much society, but he must make great exertions to gain it when he is alone; without it, I am convinced, solitude is not to be endured.'"—*Lady Holland's Memoir*, p. 113.

me unhappy; but, 1st. There is much unhappiness in human life: how can school be exempt? 2dly. Boys are apt to take a particular moment of depression for a general feeling, and they are in fact rarely unhappy; at the moment I write, perhaps he is playing about in the highest spirits. 3dly. When he comes to state his grievance, it will probably have vanished, or be so trifling, that it will yield to argument or expostulation. 4thly. At all events, if it is a real evil which makes him unhappy, I must find out what it is, and proceed to act upon it; but I must wait till I can, either in person or by letter, find out what it is.

Not only is religion calm and tranquil, but it has an extensive atmosphere round it, whose calmness and tranquillity must be preserved, if you would avoid misrepresentation.

Not only study that those with whom you live should habitually respect you, but cultivate such manners as will secure the respect of persons with whom you occasionally converse. Keep up the habit of being respected, and do not attempt to be more amusing and agreeable than is consistent with the preservation of respect.

I am come to the age of seventy; have attained enough reputation to make me somebody: I should not like a vast reputation, it would plague me to death. I hope to care less for the outward world.

Hope.

Don't be too severe upon yourself and your own failings; keep on, don't faint, be energetic to the last.

If you wish to keep mind clear and body healthy, abstain from all fermented liquors.

Fight against sloth, and do all you can to make friends.

If old age is even a state of suffering, it is a state of superior wisdom, in which man avoids all the rash and foolish things he does in his youth, and which make life dangerous and painful.

Death must be distinguished from dying, with which it is often confounded.

Reverence and stand in awe of yourself.

How Nature delights and amuses us by varying even the character of insects; the ill-nature of the wasp, the sluggishness of the drone, the volatility of the butterfly, the slyness of the bug.

Take short views, hope for the best, and trust in God.

MODERN CHANGES.*

"The good of ancient times let others state,
I think it lucky I was born so late."

MR. EDITOR: It is of some importance at what period a man is born. A young man, alive at this period, hardly knows to what improvements of human life he has been introduced: and I would bring before his notice the following eighteen changes which have taken place in England, since I first began to breathe in it the breath of life—a period amounting now to nearly seventy-three years.

Gas was unknown: I groped about the streets of London in all but the utter darkness or a twinkling oil lamp, under the protection of watchmen, in their grand climacteric, and exposed to every species of depredation and insult.

I have been nine hours in sailing from Dover to Calais, before the invention of steam. It took me nine hours to go from Taunton to Bath, before the invention of railroads, and I now go, in six hours, from Taunton to London! In going from Taunton to Bath, I suffered between ten thousand and twelve thousand severe contusions, before stone-breaking Macadam was born.

I paid fifteen pounds, in a single year, for repairs of carriage-springs on the pavement of London; and I now glide, without noise or fracture, on wooden pavements.

I can walk, by the assistance of the police, from one end of London to the other, without molestation; or, if tired, get into a cheap and active cab, instead of those cottages on wheels, which the hackney-coaches were at the beginning of my life.

I had no umbrella! They were little used, and very dear. There were no waterproof hats, and *my* hat has often been reduced by rains into its primitive pulp.

I could not keep my smallclothes in their proper place, for braces were unknown. If I had the gout, there was no colchicum. If I was bilious, there was no calomel. If I was attacked by ague, there was no quinine. There were filthy coffeehouses instead of elegant clubs. Game could not be bought. Quarrels about un-

---

* This is published in Longman's octavo edition of Sydney Smith's works It was written for a London newspaper the year before the author's death.

commuted tithes were endless. The corruption of Parliament, before Reform, infamous.

There were no banks to receive the savings of the poor. The Poor-Laws were gradually sapping the vitals of the country; and whatever miseries I suffered, I had no post to whisk my complaints, for a single penny, to the remotest corners of the empire; and yet, in spite of all these privations, I lived on quietly, and am now ashamed that I was not more discontented, and utterly surprised that all these changes and inventions did not occur two centuries ago.

I forgot to add, that as the basket of stage-coaches, in which luggage was then carried, had no springs, your clothes were rubbed all to pieces; and that, even in the best society, one third of the gentlemen, at least, were always drunk.

PASSAGES FROM PETER PLYMLEY.*

INTRODUCTION.

DEAR ABRAHAM: A worthier and better man than yourself does not exist; but I have always told you, from the time of our boyhood, that you were a bit of a goose. Your parochial affairs are governed with exemplary order and regularity; you are as powerful in the vestry as Mr. Perceval is in the House of Commons — and, I must say, with much more reason; nor do I know any church where the faces and smock-frocks of the congregation are so clean, or their eyes so uniformly directed to the preacher. There is another point upon which I will do you ample justice; and that is, that the eyes so directed toward you are wide open; for the rustic has, in general, good principles, though he cannot control his animal habits; and however loud he may snore, his face is perpetually turned toward the fountain of orthodoxy.

Having done you this act of justice, I shall proceed, according to our ancient intimacy and familiarity, to explain to you my opinions about the Catholics, and to reply to yours.

In the first place, my sweet Abraham, the Pope is not landed, nor are there any curates sent out after him — nor has he been hid at St. Alban's by the Dowager Lady Spencer — nor dined privately at Holland House — nor been seen near Dropmore.† If these fears exist (which I do not believe), they exist only in the mind of the Chancellor of the Exchequer; they emanate from his zeal for the Protestant interest; and though they reflect the high-

---

* " Letters on the Subject of the Catholics, to My Brother Abraham, who lives in the Country." By Peter Plymley.

† The seat of Lord Grenville, who advocated concessions to the Catholics

est honour upon the delicate irritability of his faith, must certainly be considered as more ambiguous proofs of the sanity and vigour of his understanding. By this time, however, the best-informed clergy in the neighbourhood of the metropolis are convinced that the rumour is without foundation; and, though the Pope is probably hovering about our coast in a fishing smack, it is most likely he will fall a prey to the vigilance of our cruisers; and it is certain he has not yet polluted the Protestantism of our soil.

Exactly in the same manner, the story of the wooden gods seized at Charing Cross, by an order from the Foreign Office, turns out to be without the shadow of a foundation; instead of the angels and archangels, mentioned by the informer, nothing was discovered but a wooden image of Lord Mulgrave, going down to Chatham, as a head-peace for the Spanker gun-vessel; it was an exact resemblance of his lordship in his military uniform; and *therefore* as little like a god as can well be imagined.

CATHOLIC AND PROTESTANT PERSECUTIONS.

I FOUND in your letter the usual remarks about fire, fagot, and bloody Mary. Are you aware, my dear priest, that there were as many persons put to death for religious opinions under the mild Elizabeth, as under the bloody Mary? The reign of the former was, to be sure, ten times as long; but I only mention the fact, merely to show you that something depends upon the age in which men live, as well as on their religious opinions. Three hundred years ago, men burned and hanged each other for these opinions. Time has softened Catholic as well as Protestant; they both required it, though each perceives only his own improvement, and is blind to that of the other. We are all the creatures of circumstances. I know not a kinder and better man than yourself; but you (if you had lived in those times) would certainly have roasted your Catholic; and I promise you, if the first exciter of this religious mob had been as powerful then as he is now, you would soon have been elevated to the mitre. I do not go the length of saying that the world has suffered as much from Protestant as from Catholic persecution; far from it; but you should remember the Catholics had all the power, when the idea first started up in the world, that there could be two modes of faith; and that it was much more natural that **they** should attempt to crush this diversity of opinion by great and cruel efforts, than that the Protestants should rage against those who differ from them, when the very basis of their system was complete freedom in all spiritual matters.

THE CHURCH IN DANGER.

THE English, I believe, are as truly religious as any nation in Europe; I know no greater blessing; but it carries with it this evil in its train, that any villain who will bawl out " *The church is in danger!*" may get a place, and a good pension; and that any administration who will do the same thing, may bring a set of men into power who, at a moment of stationary and passive piety, would be hooted by the very boys in the streets. But it is not all religion; it is, in great part, that narrow and exclusive spirit, which delights to keep the common blessings of sun, and air, and freedom, from other human beings. "Your religion has always been degraded; you are in the dust, and I will take care you never rise again. I should enjoy less the possession of an earthly good, by every additional person to whom it was extended." You may not be aware of it yourself, most reverend Abraham, but you deny their freedom to the Catholics upon the same principle that Sarah your wife refuses to give the receipt for a ham or a gooseberry dumpling; she values her receipts, not because they secure to her a certain flavour, but because they remind her that her neighbours want it—a feeling laughable in a priestess, shameful in a priest; venial when it withholds the blessings of a ham, tyrannical and execrable when it narrows the boon of religious freedom.

A GOOD MAN AND BAD MINISTER.

YOU spend a great deal of ink about the character of the present Prime Minister. Grant you all that you write; I say, I fear he will ruin Ireland, and pursue a line of policy destructive to the true interest of his country: and then you tell me he is faithful to Mrs. Perceval, and kind to the Master Percevals! These are, undoubtedly, the first qualifications to be looked to in a time of the most serious public danger; but somehow or another (if public and private virtue must always be incompatible), I should prefer that he destroyed the domestic happiness of Wood or Cockell, owed for the veal of the preceding year, whipped his boys, and saved his country.

SOLDIERS AND THEOLOGY.

WHAT is it the Catholics ask of you?* Do not exclude us from the honours and emoluments of the state, because we worship God in one way, and you worship him in another—in a period of the deepest peace, and the fattest prosperity, this would be a fair request; it should be granted, if Lord Hawkesbury † had reached Paris, if Mr. Canning's interpreter had threatened the Senate in an opening speech, or Mr. Perceval explained to them the improvements he meant to introduce into the Catholic religion; but to deny the Irish this justice now, in the present state of Europe, and in the summer months, just as the season for destroying kingdoms is coming on, is (beloved Abraham), whatever you may think of it, little short of positive insanity.

Here is a frigate attacked by a corsair of immense strength and size, rigging cut, masts in danger of coming by the board, four feet water in the hold, men dropping off very fast; in this dreadful situation how do you think the captain acts (whose name shall be Perceval)? He calls all hands upon deck; talks to them of king, country, glory, sweethearts, gin, French prisons, wooden shoes, old England, and hearts of oak; they give three cheers, rush to their guns, and after a tremendous conflict, succeed in beating off the enemy. Not a syllable of all this; this is not the manner in which the honourable commander goes to work; the first thing he does is to secure twenty or thirty of his prime sailors, who happen to be Catholics, to clap them in irons, and set over them a guard of as many Protestants; having taken this admirable method of defending himself against his infidel opponents, he goes upon deck, reminds the sailors, in a very bitter harangue, that they are of different religions; exhorts the Episcopal gunner not to trust to

---

* A Catholic Naval and Military Service Bill, allowing Catholics to hold commissions in the army and navy, was under discussion in Parliament.

† The "lesser of the two Jenkinsons," soon after (on the death of his father) Lord Liverpool. He was Home Secretary at the date of the Plymley Letters.

the Presbyterian quarter-master; issues positive orders that the Catholics should be fired at upon the first appearance of discontent; rushes through blood and brains, examining his men in the catechism and thirty-nine articles, and positively forbids every one to sponge or ram who has not taken the sacrament according to the Church of England. Was it right to take out a captain made of excellent British stuff, and to put in such a man as this? Is not he more like a parson, or a talking lawyer, than a thorough-bred seaman? And built as she is of heart of oak, and admirably manned, is it possible, with such a captain, to save this ship from going to the bottom?

MR. CANNING AND HIS PARASITES.

NATURE descends down to infinite smallness. Mr. Canning has his parasites; and if you take a large buzzing blue-bottle fly, and look at it in a microscope, you may see twenty or thirty little ugly insects crawling about it, which doubtless think their fly to be the bluest, grandest, merriest, most important animal in the universe, and are convinced the world would be at an end if it ceased to buzz.

SUBSTITUTE THE CLAPHAMITES FOR THE CATHOLICS.

I ADMIT there is a vast luxury in selecting a particular set of Christians, and in worrying them as a boy worries a puppy-dog; it is an amusement in which all the young English are brought up from their earliest days. I like the idea of saying to men who use a different hassock from me, that till they change their hassock, they shall never be colonels, aldermen, or parliament-men. While I am gratifying my personal insolence respecting religious forms, I fondle myself into an idea that I am religious, and that I am doing my duty in the most exemplary (as I certainly am in the most easy) way. But then, my good Abraham, this sport, admirable as it is, is become, with respect to the Catholics, a little dangerous; and if we are not extremely careful in taking the amusement, we shall tumble into the holy water, and be drowned. As it seems necessary to your idea of an established church to have somebody to worry and torment, suppose we were to select for this purpose

William Wilberforce, Esq., and the patent Christians of Clapham.* We shall by this expedient enjoy the same opportunity for cruelty and injustice, without being exposed to the same risks; we will compel them to abjure vital clergymen by a public test, to deny that the said William Wilberforce has any power of working miracles, touching for barrenness or any other infirmity, or that he is endowed with any preternatural gift whatever. We will swear them to the doctrine of good works, compel them to preach common sense, and to hear it; to frequent bishops, deans, and other high churchmen; and to appear (once in the quarter at the least) at some melodrame, opera, pantomime, or other light scenical representation; in short, we will gratify the love of insolence and power; we will enjoy the old orthodox sport of witnessing the impotent anger of men compelled to submit to civil degradation, or to sacrifice their notions of truth to ours. And all this we may do without the slightest risk, because their numbers are (as yet) not very considerable. Cruelty and injustice must, of course, exist; but why connect them with danger? Why torture a bull-dog when you can get a frog or a rabbit? I am sure my proposal will meet with the most universal approbation. Do not be apprehensive of any opposition from ministers. If it is a case of hatred, we are sure that one man will defend it by the Gospel; if it abridges human freedom, we know that another will find precedents for it in the Revolution.

MR. ISAAC HAWKINS BROWN.

Then comes Mr. Isaac Hawkins Brown (the gentleman who danced so badly† at the court of Naples), and asks, if it is not an

* "The Clapham Sect" is the subject of an eloquent article by James Stephen, in the Edinburgh Review for July, 1844. The designation was given to an eminent circle of friends —" men whom the second generation of the Evangelical party acknowledged as their secular chiefs"— who met at the villas at Clapham, in the neighbourhood of London, occupied by Henry Thornton, William Wilberforce, and Granville Sharpe. Thomas Clarkson, Zachary Macaulay (father of the historian), Mr. Stephen (father of the reviewer), Isaac Milner, Dean of Carlisle, and Charles Simeon of Cambridge, were honoured members of the society to which Perceval the minister, "the evangelical Perceval," as Smith styles him, was also, in a measure, attached.

† In the third year of his present majesty, and in the thirtieth of his own

anomaly to educate men in another religion than your own? It certainly is our duty to get rid of error, and above all, of religious error; but this is not to be done *per saltum*, or the measure will miscarry, like the queen. It may be very easy to dance away the royal embryo of a great kingdom; but Mr. Hawkins Brown, must look before he leaps, when his object is to crush an opposite sect in religion; false steps aid the one effect as much as they are fatal to the other; it will require not only the lapse of Mr. Hawkins Brown, but the lapse of centuries, before the absurdities of the Catholic religion are laughed at as much as they deserve to be; but surely, in the meantime, the Catholic religion is better than none; four millions of Catholics are better than four millions of wild beasts; two hundred priests, educated by our own government, are better than the same number educated by the man who means to destroy us.

EXAMPLE OF SCOTLAND.

If the great mass of the people, environed as they are on every side with Jenkinsons, Percevals, Melvilles, and other perils, were to pray for Divine illumination and aid, what more could Providence in its mercy do than send them the example of Scotland? For what a length of years was it attempted to compel the Scotch to change their religion? horse, foot, artillery, and armed prebendaries, were sent out after the Presbyterian parsons and their congregations. The Percevals of those days called for blood; this call is never made in vain, and blood was shed; but, to the astonishment and horror of the Percevals of those days, they could not introduce the Book of Common Prayer, nor prevent that metaphysical people from going to heaven their true way, instead of our true way. With a little oatmeal for food, and a little sulphur for friction, allaying cutaneous irritation with the one hand, and

age, Mr. Isaac Hawkins Brown, then upon his travels, danced one evening at the court of Naples. His dress was a volcano silk with lava buttons. Whether (as the Neapolitan wits said) he had studied dancing under St. Vitus, or whether David, dancing in a linen vest, was his model, is not known; but Mr. Brown danced with such inconceivable alacrity and vigour, that he threw the Queen of Naples into convulsions of laughter, which terminated in a miscarriage, and changed the dynasty of the Neapolitan throne.—*Author's Note* holding his Calvinistical Creed in the other, Sawney ran away to his flinty hills, sung his psalm out of tune his own way, and listened to his sermon of two hours long, amid the rough and imposing melancholy of the tallest thistles. But Sawney brought up his unbreeched offspring in a cordial hatred of his oppressors; and Scotland was as much a part of the weakness of England then as Ireland is at this moment. The true and the only remedy was applied; the Scotch were suffered to worship God after their own tiresome manner, without pain, penalty, and privation. No lightnings descended from heaven; the country was not ruined; the world is not yet come to an end; the dignitaries, who foretold all these consequences, are utterly forgotten; and Scotland has ever since been an increasing source of strength to Great Britain. In the six hundredth year of our empire over Ireland, we are making laws to transport a man, if he is found out of his house after eight o'clock at night. That this is necessary, I know too well; but tell me why it is necessary? It is not necessary in Greece where the Turks are masters.

ENGLAND IN AN INVASION.

You cannot imagine, you say, that England will ever be ruined and conquered; and for no other reason that I can find, but because it seems so very odd it should be ruined and conquered Alas! so reasoned, in their time, the Austrian, Russian, and Prussian Plymleys. But the English are brave; so were all these nations. You might get together a hundred thousand men individually brave; but without generals capable of commanding such a machine, it would be as useless as a first-rate man-of-war manned by Oxford clergyman or Parisian shopkeepers. I do not say this to the disparagement of English officers; they have had no means of acquiring experience; but I do say it to create alarm; for we do not appear, to me, to be half alarmed enough, or to entertain that sense of our danger which leads to the most obvious means of self-defence. As for the spirit of the peasantry, in making a gallant defence behind hedge-rows, and through plate-racks and hen-coops, highly as I think of their bravery, I do not know any nation in Europe so likely to be struck with panic as the English; and this from their total unacquaintance with the science of war. Old wheat and beans blazing for twenty miles round; cart mares shot; sows of Lord Somerville's* breed running wild over the country; the minister of the parish wounded sorely in his hinder parts; Mrs. Plymley in fits; all these scenes of war an Austrian or a Russian has seen three or four times; but it is now three centuries since an English pig has fallen in a fair battle upon English ground, or a farmhouse been rifled, or a clergyman's wife been subjected to any other proposals of love than the connubial endearments of her sleek and orthodox mate. The old edition of Plutarch's Lives, which lies in the corner of your parlour window, has contributed to work you up to the most romantic expectations of our Roman behaviour. You are persuaded that Lord Amherst will defend Kew Bridge like Cocles; that some maid of honour will break away from her captivity, and swim over the Thames; that the Duke of York will burn his capitulating hand; and little Mr. Sturges Bourne† give forty years' purchase for Moulsham Hall, while the French are encamped upon it. I hope we shall witness all this, if the French do come; but, in the meantime, I am so enchanted with the ordinary English behaviour of these invaluable persons, that I earnestly pray no opportunity may be given them for Roman valour, and for those very un-Roman pensions which they would all, of course, take especial care to claim in consequence. But whatever was our conduct, if every ploughman was as great a hero as he who was called from his oxen to save Rome from her enemies, I should still say, that at such a crisis you want the affections of all your subjects in both islands; there is no spirit which you must alienate, no heart you must avert; every man must feel he has a country, and that there is an urgent and pressing cause why he should expose himself to death.

* John, fifteenth Lord Somerville, 1765–1819. He was eminent for his interest in agricultural affairs, and the author of several publications on those subjects. His family residence was in Somersetshire, but he had a seat on the Tweed, near Abbotsford, where he enjoyed the warm friendship of Sir Walter Scott, who called him, his "master in the art of planting." Scott edited the family history, "The Memorie of the Somervilles," of which Lockhart says: "as far as I know, the best of its class in any language."

† There is nothing more objectionable in Plymley's Letters, than the abuse of Mr. Sturges Bourne, who is an honourable, able, and excellent person; but such are the malevolent effects of party spirit.—*Author's Note*. Sturges Bourne, the *protégé* and political friend of Canning, had, at several times, a seat in the cabinet. He died in 1845, at the age of seventy-six.

IDLE FEARS OF POPERY.

As fo the enormous wax candles, and superstitious mummeries, and painted jackets of the Catholic priests, I fear them not. Tell me that the world will return again under the influence of the small-pox; that Lord Castlereagh will hereafter oppose the power of the court; that Lord Howick* and Mr. Grattan will do each of them a mean and dishonourable action; that anybody who has heard Lord Redesdale† speak once will knowingly and willingly hear him again; that Lord Eldon has assented to the fact of two and two making four, without shedding tears, or expressing the smallest doubt or scruple; tell me any other thing absurd or incredible, but, for the love of common sense, let me hear no more of the danger to be apprehended from the general diffusion of Popery. It is too absurd to be reasoned upon; every man feels it is nonsense when he hears it stated, and so does every man while he is stating it.

A RED-HAIR DISQUALIFICATION.

I HAVE often thought, if the *wisdom of our ancestors* had excluded all persons with red hair from the House of Commons, of the throes and convulsions it would occasion to restore them to their natural rights. What mobs and riots would it produce? To what infinite abuse and obloquy would the capillary patriot be exposed? what wormwood would distil from Mr. Perceval, what froth would drop from Mr. Canning; how (I will not say *my*, but *our* Lord Hawkesbury, for he belongs to us all), how our Lord Hawkesbury would work away about the hair of King William and Lord Somers, and the authors of the great and glorious Revolution; how Lord Eldon would appeal to the Deity and his own virtues, and to the hair of his children: some would say that red-haired men were superstitious; some would prove they were atheists; they would be petitioned against as the friends of slavery, and the advocates for revolt; in short, such a corrupter of the heart and the understanding is the spirit

---

* Afterward Earl Grey.
† John Mitford, Lord Redesdale, brother of Mitford the historian of Greece, was Lord-High-Chancellor of Ireland; raised to the Peerage in 1802 He died in 1830, at the age of eighty-one.

of persecution, that these unfortunate people (conspired against by their fellow-subjects of every complexion), if they did not emigrate to countries where hair of another colour was persecuted, would be driven to the falsehood of perukes, or the hypocrisy of the Tricosian fluid.

THE CATHOLICS ASKING FOR MORE—AN APOLOGUE.

WHAT amuses me the most is, to hear of the *indulgences* which the Catholics have received, and their exorbitance in not being satisfied with those indulgences: now if you complain to me that a man is obtrusive and shameless in his requests, and that it is impossible to bring him to reason, I must first of all hear the whole of your conduct toward him; for you may have taken from him so much in the first instance, that, in spite of a long series of restitution, a vast latitude for petition may still remain behind.

There is a village (no matter where) in which the inhabitants, on one day in the year, sit down to a dinner prepared at the common expense; by an extraordinary piece of tyranny (which Lord Hawkesbury would call the wisdom of the village ancestors), the inhabitants of three of the streets, about a hundred years ago, seized upon the inhabitants of the fourth street, bound them hand and foot, laid them upon their backs, and compelled them to look on while the rest were stuffing themselves with beef and beer; the next year, the inhabitants of the persecuted street (though they contributed an equal quota of the expense) were treated precisely in the same manner. The tyranny grew into a custom; and (as the manner of our nature is) it was considered as the most sacred of all duties to keep these poor fellows without their annual dinner; the village was so tenacious of this practice, that nothing could induce them to resign it; every enemy to it was looked upon as a disbeliever in Divine Providence, and any nefarious church-warden who wished to succeed in his election had nothing to do but to represent his antagonist as an abolitionist, in order to frustrate his ambition, endanger his life, and throw the village into a state of the most dreadful commotion. By degrees, however, the obnoxious street grew to be so well-peopled, and its inhabitants so firmly united, that their oppressors, more afraid of injustice, were more disposed to be just. At the next dinner they are unbound, the year after allowed to sit upright, then a bit of bread and a glass of water; till at last, after a long series of concessions, they are emboldened to ask, in pretty plain terms, that they may be allowed to sit down at the bottom of the table, and to fill their bellies as well as the rest. Forthwith a general cry of shame and scandal: "Ten years ago, were you not laid upon your backs? Don't you remember what a great thing you thought it to get a piece of bread? How thankful you were for cheese-parings? Have you forgotten that memorable era, when the lord of the manor interfered to obtain for you a slice of the public pudding? And now, with an audacity only equalled by your ingratitude, you have the impudence to ask for knives and forks, and to request, in terms too plain to be mistaken, that you may sit down to table with the rest, and be indulged even with beef and beer: there are not more than half a dozen dishes which we have reserved for ourselves; the rest has been thrown open to you in the utmost profusion; you have potatoes, and carrots, suet-dumplings, sops in the pan, and delicious toast and water, in incredible quantities. Beef, mutton, lamb, pork, and veal, are ours; and if you were not the most restless and dissatisfied of human beings, you would never think of aspiring to enjoy them."

Is not this, my dainty Abraham, the very nonsense, and the very insult, which is talked to and practised upon the Catholics? You are surprised that men who have tasted of partial justice, should ask for perfect justice; that he who has been robbed of coat and cloak will not be contented with the restitution of one of his garments. He would be a very lazy blockhead if he were content, and I (who, though an inhabitant of the village, have preserved, thank God, some sense of justice) most earnestly counsel these half-fed claimants to persevere in their just demands, till they are admitted to a more complete share of a dinner for which they pay as much as the others; and if they see a little attenuated lawyer squabbling at the head of their opponents, let them desire him to empty his pockets, and to pull out all the pieces of duck, fowl, and pudding, which he has filched from the public feast to carry home to his wife and children.

CANNING.

Dear Abraham: In the correspondence which is passing between us, you are perpetually alluding to the foreign secretary; and in answer to the dangers of Ireland which I am pressing upon your notice, you have nothing to urge but the confidence which you repose in the discretion and sound sense of this gentleman. I can only say, that I have listened to him long and often, with the greatest attention; I have used every exertion in my power to take a fair measure of him, and it appears to me impossible to hear him upon any arduous topic without perceiving that he is eminently deficient in those solid and serious qualities upon which, and upon which alone, the confidence of a great country can properly repose. He sweats and labours, and works for sense; and Mr. Ellis* seems always to think it is coming, but it does not come; the machine can't draw up what is not to be found in the spring; Providence has made him a light, jesting, paragraph-writing man, and that he will remain to his dying day. When he is jocular he is strong, when he is serious he is like Samson in a wig; any ordinary person is a match for him; a song, an ironical letter, a burlesque ode, an attack in the newspaper upon Nicoll's eye, a smart speech of twenty minutes, full of gross misrepresentations and clever turns, excellent language, a spirited manner, lucky quotation, success in provoking dull men, some half information picked up in Pall Mall in the morning; these are your friend's natural weapons; all these things he can do; here I allow him to be truly great; nay, I will be just, and go still farther, if he would confine himself to these things, and consider the *facete* and the playful to be the basis of his character, he would, for that species of man, be universally regarded as a person of a very good understanding; call him a legislator, a reasoner, and the conductor of the affairs of a great nation, and it seems to me as absurd as if a butterfly were to teach bees to make honey. That he is an extraordinary writer of small poetry, and a diner-out of the highest lustre, I do most readily admit. After George Selwyn, and perhaps Tickell,† there has been no such man for this half century.

---

* George Ellis, Editor of the Early English Poets and Metrical Romances, an associate of Canning in the poetry of the Anti-Jacobin, and his warm friend through life.

† Richard Tickell is less known than Selwyn to readers of the present

The foreign secretary is a gentleman, a respectable as well as a highly agreeable man in private life; but you may as well feed me with decayed potatoes as console me for the miseries of Ireland by the resources of his *sense* and his *discretion*. It is only the public situation which this gentleman holds which entitles me or induces me to say so much about him. He is a fly in amber; nobody cares about the fly: the only question is, How the devil did it get there? Nor do I attack him from the love of glory, but from the love of utility, as a burgomaster hunts a rat in a Dutch dyke, for fear it should flood a province.*

VIGOUR IN IRELAND.

I CANNOT describe the horror and disgust which I felt at hearing Mr. Perceval call upon the then ministry for measures of vigour in Ireland. If I lived at Hampstead upon stewed meats and claret; if I walked to church every Sunday before eleven young gentlemen of my own begetting, with their faces washed, and their hair pleasingly combed; if the Almighty had blessed me with every earthly comfort — how awfully would I pause be-

day. He was brother-in-law of Richard Brinsley Sheridan and the grandson of Addison's friend and associate in the Spectator. He was patronized by Lord North, wrote "Anticipation," a parody on the speeches at the opening of Parliament and a satire of the opposition, some other squibs of the kind, and two plays which have given him a niche in the Biographia Dramatica.

* Set a wit to catch a wit! This character of Canning seems scant measure from the mirthful Plymley. The 'fly' was destined for a more precious bit of amber in the national annals. But no one will be content with history or biography in a single political skirmish. Canning's witty effusions were freely scattered in society. The chief monument of them which remains are his brilliant contributions with his old friend of the microcosm, Frere, and others, to the poetry of the Anti-Jacobin. Sydney Smith, by the way, in a passage from the Edinburgh Review (ante p. 160) speaks of Canning as an Irishman. He was of Irish parentage and "accidentally," as he himself said, born in London. His father, however, at the time of his marriage had been a number of years a resident in the British metropolis, where among other occupations he had sustained with some ability the part of a literary adventurer. He wrote poems and a political pamphlet, "On the Connection between Great Britain and her American Colonies," in the "general manner" of which Mr. Robert Bell finds traces of "a curious resemblance to some peculiarities in the style of George Canning the son." — (Life of Canning, chapter i.)

fore I sent forth the flame and the sword over the cabins of the poor, brave, generous, open-hearted peasants of Ireland! How easy it is to shed human blood—how easy it is to persuade ourselves that it is our duty to do so—and that the decision has cost us a severe struggle—how much, in all ages, have wounds and shrieks and tears been the cheap vulgar resources of the rulers of mankind—how difficult and how noble it is to govern in kindness, and to found an empire upon the everlasting basis of justice and affection!—But what do men call vigour? To let loose hussars and to bring up artillery, to govern with lighted matches, and to cut, and push, and prime—I call this, not vigour, but the *sloth of cruelty and ignorance.* The vigour I love consists in finding out wherein subjects are aggrieved, in relieving them, in studying the temper and genius of a people, in consulting their prejudices, in selecting proper persons to lead and manage them, in the laborious, watchful, and difficult task of increasing public happiness by allaying each particular discontent. In this way Hoche pacified La Vendée—and in this way only will Ireland ever be subdued. But this, in the eyes of Mr. Perceval, is imbecility and meanness; houses are not broken open—women are not insulted—the people seem all to be happy; they are not rode over by horses, and cut by whips. Do you call this vigour?—Is this government?

GOD SAVE THE KING.

Do not imagine, by these observations, that I am not loyal, without joining in the common cant of the best of kings, I respect the king most sincerely as a good man. His religion is better than the religion of Mr. Perceval, his old morality very superior to the old morality of Mr. Canning, and I am quite certain he has a safer understanding than both of them put together. Loyalty, within the bounds of reason and moderation, is one of the great instruments of English happiness; but the love of the king may easily become more strong than the love of the kingdom, and we may lose sight of the public welfare in our exaggerated admiration of him who is appointed to reign only for its promotion and support. I detest Jacobinism; and if I am doomed to be a slave at all, I would rather be the slave of a king than a cobler. God save the king, you say, warms your heart like the sound of a trumpet. I cannot make use of so violent a metaphor; but I am delighted to hear it, when it is the cry of genuine affection; I am delighted to hear it, when they hail not only the individual man, but the outward and living sign of all English blessings. These are noble feelings, and the heart of every good man must go with them; but God save the king, in these times, too often means God save my pension and my place, God give my sisters an allowance out of the privy purse—make me clerk of the irons, let me survey the meltings, let me live upon the fruits of other men's industry, and fatten upon the plunder of the public.

MEDICAL STATESMANSHIP.

WHAT is it possible to say to such a man as the gentleman of Hampstead, who really believes it feasible to convert the four million Irish Catholics to the Protestant religion, and considers this as the best remedy for the disturbed state of Ireland? It is not possible to answer such a man with arguments; we must come out against him with beads, and a cowl, and push him into a hermitage. It is really such trash, that it is an abuse of the privilege of reasoning to reply to it. Such a project is well worthy the statesman who would bring the French to reason by keeping them without rhubarb, and exhibit to mankind the awful spectacle of a nation deprived of neutral salts. This is not the dream of a wild apothecary indulging in his own opium; this is not the distempered fancy of a pounder of drugs, delirious from smallness of profits; but it is the sober, deliberate, and systematic scheme of a man to whom the public safety is intrusted, and whose appointment is considered by many as a masterpiece of political sagacity. What a sublime thought, that no purge can now be taken between the Weser and the Garonne; that the bustling pestle is still, the canorous mortar mute, and the bowels of mankind locked up for fourteen degrees of latitude! When, I should be curious to know, were all the powers of crudity and flatulence fully explained to his majesty's ministers? At what period was this great plan of conquest and constipation fully developed? In whose mind was the idea of destroying the pride and the plasters of France first engendered? Without castor oil they might, for some months, to be sure, have carried on a lingering war; but can they do without bark? Will the people live under a government where antimonial powders cannot be procured? Will they bear the loss of mercury? "There's the rub." Depend upon it, the absence of the materia medica will soon bring them to their senses, and the cry of *Bourbon and bolus* burst forth from the Baltic to the Mediterranean.*

* Napier, in his History of the War in the Peninsula (book xiv.) says of Perceval's administration: "Narrow, harsh, factious, and illiberal, in everything relating to public matters, this man's career was one of unmixed evil. His bigotry taught him to oppress Ireland, but his religion did not deter him from passing a law to prevent the introduction of medicines into France during a pestilence." A further discussion of Perceval's "Jesuit's Bark Bill," with citations of contemporary orators and writers — strengthening Smith's attack — will be found among Napier's appendices.

REFORM SPEECHES.

A COUNTRY PROSPEROUS IN SPITE OF POLITICAL EVILS.*

They tell you, gentlemen, that you have grown rich and powerful with these rotten boroughs, and that it would be madness to part with them, or to alter a constitution which had produced such happy effects. There happens, gentlemen, to live near my parsonage, a labouring man of very superior character and understanding to his fellow-labourers; and who has made such good use of that superiority, that he has saved what is (for his station in life) a very considerable sum of money, and if his existence is extended to the common period, he will die rich. It happens, however, that he is (and long has been) troubled with violent stomachic pains, for which he has hitherto obtained no relief, and which really are the bane and torment of his life. Now, if my excellent labourer were to send for a physician, and to consult him respecting this malady, would it not be very singular language if our doctor were to say to him, "My good friend, you surely will not be so rash as to attempt to get rid of these pains in your stomach. Have you not grown rich with these pains in your stomach? have not you risen under them from poverty to prosperity? has not your situation, since you were first attacked, been improving every year? You surely will not be so foolish and so indiscreet as to part with the pains in your stomach?"—Why, what would be the answer of the rustic to this nonsensical monition? "Monster of rhubarb!" he would say, "I am not rich in consequence of the pains in my stomach, but in spite of the pains in my stomach; and I should have been ten times richer, and fifty times happier, if I had never had any pains in my

* From a speech on the Reform Bill, at Taunton.

stomach at all." Gentlemen, these rotten boroughs are your pains in the stomach—and you would have been a much richer and greater people if you had never had them at all. Your wealth and your power have been owing, not to the debased and corrupted parts of the House of Commons, but to the many independent and honourable members whom it has always contained within its walls. If there had been a few more of these very valuable members for close boroughs, we should, I verily believe, have been by this time about as free as Denmark, Sweden, or the Germanized states of Italy.

SPEECH AT TAUNTON.*

Mr. Bailiff, I have spoken so often on this subject, that I am sure both you and the gentlemen here present will be obliged to me for saying but little, and that favour I am as willing to confer as you can be to receive it. I feel most deeply the event which has taken place, because, by putting the two houses of Parliament in collision with each other, it will impede the public business, and diminish the public prosperity. I feel it as a churchman, because I cannot but blush to see so many dignitaries of the church arrayed against the wishes and happiness of the people. I feel it more than all, because I believe it will sow the seeds of deadly hatred between the aristocracy and the great mass of the people. The loss of the bill I do not feel, and for the best of all possible reasons —because I have not the slightest idea that it is lost. I have no more doubt, before the expiration of the winter, that this bill will pass, than I have that the annual tax bills will pass, and greater certainty than this no man can have, for Franklin tells us there are but two things certain in this world—death and taxes. As for the possibility of the House of Lords preventing, ere long, a reform of Parliament, I hold it to be the most absurd notion that ever entered into human imagination. I do not mean to be disrespectful, but the attempt of the lords to stop the progress of reform, reminds me very forcibly of the great storm of Sidmouth, and of the conduct of the excellent Mrs. Partington on that occasion. In the winter of 1824, there set in a great flood upon that town—the tide rose to an incredible height—the waves rushed in

* Reported in the Taunton Courier, Oct. 12, 1831.

upon the houses, and everything was threatened with destruction. In the midst of this sublime and terrible storm, Dame Partington, who lived upon the beach, was seen at the door of her house, with mop and pattens, trundling her mop, squeezing out the sea-water, and vigourously pushing away the Atlantic ocean. The Atlantic was roused. Mrs. Partington's spirit was up; but I need not tell you that the contest was unequal. The Atlantic Ocean beat Mrs. Partington. She was excellent at a slop, or a puddle, but she should not have meddled with a tempest. Gentlemen, be at your ease—be quiet and steady. You will beat Mrs. Partington.*

They tell you, gentlemen, in the debates by which we have been lately occupied, that the bill is not justified by experience. I do not think this true, but if it were true, nations are sometimes compelled to act without experience for their guide, and to trust to their own sagacity for the anticipation of consequences. The instances where this country has been compelled thus to act have been so eminently successful, that I see no cause for fear, even if we were acting in the manner imputed to us by our enemies. What precedents and what experience were there at the Reformation, when the country, with one unanimous effort, pushed out the Pope, and his grasping and ambitious clergy?—What experience, when, at the Revolution, we drove away our ancient race of kings, and

* Did Sydney Smith invent Mrs. Partington? A communication in Notes and Queries (Nov. 16, 1850), may seem to establish Mrs. Partington as a real personage, but the evidence is not conclusive. The writer says, the original Mrs. P. was a respectable old lady, living at Sidmouth, in Devonshire, and her encounter with the ocean, when mop and broom failed, and she was driven to take refuge in the second story of her cottage on the beach, occurred, to the best of his recollection, during an awful storm in November, 1824, when some fifty or sixty ships were lost at Plymouth. He well recollects, he adds, reading in the Devonshire newspapers of the time, an account of Mrs. Partington; but he may have read only Smith's speech, which he wrongly ascribes to Lord Brougham.

Mrs. Partington has acquired additional celebrity by the pleasant sayings in the vein of Mrs. Malaprop, which have been widely scattered over the world, in the newspapers. This peculiar pleasantry, a humourous dislocation of the English language, with grotesque associations of ideas, has had various imitators; but the original American Mrs. Partington owes her graces to Mr. B. P. Shillaber, for several years associated with the *Boston Post*, in which the genuine sayings are recorded. They were collected into a volume in 1854, with the title, "The Life and Sayings of Mrs. Partington, and others of the Family."

chose another family more congenial to our free principles?— And yet to those two events, contrary to experience, and unguided by precedents, we owe all our domestic happiness, and civil and religious freedom — and having got rid of corrupt priests and despotic kings, by our sense and our courage, are we now to be intimidated by the awful danger of extinguishing boroughmongers, and shaking from our necks the ignominious yoke which their baseness has imposed upon it? Go on, they say, as you have done for these hundred years last past. I answer, it is impossible — five hundred people now write and read where one hundred wrote and read fifty years ago. The iniquities and enormities of the borough system are now known to the meanest of the people. You have a different sort of men to deal with — you must change, because the beings whom you govern are changed. After all, and to be short, I must say, that it has always appeared to me to be the most absolute nonsense, that we cannot be a great, or a rich and happy nation, without suffering ourselves to be bought and sold every five years, like a pack of negro-slaves. I hope I am not a very rash man, but I would launch boldly into this experiment without any fear of consequences, and I believe there is not a man here present who would not cheerfully embark with me. As to the enemies of the bill, who pretend to be reformers, I know them, I believe, better than you do, and I earnestly caution you against them. You will have no more of reform than they are compelled to grant — you will have no reform at all, if they can avoid it — you will be hurried into a war to turn your attention from reform. They do not understand you — they will not believe in the improvement you have made — they think the English of the present day are as the English of the times of Queen Anne or George the First. They know no more of the present state of their own country, than of the state of the Esquimaux Indians. Gentlemen, I view the ignorance of the present state of the country with the most serious concern, and I believe they will one day or another waken into conviction with horror and dismay. I will omit no means of rousing them to a sense of their danger; for this object I cheerfully sign the petition proposed by Dr. Kinglake, which I consider to be the wisest and most moderate of the two.

SPEECH ON THE REFORM BILL.

Stick to the Bill—it is your Magna Charta, and your Runnymede. King John made a present to the barons. King William has made a similar present to you. Never mind, common qualities good in common times. If a man does not vote for the Bill, he is unclean—the plague-spot is upon him—push him into the Lazaretto of the last century, with Wetherell and Sadler—purify the air before you approach him—bathe your hands in chloride of lime, if you have been contaminated by his touch.

So far from its being a merely theoretical improvement, I put it to any man, who is himself embarked in a profession, or has sons in the same situation, if the unfair influence of boroughmongers has not perpetually thwarted him in his lawful career of ambition, and professional emolument? "I have been in three general engagements at sea," said an old sailor, "have been twice wounded: I commanded the boats when the French frigate, the Astrolabe, was cut out so gallantly." "Then you are made a post-captain?" "No; I was very near it, but—Lieutenant Thomson cut me out, as I cut out the French frigate; his father is townclerk of the borough, for which Lord F—— is member, and there my chance was finished." In the same manner, all over England, you will find great scholars rotting on curacies—brave captains starving in garrets—profound lawyers decayed and mouldering in the Inns of Court, because the parsons, warriors, and advocates, of boroughmongers, must be crammed to saturation, before there is a morsel of bread for the man who does not sell his votes, and put his country up at auction; and though this is of every-day occurrence, the borough system, we are told, is no practical evil.

Who can bear to walk through a slaughterhouse? blood, garbage, stomachs, entrails, legs, tails, kidneys, horrors—I often walk a mile about to avoid it. What a scene of disgust and horror is an election—the base and infamous traffic of principles—a candidate of high character reduced to such means—the perjury and evasion of agents—the detestable rapacity of voters—the ten days' dominion, of mammon, and Belial. The Bill lessens it—begins the destruction of such practices—affords some chance, and some means of turning public opinion against bribery, and of rendering it infamous.

But the thing I cannot, and will not bear, is this; what right has *this* lord or *that* marquis to buy ten seats in Parliament, in the shape of boroughs, and then to make laws to govern me? And how are these masses of power re-distributed? The eldest son of my lord is just come from Eton—he knows a good deal about Æneas, and Dido, Apollo, and Daphne—and that is all and to this boy, his father gives a six-hundredth part of the power of making laws, as he would give him a horse, or a double-barrelled gun. Then Vellum, the steward, is put in—an admirable man; he has raised the estates, watched the progress of the family road, and canal bills—and Vellum shall help to rule over the people of Israel. A neighbouring country gentleman, Mr. Plumpkin, hunts with my lord—opens him a gate or two, while the hounds are running—dines with my lord—agrees with my lord—wishes he could rival the Southdown sheep of my lord—and upon Plumpkin is conferred a portion of the government. Then there is a distant relation of the same name, in the county militia, with white teeth, who calls up the carriage at the opera, and is always wishing O'Connell was hanged, drawn, and quartered; then a barrister, who has written an article in the Quarterly, and is very likely to speak and refute M'Culloch; and these five people, in whose nomination I have no more agency than I have in the nomination of the tollkeepers of the Bosphorus, are to make laws for me and my family —to put their hands in my purse, and to sway the future destinies of this country; and when the neighbors step in, and beg permission to say a few words before these persons are chosen, there is a universal cry of ruin, confusion, and destruction; we have become a great people under Vellum and Plumpkin—under Vellum and Plumpkin our ships have covered the ocean—under Vellum and Plumpkin our armies have secured the strength of the hills—to turn out Vellum and Plumpkin is not reform, but revolution.

Was there ever such a ministry? Was there ever before a real ministry of the people? Look at the condition of the country when it was placed in their hands: the state of the house when the incoming tenant took possession: windows broken, chimneys on fire, mobs round the house threatening to pull it down, roof tumbling, rain pouring in. It was courage to occupy it; it was a miracle to save it; it will be the glory of glories to enlarge and expand it, and to make it the eternal palace of wise and temperate freedom.

Proper examples have been made among the unhappy and misguided disciples of Swing: a rope has been carried round O'Connell's legs, and a ring inserted in Cobbett's nose. Then the game laws! Was ever conduct so shabby as that of the two or three governments which preceded that of Lord Grey? The cruelties and enormities of this code had been thoroughly exposed; and a general conviction existed of the necessity of a change. Bills were brought in by various gentlemen, containing some trifling alteration in this abominable code, and even these were sacrificed to the tricks and manœuvres of some noble Nimrod, who availed himself of the emptiness of the town in July, and flung out the Bill. Government never stirred a step. The fullness of the prisons, the wretchedness and demoralization of the poor, never came across them. The humane and considerate Peel never once offered to extend his ægis over them. It had nothing to do with the state of party; and some of their double-barrelled voters might be offended. In the meantime, for every ten pheasants which fluttered in the wood, one English peasant was rotting in jail. No sooner is Lord Althorp chancellor of the exchequer, than he turns out of the house a trumpery and (perhaps) an insidious bill for the improvement of the game laws; and in an instant offers the assistance of government for the abolition of the whole code.

Then look at the gigantic Brougham, sworn in at twelve o'clock, and before six, has a bill on the table abolishing the abuses of a court which has been the curse of the people of England for centuries. For twenty-five long years did Lord Eldon sit in that court, surrounded with misery and sorrow, which he never held up a finger to alleviate. The widow and the orphan cried to him as vainly as the town-crier cries when he offers a small reward for a full purse; the bankrupt of the court became the lunatic of the court; estates mouldered away, and mansions fell down; but the fees came in, and all was well. But in an instant the iron mace of Brougham shivered to atoms this house of fraud and of delay; and this is the man who will help to govern you; who bottoms his reputation on doing good to you; who knows, that to reform abuses is the safest basis of fame and the surest instrument of power; who uses the highest gifts of reason, and the most splendid efforts of genius, to rectify those abuses, which all the genius and talent of the profession* have hitherto been employed to justify, and to protect. Look to Brougham, and turn you to that side where he waves his long and lean finger, and mark well that face which nature has marked so forcibly — which dissolves pensions — turns jobbers into honest men — scares away the plunderer of the public — and is a terror to him who doeth evil to the people. But, above all, look to the northern Earl,† victim, before this honest and manly reign, of the spitefulness of the court. You may now, for the first time, learn to trust in the professions of a minister; you are directed by a man who prefers character to place, and who has given such unequivocal proofs of honesty and patriotism, that his image ought to be amongst your household gods, and his name to be lisped by your children; two thousand years hence it will be a legend like the fable of Perseus and Andromeda; Britannia chained to a mountain — two hundred rotten animals menacing her destruction, till a tall Earl, armed with schedule A., and followed by his page Russell, drives them into the deep, and delivers over Britannia in safety to crowds of ten-pound renters, who deafen the air with their acclamations. Forthwith, Latin verses upon this — school exercises — boys whipped, and all the usual absurdities of education. Don't part with an administration composed of Lord Grey and Lord Brougham; and not only these, but look at them all — the mild wisdom of Lansdowne — the genius and extensive knowledge of Holland, in whose bold and honest life there is no varying nor shadow of change — the unexpected and exemplary activity of Lord Melbourne — and the rising parliamentary talents of Stanley. You are ignorant of your best interests, if every vote you can bestow is not given to such a ministry as this.

You will soon find an alteration of behaviour in the upper orders when elections become real. You will find that you are raised to the importance to which you ought to be raised. The merciless ejector, the rural tyrant, will be restrained within the limits of decency and humanity, and will improve their own characters at the same time that they better your condition.

* Lord Lyndhurst is an exception; I firmly believe he had no wish to perpetuate the abuses of the Court of Chancery. — *Author's Note*
† Lord Grey.

It is not the power of aristocracy that will be destroyed by these measures, but the unfair power. If the Duke of Newcastle is kind and obliging to his neighbours, he will probably lead his neighbours; if he is a man of sense, he will lead them more certainly, and to a better purpose. All this is as it should be; but the Duke of Newcastle, at present, by buying certain old houses, could govern his neighbours and legislate for them, even if he had not five grains of understanding, and if he were the most churlish and brutal man under heaven. The present state of things renders unnecessary all those important virtues, which rich and well-born men, under a better system, would exercise for the public good. The Duke of Newcastle (I mention him only as an instance), Lord Exeter will do as well, but either of those noblemen, depending not upon walls, arches, and abutments, for their power—but upon mercy, charity, forbearance, indulgence, and example—would pay this price, and lead the people by their affections; one would be the god of Stamford, and the other of Newark. This union of the great with the many is the real healthy state of a country; such a country is strong to invincibility—and this strength the borough system entirely destroys.

Cant words creep in, and affect quarrels; the changes are rung between revolution and reform; but, first settle whether a wise government ought to attempt the measure—whether anything is wanted—whether less would do—and, having settled this, mere nomenclature becomes of very little consequence. But, after all, if it is revolution, and not reform, it will only induce me to receive an old political toast in a twofold meaning, and with twofold pleasure. When King William and the great and glorious Revolution are given, I shall think not only of escape from bigotry, but exemption from corruption; and I shall thank Providence, which has given us a second King William for the destruction of vice, as the other, of that name, was given us for the conservation of freedom.

All formal political changes, proposed by these very men, it is said, were mild and gentle, compared to this; true, but are you on Saturday night to seize your apothecary by the throat and to say to him, "Subtle compounder, fraudulent posologist, did not you order me a drachm of this medicine on Monday morning, and now you declare that nothing short of an ounce can do me any good?" "True enough," would he of the vials reply, "*but you did not take the drachm on Monday morning*—that makes all the difference, my dear sir; if you had done as I advised you at first, the small quantity of medicine would have sufficed; and instead of being in a night-gown and slippers up-stairs, you would have been walking vigourously in Piccadilly. Do as you please—and die if you please; but don't blame me because you despised my advice, and by your own ignorance and obstinacy have entailed upon yourself tenfold rhubarb and unlimited infusion of senna."

Now see the consequences of having a manly leader, and a manly Cabinet. Suppose they had come out with a little ill-fashioned seven months' reform; what would have been the consequence? The same opposition from the Tories—that would have been quite certain—and not a single Reformer in England satisfied with the measure. You have now a real Reform, and a fair share of power delegated to the people.

The Anti-Reformers cite the increased power of the press—this is the very reason why I want an increased power in the House of Commons. The Times, Herald, Advertiser, Globe, Sun, Courier, and Chronicle, are a heptarchy which governs this country, and governs it because the people are so badly represented. I am perfectly satisfied, that with a fair and honest House of Commons the power of the press would diminish—and that the greatest authority would centre in the highest place.

Is it possible for a gentleman to get into Parliament, at present, without doing things he is utterly ashamed of—without mixing himself up with the lowest and basest of mankind? Hands accustomed to the scented lubricity of soap, are defiled with pitch, and contaminated with filth. Is there not some inherent vice in a Government, which cannot be carried on but with such abominable wickedness, in which no gentleman can mingle without moral degradation, and the practice of crimes, the very imputation of which, on other occasions, he would repel at the hazard of his life?

What signifies a small majority in the House? The miracle is, that there should have been any majority at all; that there was not an immense majority on the other side. It was a very long period before the courts of justice in Jersey could put down smuggling, and why? The judges, counsel, attorneys, crier of the court, grand and petty jurymen, were all smugglers, and the high-sheriff and constables were running goods every moonlight night.

How are you to do without a government? And what other government, if this Bill be ultimately lost, could possibly be found? How could any country defray the ruinous expense of protecting, with troops and constables, the Duke of Wellington and Sir Robert Peel, who literally would not be able to walk from the Horse-Guards to Grosvenor Square, without two or three regiments of foot to screen them from the mob; and in these hollow squares the Hero of Waterloo would have to spend his political life? By the whole exercise of his splendid military talents, by strong batteries, at Boodle's and White's, he might, on nights of great debate, reach the House of Lords; but Sir Robert would, probably, be cut off, and nothing could save Twiss and Lewis.

The great majority of persons returned by the new Boroughs would either be men of high reputation for talents, or persons of fortune known in the neighbourhood; they have property and character to lose. Why are they to plunge into mad revolutionary projects of pillaging the public creditor? It is not the interest of any such man to do it; he would lose more by the destruction of public credit than he would gain by a remission of what he paid for the interest of the public debt. And if it is not the interest of any one to act in this manner, it is not the interest of the mass. How many, also, of these new legislators would there be, who were not themselves creditors of the state? Is it the interest of such men to create a revolution, by destroying the constitutional power of the House of Lords, or of the king? Does there exist in persons of that class, any disposition for such changes? Are not all their feelings, and opinions, and prejudices, on the opposite side? The majority of the new members will be landed gentlemen: their genus is utterly distinct from the revolutionary tribe; they have molar teeth; they are destitute of the carnivorous and incisive jaws of political adventurers.

There will be mistakes at first, as there are in all changes. All young ladies will imagine (as soon as this bill is carried) that they will be instantly married. Schoolboys believe that gerunds and supines will be abolished, and that currant tarts must ultimately come down in price; the corporal and sergeant are sure of double pay; bad poets will expect a demand for their epics; fools will be disappointed, as they always are; reasonable men, who know what to expect, will find that a very serious good has been obtained.

What good to the hewer of wood and the drawer of water? How is he benefited, if Old Sarum is abolished, and Birmingham members created? But if you ask this question of reform, you must ask it of a great number of other great measures. How is he benefited by Catholic emancipation, by the repeal of the Corporation and Test Act, by the Revolution of 1688, by any great political change? by a good government? In the first place, if many are benefited, and the lower orders are not injured, this alone is reason enough for the change. But the hewer of wood and the drawer of water *are* benefited by reform. Reform will produce economy and investigation; there will be fewer jobs, and a less lavish expenditure; wars will not be persevered in for years after the people are tired of them; taxes will be taken off the poor and laid upon the rich: demotic habits will be more common in a country where the rich are forced to court the poor for political power; cruel and oppressive punishments (such as those for night poaching) will be abolished. If you steal a pheasant, you will be punished as you ought to be, but not sent away from your wife and children for seven years. Tobacco will be two pence per pound cheaper. Candles will fall in price. These last results of an improved government will be felt. We do not pretend to abolish poverty, or to prevent wretchedness; but if peace, economy, and justice, are the results of reform, a number of small benefits, or rather of benefits which appear small to us but not to them, will accrue to millions of the people; and the connection between the existence of John Russell, and the reduced price of bread and cheese, will be as clear as it has been the object of his honest, wise, and useful life to make it.

Don't be led away by such nonsense; all things are dearer under a bad government, and cheaper under a good one. The real question they ask you is, What difference can any change of government make to you? They want to keep the bees from buzzing and stinging, in order that they may rob the hive in peace.

Work well! How does it work well, when every human being in doors and out (with the exception of the Duke of Wellington) says it must be made to work better, or it will soon cease to work at all?

It is little short of absolute nonsense to call a government good, which the great mass of Englishmen would before twenty years were elapsed, if reform were denied, rise up and destroy. Of what use have all the cruel laws been of Perceval, Eldon, and Castlereagh, to extinguish reform? Lord John Russell and his abettors, would have been committed to jail twenty years ago for half only of his present reform; and now relays of the people would drag them from London to Edinburgh; at which latter city we are told by Mr. Dundas, that there is no eagerness for reform. Five minutes before Moses struck the rock, this gentleman would have said that there was no eagerness for water.

There are two methods of making alterations; the one is to despise the applicants, to begin with refusing every concession, then to relax to making concessions which are always too late; by offering in 1831 what is then too late, but would have been cheerfully accepted in 1830 — gradually to O'Connellize the country, till at last, after this process has gone on for some time, the alarm becomes too great, and everything is conceded in hurry and confusion. In the meantime, fresh conspiracies have been hatched by the long delay, and no gratitude is expressed for what has been extorted by fear. In this way, peace was concluded with America, and emancipation granted to the Catholics; and in this way the war of complexion will be finished in the West Indies. The other method is, to see at a distance that the thing must be done, and to do it effectually, *and at once;* to take it out of the hands of the common people, and to carry the measure in a manly liberal manner, so as to satisfy the great majority.—The merit of this belongs to the administration of Lord Grey. He is the only minister I know of who has begun a great measure in good time, conceded at the beginning of twenty years what would have been extorted at the end of it, and prevented that folly, violence, and ignorance, which emanate from a long denial and extorted concession of justice to great masses of human beings. I believe the question of reform, or any dangerous agitation of it, is set at rest for thirty or forty years; and this is an eternity in politics.

Boroughs are not the power proceeding from wealth. Many men, who have no boroughs, are infinitely richer than those who have—but it is the artifice of wealth in seizing hold of certain localities. The boroughmonger is like rheumatism, which owes its power not so much to the intensity of the pain as to its peculiar position; a little higher up, or a little lower down, the same pain would be trifling; but it fixes in the joints, and gets into the head-quarters of motion and activity. The boroughmonger knows the importance of arthritic positions; he disdains muscle, gets into the joints, and lords it over the whole machine by felicity of place. Other men are as rich—but those riches are not fixed in the critical spot.

I live a good deal with all ranks and descriptions of people; I am thoroughly convinced that the party of democrats and republicans is very small and contemptible; that the English love their institutions—that they not only love this king (who would not love him?) but the kingly office—that they have no hatred to the aristocracy. I am not afraid of trusting English happiness to English gentlemen. I believe that the half million of new voters will choose much better for the public than the twenty or thirty peers, to whose usurped power they succeed.

If any man doubts the power of reform, let him take these two memorable proofs of its omnipotence. First, but for the declaration against it, I believe the Duke of Wellington might this day have been in office; and, secondly, in the whole course of the debates at county meetings and in Parliament, there are not twenty men who have declared against reform. Some advance an inch, some a foot, some a yard—but nobody stands still—nobody says, We ought to remain just where we were—everybody discovers that he is a reformer, and has long been so—and appears infinitely delighted with this new view of himself. Nobody appears without the cockade—bigger or less—but always the cockade.

An exact and elaborate census is called for—vast information should have been laid upon the table of the house—great time should have been given for deliberation. All these objections, being turned into English, simply mean, that the chances of another year should have been given for defeating the bill. In that time the Poles may be crushed, the Belgians Orangized, Louis Philippe dethroned; war may rage all over Europe—the popular spirit may be diverted to other objects. It is certainly provoking that the ministry foresaw all these possibilities, and determined to model the iron while it was red and glowing.

It is not enough that a political institution works well practically:

it must be defensible; it must be such as will bear discussion, and not excite ridicule and contempt. It might work well for aught I know, if, like the savages of Onelashka, we sent out to catch a king: but who could defend a coronation by chase? who can defend the payment of forty thousand pounds for the three-hundredth part of the power of Parliament, and the re-sale of this power to government for places to the Lord Williams, and Lord Charles's, and others of the Anglophagi? Teach a million of the common people to read—and such a government (work it ever so well) must perish in twenty years. It is impossible to persuade the mass of mankind, that there are not other and better methods of governing a country. It is so complicated, so wicked, such envy and hatred accumulate against the gentlemen who have fixed themselves on the joints, that it cannot fail to perish, and to be driven as it *is* driven from the country, by a general burst of hatred and detestation. I meant, gentlemen, to have spoken for another half-hour, but I am old and tired. Thank me for ending—but, gentlemen, bear with me for another moment; one word more before I end. I am old, but I thank God I have lived to see more than my observations on human nature taught me I had any right to expect. I have lived to see an honest king, in whose word his ministers can trust; who disdains to deceive those men whom he has called to the public service, but makes common cause with them for the common good; and exercises the highest powers of a ruler for the dearest interests of the state. I have lived to see a king with a good heart, who, surrounded by nobles, thinks of common men; who loves the great mass of English people, and wishes to be loved by them; who knows that his real power, as he feels that his happiness, is founded on their affection. I have lived to see a king, who, without pretending to the pomp of superior intellect, has the wisdom to see, that the decayed institutions of human policy require amendment; and who, in spite of clamour, interest, prejudice, and fear, has the manliness to carry these wise changes into immediate execution. Gentlemen, farewell: shout for the king.

LETTERS TO ARCHDEACON SINGLETON.*

BISHOPS AND PATRONAGE.

NEVER dreaming of such sudden revolutions as these, a prebendary brings up his son to the church, and spends a large sum of money in his education, which, perhaps, he can ill afford. His hope is (wicked wretch!) that, according to the established custom of the body to which he (immoral man!) belongs, the chapter will (when his turn arrives), if his son be of fair attainments and good character attend to his nefarious recommendation, and confer the living upon the young man; and in an instant all his hopes are destroyed, and he finds his preferment seized upon, under the plea of public good, by a stronger churchman than himself. I can call this by no other name than that of tyranny and oppression. I know very well that this is not the theory of patronage; but who does better?—do individual patrons?—do colleges who give in succession?—and as for bishops, lives there the man so weak and foolish, so little observant of the past, as to believe (when this tempest of purity and perfection has blown over) that the name of Blomfield will not figure in benefices from which the names of Copleston, Blomberg, Tate, and Smith, have been so virtuously excluded? I have no desire to make odious comparisons between the purity of one set of patrons and another, but they are forced upon me by the injustice of the commissioners. I must either make such comparisons or yield up, without remonstrance, those rights to which I am fairly entitled.

It may be said that the bishops will do better in future; that

* Letters to Archdeacon Singleton on the Ecclesiastical Commission. 1837.

now the *public eye* is upon them, they will be ashamed into a more lofty and anti-nepotic spirit; but, if the argument of past superiority is given up, and the hope of future amendment resorted to, why may we not improve as well as our masters? but the commission say, "These excellent men" (meaning themselves) "have promised to do better, and we have an implicit confidence in their word: we must have the patronage of the cathedrals." In the meantime, we are ready to promise as well as the bishops.

With regard to that common newspaper phrase, *the public eye* —there's nothing (as the bench well know) more wandering and slippery than the *public eye*. In five years hence, the public eye will no more see what description of men are promoted by bishops, than it will see what doctors of law are promoted by the Turkish Ulhema; and at the end of this period (such is the example set by the commission), the *public eye*, turned in every direction, may not be able to see any bishops at all.

In many instances, chapters are better patrons than bishops, because their preferment is not given exclusively to one species of incumbents. I have a diocese now in my private eye which has undergone the following changes. The first of three bishops whom I remember was a man of careless, easy temper, and how patronage went in those early days may be conjectured by the following letters; which are not his, but serve to illustrate a system:

THE BISHOP TO LORD A——

My dear Lord,

I have noticed with great pleasure the behaviour of your lordship's second son, and am most happy to have it in my power to offer to him the living of ＊＊＊. He will find it of considerable value; and there is, I understand a very good house upon it, &c., &c.

This is to confer a living upon a man of real merit out of the family; into which family, apparently sacrificed to the public good, the living is brought back by the second letter:—

THE SAME TO THE SAME, A YEAR AFTER.

My dear Lord,

Will you excuse the Liberty I take in soliciting promotion for my grandson? He is an officer of great skill and gallantry, and can bring the most ample testimonials from some of the best men in the profession: the Arethusa frigate is, I understand, about to be commissioned; and if, &c., &c.

Now I am not saying that hundreds of prebendaries have not committed such enormities and stupendous rimes as this (a declaration which will fill the whig cabinet with horror); all that I mean to contend for is, that such is the practice of bishops quite as much as it is of inferior patrons.

The second bishop was a decided enemy of Calvinistical doctrines, and no clergyman so tainted had the slightest chance of preferment in his diocese.

The third bishop could endure no man whose principles were not strictly Calvinistic, and who did not give to the articles that kind of interpretation. Now here were a great mass of clergy naturally alive to the emoluments of their profession, and not knowing which way to look or stir, because they depended so entirely upon the will of one person. Not otherwise is it with a very whig bishop, or a very tory bishop; but the worst case is that of a superannuated bishop; here the preferment is given away, and must be given away, by wives and daughters, or by sons, or by butlers, perhaps, and valets, and the poor dying patron's paralytic hand is guided to the signature of papers, the contents of which he is utterly unable to comprehend. In all such cases as these, the superiority of bishops as patrons will not assist that violence which the commissioners have committed upon the patronage of cathedrals.

ADVICE TO BISHOPS.

There is a practice among some bishops, which may as well be mentioned here as anywhere else, but which, I think, cannot be too severely reprobated. They send for a clergyman, and insist upon his giving evidence respecting the character and conduct of his neighbour. Does he hunt? Does he shoot? Is he in debt? Is he temperate? Does he attend to his parish? &c., &c. Now, what is this, but to destroy for all clergymen the very elements of social life — to put an end to all confidence between man and man — and to disseminate among gentlemen, who are bound to live in concord, every feeling of resentment, hatred, and suspicion? But the very essence of tyranny is to act as if the finer feelings, like the finer dishes, were delicacies only for the rich and great, and that little people have no taste for them, and no right to them. A good and honest bishop (I thank God there are many who deserve that character!) ought to suspect himself, and carefully to watch his own heart. He is all of a sudden elevated from being a tutor, dining at an early hour with his pupil (and occasionally, it is believed, on cold meat), to be a spiritual lord; he is dressed in a magnificent dress, decorated with a title, flattered by chaplains, and surrounded by little people looking up for the things which he has to give away; and this often happens to a man who has had no opportunities of seeing the world, whose parents were in very humble life, and who has given up all his thoughts to the Frogs of Aristophanes and the Targum of Onkelos. How is it possible that such a man should not lose his head? that he should not swell? that he should not be guilty of a thousand follies, and worry and tease to death (before he recovers his common sense) a hundred men as good, and as wise, and as able as himself.

THE DUTCH CHRONICLE OF DORT.

I MET, the other day, in an old Dutch chronicle, with a passage so apposite to this subject, that though it is somewhat too light for the occasion, I cannot abstain from quoting it. There was a great meeting of all the clergy at Dordrecht, and the chronicler thus describes it, which I give in the language of the translation: "And there was great store of bishops in the town, in their robes goodly to behold, and all the great men of the state were there, and folks poured in in boats on the Meuse, the Merve, the Rhine, and the Linge, coming from the Isle of Beverlandt, and Isselmond, and from all quarters in the Bailiwick of Dort; Arminians and Gomarists, with the friends of John Barneveldt and of Hugh Grote. And before my lords the bishops, Simon of Gloucester, who was a bishop in those parts, disputed with Vorstius, and Leoline the Monk, and many texts of Scripture were bandied to and fro; and when this was done, and many propositions made, and it waxed toward twelve of the clock, my lords the bishops prepared to set them down to a fair repast, in which was great store of good things, — and among the rest a roasted peacock, having, in lieu of a tail, the arms and banners of the archbishop, which was a goodly sight to all who favoured the church — and then the archbishop would say a grace, as was seemly to do, he being a very holy man; but ere he had finished, a great mob of townspeople and folks from the country, who were gathered under the window, cried out, *Bread! bread!* for there was a great famine, and wheat had risen to three

times the ordinary price of the *sleich;** and when they had done
crying *Bread! bread!* they called out *No bishops!*—and began
to cast up stones at the windows. Whereat my lords the bishops
were in a great fright, and cast their dinner out of the window to
appease the mob, and so the men of that town were well pleased,
and did devour the meats with great appetite; and then you might
have seen my lords standing with empty plates, and looking wistfully at each other, till Simon of Gloucester, he who disputed with
Leoline the Monk, stood up among them and said, '*Good, my lords,
is it your pleasure to stand here fasting, and that those who count
lower in the church than you do, should feast and fluster? Let us
order to us the dinner of the deans and canons, which is making
ready for them in the chamber below.*' And this speech of Simon
of Gloucester pleased the bishops much; so that they sent for the
host, one William of Ypres, and told him it was for the public
good, and he, much fearing the bishops, brought them the dinner
of the deans and canons; and so the deans and canons went away
without dinner, and were pelted by the men of the town, because
they had not put any meat out of the window like the bishops; and
when the count came to hear of it, he said it was a pleasant conceit, *and that the bishops were right cunning men, and had ding'd
the canons well.*"

YOUNG CRUMPET'S ASCENT TO ST. PAUL'S.

I AM surprised it does not strike the mountaineers how very
much the great emoluments of the church are flung open to the
lowest ranks of the community. Butchers, bakers, publicans,
schoolmasters, are perpetually seeing their children elevated to the
mitre. Let a respectable baker drive through the city from the
west end of the town, and let him cast an eye on the battlements
of Northumberland House, has his little muffin-faced son the smallest chance of getting in among the Percies, enjoying a share of
their luxury and splendour, and of chasing the deer with hound
and horn upon the Cheviot Hills? But let him drive his alumsteeped loaves a little farther, till he reaches St. Paul's Church-

---

* A measure in the bailiwick of Dort, containing two gallons one pint
English dry measure.—*Author's Note.* The whole passage from the Chronicle, of course, a pleasant invention.

yard, and all his thoughts are changed when he sees that beautiful fabric; it is not impossible that his little penny roll may be introduced into that splendid oven. Young Crumpet is sent to school—takes to his books—spends the best years of his life, as all eminent Englishmen do, in making Latin verses—knows that the *crum* in crumpet is long, and the *pet* short—goes to the University—gets a prize for an Essay on the Dispersion of the Jews—takes orders—becomes a bishop's chaplain—has a young nobleman for his pupil—publishes a useless classic, and a serious call to the unconverted—and then goes through the Elysian transitions of prebendary, dean, prelate, and the long train of purple, profit, and power.

LORD MELBOURNE.

VISCOUNT MELBOURNE declared himself quite satisfied with the church as it is; but if the public had any desire to alter it, they might do as they pleased. He might have said the same thing of the monarchy, or of any other of our institutions; and there is in the declaration a permissiveness and good humour which, in public men, have seldom been exceeded. Carelessness, however, is but a poor imitation of genius, and the formation of a wise and well-reflected plan of reform conduces more to the lasting fame of a minister than that affected contempt of duty which every man sees to be mere vanity, and a vanity of no very high description.

But if the truth must be told, our Viscount is somewhat of an impostor. Everything about him seems to betoken careless desolation; any one would suppose from his manner that he was playing at chuck-farthing with human happiness; that he was always on the heel of pastime; that he would giggle away the great charter, and decide by the method of tee-totum whether my lords the bishops should or should not retain their seats in the House of Lords. All this is the mere vanity of surprising, and making us believe that he can play with kingdoms as other men can with nine-pins. Instead of this lofty nebulo, this miracle of moral and intellectual felicities, he is nothing more than a sensible, honest man, who means to do his duty to the sovereign and to the country; instead of being the ignorant man he pretends to be, before he meets the deputation of tallow-chandlers in the morning, he sits up half the night talking with Thomas Young about melting and skimming, and then, though he has acquired knowledge enough to work off a whole vat of prime Leicester tallow, he pretends next morning not to know the difference between a dip and a mould. In the same way, when he has been employed in reading acts of Parliament, he would persuade you that he has been reading *Cleghorn on the Beatitudes*, or *Pickler on the Nine Difficult Points*. Neither can I allow to this minister (however he may be irritated by the denial) the extreme merit of indifference to the consequences of his measures. I believe him to be conscientiously alive to the good or evil that he is doing, and that his caution has more than once arrested the gigantic projects of the Lycurgus of the Lower House. I am sorry to hurt any man's feelings, and to brush away the magnificent fabric of levity and gayety he has reared; but I accuse our minister of honesty and diligence; I deny that he is careless or rash: he is nothing more than a man of good understanding, and good principle, disguised in the eternal and somewhat wearisome affectation of a political roué.

RUSSELL AND THE BISHOPS — AN APOLOGUE.

THIS is very good episcopal reasoning; but is it true? The bishops and commissioners wanted a fund to endow small livings; they did not touch a farthing of their own incomes, only distributed them a little more equally; and proceeded lustily at once to confiscate cathedral property. But why was it necessary, if the fund for small livings was such a paramount consideration, that the future archbishops of Canterbury should be left with two palaces, and £15,000 per annum? Why is every future bishop of London to have a palace in Fulham, a house in St. James's Square, and £10,000 a-year? Could not all the episcopal functions be carried on well and effectually with the half of these incomes? Is it necessary that the Archbishop of Canterbury should give feasts to aristocratic London; and that the domestics of the prelacy should stand with swords and bag-wigs round pig, and turkey, and venison, to defend, as it were, the orthodox gastronome from the fierce Unitarian, the fell Baptist, and all the famished children of dissent? I don't object to all this; because I am sure that the method of **prizes and blanks is the best method** of supporting a church, which must be considered as very slenderly endowed, if the whole were equally divided among the parishes; but if my opinion were different—if I thought the important improvement was to equalize preferment in the English church—that such a measure was not the one thing foolish, but the one thing needful—I should take care, as a mitred commissioner, to reduce my own species of preferment to the narrowest limits, before I proceeded to confiscate the property of any other grade of the church. I could not, as a conscientious man, leave the Archbishop of Canterbury with £15,000 a-year, and make a fund by annihilating residentiaries at Bristol of £500. This comes of calling a meeting of one species of cattle only. The horned cattle say—" If you want any meat, kill the sheep; don't meddle with us, there is no beef to spare." They said this, however, to the lion; and the cunning animal, after he had gained all the information necessary for the destruction of the muttons, and learned how well and widely they pastured, and how they could be most conveniently eaten up, turns round and informs the cattle, who took him for their best and tenderest friend, that he means to eat them up also. Frequently did Lord John meet the destroying bishops; much did he commend their daily heap of ruins; sweetly did they smile on each other, and much charming talk was there of meteorology and catarrh, and the particular cathedral they were pulling down at each period;* till one fine day, the Home Secretary, with a voice more bland, and a look more ardently affectionate, than that which the masculine mouse bestows on his nibbling female, informed them that the government meant to take all the church property into their own hands, to pay the rates out of it, and deliver the residue to the rightful possessors. Such an effect, they say, was never before produced by a *coup de théâtre*. The commission was separated in an instant: London clinched his fist; Canterbury was hurried out by his chaplains, and put into a warm bed; a solemn vacancy spread itself over the face of Gloucester; Lincoln was taken out in strong hysterics. What a noble scene Serjeant Talfourd would have made of this! Why are such talents wasted on *Ion* and the *Athenian Captive*?

* " What cathedral are we pulling down to-day?" was the standing question at the Commission.

PAYING THE BISHOPS.

There is some safety in dignity. A church is in danger when it is degraded. It costs mankind much less to destroy it when an institution is associated with mean, and not with elevated ideas. I should like to see the subject in the hands of H. B. I would entitle the print:—

"The Bishop's Saturday Night; or, Lord John Russell at the Pay-Table."

The bishops should be standing before the pay-table, and receiving their weekly allowance; Lord John and Spring Rice counting, ringing, and biting the sovereigns, and the Bishop of Exeter insisting that the chancellor of the exchequer has given him one which was not weight. Viscount Melbourne, in high chuckle, should be standing, with his hat on, and his back to the fire, delighted with the contest; and the deans and canons should be in the background, waiting till their turn came, and the bishops were paid; and among them a canon, of large composition, urging them on not to give way too much to the bench. Perhaps I should add the President of the Board of Trade, recommending the truck principle to the bishops, and offering to pay them in hassocks, cassocks, aprons, shovel-hats, sermon-cases, and such like ecclesiastical gear.

But the madness and folly of such a measure is in the revolutionary feeling which it excites. A government taking into its hands such an immense value of property! What a lesson of violence and change to the mass of mankind! Do you want to accustom Englishmen to lose all confidence in the permanence of their institutions—to inure them to great acts of plunder—and to draw forth all the latent villanies of human nature? The whig leaders are honest men, and cannot mean this; but these foolish and inconsistent measures are the horn-book and infantile lessons of revolution; and remember, it requires no great time to teach mankind to rob and murder on a great scale.

A FOOLOMETER.

I am astonished that these ministers neglect the common precaution of a foolometer,* with which no public man should be un-

* Mr. Fox very often used to say, "I wonder what Lord B. will think of this." Lord B. happened to be a very stupid person, and the curiosity of

provided; I mean, the acquaintance and society of three or four regular British fools as a test of public opinion. Every cabinet-minister should judge of all his measures by his foolometer, as a navigator crowds or shortens sail by the barometer in his cabin. I have a very valuable instrument of that kind myself, which I have used for many years; and I would be bound to predict, with the utmost nicety, by the help of this machine, the precise effect which any measure would produce upon public opinion. Certainly, I never saw anything so decided as the effects produced upon my machine by the rate bill. No man who had been accustomed in the smallest degree to handle philosophical instruments could have doubted of the storm which was coming on, or of the thoroughly un-English scheme in which the ministry had so rashly engaged themselves.

INEQUALITIES OF THE CHURCH — CURATES.

I HAVE no manner of doubt, that the immediate effect of passing the dean and chapter bill will be, that a great number of fathers and uncles, judging, and properly judging, that the church is a very altered and deteriorated profession, will turn the industry and capital of their *élèves* into another channel. My friend, Robert Eden, says "this is of the earth earthy:" be it so; I cannot help it, I paint mankind as I find them, and am not answerable for their defects. When an argument, taken from real life, and the actual condition of the world, is brought among the shadowy discussions of ecclesiastics, it always occasion terror and dismay; it is like Æneas stepping into Charon's boat, which carried only ghosts and spirits.

"Gemuit sub pondere cymba
Sutilis."

The whole plan of the Bishop of London is a ptochogony—a generation of beggars. He purposes, out of the spoils of the cathedral, to create a thousand livings, and to give to the thou-

---

Mr. Fox's friends was naturally excited to know why he attached such importance to the opinion of such an ordinary commonplace person. "His opinion," said Mr. Fox, "is of much more importance than you are aware of. He is an exact representative of all commonplace English prejudices, and what Lord B. thinks of any measure, the great majority of English people will think of it." It would be a good thing if every cabinet of philosophers had a Lord B. among them.—*Author's Note.*

sand clergymen £130 per annum each; a Christian bishop proposing, in cold blood, to create a thousand livings of £130 per annum each;—to call into existence a thousand of the most unhappy men on the face of the earth—the sons of the poor, without hope, without the assistance of private fortune, chained to the soil, ashamed to live with their inferiors, unfit for the society of the better classes, and dragging about the English curse of poverty, without the smallest hope that they can ever shake it off. At present, such livings are filled by young men who have better hopes—who have reason to expect good property—who look forward to a college or a family living—who are the sons of men of some substance, and hope so to pass on to something better—who exist under the delusion of being hereafter deans and prebendaries—who are paid once by money, and three times by hope. Will the Bishop of London promise to the progeny of any of these thousand victims of the *holy innovation* that, if they behave well, one of them shall have his butler's place? another take care of the cedars and hyssops of his garden? Will he take their daughters for his nurserymaids? and may some of the sons of these "labourers of the vineyard" hope one day to ride the leaders from St. James's to Fulham? Here is hope—here is room for ambition—a field for genius, and a ray of amelioration! If these beautiful feelings of compassion are throbbing under the cassock of the bishop, he ought, in common justice to himself, to make them known.

If it were a scheme for giving ease and independence to any large bodies of clergymen, it might be listened to; but the revenues of the English church are such as to render this wholly and entirely out of the question. If you place a man in a village in the country, require that he should be of good manners and well educated, that his habits and appearance should be above those of the farmers to whom he preaches, if he has nothing else to expect (as would be the case in a church of equal division); and if, upon his village income, he is to support a wife and educate a family, without any power of making himself known in a remote and solitary situation, such a person ought to receive £500 per annum, and be furnished with a house. There are about 10,700 parishes in England and Wales, whose average income is £285 per annum. Now, to provide these incumbents with decent houses, to keep them in repair, and to raise the income of the incumbent to £500 per annum, would require (if all the incomes of the bishops, deans and chapters of separate dignitaries, of sinecure rectories, were confiscated, and if the excess of all the livings in England above £500 per annum were added to them) a sum of two millions and a half in addition to the present income of the whole church; and no power on earth could persuade the present Parliament of Great Britain to grant a single shilling for that purpose. Now, is it possible to pay such a church upon any other principle than that of unequal division? The proposed pillage of the cathedral and college churches (omitting all consideration of the separate estate of dignitaries) would amount, divided among all the benefices of England to about £5 12s. 6½d. per man: and this, which would not stop an hiatus in a cassock, and would drive out of the parochial church ten times as much as it brought into it, is the panacea for pauperism recommended by her majesty's commissioners.

But if this plan were to drive men of capital out of the church, and to pauperize the English clergy, where would the harm be? Could not all the duties of religion be performed as well by poor clergymen as by men of good substance? My great and serious apprehension is, that such would not be the case. There would be the greatest risk that your clergy would be fanatical, and ignorant; that their habits would be low and mean, and that they would be despised.

Then a picture is drawn of a clergyman with £130 per annum, who combines all moral, physical, and intellectual advantages; a learned man, dedicating himself intensely to the care of his parish —of charming manners and dignified deportment—six feet two inches high, beautifully proportioned, with a magnificent countenance expressive of all the cardinal virtues and the Ten Commandments—and it is asked, with an air of triumph, if such a man as this will fall into contempt on account of his poverty? But substitute for him an average, ordinary, uninteresting minister; obese, dumpy, neither ill-natured nor good-natured; neither learned nor ignorant, striding over the stiles to church, with a second-rate wife—dusty and deliquescent—and four parochial children, full of catechism and bread and butter; or let him be seen in one of those Shem-Ham-and-Japhet buggies, made on Mount Ararat soon after the subsidence of the waters, driving in the High Street of Edmonton;—among all his pecuniary, saponaceous, oleaginous parishioners. Can any man of common sense say that all these outward circumstances of the ministers of religion have no bearing on religion itself? *

REPLY TO THE BISHOP OF GLOUCESTER.

You must have read an attack upon me by the Bishop of Gloucester,† in the course of which he says that I have not been appointed to my situation as canon of St. Paul's for my piety and learning, but because I am a scoffer and a jester. Is not this rather strong for a bishop, and does it not appear to you, Mr. Archdeacon, as rather too close an imitation of that language which is used in the apostolic occupation of trafficking in fish? Whether I have been appointed for my piety or not, must depend upon what this poor man means by piety. He means by that word, of course, a defence of all the tyrannical and oppressive abuses of the church which have been swept away within the last fifteen or twenty years of my life; the corporation and test acts; the penal laws against the Catholics; the compulsory marriages of dissenters, and all those disabling and disqualifying laws which were the disgrace of our church, and which he has always looked up to as the consummation of human wisdom. If piety consisted in the defence of these — if it was impious to struggle for their abrogation, I have, indeed, led an ungodly life.

There is nothing pompous gentlemen are so much afraid of as a little humour. It is like the objection of certain cephalic animalculæ to the use of small-tooth combs — " Finger and thumb, precipitate powder, or anything else you please; but for Heaven's

---

* Compare Smith's picture of A Curate, in his article "Persecuting Bishops" (Ed. Rev. Nov. 1822):—

"A curate—there is something which excites compassion in the very name of a curate !!! How any man of purple, palaces, and preferment, can let himself loose against this poor workman of God, we are at a loss to conceive —a learned man in a hovel, with sermons and saucepans, lexicons and bacon, Hebrew books and ragged children — good and patient — a comforter and a preacher—the first and purest pauper in the hamlet, and yet showing, that, in the midst of his worldly misery, he has the heart of a gentleman and the spirit of a Christian, and the kindness of a pastor."

† James Henry Monk, appointed Bishop of Gloucester in 1830. He has published various sermons and charges, an edition of the Alcestis of Euripides, and a life of Richard Bentley.

sake no small-tooth combs!" After all, I believe Bishop Monk has been the cause of much more laughter than ever I have been; I cannot account for it, but I never see him enter a room without exciting a smile on every countenance within it.

Dr. Monk is furious at my attacking the heads of the church: but how can I help it? If the heads of the church are at the head of the mob, if I find the best of men doing that which has in all times drawn upon the worst enemies of the human race the bitterest curses of history, am I to stop because the motives of these men are pure, and their lives blameless? I wish I could find a blot in their lives, or a vice in their motives. The whole power of the motion is in the character of the movers; feeble friends, false friends, and foolish friends, all cease to look into the measure, and say, "Would such a measure have been recommended by such men as the prelates of Canterbury and London, if it were not for the public advantage?" And in this way the great good of a religious establishment, now rendered moderate and compatible with all men's liberties and rights, is sacrificed to names; and the church destroyed from good breeding and etiquette! the real truth is, that Canterbury and London have been frightened—they have overlooked the effect of time and delay—they have been betrayed into a fearful and ruinous mistake. Painful as it is to teach men who ought to teach us, the legislature ought, while there is yet time, to awake and read them this lesson.

It is dangerous for a prelate to write; and whoever does it ought to be a very wise one. He has speculated why I was made a canon of St. Paul's. Suppose I were to follow his example, and, going through the bench of bishops, were to ask for what reason each man had been made a bishop; suppose I were to go into the county of Gloucester, &c., &c., &c.!!!!!

I was afraid the bishop would attribute my promotion to the Edinburgh Review; but upon the subject of promotion by reviews, he preserves an impenetrable silence. If my excellent patron, Earl Grey, had any reasons of this kind, he may at least be sure that the reviews commonly attributed to me, were really written by me. I should have considered myself as the lowest of created beings, to have disguised myself in another man's wit and sense, and to have received a reward to which I was not entitled.*

* I understand that the bishop bursts into tears every now and then, and

I presume that what has drawn upon me the indignation of this prelate, is the observations I have, from time to time, made on the conduct of the Commissioners, of which he positively asserts himself to have been a member; but whether he was, or was not, a member, I utterly acquit him of all possible blame, and of every species of imputation which may attach to the conduct of the Commission In using that word, I have always meant the Archbishop of Canterbury, the Bishop of London, and Lord John Russell; and have, honestly speaking, given no more heed to the Bishop of Gloucester, than if he had been sitting in a commission of Bonzes in the Court of Pekin.

To read, however, his Lordship a lesson of good manners, I had proposed for him a chastisement which would have been echoed from the *Seagrave* who banqueteth in the Castle to the idiot who spitteth over the bridge at Gloucester; but the following appeal struck my eye, and stopped my pen: "Since that time my inadequate qualifications have sustained an appalling diminution by the affection of my eyes, which has impaired my vision, and the progress of which threatens to consign me to darkness; I beg the benefit of your prayers to the Father of all mercies, that he will restore to me the better use of the visual organs, to be employed on his service; or that he will inwardly illumine the intellectual vision, with a particle of that divine ray, which his Holy Spirit can alone impart."

It might have been better taste, perhaps, if a mitred invalid, in describing his bodily infirmities before a church full of clergymen, whose prayers he asked, had been a little more sparing in the abuse of his enemies; but a good deal must be forgiven to the sick. I wish that every Christian was as well aware as this poor bishop of what he needed from Divine assistance; and in his supplication for the restoration of his sight, and the improvement of his understanding, I most fervently and cordially join.

says that I have set him the name of Simon [ante. p. 333], and that all the bishops now call him Simon. Simon of Gloucester, however, after all, is a real writer, and how could I know that Dr. Monk's name was Simon? When tutor in Lord Carrington's family, he was called by the endearing, though somewhat unmajestic name of *Dick;* and if I had thought about his name at all, I should have called him Richard of Gloucester.—*Author's Note.*

LETTERS ON RAILWAYS.

"LOCKING IN" ON RAILWAYS.

To the Editor of the Morning Chronicle:—

SIR: It falls to my lot to travel frequently on the Great Western Railway, and I request permission, through the medium of your able and honest journal, to make a complaint against the directors of that company. It is the custom on that railway to lock the passengers in on both sides—a custom which, in spite of the dreadful example at Paris, I have every reason to believe they mean to continue without any relaxation.

In the course of a long life I have no recollection of any accident so shocking as that on the Paris railway[*]—a massacre so sudden, so full of torment—death at the moment of pleasure—death aggravated by all the amazement, fear, and pain, which can be condensed into the last moments of existence.

Who can say that the same scene may not be acted over again on the Great Western Railroad?—that in the midst of their tunnel of three miles length, the same scene of slaughter and combustion may not scatter dismay and alarm over the whole country?

It seems to me perfectly monstrous that a board of ten or twelve monopolists can read such a description, and say to the public, "You must run your chance of being burnt or mutilated. We

---

[*] The accident in May, 1842, on the Versailles line, near Meudon. By the breaking of the axle of the first engine, the other engine and cars attached were forced forward and set fire to. In consequence of keeping the doors of the cars locked, more than a hundred persons were burnt alive, without possibility of escape

have arranged our plan upon the locking-in system, and we shall not incur the risk and expense of changing it."

The plea is, that rash or drunken people will attempt to get out of the carriages which are not locked, and that this measure really originates from attention to the safety of the public; so that the lives of two hundred persons who are not drunk, and are not rash, are to be endangered for the half-yearly preservation of some idiot, upon whose body the coroner is to sit, and over whom the sudden-death man is to deliver his sermon against the directors.

The very fact of locking the doors will be a frequent source of accidents. Mankind, whatever the directors may think of that process, are impatient of combustion. The Paris accident will never be forgotten. The passengers will attempt to escape through the windows, and ten times more of mischief will be done than if they had been left to escape by the doors in the usual manner.

It is not only the locking of the doors which is to be deprecated; but the effects which it has upon the imagination. Women, old people, and the sick, are all forced to travel by the railroad; and for two hundred miles they live under the recollection, not only of impending danger, but under the knowledge that escape is impossible — a journey comes to be contemplated with horror. Men cannot persuade the females of their families to travel by the railroad; it is inseparably connected with abominable tyranny and perilous imprisonment.

Why does the necessity of locking both doors exist only on the Great Western? Why is one of the doors left open on all other railways?

The public have a right to every advantage under permitted monopoly which they would enjoy under free competition; and they are unjust to themselves if they do not insist upon this right. If there were two parallel railways, the one locking you in, and the other not, is there the smallest doubt which would carry away all the business? Can there be any hesitation in which timid women, drunken men, sages, philosophers, bishops, and all combustible beings, would place themselves?

I very much doubt the legality of locking doors, and refusing to open them. I arrive at a station where others are admitted; but I am not suffered to get out, though perhaps at the point of death. In all other positions of life there is egress where there is ingress.

Man is universally the master of his own body, except he chooses to go from Paddington to Bridgewater: there only the Habeas Corpus is refused.

Nothing, in fact, can be more utterly silly or mistaken than this over-officious care of the public; as if every man, who was not a railway director, was a child or a fool. But why stop here? Why are not strait-waistcoats used? Why is not the accidental traveller strapped down? Why do contusion and fracture still remain physically possible?

Is not this extreme care of the public new? When first mail-coaches began to travel twelve miles an hour, the *outsides* (if I remember rightly) were never tied to the roof. In packets, landsmen are not locked into the cabin to prevent them from tumbling overboard. This affectionate nonsense prevails only on the Great Western. It is there only that men, women, and children (seeking the only mode of transit which remains), are, by these tender-hearted monopolists, immediately committed to their locomotive prisons. Nothing can, in fact, be so absurd as all this officious zeal. It is the duty of the directors to take all reasonable precautions to warn the public of danger — to make it clear that there is no negligence on the part of the railroad directors; and then, this done, if a fool-hardy person choose to expose himself to danger, so be it. Fools there will be on roads of iron, and on roads of gravel, and they must suffer for their folly; but why are Socrates, Solon, and Solomon, to be locked up?

But is all this, which appears so philanthropical, mere philanthropy? Does not the locking of the doors save servants and policemen? Does not economy mingle with these benevolent feelings? Is it to save a few fellow-creatures, or a few pounds, that the children of the West are to be hermetically sealed in the locomotives? I do not say it is so; but I say it deserves a very serious examination whether it be so or not. Great and heavy is the sin of the directors of this huge monopoly, if they repeat upon their own iron the tragedy of Paris, in order to increase their dividends a few shillings per cent.

The country has (perhaps inevitably) given way to this great monopoly. Nothing can make it tolerable for a moment, but the most severe and watchful jealousy of the manner in which its powers are exercised. We shall have tyrannical rules, vexatious rules, ill-temper, pure folly, and meddling and impertinent paternity. It is the absolute duty of Lord Ripon and Mr. Gladstone (if the directors prove themselves to be so inadequate to the new situation in which they are placed) to restrain and direct them by law; and if these two gentlemen are afraid of the responsibility of such laws, they are deficient in the moral courage which their office requires, and the most important interests of the public are neglected. I am, sir, your obedient servant,

SYDNEY SMITH.

MAY 21, 1842.

"LOCKING-IN" ON RAILWAYS.

To the Editor of the Morning Chronicle:—

SIR: Since the letter upon railroads which you were good enough to insert in your paper, I have had some conversation with two gentlemen officially connected with the Great Western. Though nothing could be more courteous than their manner, nor more intelligible than their arguments, I remain unshaken as to the necessity of keeping the doors open.

There is in the first place, the effect of imagination, the idea that all escape is impossible, that (let what will happen) you must sit quiet in first class No. 2, whether they are pounding you into a jam, or burning you into a cinder, or crumbling you into a human powder. These excellent directors, versant in wood and metal, seem to require that the imagination should be sent by some other conveyance, and that only loads of unimpassioned, unintellectual flesh and blood should be darted along on the Western rail; whereas, the female *homo* is a screaming, parturient, interjectional, hysterical animal, whose delicacy and timidity monopolists (even much as it may surprise them) must be taught to consult. The female, in all probability, never would jump out; but she thinks she may jump out when she pleases; and this is intensely comfortable.

There are two sorts of dangers which hang over railroads. The one, retail dangers, where individuals only are concerned; the other, wholesale dangers, where the whole train, or a considerable part of it, is put in jeopardy. For the first danger there is a remedy in the prudence of individuals; for the second, there is none.

No man need be drunk, nor need he jump out when the carriage is in motion, but in the present state of science it is impossible to guard effectually against the fracture of the axletree, or the explosion of the engine; and if the safety of the one party cannot be consulted but by the dangers of the other, if the foolish cannot be restrained but by the unjust incarceration of the wise, the prior consideration is due to those who have not the remedy for the evil in their own hands.

But the truth is—and so (after a hundred monopolizing experiments on public patience) the railroad directors will find it—there can be no other dependence for the safety of the public than the care which every human being is inclined to take of his own life and limbs. Everything beyond this is the mere lazy tyranny of monopoly, which makes no distinction between human beings and brown paper parcels. If riding were a monopoly, as travelling in carriages is now become, there are many gentlemen whom I see riding in the Park upon such false principles, that I am sure the cantering and galloping directors would strap them, in the ardour of their affection, to the saddle, padlock them to the stirrups, or compel them to ride behind a policeman of the stables; and nothing but a motion from O'Brien, or an order from Gladstone, could release them.

Let the company stick up all sorts of cautions and notices within their carriages and without; but, after that, no doors locked. If one door is allowed to be locked, the other will soon be so too; there is no other security to the public than absolute prohibition of the practice. The directors and agents of the Great Western are individually excellent men; but the moment men meet in public boards, they cease to be collectively excellent. The fund of morality becomes less, as the individual contributors increase in number. I do not accuse such respectable men of any wilful violation of truth, but the memoirs which they are about to present will be, without the scrupulous cross-examination of a committee of the House of Commons, mere waste-paper.

But the most absurd of all legislative enactments is this hemiplegian law—an act of Parliament to protect one side of the body and not the other. If the wheel comes off on the right, the open door is uppermost, and every one is saved. If, from any sudden avalanche on the road, the carriage is prostrated to the left, the locked door is uppermost, all escape is impossible, and the railroad martyrdom begins.

Leave me to escape in the best way I can, as the fire-officers very kindly permit me to do. I know very well the danger of getting out on the off-side; but escape is the affair of a moment: suppose a train to have passed at that moment, I know I am safe from any other trains for twenty minutes or half an hour; and if I do get out on the off-side I do not remain in the valley of death between the two trains, but am over to the opposite bank in an instant— only half-roasted or merely browned, certainly not done enough for the Great Western directors.

On Saturday morning last, the wheel of the public carriage, in which a friend of mine was travelling, began to smoke, but was pacified by several buckets of water, and proceeded. After five more miles, the whole carriage was full of smoke, the train was with difficulty stopped, and the flagrant vehicle removed. The axle was nearly in two, and in another mile would have been severed.

Railroad travelling is a delightful improvement of human life. Man is become a bird; he can fly longer and quicker than a Solan goose. The mamma rushes sixty miles in two hours to the aching finger of her conjugating and declining grammar-boy. The early Scotchman scratches himself in the morning mists of the north, and has porridge in Piccadilly, before the setting sun. The Puseyite priest, after a rush of one hundred miles, appears with his little volume of nonsense at the breakfast of his bookseller. Everything is near, everything is immediate—time, distance, and delay, are abolished. But, though charming and fascinating as all this is, we must not shut our eyes to the price we shall pay for it. There will be every three or four years some dreadful massacre—whole trains will be hurled down a precipice, and two hundred or three hundred persons will be killed on the spot. There will be every now and then a great combustion of human bodies, as there has been at Paris; then all the newspapers up in arms—a thousand regulations forgotten as soon as the directors dare—loud screams of the velocity whistle—monopoly locks and bolts as before.

The locking plea of directors is philanthropy; and I admit that to guard men from the commission of moral evil is as philanthropical as to prevent physical suffering. There is, I allow, a strong propensity in mankind to travel on railroads without paying; and to lock mankind in till they have completed their share of the contract, is benevolent, because it guards the species from degrading and immoral conduct; but to burn or crush a whole train, merely to prevent a few immoral insides from not paying, is, I hope, a little more than Ripon or Gladstone will bear.

We have been, up to this point, very careless of our railway regulations. The first person of rank who is killed will put everything in order, and produce a code of the most careful rules. I hope it will not be one of the bench of bishops; but should it be so destined, let the burned bishop—the unwilling Latimer—remember that, however painful gradual concoction by fire may be, his death will produce unspeakable benefit to the public. Even Sodor and Man will be better than nothing. From that moment the bad effects of the monopoly are destroyed; no more fatal deference to the directors; no despotic incarceration; no barbarous inattention to the anatomy and physiology of the human body; no commitment to locomotive prisons, with warrant. We shall then find it possible—

"Voyager libre sans mourir."

SYDNEY SMITH

JUNE 7, 1842.

BURNING ALIVE ON RAILROADS.

To the Editor of the Morning Chronicle:—

SIR:—Having gradually got into this little controversy respecting the burning human beings alive on the railroads, I must beg leave, preparatory to the introduction of the bill, to say a few more words on the subject. If I could have my will in these matters, I would introduce into the bill a clause absolutely prohibitory of all locking doors on railroads; but as that fascinating board, the Board of Trade, does not love this, and as the public may, after some repetitions of roasted humanity, be better prepared for such peremptory legislation, the better method, perhaps, will be, to give to the Board of Trade the power of opening doors (one or both), with the customary penalties against the companies for disobedience of orders, and then the Board may use this power as the occasion may require.

To pass a one-legged law, giving power over one door, and not the other, would, perhaps be too absurd for human endurance. If railroad companies were aware of their real and extended interests, they would not harass the public by vexatious regulations, nor, under the plea of humanity (though really for purposes of economy), expose them to serious peril. The country are very angry with themselves for having granted the monopoly, and very angry for the instances of carelessness and oppression which have appeared in the working of the system: the heaviest fines are inflicted by coroner's juries, the heaviest damages are given by common juries. Railroads have daily proof of their unpopularity. If Parliament get out of temper with these metallic ways, they will visit them with laws of iron, and burst upon them with the high pressure of despotism.

The wayfaring men of the North will league with the wayfaring men of the West—South and East will join hand in hand against them. All the points of the compass will combine against these venders of velocity and traders in transition. I hope a clause will be introduced, compelling the Board of Trade to report twice a year to Parliament, upon the accidents of railroads, their causes, and their prevention. The public know little or nothing of what happens on the rail. All the men with letters upon the collars of their coats are sworn to secrecy—nothing can be extracted from them; when anything happens they neither appear to see nor hear you.

In case of conflagration, you would be to them as so many joints on the spit. It has occurred to five hundred persons, that soft impediments behind and before (such as wool), would prevent the dangers of meeting or overtaking. It is not yet understood why a carriage on fire at the end of the train cannot be seen by the driver of the engine. All this may be great nonsense; but the public ought to know that these points have been properly considered; they should know that there are a set of officers paid to watch over their interests, and to guard against the perpetual encroachments, the carelessness, the insolence, and the avarice of monopoly.

Why do not our dear Ripon and our youthful Gladstone see this, and come cheerfully to the rescue? and instead of wrapping themselves up in transcendental philosophy, and the principles of letting-aloneness, why do they not at once do what ought to be done —what must be done—and what, after many needless butcheries, they will at last be compelled to do? Yours, SYDNEY SMITH.

JUNE 18, 1842.

[Sir Robert Peel having insinuated, in the House of Commons, that the zeal of Sydney Smith in the Railway Question might be owing to personal fear, the following characteristic reply appeared in a daily paper.]

To Sir Robert Peel:—

A cruel attack upon me, Sir Robert, to attribute all my interference with the arbitrary proceedings of railroads to personal fear. Nothing can be more ungrateful and unkind. I thought only of you, and for you, as many whig gentlemen will bear me testimony, who rebuked me for my anxiety. I said to myself and to them, "Our lovely and intrepid minister may be overthrown on the rail. The locked door may be uppermost. He will kick and call on the Speaker and Sergeant-at-Arms in vain. Nothing will remain of all his graces, his flexibility, his fascinating, facetious fun, his social warmth; nothing of his flow of soul, of his dear heavy pleasantry, of his prevailing skill to impart disorderly wishes to the purest heart. Nothing will remain of it at all, but a heap of ashes for the parish church of Tamworth. He perishes at the moment he is becoming as powerful in the drawing-room of Court as in the House of Parliament—at the moment when Hullah (not without hopes of ultimate success), is teaching him to sing and Melnotte to dance."

I have no doubt of your bravery, Sir Robert, though you have of mine; but then consider what different lives we have led, and what a school of courage is that troop of yeomanry at Tamworth, the Tory Fencibles. Who can doubt of your courage who has seen you at their head, marching up Pitt street, through Dundas square, on the Liverpool lane, and looking all the while like those beautiful medals of *Bellona Frigida* and *Mars sine sanguine*, the very horses looking at you as if you were going to take away three per cent. of their oats! After such spectacles as these, the account you give of your own courage cannot be doubted. The only little circumstance which I cannot entirely reconcile to the possession of this very high attribute in so eminent a degree is, that you should have selected, for your uncourteous attack, enemies who cannot resent, and a place where there can be no reply.

I am, sir, your obedient servant,
SYDNEY SMITH.

LETTERS ON AMERICAN DEBTS.

The Humble Petition *of the* Rev. Sydney Smith *to the* House of Congress *at* Washington.

I petition your honourable House to institute some measures for the restoration of American credit, and for the repayment of debts incurred and repudiated by several of the States. Your Petitioner lent to the State of Pennsylvania a sum of money, for the purpose of some public improvement. The amount, though small, is to him important, and is a saving from a life income, made with difficulty and privation. If their refusal to pay (from which a very large number of English families are suffering) had been the result of war, produced by the unjust aggression of powerful enemies; if it had arisen from civil discord; if it had proceeded from an improvident application of means in the first years of self-government; if it were the act of a poor State struggling against the barrenness of nature — every friend of America would have been contented to wait for better times; but the fraud is committed in the profound peace of Pennsylvania, by the richest State in the Union, after the wise investment of the borrowed money in roads and canals, of which the repudiators are every day reaping the advantage. It is an act of bad faith which (all its circumstances considered) has no parallel, and no excuse.

Nor is it only the loss of property which your Petitioner laments. He laments still more that immense power which the bad faith of America has given to aristocratical opinions, and to the enemies of free institutions in the old world. It is vain any longer to appeal to history, and to point out the wrongs which the many have received from the few. The Americans, who boast to have improved the institutions of the old world, have at least equalled its crimes. A great nation, after trampling under foot all earthly tyranny, has been guilty of a fraud as enormous as ever disgraced the worst king of the most degraded nation of Europe.

It is most painful to your Petitioner to see that American citizens excite, wherever they may go, the recollection that they belong to a dishonest people, who pride themselves on having tricked and pillaged Europe; and this mark is fixed by their faithless legislators on some of the best and most honourable men in the world, whom every Englishman has been eager to see and proud to receive.

It is a subject of serious concern to your Petitioner that you are losing all that power which the friends of freedom rejoiced that you possessed, looking upon you as the ark of human happiness, and the most splendid picture of justice and of wisdom that the world had yet seen. Little did the friends of America expect it, and sad is the spectacle to see you rejected by every State in Europe, as a nation with whom no contract can be made, because none will be kept; unstable in the very foundations of social life, deficient in the elements of good faith, men who prefer any load of infamy however great, to any pressure of taxation however light.

Nor is it only this gigantic bankruptcy for so many degrees of longitude and latitude which your petitioner deplores, but he is alarmed also by that total want of shame with which these things have been done; the callous immorality with which Europe has been plundered, that deadness of the moral sense which seems to preclude all return to honesty, to perpetuate this new infamy, and to threaten its extension over every State in the Union.

To any man of real philanthropy, who receives pleasure from the improvements of the world, the repudiation of the public debts of America, and the shameless manner in which it has been talked of and done, is the most melancholy event which has happened during the existence of the present generation. Your Petitioner sincerely prays that the great and good men still existing among you may, by teaching to the United States the deep disgrace they have incurred in the whole world, restore them to moral health, to that high position they have lost, and which, for the happiness of mankind, it is so important they should ever maintain; for the United States are now working out the greatest of all political problems, and upon that confederacy the eyes of thinking men are intensely fixed, to see how far the mass of mankind can be trusted with the management of their own affairs, and the establishment of their own happiness.

May 18, 1843.

LETTER I.

To the Editor of the Morning Chronicle:—

Sir: You did me the favour, some time since, to insert in your valuable journal a petition of mine to the American Congress, for the repayment of a loan made by me, in common with many other unwise people, to the State of Pennsylvania. For that petition I have been abused in the grossest manner by many of the American papers. After some weeks' reflection, I see no reason to alter my opinions, or to retract my expressions. What I then said was not wild declamation, but measured truth. I repeat again, that no conduct was ever more profligate than that of the State of Pennsylvania. History cannot pattern it: and let no deluded being imagine that they will ever repay a single farthing—their people have tasted of the dangerous luxury of dishonesty, and they will never be brought back to the homely rule of right. The money transactions of the Americans are become a by-word among the nations of Europe. In every grammar-school of the old world *ad Græcas Calendas* is translated—the American dividends.

I am no enemy to America. I loved and admired honest America when she respected the laws of pounds, shillings, and pence; and I thought the United States the most magnificent picture of human happiness: I meddle now in these matters because I hate fraud—because I pity the misery it has occasioned—because I mourn over the hatred it has excited against free institutions.

Among the discussions to which the moral lubricities of this insolvent people have given birth, they have arrogated to themselves the right of sitting in judgment upon the property of their creditors—of deciding who among them is rich, and who poor.

and who are proper objects of compassionate payment; but in thé name of Mercury, the great god of thieves, did any man ever hear of debtors alleging the wealth of the lender as a reason for eluding the payment of the loan? Is the Stock Exchange a place for the tables of the money-lenders; or is it a school of moralists, who may amerce the rich, exalt the poor, and correct the inequalities of fortune? Is *Biddle* an instrument in the hand of Providence to exalt the humble, and send the rich empty away? Does American Providence work with such instruments as *Biddle?*

But the only good part of this bad morality is not acted upon. The rich are robbed, but the poor are not paid: they growl against the dividends of Dives, and don't lick the sores of Lazarus. They seize, with loud acclamations, on the money-bags of Jones Loyd, Rothschild, and Baring, but they do not give back the pittance of the widow, and the bread of the child. Those knaves of the setting sun may call me rich, for I have a twentieth part of the income of the Archbishop of Canterbury; but the curate of the next parish is a wretched soul, bruised by adversity; and the three hundred pounds for his children, which it has taken his life to save, is eaten and drunken by the mean men of Pennsylvania—by men who are always talking of the virtue and honour of the United States—by men who soar above others in what they say, and sink below all nations in what they do—who, after floating on the heaven of declamation, fall down to feed on the offal and garbage of the earth.

Persons who are not in the secret are inclined to consider the abominable conduct of the repudiating States to proceed from exhaustion — "They don't pay because they cannot pay; whereas, from estimates which have just now reached this country, this is the picture of the finances of the insolvent states. Their debts may be about 200 millions of dollars; at an interest of 6 per cent., this makes an annual charge of 12 millions of dollars, which is little more than 1 per cent. of their income in 1840, and may be presumed to be less than 1 per cent. of their present income; but if they were all to provide funds for the punctual payment of interest, the debt could readily be converted into a 4 or 5 per cent. stock, and the excess, converted into a sinking fund, would discharge the debt in less than thirty years. The debt of Pennsylvania, estimated at 40 millions of dollars, bears, at 5 per cent..

an annual interest of 2 millions. The income of this State was, in 1840, 131 millions of dollars, and is probably at this time not less than 150 millions: a net revenue of only $1\frac{1}{2}$ per cent. would produce the 2 millions required. So that the price of national character in Pennsylvania is $1\frac{1}{2}$ per cent. on the net income; and if this market price of morals were established here, a gentleman of a thousand a year would deliberately and publicly submit to infamy for £15 per annum; and a poor man, who by laborious industry had saved one hundred a year, would incur general disgrace and opprobrium for thirty shillings by the year. There really should be lunatic asylums for nations as well as for individuals.

But they begin to feel all this: their tone is changed; they talk with bated breath and whispering apology, and allay with some cold drops of modesty their skipping spirit. They strutted into this miserable history, and begin to think of sneaking out.

And then the subdolous press of America contends that the English under similar circumstances would act with their own debt in the same manner; but there are many English constituencies where are thousands not worth a shilling, and no such idea has been broached among them, nor has any petition to such effect been presented to the legislature. But what if they did act in such a manner, would it be a conduct less wicked than that of the Americans? Is there not one immutable law of justice?—is it not written in the book? Does it not beat in the heart?—are the great guide-marks of life to be concealed by such nonsense as this? I deny the fact on which the reasoning is founded; and if the facts were true, the reasoning would be false.

I never meet a Pennsylvanian at a London dinner without feeling a disposition to seize and divide him;—to allot his beaver to one sufferer and his coat to another—to appropriate his pocket-handkerchief to the orphan, and to comfort the widow with his silver watch, Broadway rings, and the London Guide, which he always carries in his pockets. How such a man can set himself down at an English table without feeling that he owes two or three pounds to every man in company I am at a loss to conceive: he has no more right to eat with honest men than a leper has to eat with clean men. If he has a particle of honour in his composition he should shut himself up, and say, " I cannot mingle with you, I belong to a degraded people — I must hide myself — I am a plunderer from Pennsylvania."

Figure to yourself a Pennsylvanian receiving foreigners in his own country, walking over the public works with them, and showing them Larcenous Lake, Swindling Swamp, Crafty Canal, and Rogues' Railway, and other dishonest works. "This swamp we gained," says the patriotic borrower, "by the repudiated loan of 1828. Our canal robbery was in 1830; we pocketed your good people's money for the railroad only last year." All this may seem very smart to the Americans; but if I had the misfortune to be born among such a people, the land of my fathers should not retain me a single moment after the act of repudiation. I would appeal from my fathers to my forefathers. I would fly to Newgate for greater purity of thought, and seek in the prisons of England for better rules of life.

This new and vain people can never forgive us for having preceded them 300 years in civilization. They are prepared to enter into the most bloody wars in England, not on account of Oregon, or boundaries, or right of search, but because our clothes and carriages are better made, and because Bond Street beats Broadway. Wise Webster does all he can to convince the people that these are not lawful causes of war; but wars, and long wars, they will one day or another produce; and this, perhaps, is the only advantage of repudiation. The Americans cannot gratify their avarice and ambition at once; they cannot cheat and conquer at the same time. The warlike power of every country depends on their Three per cents. If Cæsar were to reappear upon earth, Wettenhall's List would be more important than his Commentaries; Rothschild would open and shut the temple of Janus; Thomas Baring, or Bates would probably command the Tenth Legion, and the soldiers would march to battle with loud cries of Scrip and Omnium reduced, Consols and Cæsar! Now, the Americans have cut themselves off from all resources of credit. Having been as dishonest as they can be, they are prevented from being as foolish as they wish to be. In the whole habitable globe they cannot borrow a guinea, and they cannot draw the sword because they have not money to buy it.

If I were an American of any of the honest States, I would never rest till I had compelled Pennsylvania to be as honest as myself. The bad faith of that State brings disgrace on all; just as common snakes are killed because vipers are dangerous. I have a general feeling, that by that breed of men I have been robbed and ruined, and I shudder and keep aloof. The pecuniary credit of every State is affected by Pennsylvania. Ohio pays; but with such a bold bankruptcy before their eyes, how long will Ohio pay? The truth is, that the eyes of all capitalists are averted from the United States. The finest commercial understandings will have nothing to do with them. Men rigidly just, who penetrate boldly into the dealings of nations, and work with vigour and virtue for honourable wealth—great and high-minded merchants—will loathe, and are now loathing, the name of America: it is becoming, since its fall, the common-shore of Europe, and the native home of the needy villain.

And now, drab-coloured men of Pennsylvania, there is yet a moment left: the eyes of all Europe are anchored upon you—

"Surrexit mundus justis furiis:"

start up from that trance of dishonesty into which you are plunged; don't think of the flesh which walls about your life, but of that sin which has hurled you from the heaven of character, which hangs over you like a devouring pestilence, and makes good men sad, and ruffians dance and sing. It is not for Gin Sling and Sherry Cobler alone that man is to live, but for those great principles against which no argument can be listened to—principles which give to every power a double power above their functions and their offices, which are the books, the arts, the academies that teach, lift up, and nourish the world—principles (I am quite serious in what I say) above cash, superior to cotton, higher than currency—principles, without which it is better to die than to live which every servant of God, over every sea and in all lands, should cherish—*usque ad abdita spiramenta animæ.*

         Yours, &c. SYDNEY SMITH.
NOVEMBER 3, 1843.

LETTER II.
To the Editor of the Morning Chronicle:—

SIR: Having been unwell for some days past, I have had no opportunity of paying my respects to General Duff Green, who (whatever be his other merits) has certainly not shown himself a Washington in defence of his country. The General demands, with a beautiful simplicity, " *Whence this morbid hatred of America?*" But this question, all-affecting as it is, is stolen from Pilpay's fables. " A fox," says Pilpay, " caught by the leg in a trap near the farm-yard, uttered the most piercing cries of distress; forthwith all the birds of the yard gathered round him, and seemed to delight in his misfortune; hens chuckled, geese hissed, ducks quacked, and chanticleer with shrill cockadoodles rent the air. 'Whence,' said the fox, stepping forward with infinite gravity, 'whence this morbid hatred of the fox? What have I done? Whom have I injured? I am overwhelmed with astonishment at these symptoms of aversion.' 'Oh, you old villain,' the poultry exclaimed, ' Where are our ducklings? Where are our goslings? Did not I see you running away yesterday with my mother in your mouth? Did you not eat up all my relations last week? You ought to die the worst of deaths—to be pecked into a thousand pieces.'" Now hence, General Green, comes the morbid hatred of America, as you term it—because her conduct has been predatory—because she has ruined so many helpless children, so many miserable women, so many aged men—because she has disturbed the order of the world, and rifled those sacred treasures which human virtue had hoarded for human misery. Why is such hatred morbid? Why, is it not just, inevitable, innate? Why, is it not disgraceful to want it? Why, is it not honourable to feel it?

Hate America!!! I have loved and honoured America all my life; and in the *Edinburgh Review*, and at all opportunities which my trumpery sphere of action has afforded, I have never ceased to praise and defend the United States; and to every American to whom I have had the good fortune to be introduced, I have proffered all the hospitality in my power. But I cannot shut my eyes to enormous dishonesty; nor, remembering their former state, can I restrain myself from calling on them (though I copy Satan) to spring up from the gulf of infamy in which they are rolling—

" Awake, arise, or be for ever fallen."

I am astonished that the honest States of America do not draw a *cordon sanitaire* round their unpaying brethren—that the truly mercantile New-Yorkers, and the thoroughly honest people of Massachusetts, do not in their European visits wear a uniform with " S. S., or Solvent States," worked in gold letters upon the coat, and receipts in full of all demands tamboured on the waistcoats, and "our own property" figured on their pantaloons.

But the General seems shocked that I should say the Americans cannot go to war without money: but what do I mean by war? Not irruptions into Canada—not the embodying of militia in Oregon; but a long, tedious, maritime war of four or five years' duration. Is any man so foolish as to suppose that Rothschild has nothing to do with such wars as these? And that a bankrupt State, without the power of borrowing a shilling in the world, may not be crippled in such a contest? We all know that the Americans can fight. Nobody doubts their courage. I see now in my mind's eye a whole army on the plains of Pennsylvania in battle array, immense corps of insolvent light infantry, regiments of heavy horse debtors, battalions of repudiators, brigades of bankrupts, with *Vivre sans payer, ou mourir*, on their banners, and *ære alieno* on their trumpets: all these desperate debtors would fight to the death for their country, and probably drive into the sea their invading creditors. Of their courage, I repeat again, I have no doubt. I wish I had the same confidence in their wisdom. But I believe they will become intoxicated by the flattery of unprincipled orators; and, instead of entering with us into a noble competition in making calico (the great object for which the Anglo-Saxon race appears to have been created) they will waste their happiness and their money (if they can get any) in years of silly, bloody, foolish, and accursed war, to prove to the world that Perkins is a real fine gentleman, and that the carronades of the Washington steamer will carry farther than those of the Britisher Victoria, or the Robert Peel vessel-of-war.

I am accused of applying the epithet repudiation to States which have not repudiated. Perhaps so; but then these latter States have not paid. But what is the difference between a man who says, "I don't owe you anything, and will not pay you," and another who says, "I do owe you a sum," and who, having admitted the debt, never pays it? There seems in the first to be some slight colour of right; but the second is broad, blazing, refulgent, meridian fraud.

It may be very true that rich and educated men in Pennsylvania wish to pay the debt, and that the real objectors are the Dutch and German agriculturists, who cannot be made to understand the effect of character upon clover. All this may be very true, but it is a domestic quarrel. Their church-wardens of reputation must make a private rate of infamy for themselves—we have nothing to do with this rate. The real quarrel is the Unpaid World *versus* the State of Pennsylvania.

And now, dear Jonathan, let me beg of you to follow the advice of a real friend, who will say to you what Wat Tyler had not the virtue to say, and what all speakers in the eleven recent Pennsylvanian elections have cautiously abstained from saying—" Make a great effort; book up at once, and pay." You have no conception of the obloquy and contempt to which you are exposing yourselves all over Europe. Bull is naturally disposed to love you, but he loves nobody who does not pay him. His imaginary paradise is some planet of punctual payment, where ready money prevails, and where debt and discount are unknown. As for me, as soon as I hear that the last farthing is paid to the last creditor, I will appear on my knees at the bar of the Pennsylvanian Senate in the plumeopicean robe of American controversy. Each Conscript Jonathan shall trickle over me a few drops of tar, and help to decorate me with those penal plumes in which the vanquished reasoner of the transatlantic world does homage to the physical superiority of his opponents. And now, having eased my soul of its indignation, and sold my stock at 40 per cent. discount, I sulkily retire from the subject, with a fixed intention of lending no more money to free and enlightened republics, but of employing my money henceforth in buying up Abyssinian bonds, and purchasing into the Turkish Fours, or the Tunis Three-and-a-half per Cent. funds.

SYDNEY SMITH.

NOVEMBER 22, 1843.

A FRAGMENT ON
THE IRISH ROMAN CATHOLIC CHURCH.*

THE revenue of the Irish Roman Catholic Church is made up of half-pence, potatoes, rags, bones, and fragments of old clothes,

* This unrevised fragment was found among the papers of Sydney Smith after his death. It was first published in April, 1845, with the prefatory remark that, "if it serve no other purpose, will, at least, prove that his *last*, as well as his earliest efforts, were exerted for the promotion of religious freedom, and may satisfy those who have objected to his later writings, because his own interest appeared to be bound up with his opinions, that he did not hesitate to the last moment of his life, boldly to advocate what he considered to be justice to others." The manuscript was accompanied by the following Private Memoranda of Subjects intended to have been introduced in the Pamphlet, &c. The subjects marked by a star are treated of in the Fragment.

Debates in the House of Commons in 1825, on the motion of Lord F. Egerton, for the support of the Roman Catholic clergy. Printed separately, I believe, in Ireland.

Evidence before the House of Commons, in 1824 and 1825, including Doyle's.

A Speech of Charles Grant's, in 1819, on a motion of James Daly to enforce the Insurrection Act.

Debates on Maynooth, in February last (1844).

Hard case of the priest's first year.

Provision offered by Pitt and Castlereagh, and accepted by the hierarchy.

* Send ambassadors to Constantinople, and refuse to send them to Rome.

England should cast off its connection with the Irish Church.

Lord F. Egerton's plan for paying the Roman Catholic clergy in 1825. The prelates agree to take the money.

* Old mode of governing by Protestants at an end.
* Vast improvements since the Union, and fully specified in Martin, page 35.
* Priests dare not thwart the people, for fear of losing money.
* Dreadful oppression of the people.
* Bishops dare not enforce their rules. They must have money.

and those Irish old clothes. They worship often in hovels, or in the open air, from the *want* of any place of worship. Their religion is the religion of three fourths of the population! Not far off, in a well-windowed and well-roofed house, is a well-paid Protestant clergyman, preaching to stools and hassocks, and crying in the wilderness; near him the clerk, near him the sexton, near him the sexton's wife—furious against the errors of Popery, and willing to lay down their lives for the great truths established at the Diet of Augsburg.

There is a story in the Leinster family which passes under the name of

"*She is not well.*"

A Protestant clergyman, whose church was in the neighbourhood, was a guest at the house of that upright and excellent man, the Duke of Leinster. He had been staying there three or four days; and on Saturday night, as they were all retiring to their rooms, the duke said, "We shall meet to-morrow at breakfast." "Not so," said our Milesian Protestant; "your hour, my lord, is a little too late for me; I am very particular in the discharge of my duty, and your breakfast will interfere with my church." The duke was pleased with the very proper excuses of his guest, and they separated for the night; his grace, perhaps, deeming his palace more safe from all the evils of life for containing in its bosom such an exemplary son of the Church. The first person, however, whom the duke saw in the morning, upon entering the breakfast-room, was our punctual Protestant, deep in rolls and butter, his finger in an egg, and a large slice of the best Tipperary ham secured on his plate. "Delighted to see you, my dear vicar," said the duke; "but I must say as much surprised as delighted." "Oh, don't you know what has happened?" said the sacred breakfaster, "*she is not well.*" "Who is not well?" said the duke: "you are not married—you have no sister living—I'm quite uneasy; tell me who is not well." "Why, the fact is, my lord duke, that my congregation consists of the clerk, the sexton, and the sexton's wife. Now the sexton's wife is in very delicate health: when she cannot attend, we cannot muster the number mentioned in the rubric; and we have, therefore, no service on that day. The good woman had a cold and sore throat this morning, and, as I had breakfasted but slightly, I thought I might as well hurry back to the regular family dejeuner." I don't know that the clergyman behaved improperly; but such a church is hardly worth an insurrection and civil war every ten years.

Sir Robert did well in fighting it out with O'Connell. He was too late; but when he began he did it boldly and sensibly, and I, for one, am heartily glad O'Connell has been found guilty and imprisoned. He was either in earnest about Repeal or he was not. If he *was* in earnest, I entirely agree with Lord Grey and Lord Spencer, that civil war is preferable to Repeal. Much as I hate wounds, dangers, privations, and explosions—much as I love regular hours of dinner—foolish as I think men covered with the feathers of the male *Pullus domesticus*, and covered with lace in the course of the ischiatic nerve—much as I detest all these follies and ferocities, I would rather turn soldier myself than acquiesce quietly in such a separation of the empire.

It is *such* a piece of nonsense, that no man can have any reverence for himself who would stop to discuss such a question. It is such a piece of anti-British villany, that none but the bitterest enemy of our blood and people could entertain such a project! It is to be met only with round and grape—to be answered by Shrapnel and Congreve; to be discussed in hollow squares, and refuted by battalions four deep; to be put down by the *ultima ratio* of that armed Aristotle, the Duke of Wellington.

O'Connell is released; and released, I have no doubt, by the conscientious decision of the law lords. If he was unjustly (even from some technical defect) imprisoned, I rejoice in his liberation. England is, I believe, the *only* country in the world where such an event *could* have happened, and a wise Irishman (if there be a wise Irishman) should be slow in separating from a country whose spirit can produce, and whose institutions can admit, of such a result. Of his guilt no one doubts, but guilty men must be hung technically and according to established rules; upon a statutable gibbet, with parliament rope, and a legal hangman, sheriff, and chaplain on the scaffold, and a mob in the foreground.

But, after all, I have no desire my dear Daniel should come to any harm, for I believe there is a great deal of virtue and excellent meaning in him, and I must now beg a few minutes' conversation with him. "After all, my dear Daniel, what is it you want? — a separation of the two countries?—for what purpose?—for your own aggrandizement?—for the gratification of your personal vanity? You don't know yourself; you are much too honourable and moral a man, and too clearsighted a person for such a business as this: the empire will be twisted out of your hands by a set of cut-throat villains, and you will die secretly by a poisoned potato, or be pistolled in the streets. You have too much sense, and taste, and openness, to endure for a session, the stupid and audacious wickedness and nonsense of your associates. If you want fame, you must be insatiable! Who is so much known in all Europe, or so much admired by honest men for the *real* good you had done to your country, before this insane cry of Repeal? And don't imagine you can intimidate this government; whatever be their faults or merits, you may take my word for it, you will *not* intimidate them. They will prosecute you again, and put down your Clontarf meetings, and they will be quite right in doing so. They may make concessions, and I think they will; but they would fall into utter contempt, if they allowed themselves to be terrified into a dissolution of the Union. They know full well that the English nation are unanimous and resolute upon this point, and that they would prefer war to a Repeal. And now, dear Daniel, sit down quietly at Derrynane, and tell me, when the bodily frame is refreshed with the wine of Bordeaux, whether all this is worth while. What is the object of all government? The object of all government is roast mutton, potatoes, claret, a stout constable, an honest justice, a clear highway, a free chapel. What trash to be bawling in the streets about the Green Isle, the Isle of the Ocean! the bold anthem of *Erin go Bragh!* A far better anthem would be Erin go bread and cheese, Erin go cabins that will keep out the rain, Erin go pantaloons without holes in them! What folly to be making eternal declamations about governing yourselves! If laws are good and well administered, is it worth while to rush into war and rebellion, in order that no better laws may be made in another place? Are you an Eton boy, who has just come out, full of Plutarch's Lives, and considering in every case how Epaminondas or Philopœmen would have acted, or are you our own dear Daniel, drilled in all the business and bustle of life? I am with you heart and soul in my detestation of all injustice done to Ireland. Your priests shall be fed and paid, the liberties of your Church be scrupulously guarded, and in civil affairs the most even justice be preserved between Catholic and Protestant. Thus far I am a thorough rebel as well as yourself; but when you come to the perilous nonsense of *Repeal*, in common with every honest man who has five grains of common sense, I take my leave."

It is entertaining enough, that although the Irish are beginning to be so clamorous about making their own laws, that the wisest and the best statutes in the books have been made since their union with England. All Catholic disabilities have been abolished; a good police has been established all over the kingdom; public courts of petty sessions have been instituted; free trade between Great Britain and Ireland has been completely carried into effect; lord lieutenants are placed in every county; church-rates are taken off Catholic shoulders; the county grand jury rooms are flung open to the public; county surveyors are of great service; a noble provision is made for educating the people. I never saw a man who had returned to Ireland after four or five years' absence, who did not say how much it had improved, and how fast it was improving; and this is the country which is to be Erin-go-bragh'd by this shallow, vain, and irritable people into bloodshed and rebellion!

The first thing to be done is to pay the priests, and after a little time they will take the money. One man wants to repair his cottage; another wants a buggy; a third cannot shut his eyes to the dilapidations of a cassock. The draft is payable at sight in Dublin, or by agents in the next market town dependent upon the commission in Dublin. The housekeeper of the holy man is importunate for money, and if it is not procured by drawing for the salary, it must be extorted by curses and comminations from the ragged worshippers, slowly, sorrowfully, and sadly. There will be some opposition at first, but the facility of getting the salary without the violence they are now forced to use, and the difficulties to which they are exposed in procuring the payment of those emoluments to which they are fairly entitled, will, in the end, overcome all obstacles.* And if it does not succeed, what harm is done by the

* Smith had a conversation with Dr. Doyle, at a time he was anxious to learn as far as possible what effect the measures he was proposing would have upon the Catholics. He proposed that Government should pay the Catholic priests. " They would not take it," said Dr. Doyle. " Do you mean to say, *that if every priest in Ireland received to-morrow morning a Government letter with a hundred pounds*, FIRST QUARTER *of their year's income*, they would re-

attempt? It evinces on the part of this country the strongest disposition to do what is just, and to apply the best remedy to the greatest evil; but the very attempt would do good, and would be felt in the great Catholic insurrection, come when it will. All rebellions and disaffections are general and terrible in proportion as one party has suffered, and the other inflicted; any great measure of conciliation, proposed in the spirit of kindness, is remembered, and renders war less terrible, and opens avenues to peace.

The Roman Catholic priest could not refuse to draw his salary from the state without incurring the indignation of his flock. "Why are you to come upon us for all this money, when you can ride over to Sligo or Belfast, and draw a draft upon government for the amount?" It is not easy to give a satisfactory answer to this, to a shrewd man who is starving to death.

Of course, in talking of a government payment to the Catholic priest, I mean it should be done with the utmost fairness and good faith; no attempt to gain patronage, or to make use of the pope as a stalking-horse for playing tricks. Leave the patronage exactly as you find it; and take the greatest possible care that the Catholic clergy have no reason to suspect you in this particular; do it like a gentleman, without shuffling and prevarication, or leave it alone altogether.

The most important step in improvement which mankind ever made, was the secession from the see of Rome, and the establishment of the Protestant religion; but though I have the sincerest admiration of the Protestant faith I have no admiration of Protestant hassocks on which there are no knees, nor of seats on which there is no superincumbent Protestant pressure, nor of whole acres of tenantless Protestant pews, in which no human being of the five hundred sects of Christians is ever seen. I have no passion for sacred emptiness, or pious vacuity. The emoluments of those livings in which there are few or no Protestants, ought, after the death of the present incumbents, to be appropriated in part to the uses of the predominant religion, or some arrangements made for superseding such utterly useless ministers immediately securing to them the emoluments they possess.

Can any honest man say, that in parishes (as is the case fre-

fuse it?" "Ah, Mr. Smith," said Dr. Doyle, "you've such a way of putting things?"—*Lady Holland's Memoir*, p. 276.

quently in Ireland) containing 3000 or 4000 Catholics and 40 or 50 Protestants, there is the smallest chance of the majority being converted? Are not the Catholics (except in the North of Ireland, where the great mass are Presbyterians) gaining everywhere on the Protestants? The tithes were originally possessed by the Catholic Church of Ireland. Not one shilling of them is now devoted to that purpose. An immense majority of the common people are Catholics; they see a church richly supported by the spoils of their own church establishments, in whose tenets not one tenth part of the people believe. Is it possible to believe this can endure?—that a light, irritable, priest-ridden people will not, under such circumstances, always remain at the very eve of rebellion, always ready to explode when the finger of Daniel touches the hair trigger?—for Daniel, be it said, though he hates shedding blood in small quantities, has no objection to provoking kindred nations to war. He very properly objects to killing or being killed by Lord Alvanly; but would urge on ten thousand Pats in civil combat against ten thousand Bulls. His objections are to small homicides; and his vow that he has registered in Heaven is only against retail destruction, and murder by piecemeal. He does not like to teaze Satan by driblets; but to earn eternal torments by persuading eight million Irish, and twelve million Britons no longer to buy and sell oats and salt meat, but to butcher each other in God's name to extermination. And what if Daniel dies, of what use his death? Does Daniel make the occasion, or does the occasion make Daniel?—Daniels are made by the bigotry and insolence of England to Ireland; and till the monstrous abuses of the Protestant Church in that country are rectified, there will always *be* Daniels, and they will always come out of their dens more powerful and more popular than when you cast them in.

I do not mean by this unjustly and cowardly to run down O'Connell. He has been of eminent service to his country in the question of Catholic Emancipation, and I am by no means satisfied that with the gratification of vanity there are not mingled genuine feelings of patriotism and a deep sense of the injustice done to his country. His first success, however, flung him off his guard; and perhaps he trusted too much in the timidity of the present government, who are by no means composed of irresolute or weak men.

If I thought Ireland quite safe, I should still object to injustice. I could never endure in silence that the Catholic Church of Ireland should be left in its present state; but I am afraid France and England can now afford to fight; and having saved a little money, they will, of course, spend it in fighting. That puppy of the waves, young Joinville, will steam over in a high-pressure fleet!—and then comes an immense twenty per cent. income-tax war, a universal insurrection in Ireland, and a crisis of misery and distress, in which life will hardly be worth having. The struggle *may* end in our favour, but it may *not;* and the object of political wisdom is to avoid these struggles. I want to see jolly Roman Catholic priests secure of their income without any motive for sedition or turbulence. I want to see Patricks at the loom; cotton and silk factories springing up in the bogs; Ireland a rich, happy, quiet country!—scribbling, carding, cleaning, and making calico, as if mankind had only a few days more allotted to them for making clothes, and were ever after to remain stark naked.

Remember that between your impending and your past wars with Ireland there is this remarkable difference. You have given up your Protestant auxiliaries; the Protestants enjoyed in former disputes all the patronage of Ireland: they fought not only from religious hatred, but to preserve their monopoly;—that monopoly is gone; you have been candid and just for thirty years, and have lost those friends whose swords were always ready to defend the partiality of the government and to stifle the cry of justice. The next war will not be between Catholic and Protestant, but between Ireland and England.

I have some belief in Sir Robert. He is a man of great understanding, and *must* see that this eternal O'Connelling will never do, that it is impossible it can last. We are in a transition state, and the Tories may be assured that the baronet will not go too fast. If Peel tells them that the thing must be done, they may be sure it is high time to do it;—they may retreat mournfully and sullenly before common justice and common sense, but retreat they must when Tamworth gives the word—and in quick-step too, and without loss of time.

And let me beg of my dear Ultras not to imagine that they survive for a single instant without Sir Robert—that they could form an ultra-tory administration. Is there a Chartist in Great

Britain who would not, upon the first intimation of such an attempt, order a new suit of clothes, and call upon the baker and milkman for an extended credit? Is there a political reasoner who would not come out of his hole with a new constitution? Is there one ravenous rogue who would not be looking for his prey? Is there one honest man of common sense who does not see that universal disaffection and civil war would follow from the blind fury, the childish prejudices and the deep ignorance of such a sect? I have a high opinion of Sir Robert Peel, but he must summon up all his political courage, and do something next session for the payment of the Roman Catholic priests. He must run some risk of shocking public opinion; no greater risk, however, than he did in Catholic Emancipation. I am sure the Whigs would be true to him, and I think I observe that very many obtuse country gentlemen are alarmed by the state of Ireland, and the hostility of France and America.

Give what you please to the Catholic priests, habits are not broken in a day. There must be time as well as justice, but in the end these things have their effect. A buggy, a house, some field near it, a decent income paid quarterly; in the long run these are the cures of sedition and disaffection; men don't quit the common business of life, and join bitter political parties, unless they have something justly to complain of.

But where is the money — about £100,000 per annum — to come from? Out of the pockets of the best of men, Mr. Thomas Grenville, out of the pockets of the bishops, of Sir Robert Inglis, and all other men who pay all other taxes; and never will public money be so well and wisely employed!

It turns out that there is no law to prevent entering into diplomatic engagements with the pope. The sooner we become acquainted with a gentleman who has so much to say to eight millions of our subjects, the better! Can anything be so childish and absurd as a horror of communicating with the pope, and all the hobgoblins we have imagined of premunires and outlawries for this contraband trade in piety? Our ancestors (strange to say, wiser than ourselves), have left us to do as we please, and the sooner government do what they can do legally, the better. A thousand opportunities of doing good in Irish affairs have been lost, from our having no avowed and dignified agent at the Court of Rome.

If it depended upon me, I would send the Duke of Devonshire there to-morrow, with nine chaplains and several tons of Protestant theology. I have no love of popery, but the pope is at all events better than the idol of Juggernaut, whose chaplains I believe we pay, and whose chariot I dare say is made in Long Acre. We pay £10,000 a year to our ambassador at Constantinople, and are startled with the idea of communicating diplomatically with Rome, deeming the Sultan a better Christian than the pope!

The mode of exacting clerical dues in Ireland is quite arbitrary and capricious. Uniformity is out of the question; everything depends on the disposition and temper of the clergyman. There are salutary regulations put forth in each diocese respecting church dues and church discipline, and put forth by Episcopal and synodical authority. Specific sums are laid down for mass, marriage, and the administration of the Eucharist. These authorized payments are moderate enough, but every priest, in spite of these rules, makes the most he can of his ministry, and the *strangest* discrepancy prevails, even in the same diocese, in the demands made upon the people. The priest and his flock are continually coming into collision on pecuniary matters. Twice a year the holy man collects confession money under the denomination of Christmas and Easter offerings. He selects, in every neighbourhood, one or two houses in which he holds stations of confession. Very disagreeable scenes take place when additional money is demanded, or when additional time for payment is craved. The first thing done when there is a question of marrying a couple is, to make a *bargain* about the marriage money. The wary minister watches the palpitations, puts on a shilling for every sigh, and two-pence on every tear, and maddens the impetuosity of the young lovers up to a pound sterling. The remuneration prescribed by the diocesan statutes, is never thought of for a moment; the priest makes as hard a bargain as he can, and the bed the poor peasants are to lie upon is sold, to make their concubinage lawful;—but every one present at the marriage is to contribute;—the minister, after begging and entreating some time to little purpose, gets into a violent rage, abuses and is abused;—and in this way is celebrated one of the sacraments of the Catholic Church!—The same scenes of altercation and abuse take place when gossip-money is refused at baptisms; but the most painful scenes take place at extreme unction, a ceremony to which the common people in Ireland attach the utmost importance. " Pay me beforehand—this is not enough —I insist upon more, I know you can afford it, I insist upon a larger fee!"—and all this before the dying man, who feels he has not an hour to live! and believes that salvation depends upon the timely application of this sacred grease.

Other bad consequences arise out of the present system of Irish Church support. Many of the clergy are constantly endeavouring to overreach and undermine one another. Every man looks to his own private emolument, regardless of all covenants, expressed or implied. The curate does not make a fair return to the parish priest, nor the parish priest to the curate. There is a universal scramble!—every one gets what he can, and seems to think he would be almost justified in appropriating the whole to himself. And how can all this be otherwise? How are the poor, wretched clergy to live, but by setting a high price on their theological labours, and using every incentive of fear and superstition to extort from six millions of beggars the little payments wanted for the bodies of the poor, and the support of life! I maintain that it is shocking and wicked to leave the religious guides of six millions of people in such a state of destitution!—to bestow no more thought upon them than upon the clergy of the Sandwich Islands! If I were a member of the cabinet, and met my colleagues once a week, to eat birds and beasts, and to talk over the state of the world, I should begin upon Ireland before the soup was finished, go on through fish, turkey, and saddle of mutton, and never end till the last thimbleful of claret had passed down the throat of the incredulous Haddington: but there they sit, week after week; there they come, week after week; the Piccadilly Mars, the Scotch Neptune, Themis Lyndhurst, the Tamworth baronet, dear Goody, and dearer Gladdy,* and think no more of paying the Catholic clergy, than a man of real fashion does of paying his tailor! And there is no excuse for this in fanaticism. There is only one man in the cabinet who objects from reasons purely fanatical, because the Pope is the Scarlet Lady, or the Seventh Vial, or the Little Horn. All the rest are entirely of opinion that it *ought* to be done—that it is the one thing needful; but they are afraid of bishops and

* Lord Goderich and the Right Hon. William Ewart Gladstone

county meetings, newspapers, and pamphlets, and reviews; all fair enough objects of apprehension, but they must be met, and encountered, and put down. It is impossible that the subject can be much longer avoided, and that every year is to produce a deadly struggle with the people, and a long trial in time of peace with O' somebody, the patriot for the time being, or the general, perhaps, in time of a foreign war.

If I were a bishop, living beautifully in a state of serene plenitude, I don't think I could endure the thought of so many honest, pious, and laborious clergymen of another faith, placed in such disgraceful circumstances! I could not get into my carriage with jelly-springs, or see my two courses every day, without remembering the buggy and the bacon of some poor old Catholic bishop, ,en times as laborious, and with much more, perhaps, of theological learning than myself, often distressed for a few pounds! and burthened with duties utterly disproportioned to his age and strength. I think, if the extreme comfort of my own condition did not extinguish all feeling for others, I should sharply commiserate such a church, and attempt with ardour and perseverance to apply the proper remedy. Now let us bring names and well-known scenes before the English reader, to give him a clearer notion of what passes in Catholic Ireland. The living of St. George's, Hanover Square, is a benefice of about £1500 per annum, and a good house. It is in the possession of Dr. Hodgson, who is also Dean of Carlisle, worth, I believe, about £1500 more. A more comfortable existence can hardly be conceived. Dr. Hodgson is a very worthy, amiable man, and I am very glad he is as rich as he is: but suppose he had no revenues but what he got off his own bat — suppose that instead of tumbling through the skylight, as his income now does, it was procured by Catholic methods. The Doctor tells Mr. Thompson he will not marry him to Miss Simpson under £30; Thompson demurs, and endeavours to beat him down. The Doctor sees Miss Simpson; finds her very pretty; thinks Thompson hasty, and after a long and undignified negotiation, the Doctor gets his fee. Soon after this he receives a message from Place, the tailor, to come and anoint him with extreme unction. He repairs to the bed-side, and tells Mr. Place that he will not touch him under a suit of clothes, equal to £10: the family resist, the altercation goes on before the perishing artisan, the price is reduced to

£8, and Mr. Place is oiled. On the ensuing Sunday the child of Lord B. is to be christened; the godfathers and godmothers will only give a sovereign each; the Doctor refuses to do it for the money, and the church is a scene of clamour and confusion. These are the scenes which, under similar circumstances, *would* take place here, for the congregation want the comforts of religion without fees, and will cheat the clergyman if they can; and the clergyman who means to live, must meet all these artifices with stern resistance. And this is the wretched state of the Irish Roman Catholic clergy!—a miserable blot and stain on the English nation What a blessing to this country would a real bishop be! A man who thought it the first duty of Christianity to allay the bad passions of mankind, and to reconcile contending sects with each other. What peace and happiness such a man as the Bishop of London might have conferred on the empire, if, instead of changing black dresses for white dresses, and administering to the frivolous disputes of foolish zealots, he had laboured to abate the hatred of Protestants for the Roman Catholics, and had dedicated his powerful understanding to promote religious peace in the two countries. Scarcely any bishop is sufficiently a man of the world to deal with fanatics. The way is not to reason with them, but to ask them to dinner. They are armed against logic and remonstrance, but they are puzzled in a labyrinth of wines, disarmed by facilities and concessions, introduced to a new world, come away thinking more of hot and cold, and dry and sweet, than of Newman, Keble, and Pusey. So mouldered away Hannibal's army at Capua! So the primitive and perpendicular prig of Puseyism is softened into practical wisdom, and coaxed into common sense. Providence gives us generals, and admirals, and chancellors of the exchequer; but I never remember in my time a real bishop—a grave, elderly man, full of Greek, with sound views of the middle voice and preterperfect tense, gentle and kind to his poor clergy, of powerful and commanding eloquence; in Parliament never to be put down when the great interests of mankind were concerned; leaning to the government when *it* was right, leaning to the people when *they* were right; feeling that the Spirit of God had called him to that high office, he was called for no mean purpose, but rather that, seeing clearly and acting boldly, and intending purely, he might confer lasting benefits upon mankind.

We consider the Irish clergy as factious, and as encouraging the bad anti-British spirit of the people. How can it be otherwise? They live by the people; they have nothing to live upon but the voluntary oblations of the people; and they must fall into the same spirit as the people, or they would be starved to death. No marriage; no mortuary masses; no unctions to the priest who preached against O'Connell!

Give the clergy a maintenance separate from the will of the people, and you will then enable them to oppose the folly and madness of the people. The objection to the state provision does not really come from the clergy, but from the agitators and repealers: these men see the immense advantage of carrying the clergy with them in their agitation, and of giving the sanction of religion to political hatred; they know that the clergy, moving in the same direction with the people, have an immense influence over them; and they are very wisely afraid, not only of losing this co-operating power, but of seeing it, by a state provision, arrayed against them. I am fully convinced that a state payment to the Catholic clergy, by leaving to that laborious and useful body of men the exercise of their free judgment, would be the severest blow that Irish agitation could receive.

For advancing these opinions, I have no doubt I shall be assailed by Sacerdos, Vindex, Latimer, Vates, Clericus, Aruspex, and be called atheist, deist, democrat, smuggler, poacher, highwayman, Unitarian, and Edinburgh Reviewer! Still, *I am in the right—* and what I say requires excuse for being trite and obvious, not for being mischievous and paradoxical. I write for three reasons; first, because I really wish to do good; secondly, because, if I don't write, I know nobody else will; and thirdly, because it is the nature of the animal to write, and I cannot help it. Still, in looking back I see no reason to repent. What I have said *ought* to be done, generally *has* been done, but always twenty or thirty years too late; done, not, of course, because I have said it, but because it was no longer *possible* to avoid doing it. Human beings cling to their delicious tyrannies, and to their exquisite nonsense, like a drunkard to his bottle, and go on till death stares them in the face. The monstrous state of the Catholic Church in Ireland will probably remain till some monstrous ruin threatens the very existence of the empire, and Lambeth and Fulham are cursed by the affrighted people.

I have always compared the Protestant church in Ireland (and I believe my friend, Thomas Moore, stole the simile from me) to the institution of butchers' shops in all the villages of our Indian empire. "We *will* have a butcher's shop in every village, and you, Hindoos, shall pay for it. We know that many of you do not eat meat at all, and that the sight of beef-steaks is particularly offensive to you; but still, a stray European may pass through your village, and want a steak or a chop: the shop *shall* be established; and you shall pay for it." This is English legislation for Ireland!! There is no abuse like it in all Europe, in all Asia, in all the discovered parts of Africa, and in all we have heard of Timbuctoo! It is an error that requires twenty thousand armed men for its protection in time of peace; which costs more than a million a year; and which, in the first French war, in spite of the puffing and panting of fighting steamers, will and *must* break out into desperate rebellion.

It is commonly said, if the Roman Catholic priests are paid by the state, they will lose their influence over their flocks; not their *fair* influence—not that influence which any wise and good man would wish to see in all religions—not the dependence of humble ignorance upon prudence and piety—only fellowship in faction, and fraternity in rebellion; all *that* will be lost. A peep-of-day clergyman will no longer preach to a peep-of-day congregation—a Whiteboy vicar will no longer lead the psalm to Whiteboy vocalists; but everything that is good and wholesome will remain. This, however, is not what the anti-British faction want; they want all the animation which piety can breathe into sedition, and all the fury which the priesthood can preach to diversity of faith: and *this* is what they mean by a clergy losing their influence over the people! The less a clergyman exacts of his people, the more his payments are kept out of sight, the less will be the friction with which he exercises the functions of his office. A poor Catholic may respect a priest the more who marries, baptizes, and anoints; but he respects him because he associates with his name and character the performance of sacred duties, not because he exacts heavy fees for doing so. Double fees would be a very doubtful cure for skepticism; and though we have often seen the tenth of the earth's produce carted away for the benefit of the clergyman, we do not remember any very lively marks of satisfaction and delight which it produced in the countenance of the decimated person. I am thoroughly convinced that state payments to the Catholic clergy would remove a thousand causes of hatred between the priest and his flock, and would be as favourable to the increase of his useful authority, as it would be fatal to his factious influence over the people.

SIR JAMES MACKINTOSH.

LETTER ON THE CHARACTER OF SIR JAMES MACKINTOSH.*

MY DEAR SIR: You ask for some of your late father's letters: I am sorry to say I have none to send you. Upon principle, I keep no letters except those on business. I have not a single letter from him, nor from any human being in my possession.

The impression which the great talents and amiable qualities of your father made upon me, will remain as long as I remain. When I turn from living spectacles of stupidity, ignorance, and

---

* It may assist the reader to recall the chief facts of Mackintosh's Life. He was born in the county of Inverness, Scotland, in 1765. He was educated at Aberdeen and in Edinburgh, where he took the degree of Doctor of medicine in 1787. He was called to the English bar in 1795; in 1803 received the honour of knighthood, on his appointment as Recorder of Bombay; discharged the duties of that office, in India, from 1804 till 1811; returned to Britain in 1812; in the following year was elected Member of Parliament for Nairnshire. In 1818, he became Professor of Law and General Politics, at Hayleybury College, an institution for the civil servants of the East India Company, and was, the same year, chosen Member of Parliament for Knaresborough, which he continued to represent till his death. He was chosen Lord-Rector of the University of Glasgow in 1823, and made Privy-Councillor by Canning, in 1827. He died in 1832. His chief writings were his Vindiciæ Gallicæ, a reply to Burke's Reflections on the French Revolution, at the age of twenty-six, in 1791; his Introductory Discourse on the Law of Nature and Nations; a Dissertation on the History and Progress of Ethical Philosophy, a History of the early English Reigns for Lardner's Cabinet Cyclopædia, a Life of Sir Thomas More, and various articles in the Edinburgh Review. His Life, Correspondence, and Journals, were published by his son, Robert James Mackintosh, to which work this Letter, by Sydney Smith, was an important contribution.

malice, and wish to think better of the world — I remember my great and benevolent friend Mackintosh.

The first points of character which everybody noticed in him were the total absence of envy, hatred, malice, and uncharitableness. He could not hate — he did not know how to set about it. The gall-bladder was omitted in his composition, and if he could have been persuaded into any scheme of revenging himself upon an enemy, I am sure (unless he had been narrowly watched) it would have ended in proclaiming the good qualities, and promoting the interests of his adversary. Truth had so much more power over him than anger, that (whatever might be the provocation) he could not misrepresent, nor exaggerate. In questions of passion and party, he stated facts as they were, and reasoned fairly upon them, placing his happiness and pride in equitable discrimination. Very fond of talking, he heard patiently, and, not averse to intellectual display, did not forget that others might have the same inclination as himself.

Till subdued by age and illness, his conversation was more brilliant and instructive than that of any human being I ever had the good fortune to be acquainted with. His memory (vast and prodigious as it was) he so managed as to make it a source of pleasure and instruction, rather than that dreadful engine of colloquial oppression into which it is sometimes erected. He remembered things, words, thoughts, dates, and everything that was wanted. His language was beautiful, and might have gone from the fireside to the press; but though his ideas were always clothed in beautiful language, the clothes were sometimes too big for the body, and common thoughts were dressed in better and larger apparel than they deserved. He certainly had this fault, but it was not one of frequent commission.*

---

* There is a bit of humour in Smith's Memoirs on this text. Writing to Lord Holland, in 1826, he says: "It struck me last night, as I was lying in bed, that Mackintosh, if he were to write on pepper, would thus describe it ·

"'Pepper may philosophically be described as a dusty and highly-pulverized seed of an Oriental fruit; an article rather of condiment than diet, which, dispersed lightly over the surface of food, with no other rule than the caprice of the consumer, communicates pleasure, rather than affords nutrition; and, by adding a tropical flavour to the gross and succulent viands of the North, approximates the different regions of the earth, explains the objects of commerce, and justifies the industry of man.'"

He had a method of putt'ng things so mildly and interrogatively, that he always procured the readiest reception for his opinions. Addicted to reasoning in the company of able men, he had two valuable habits, which are rarely met with in great reasoners — he never broke in upon his opponent, and always avoided strong and vehement assertions. His reasoning commonly carried conviction, for he was cautious in his positions, accurate in his deductions, aimed only at truth. The ingenious side was commonly taken by some one else; the interests of truth were protected by Mackintosh.

His good-nature and candour betrayed him into a morbid habit of eulogizing everybody — a habit which destroyed the value of commendations, that might have been to the young (if more sparingly distributed) a reward of virtue and a motive to exertion.*

* Smith hit off this trait of his friend in a parody. The following is from Lady Holland's Memoir : —
"What a loss you had in not knowing Mackintosh! how was it?... Yes, his manner was cold; his shake of the hand came under the genus 'mortmain;' but his heart was overflowing with benevolence. I like that simile I made on him in my letter, of 'a great ship cutting its cable;' it is fine, and it well described Mackintosh. His chief foible was indiscriminate praise. I amused myself the other day,' said he, laughing, 'in writing a termination of a speech for him; would you like to hear it? I will read it to you : —
"'It is impossible to conclude these observations without expressing the obligations I am under to a person in a much more humble scene of life — I mean, sir, the hackney-coachman by whom I have been driven to this meeting. To pass safely through the streets of a crowded metropolis must require, on the part of the driver, no common assemblage of qualities. He must have caution without timidity, activity without precipitation, and courage without rashness; he must have a clear perception of his object, and a dexterous use of his means. I can safely say of the individual in question, that, for a moderate reward, he has displayed unwearied skill; and to him I shall never forget that I owe unfractured integrity of limb, exemption from pain, and perhaps prolongation of existence.
"'Nor can I pass over the encouraging cheerfulness with which I was received by the waiter, nor the useful blaze of light communicated by the linkboys, as I descended from the carriage. It was with no common pleasure that I remarked in these men, not the mercenary bustle of venal service, but the genuine effusions of untutored benevolence; not the rapacity of subordinate agency, but the alacrity of humble friendship. What may not be said of a country where all the little accidents of life bring forth the hidden qualities of the heart — where her vehicles are driven, her streets illumined, and her bells answered, by men teeming with all the refinements of civilized life?

Occasionally he took fits of an opposite nature; and I have seen him abating and dissolving pompous gentlemen with the most successful ridicule. He certainly had a good deal of humour; and I remember, amongst many other examples of it, that he kept us for two or three hours in a roar of laughter, at a dinner-party at his own house, playing upon the simplicity of a Scotch cousin, who had mistaken me for my gallant synonym, the hero of Acre. I never saw a more perfect comedy, nor heard ridicule so long and so well sustained.* Sir James had not only humour, but he had wit also; at least, new and sudden relations of ideas flashed across his mind in reasoning, and produced the same effect as wit, and would have been called wit, if a sense of their utility and im-

"'I can not conclude, sir, without thanking you for the very clear and distinct manner in which you have announced the proposition on which we are to vote. It is but common justice to add that public assemblies rarely witness articulation so perfect, language so select, and a manner so eminently remarkable for everything that is kind, impartial, and just.'"

* This was in his early days at London, about the year 1807. Lady Holland (Memoir, p. 87) tells the story:—

"It was on occasion of one of these suppers that Sir James Mackintosh happened to bring with him a raw Scotch cousin, an ensign in a Highland regiment. On hearing the name of his host he suddenly turned round, and, nudging Sir James, said in an audible whisper, 'Is that the great Sir Sudney?' 'Yes, yes,' said Sir James, much amused; and giving my father the hint, on the instant he assumed the military character, performed the part of the hero of Acre to perfection, fought all his battles over again, and showed how he had charged the Turks, to the infinite delight of the young Scotchman, who was quite enchanted with the kindness and condescension of 'the great Sir Sudney,' as he called him, and to the absolute torture of the other guests, who were bursting with suppressed laughter at the scene before them. At last, after an evening of the most inimitable acting on the part both of my father and Sir James, nothing would serve the young Highlander but setting off, at twelve o'clock at night, to fetch the piper of his regiment to pipe to 'the great Sir Sudney,' who said he had never heard the bagpipes, upon which the whole party broke up and dispersed instantly, for Sir James said his Scotch cousin would infallibly cut his throat if he discovered his mistake. A few days afterward, when Sir James Mackintosh and his Scotch cousin were walking in the streets, they met my father with my mother on his arm. He introduced her as his wife, upon which the Scotch cousin said in a low voice to Sir James, and looking at my mother, 'I did na ken the great Sir Sudney was married.' 'Why, no,' said Sir James, a little embarrassed and winking at him, 'not ex-act-ly married — only an Egyptian slave he brought over with him; Fatima — you know — you understand.' My mother was long known in the little circle as Fatima."

portance had not often overpowered the admiration of novelty, and entitled them to the higher name of wisdom. Then the great thoughts and fine sayings of the great men of all ages were intimately present to his recollection, and came out dazzling and delighting in his conversation. Justness of thinking was a strong feature in his understanding; he had a head in which nonsense and error could hardly vegetate: it was a soil utterly unfit for them. If his display in conversation had been only in maintaining splendid paradoxes, he would soon have wearied those he lived with; but no man could live long intimately with your father without finding that he was gaining upon doubt, correcting error, enlarging the boundaries, and strengthening the foundations of truth. It was worth while to listen to a master, whom not himself, but nature had appointed to the office, and who taught what it was not easy to forget, by methods which it was not easy to resist.*

Curran, the master of the rolls, said to Mr. Grattan, "You would be the greatest man of your age, Grattan, if you would buy a few yards of red tape, and tie up your bills and papers." This was the fault or misfortune of your excellent father; he never knew the use of red tape, and was utterly unfit for the common business of life.† That a guinea represented a quantity of shil-

---

* In 1801 Smith wrote to Jeffrey: "Nothing has pleased me more in London than the conversation of Mackintosh. I never saw so theoretical a head which contained so much practical understanding. He has lived much among various men, with great observation, and has always tried his profound moral speculations by the experience of life. He has not contracted in the world a lazy contempt for theorists nor in the closet a peevish impatience of that grossness and corruptibility of mankind, which are ever marring the schemes of secluded benevolence. He does not wish for the *best* in politics or morals, but for the best which can be attained; and what that is he seems to know well. Now what *I* object to Scotch philosophers in general is, that they reason upon man as they would upon a divinity; they pursue truth without caring if it be *useful* truth. They are more fond of disputing on mind and matter than on anything which can have a reference to the real world, inhabited by real men, women, and children; a philosopher that descends to the present state of things is debased in their estimation. Look among our friends in Edinburgh, and see if there be not some truth in this. I do not speak of great prominent literary personages, but of the mass of reflecting men in Scotland."

† Smith, writing to the Countess Grey of Mackintosh's visit to Foston in 1823, says of his guest: "Mackintosh had seventy volumes in his

lings, and that it would barter for a quantity of cloth, he was well aware; but the accurate number of the baser coin, or the just measurement of the manufactured article, to which he was entitled for his gold, he could never learn, and it was impossible to teach him. Hence his life was often an example of the ancient and melancholy struggle of genius, with the difficulties of existence.

I have often heard Sir James Mackintosh say of himself, that he was born to be the professor of a university. Happy, and for ages celebrated, would have been the university, which had so possessed him, but in this view he was unjust to himself. Still, however, his style of speaking in Parliament was certainly more academic than forensic; it was not sufficiently short and quick for a busy and impatient assembly. He often spoke over the heads of his hearers—was too much in advance of feeling for their sympathies, and of reasoning for their comprehension. He began too much at the beginning, and went too much to the right and left of the question, making rather a lecture or a dissertation than a speech. His voice was bad and nasal; and though nobody was in reality more sincere, he seemed not only not to feel, but hardly to think what he was saying.

Your father had very little science, and no great knowledge of physics. His notions of his early pursuit—the study of medicine—were imperfect and antiquated, and he was but an indifferent classical scholar, for the Greek language has never crossed the Tweed in any great force. In history the whole stream of time was open before him; he had looked into every moral and metaphysical question from Plato to Paley, and had waded through morasses of international law, where the step of no living man could follow him. Political economy is of modern invention; I am old enough to recollect when every judge on the bench (Lord Eldon and Sergeant Runnington excepted), in their charges to the grand juries, attributed the then high prices of corn to the scandalous combination of farmers. Sir James knew what is commonly agreed upon by political economists, without taking much pleasure in the science, and with a disposition to blame the very speculative and metaphysical disquisitions into which it has

carriage! None of the glasses would draw up or let down, but one; and he left his hat behind him at our house."

wandered, but with a full conviction also (which many able men of his standing are without) of the immense importance of the science to the welfare of society.

I think (though, perhaps, some of his friends may not agree with me in this opinion) that he was an acute judge of character, and of the good as well as evil in character. He was, in truth, with the appearance of distraction and of one occupied with other things, a very minute observer of human nature; and I have seen him analyze, to the very springs of the heart, men who had not the most distant suspicion of the sharpness of his vision, nor a belief that he could read anything but books.

Sufficient justice has not been done to his political integrity. He was not rich, was from the northern part of the island, possessed great facility of temper, and had therefore every excuse for political lubricity, which that vice (more common in those days than I hope it will ever be again) could possibly require. Invited by every party, upon his arrival from India, he remained steadfast to his old friends the whigs, whose admission to office, or enjoyment of political power, would at that period have been considered as the most visionary of all human speculations; yet, during his lifetime, everybody seemed more ready to have forgiven the tergiversation of which he was not guilty, than to admire the actual firmness he had displayed. With all this he never made the slightest efforts to advance his interests with his political friends, never mentioned his sacrifices nor his services, expressed no resentment at neglect, and was therefore pushed into such situations as fall to the lot of the feeble and delicate in a crowd.

A high merit in Sir James Mackintosh was his real and unaffected philanthropy. He did not make the improvement of the great mass of mankind an engine of popularity, and a stepping-stone to power, but he had a genuine love of human happiness. Whatever might assuage the angry passions, and arrange the conflicting interests of nations; whatever could promote peace, increase knowledge, extend commerce, diminish crime, and encourage industry; whatever could exalt human character, and could enlarge human understanding; struck at once at the heart of your father, and roused all his faculties. I have seen him in a moment when this spirit came upon him — like a great ship of war—cut his cable, and spread his enormous canvass and launch into a wide sea of reasoning eloquence.

But though easily warmed by great schemes of benevolence and human improvement, his manner was cold to individuals. There was an apparent want of heartiness and cordiality. It seemed as if he had more affection for the species than for the ingredients of which it was composed. He was in reality very hospitable, and so fond of company, that he was hardly happy out of it; but he did not receive his friends with that honest joy which warms more than dinner or wine.*

This is the good and evil of your father which comes uppermost. If he had been arrogant and grasping; if he had been faithless and false; if he had always been eager to strangle infant genius in its cradle; always ready to betray and to blacken those with whom he sat at meat; he would have passed many men, who, in the course of his long life, have passed him; but, without selling his soul for pottage, if he only had had a little more prudence for the promotion of his interests, and more of angry passions for the punishment of those detractors who envied his fame and presumed upon his sweetness; if he had been more aware of his powers, and of that space which nature intended him to occupy: he would have acted a great part in life, and remained a character in history. As it is, he has left, in many of the best men in England, and of the continent, the deepest admiration of his talents, his wisdom, his knowledge, and his benevolence.

I remain, my dear sir, very truly yours,

Sydney Smith.

* In reference to this passage a Quarterly reviewer remarked: "Mr. Sydney Smith is remarkable for the quality he describes as wanting in Mackintosh; and to have passed a day at Combe Florey, the paragon of parsonages, is an epoch in the life of any man." (Quar. Rev., Feb., 1836.)

RECOLLECTIONS OF FRANCIS HORNER.

LETTER FROM SYDNEY SMITH TO LEONARD HORNER.

MY DEAR SIR: You desire me to commit to paper my recollections of your brother, Francis Horner. I think that the many years which have elapsed since his death, have not at all impaired my memory of his virtues, at the same time that they have afforded me more ample means of comparing him with other important human beings with whom I have become acquainted since that period.

I first made the acquaintance of Francis Horner at Edinburgh, where he was among the most conspicuous young men in that energetic and infragrant city. My desire to know him proceeded first of all from being cautioned against him by some excellent and feeble people to whom I had brought letters of introduction, and who represented him to me as a person of violent political opinions. I interpreted this to mean a person who thought for himself— who had firmness enough to take his own line in life, and who loved truth better than he loved Dundas, at that time the tyrant of Scotland. I found my interpretation to be just, and from thence till the period of his death, we lived in constant society, and friendship with each other.

There was something very remarkable in his countenance — the commandments were written on his face, and I have often told him there was not a crime he might not commit with impunity, as no judge or jury who saw him, would give the smallest degree of credit to any evidence against him: there was in his look a calm settled love of all that was honourable and good — an air of wisdom and of sweetness; you saw at once that he was a great man, whom nature had intended for a leader of human beings; you ranged yourself willingly under his banners, and cheerfully submitted to his sway.

He had an intense love of knowledge; he wasted very little of the portion of life conceded to him, and was always improving himself, not in the most foolish of all schemes of education, in making long and short verses and scanning Greek choruses, but in the masculine pursuits of the philosophy of legislation, of political economy, of the constitutional history of the country, and of the history and changes of Ancient and Modern Europe. He had read so much, and so well, that he was a contemporary of all men, and a citizen of all states.

I never saw any person who took such a lively interest in the daily happiness of his friends. If you were unwell, if there was a sick child in the nursery, if any death happened in your family, he never forgot you for an instant! You always found there was a man with a good heart who was never far from you.

He loved truth so much, that he never could bear any jesting upon important subjects. I remember one evening the late Lord Dudley and myself pretended to justify the conduct of the government in stealing the Danish fleet; we carried on the argument with some wickedness against our graver friend; he could not stand it, but bolted indignantly out of the room; we flung up the sash, and, with loud peals of laughter, professed ourselves decided Scandinavians; we offered him not only the ships, but all the shot, powder, cordage, and even the biscuit, if he would come back: but nothing could turn him; he went home; and it took us a fortnight of serious behaviour before we were forgiven.

Francis Horner was a very modest person, which men of great understanding seldom are. It was his habit to confirm his opinion by the opinions of others; and often to form them from the same source.*

* Writing to Jeffrey, in 1805, Smith says: "Horner is a very happy man; his worth and talents are acknowledged by the world at a more early period than those of any independent and upright man I ever remember. He verifies an observation I have often made, that the world do not dislike originality, liberality, and independence, so much as the *insulting arrogance* with which they are almost always accompanied. Now, Horner pleases the best judges, and does not offend the worst."

His success in the House of Commons was decided and immediate, and went on increasing to the last day of his life. Though put into Parliament by some of the great borough lords, every one saw that he represented his own real opinions: without hereditary wealth, and known as a writer in the Edinburgh Review, his independence was never questioned: his integrity, sincerity, and moderation, were acknowledged by all sides, and respected even by those impudent assassins who live only to discourage honesty and traduce virtue. The House of Commons as a near relative of mine once observed,* has more good taste than any man in it. Horner, from his manners, his ability, and his integrity, became a general favourite with the House; they suspended for him their habitual dislike of lawyers, of political adventurers, and of young men of *conseederable taalents* from the North.

Your brother was wholly without pretensions or affectation. I have lived a long time in Scotland, and have seen very few affected Scotchmen; of those few he certainly was not one. In the ordinary course of life, he never bestowed a thought upon the effect he was producing; he trusted to his own good nature, and good intentions, and left the rest to chance.

Having known him well before he had acquired a great London reputation, I never observed that his fame produced the slightest alteration in his deportment; he was as affable to me, and to all his old friends, as when we were debating metaphysics in a garret in Edinburgh. I don't think it was in the power of ermine or mace, or seals, or lawn, or lace, or of any of those emblems and ornaments with which power loves to decorate itself, to have destroyed the simplicity of his character. I believe it would have defied all the corrupting appellations of human vanity: Severe, Honourable, Right Honourable, Sacred, Reverend, Right Reverend, Lord High, Earl, Marquis, Lord Mayor, Your Grace, Your Honour, and every other vocable which folly has invented, and idolatry cherished, would all have been lavished on him in vain.

The character of his understanding was the exercise of vigorous reasoning, in pursuit of important and difficult truth. He had no wit; nor did he condescend to that inferior variety of this electric talent which prevails occasionally in the North, and which, under the name of *Wut*, is so infinitely distressing to persons of good

* His brother Robert Smith.

taste. He had no very ardent and poetical imagination, but he had that innate force, which,

> ——— "Quemvis perferre laborem
> Suasit, et induxit noctes vigilare serenas
> Quærentem dictis quibus, et quo carmine demum,
> Clara suæ possit præpandere lumina menti."*

Your late excellent father, though a very well-informed person, was not what would be called a literary man, and you will readily concede to me that none of his family would pretend to rival your brother in point of talents. I never saw more constant and high-principled attention to parents than in his instance; more habitual and respectful deference to their opinions and wishes. I never saw brothers and sisters, over whom he might have assumed a family sovereignty, treated with more cheerful and endearing equality. I mention these things, because men who do good things are so much more valuable than those who say wise ones; because the order of human excellence is so often inverted, and great talents considered as an excuse for the absence of obscure virtues.

Francis Horner was always very guarded in his political opinions; guarded, I mean, against the excesses into which so many young men of talents were betrayed by their admiration of the French revolution. He was an English Whig, and no more than an English Whig. He mourned sincerely over the crimes and madness of France, and never, for a single moment, surrendered his understanding to the novelty and nonsense which infested the world at that strange era of human affairs.

I remember the death of many eminent Englishmen, but I can safely say, I never remember an impression so general as that ex-

* Part of the address of Lucretius to Memmius in the opening of his great philosophical poem De Rerum Natura, where the author is warmed by friendship to overcome the difficulties of presenting Greek themes in Latin measures; in Creech's loose version:—

> "Yet for respect of you with great delight
> I meet these dangers, and I wake all night,
> Labouring fit numbers and fit words to find,
> To make things plain and to instruct your mind,
> And teach her to direct her curious eye
> Into coy nature's greatest privacy."

Smith has adapted the passage by some slight changes.

cited by the death of Francis Horner.* The public looked upon him as a powerful and safe man, who was labouring, not for himself or his party, but for them. They were convinced of his talents, they confided in his moderation, and they were sure of his motives; he had improved so quickly and so much, that his early death was looked upon as the destruction of a great statesman, who had done but a small part of the good which might be expected from him, who would infallibly have risen to the highest offices, and as infallibly have filled them to the public good. Then, as he had never lost a friend, and made so few enemies, there was no friction, no drawback; public feeling had its free course; the image of a good and great man was broadly before the world, unsullied by any breath of hatred; there was nothing but pure sorrow! Youth destroyed before its time, great talents and wisdom hurried to the grave, a kind and good man, who might have lived for the glory of England, torn from us in the flower of his life!—but all this is gone and past, and, as Galileo said of his lost sight, "It has pleased God it should be so, and it must please me also."

Ever truly, yours,   SYDNEY SMITH.

COMBE FLOREY, 26th August, 1842.

* Horner died at Pisa, in February, 1817, in the thirty-ninth year of his age. He was born in Edinburgh, in 1778, and was the playmate, in childhood, of Henry Brougham. Educated at the University of Edinburgh, he pursued his studies in England; wrote for the first number of the Edinburgh Review, practised law in Scotland, and was called to the English bar in 1807. He was best known by his career in the House of Commons, from 1806 to his death. He was at home on the currency, the corn laws, and other laborious questions of government and trade. His Memoir and Correspondence, edited by his brother, Leonard Horner, to which Sydney Smith's letter was a contribution, are a noble monument to his memory. Lady Holland (Memoir, p. 154) supplies these additional memoranda of Sydney Smith's affection and respect for his friend: "My father speaks of his feelings on this loss, in the following letter to Mr. Horner's younger brother: 'Foston, March, 23, 1817. I remember no misfortune of my life which I have felt so deeply as the loss of your brother. I never saw any man who combined together so much talent, worth, and warmth of heart; and we lived together in habits of great friendship and affection for many years. I shall always retain a most lively and affectionate remembrance of him to the day of my death.' Again, in a letter to Mr. John Whishaw (March 26, 1817), he says: 'I have received a melancholy fragment from poor Horner—a letter half-finished at his death. I cannot say how much I was affected by it; indeed, on looking back on my own mind, I never remember to have felt an event more deeply than his death.'"

PASSAGES FROM LETTERS.

VISITS OXFORD — CLIQUEISM.

(*To Jeffrey*, 1803.) I have been spending three or four days in Oxford, in a contested election; Horner went down with me, and was much entertained. I was so delighted with Oxford, after my long absence, that I almost resolved to pass the long vacation there, with my family, amidst the shades of the trees and the silence of the monasteries. Horner is to come down too; will you join us? We would settle the fate of nations, and believe ourselves (as all three or four men who live together do) the sole repositories of knowledge, liberality, and acuteness.

LIFE OF A PARENT.

(*To Jeffrey, London*, 1803 or 1804.) Mrs. Sydney is pretty well, and slowly recovering from her shock,* of which your kindness and your experience enabled you to ascertain the violence. Children are horribly insecure: the life of a parent is the life of a gambler.

WELL-INFORMED WOMEN.

(*To Jeffrey, London.* 1804.) —— —— is here, and will certainly settle in Scotland next winter. She is, for a woman, well-informed and very liberal: neither is she at all disagreeable; but the information of a very plain woman is so inconsiderable, that I agree with you in setting no very great store by it. I am no great

* The loss of her infant son.

physiognomist, nor have I much confidence in a science which pretends to discover the inside from the out; but where I have seen fine eyes, a beautiful complexion, grace and symmetry in women, I have generally thought them amazingly well-informed and extremely philosophical. In contrary instances, seldom or never.

JEFFREY'S ANALYSIS.

(*To Jeffrey, London*, 1804.) I certainly, my dear Jeffrey, in conjunction with the Knight of the Shaggy Eyebrows,* do protest against your increasing and unprofitable skepticism. I exhort you to restrain the violent tendency of your nature for analysis, and to cultivate synthetical propensities. What is virtue? What's the use of truth? What's the use of honour? What's a guinea, but a d—d yellow circle? The whole effort of your mind is to destroy. Because others build slightly and eagerly, you employ yourself in kicking down their houses, and contract a sort of aversion for the more honourable, useful, and difficult task of building well yourself.

TRIUMPH OF CIVILIZED LIFE.

(*To Jeffrey, London*, 1806.) Tell Murray that I was much struck with the politeness of Miss Markham the day after he went. In carving a partridge, I splashed her with gravy from head to foot; and though I saw three distinct brown rills of animal juice trickling down her cheek, she had the complaisance to swear that not a drop had reached her. Such circumstances are the triumphs of civilized life.

HINTS TO JEFFREY.

(*To Jeffrey, London*, 1806.) I must be candid with you, my dear Jeffrey, and tell you that I do not like your article on the Scotch Courts; and with me think many persons whose opinions I am sure you would respect. I subscribe to none of your reasonings, hardly, about juries; and the manner in which you have done it is far from happy. You have made, too, some egregious

* Francis Horner.

mistakes about English law, pointed out to me by one of the first lawyers of the King's Bench. I like to tell you these things, because you never do so well as when you are humbled and frightened, and if you could be alarmed into the semblance of modesty, you would charm everybody; but remember my joke against you about the moon: "D—n the solar system! bad light—planets too distant—pestered with comets—feeble contrivance; could make a better with great ease."

PAYING IN TURBOT.

(*To Jeffrey, London*, 1808.) I regret sincerely that so many years have elapsed since we met. I hope, if you possibly can, you will contrive to come to town this spring: we will keep open house for you; you shall not be molested with large parties. You have earned a very high reputation here, and you may eat it out in turbot, at great people's houses, if you please; though I well know you would prefer the quiet society of your old friends.

MAXIMS.

(*To Lady Holland, about* 1809.) I mean to make some maxims, like Rochefoucauld, and to preserve them. My first is this: After having lived half their lives respectably, many men get tired of honesty, and many women of propriety.

A SIGN OF THE STATE IN DIFFICULTY.

(*To Earl Grey*, 1809.) There is no man who thinks better of what you and your coadjutors can and will do; but I can not help looking upon it as a most melancholy proof of the miserable state of this country, when men of integrity and ability are employed. If it were possible to have gone on without them, I am sure they would never have been thought of.

ROGERS.

(*To Lady Holland*, 1815.) Many thanks for your letter. I think you very fortunate in having Rogers at Rome. Show me a more kind and friendly man; secondly, one, from good manners, knowledge, fun, taste, and observation, more agreeable; thirdly, a man of more strict political integrity, and of better character in private life. If I were to choose any Englishman in foreign parts whom I should wish to blunder upon, it should be Rogers.

SIR WALTER SCOTT.

(*To Lady Holland, Foston*, 1818.) I am sorry we cannot agree about Walter Scott. My test of a book written to amuse, is amusement; but I am rather rash, and ought not to say *I am amused*, before I have inquired whether Sharp or Mackintosh is so. Whishaw's* plan is the best: he gives no opinion for the first week, but confines himself to chuckling and elevating his chin; in the meantime, he drives diligently about the first critical stations, breakfasts in Mark Lane, hears from Hertford College, and by Saturday night is as bold as a lion, and as decisive as a court of justice.

A DINNER-PARTY AT HOLLAND HOUSE.

(*To the Countess Grey.*) We had a large party at dinner here yesterday: Dr. Wollaston, the great philosopher, who did not say one word; William Lamb; Sir Henry Bunbury; Palmella, the Portuguese ambassador; Lord Aberdeen, the Exquisite; Sir William Grant, a rake and disorderly man of the town, recently Master of the Rolls; Whishaw, a man of fashion; Frere; Hallam, of the "Middle Ages;" and myself. In spite of such heterogeneous materials, we had a pleasant party.†

* John Whishaw, the political and social friend of Mackintosh, and the Romillys. Writing to Earl Grey, at the period of the Reform Bill, Smith says, "Cultivate Whishaw; he is one of the most sensible men in England." And previously, to John Allen, in 1826: "We have seen a good deal of old Whishaw this summer; he is as pleasant as he is wise and honest. He has character enough to make him well received if he were dull, and wit enough to make him popular if he were a rogue."

† This ironical passage has given rise to a curious correspondence between the representatives of the family of one of the persons mentioned and Mrs. Austin, the editor of the Letters. A nephew of Sir William Grant, William Charles Grant complains to the lady of the slander to the memory of his rel-

TRAVELLERS IN AMERICA.

(*To the Earl Grey, Foston, Nov.* 30, 1818.) Dear Lord Grey: I will send Lady Grey the news from London when I get there. I am sure she is too wise a woman not to be fond of gossiping; I am fond of it, and have some talents for it.

I recommend you to read Hall, Palmer, Fearon, and Bradbury's Travels in America, particularly Fearon. Those four books may, with ease, be read through between breakfast and dinner. There is nothing so curious and interesting as the rapidity with which the Americans are spreading themselves over that immense continent.

It is quite contrary to all probability that America should remain in an integral state. They aim at extending from sea to sea, and have already made settlements on the Pacific. There can be no community of interest between people placed under such very different circumstances: the maritime Americans, and those who communicate with Europe by the Mississippi are at this moment, as far as interest can divide men, two separate people. There does not appear to be in America at this moment one man of any considerable talents. They are a very sensible people; and seem to have conducted their affairs, upon the whole, very well. Birkbeck's second book is not so good as his first. He deceives himself—says he *wishes* to deceive himself—and is not candid. If a man chooses to say, "I will live up to my neck in mud, fight bears, swim rivers, and combat backwoodsmen, that I may ulti-

---

ative (one of the most unexceptionable men in England in private and public life), asks for its suppression, and a public denial commensurate with the injury, adding that he supposes Sydney Smith "to have been imposed upon by some malicious person." Mrs. Austin gravely promises to omit the offending words from any future edition. The London Athenæum (April 26, 1856), which publishes the correspondence, as "The Sequel to a Jest," compares the original passage with Pope's ironical sketch (Epilogue to the Satires), when he has invoked the spirit of the detractor Arnall to "aid me while I lie":—

> "Cobham's a coward, Polwarth is a slave,
> And Lyttleton a dark designing knave,
> St. John has ever been a wealthy fool—
> But let me add, Sir Robert's mighty dull,
> Has never made a friend in private life,
> And was, besides, a tyrant to his wife."

mately gain an independence for myself and children," this is plain and intelligible; but, by Birkbeck's account, it is much like settling at Putney or Kew; only the people are more liberal and enlightened. Their economy and their cheap government will do some good in this country by way of example. Their allowance to Monroe is £5,000 per annum; and he finds his own victuals fire, and candles!

Ever yours, dear Lord Grey, most sincerely,

SYDNEY SMITH.

TO HIS SON DOUGLAS.

(*To Douglas Smith, Esq., King's Scholar at Westminster College, Foston Rectory*, 1819.) My dear Douglas: Concerning this Mr. ——, I would not have you put any trust in him, for he is not trustworthy; but so live with him as if one day or other he were to be your enemy. With such a character as his, this is a necessary precaution.

In the time you can give to English reading you should consider what it is most needful to have, what it is most shameful to want—shirts and stockings, before frills and collars. Such is the history of your own country, to be studied in Hume. then in Rapin's History of England, with Tindal's Continuation. Hume takes you to the end of James the Second, Rapin and Tindal will carry you to the end of Anne. Then, Coxe's " Life of Sir Robert Walpole," and the " Duke of Marlborough ;" and these read with attention to dates and geography. Then, the history of the other three or four enlightened nations in Europe. For the English poets, I will let you off at present with Milton, Dryden, Pope, and Shakespeare; and remember, always, in books, keep the best company. Don't read a line of Ovid till you have mastered Virgil; nor a line of Thomson till you have exhausted Pope; nor of Massinger, till you are familiar with Shakespeare.

I am glad you liked your box and its contents. Think of us as we think of you; and send us the most acceptable of all presents —the information that you are improving in all particulars.

The greatest of all human mysteries are the Westminster holidays. If you can get a peep behind the curtain, pray let us know immediately the day of your coming home.

We have had about three or four ounces of rain here, that is all. I heard of your being wet through in London, and envied you very much. The whole of this parish is pulverized from long and excessive drought. Our whole property depends upon the tranquillity of the winds: if it blow before it rains, we shall all be up in the air in the shape of dust, and shall be *transparished* we know not where.

God bless you, my dear boy! I hope we shall soon meet at Lydiard. Your affectionate father,

SYDNEY SMITH.

REVISITS EDINBURGH.

(*To Lady Mary Bennett, Dec.* 1821.) In the first place I went to Lord Grey's, and stayed with them three or four days; from thence I went to Edinburgh, where I had not been for ten years. I found a noble passage into the town, and new since my time; two beautiful English chapels, two of the handsomest library-rooms in Great Britain, and a wonderful increase of shoes and stockings, streets and houses. When I lived there, very few maids had shoes and stockings, but plodded about the house with feet as big as a family Bible, and legs as large as portmanteaus. I stayed with Jeffrey. My time was spent with the Whig leaders of the Scotch bar, a set of very honest, clever men, each possessing thirty-two different sorts of wine. My old friends were glad to see me; some had turned Methodists — some had lost their teeth — some had grown very rich — some very fat — some were dying — and, alas! alas! many were dead; but the world is a coarse enough place, so I talked away, comforted some, praised others, kissed some old ladies, and passed a very riotous week.

AN ARGILLACEOUS IMMORTALITY.

(*To John Murray, Foston,* 1821.) How little you understand young Wedgewood! If he appears to love waltzing, it is only to catch fresh figures for cream-jugs. Depend upon it, he will have Jeffrey and you upon some of his vessels, and you will enjoy an argillaceous immortality

ANTI-WAR.

(*To the Countess Grey, Foston, York, Feb.* 19, 1823.) For God's sake, do not drag me into another war! I am worn down, and worn out, with crusading and defending Europe, and protecting mankind; I *must* think a little of myself. I am sorry for the Spaniards—I am sorry for the Greeks—I deplore the fate of the Jews; the people of the Sandwich Islands are groaning under the most detestable tyranny; Bagdad is oppressed—I do not like the present state of the Delta—Thibet is not comfortable. Am I to fight for all these people? The world is bursting with sin and sorrow. Am I to be champion of the Decalogue, and to be eternally raising fleets and armies to make all men good and happy? We have just done saving Europe, and I am afraid the consequence will be, that we shall cut each other's throats. No war, dear Lady Grey!—no eloquence; but apathy, selfishness, common sense, arithmetic! I beseech you, secure Lord Grey's sword and pistols, as the housekeeper did Don Quixote's armour. If there is another war, life will not be worth having. I will go to war with the King of Denmark if he is impertinent to you, or does any injury to Howick; but for no other cause.

"May the vengeance of Heaven" overtake all the Legitimates of Verona! but, in the present state of rent and taxes, they must be *left* to the vengeance of Heaven! I allow fighting in such a cause to be a luxury; but the business of a prudent, sensible man, is to guard against luxury.

AN ORATORIO.

(*To Lady Holland*, 1823.) Nothing can be more disgusting than an Oratorio. How absurd, to see five hundred people fiddling like madmen about the Israelites in the Red Sea! Lord Morpeth pretends to say he was pleased, but I see a great change in him since the music-meeting. Pray tell Luttrell he did wrong not to come to the music. It tired me to death; it would have pleased him. He is a melodious person, and much given to sacred music.

In his fits of absence I have heard him hum the Hundredth Psalm! (Old Version.)

JEFFREY.

(*To Lady Holland*, 1827.) Jeffrey has been here with his adjectives, who always travel with him. His throat is giving way; so much wine goes down it, so many million words leap over it, how can it rest? Pray make him a judge; he is a truly great man, and is very heedless of his own interests. I lectured him on his romantic folly of wishing his friends to be preferred before himself, and succeeded, I think, in making him a little more selfish.

IRRELIGION AND IMPIETY.

(*To Messrs* ———, *Booksellers,* ——— *Foston*, 1827.) I hate the insolence, persecution, and intolerance, which so often pass under the name of religion, and (as you know) I have fought against them; but I have an unaffected horror of irreligion and impiety; and every principle of suspicion and fear would be excited in me by a man who professed himself an infidel.

TEMPERANCE.

(*To Lady Holland*, 1828.) Many thanks for your kind anxiety respecting my health. I not only was never better, but never half so well: indeed I find I have been very ill all my life, without knowing it. Let me state some of the goods arising from abstaining from all fermented liquors. First, sweet sleep; having never known what sweet sleep was, I sleep like a baby or a ploughboy. If I wake, no needless terrors, no black visions of life, but pleasing hopes and pleasing recollections: Holland House, past and to come! If I dream, it is not of lions and tigers, but of Easter dues and tithes. Secondly, I can take longer walks, and make greater exertions, without fatigue. My understanding is improved, and I comprehend Political Economy. I see better without wine and spectacles than when I used both. Only one evil ensues from it: I am in such extravagant spirits that I must lose blood, or look out for some one who will bore and depress me. Pray leave off wine: the stomach quite at rest; no heartburn no pain, no distension.

TO THOMAS MOORE.*

(*London*, 1831.) My dear Moore: By the beard of the prelate of Canterbury, by the cassock of the prelate of York, by the breakfasts of Rogers, by Luttrell's love of side-dishes, I swear that I had rather hear you sing than any person I ever heard in my life, male or female. For what is your singing but beautiful poetry floating in fine music, and guided by exquisite feeling? Call me Dissenter, say that my cassock is ill put on, that I know not the delicacies of decimation, and confound the greater and the smaller tithes; but do not think that I am insensible to your music. The truth is, that I took a solemn oath to Mrs. Beauclerk, to be there by ten, and set off, to prevent perjury, at eleven; but was seized with a violent pain in the stomach by the way, and went to bed. Yours ever, my dear Moore, very sincerely.

SYDNEY SMITH.

MALTHUS.

(*To Lady Holland, Combe Florey*, 1831.) Philosopher Malthus came here last week. I got an agreeable party for him of unmarried people. There was only one lady who had had a child; but he is a good-natured man, and, if there are no appearances of approaching fertility, is civil to every lady. Malthus is a real moral philosopher, and I would almost consent to speak as inarticulately, if I could think and act as wisely.

PREFERMENT.—AT COURT.

(*To the Countess of Morley, Bristol*, 1831.) Dear Lady Morley: I have taken possession of my preferment. The house is in Amen-corner—an awkward name on a card, and an awkward annunciation to the coachman on leaving any fashionable mansion. I find, too (sweet discovery!) that I give a dinner every Sunday, for three months in the year, to six clergymen and six singing-

* In answer to a note of Moore expressing the regret, that "he had gone away so soon from Ellis's the other night, as I had improved (i. e., in my singing) afterward, and he was one of the few I always wished to do my *best* for."—Moore's Diary, June 15, 1831.

men, at one o'clock. Do me the favour to drop in as Mrs. Morley. I did the duty at St. Paul's; the organ and music were excellent.

I went to Court, and, horrible to relate! with strings to my shoes instead of buckles—not from Jacobinism, but ignorance. I saw two or three Tory lords looking at me with dismay, was informed by the Clerk of the Closet of my sin, and gathering my sacerdotal petticoats about me (like a lady conscious of thick ankles), I escaped further observation. My residence is in February, March, and July.

EDWARD IRVING.

(*To the Countess of Morley.*) Noble countenance, expressing quite sufficient when at rest, too much when in activity. Middling voice, provincial accent, occasional bad taste; language often very happy, with flights of mere eloquence; not the vehicle of reasoning, or of profound remark. Very difficult, when the sermon was over, to know what it was about; and the whole effect rather fatiguing and tiresome.

READING IN AGE.

(*To Lady Holland, Combe Florey,* 1831.) Read Cicero's "Letters to Atticus," translated by the Abbé Mongon, with excellent notes. I sit in my beautiful study, looking upon a thousand flowers, and read agreeable books, in order to keep up arguments with Lord Holland and Allen. I thank God heartily for my comfortable situation in my old age—above my deserts, and beyond my former hopes.

TO EARL GREY IN OFFICE.

(1831.) Pray keep well, and do your best, with a gay and careless heart. What is it all, but the scratching of pismires upon a heap of earth? Rogues are careless and gay, why not honest men? Think of the Bill in the morning, and take your claret in the evening, totally forgetting the Bill. You have done admirably up to this time.

EPIGRAM ON PROFESSOR AIRY.

(*To John Murray, Combe Florey*, 1832.) We are living here with windows all open, and eating our own ripe grapes grown in the open air; but, in revenge, there is no man within twenty miles who knows anything of history, or angles, or of the mind. I send Mrs. Murray my epigram on Professor Airy,, of Cambridge, the great astronomer and mathematician, and his beautiful wife:—

> Airy alone has gained that double prize
> Which forced musicians to divide the crown;
> His works have raised a mortal to the skies,
> His marriage vows have drawn an angel down.

ANTI-CHOLERA.

(*To the Countess Grey, Combe Florey*, 1832.) The cholera will have killed by the end of the year about one person in every thousand. Therefore it is a thousand to one (supposing the cholera to travel at the same rate) that any person does not die of the cholera in any one year. This calculation is for the mass; but if you are prudent, temperate, and rich, your chance is at least five times as good that you do not die of the cholera — in other words, five thousand to one that you do not die of cholera in a year; it is not far from two millions to one that you do not die any one day from cholera. It is only seven hundred and thirty thousand to one that your house is not burnt down any one day. Therefore it is nearly three times as likely that your house should be burnt down any one day, as that you should die of cholera; or, it is as probable that your house should be burnt down three times in any one year, as that you should die of cholera.

THE HAY-FEVER.

(*To Dr. Holland, Combe Florey, June*, 1835.) I am suffering from my old complaint, the hay-fever (as it is called). My fear is, perishing by deliquescence; I melt away in nasal and lachrymal profluvia. My remedies are warm pediluvium, cathartics, topical application of a watery solution of opium to eyes, ears, and the interior of the nostrils. The membrane is so irritable, that light, dust, contradiction, an absurd remark, the sight of a Dissenter—anything, sets me sneezing; and if I begin sneezing at twelve, I don't leave off till two o'clock, and am heard distinctly in Taunton, when the wind sets that way—a distance of six miles. Turn your mind to this little curse. If consumption is too powerful for physicians, at least they should not suffer themselves to be outwitted by such little upstart disorders as the hay-fever.

OLD AGE TO BE PASSED IN THE CITY.

(*To Mrs. ——, Paris*, 1835.) I suspect the fifth act of life should be in great cities; it is there, in the long death of old age, that a man most forgets himself and his infirmities; receives the greatest consolation from the attentions of friends, and the greatest diversion from external circumstances.

AFFECTION AND THE THERMOMETER.

(*To Mrs. ——, July*, 1836.) Very high and very low temperature extinguishes all human sympathy and relations. It is impossible to feel affection beyond 78°, or below 20° of Fahrenheit; human nature is too solid or too liquid beyond these limits. Man only lives to shiver or to perspire. God send that the glass may fall, and restore me to my regard for you, which in the temperate zone is invariable.

HIS PORTRAIT.

(*To Lady Ashburton. With a Print.*) Dear Lady Ashburton: Miss Mildmay told me yesterday that you had been looking about for a print of the Rev. Sydney Smith. Here he is—pray accept him. I said to the artist, "Whatever you do, preserve the orthodox look."

DIGESTION AND THE VIRTUES.

(*To Arthur Kinglake, Combe Florey*, 1837.) I am much obliged by the present of your brother's book.* I am convinced

* Eothen.

digestion is the great secret of life; and that character, talents, virtues, and qualities, are powerfully affected by beef, mutton, pie-crust, and rich soups. I have often thought I could feed or starve men into many virtues and vices, and affect them more powerfully with my instruments of cookery than Timotheus could do formerly with his lyre.

TOWN AND COUNTRY.

(*To Miss G. Harcourt, London,* 1838.) The summer and the country, dear Georgiana, have no charms for me. I look forward anxiously to the return of bad weather, coal fires, and good society, in a crowded city. I have no relish for the country; it is a kind of healthy grave. I am afraid you are not exempt from the delusions of flowers, green turf, and birds; they all afford slight gratification, but not worth an hour of rational conversation: and rational conversation in sufficient quantities is only to be had from the congregation of a million of people in one spot. God bless you!

A PARODY.

(*To Lady Davy, London,* 1840.) Do you remember that passage in the "Paradise Lost," which is considered so beautiful?

> "As one who, long in populous cities pent,
> Where houses thick and sewers annoy the air,
> Forth issuing on a summer's morn, to breathe
> Among the pleasant villages and farms
> Adjoined, from each thing met conceives delight:
> The smell of grain, or tedded grass, or kine,
> Or flowers: each rural sight, each rural sound.
> If chance with nymph-like step fair virgin pass,
> What pleasing seemed, for her now pleases more,
> *She* most; and in her look sums all delight."

I think this simile very unjust to London, and I have amended the passage. I read it over to Lady Charlotte Lindsay and the Miss Berrys. The question was, whom the gentleman should see first when he arrived in London; and after various proposals, it was at last unanimously agreed it must be *you;* so it stands thus:—

" As one who, long in rural hamlets pent,
Where squires and parsons deep potations make,
With lengthened tale of fox or timid hare,
Or antlered stag, sore vexed by hound and horn,
Forth issuing on a winter's morn, to reach
In chaise or coach the London Babylon
Remote, from each thing met conceives delight;
Or cab, or car, or evening muffin-bell,
Or lamps: each city sight, each city sound.
If chance with nymph-like step the *Davy* pass,
What pleasing seemed, for her now pleases more.
She most; and in her look sums all delight."

I tried the verses with names of other ladies, but the universal opinion was, in the conclave of your friends, that it must be you; and this told, now tell me, dear Lady Davy, how do you do? Shall we ever see you again? We are dying very fast here; come and take another look at us. Mrs. Sydney is in the country in rather bad health; I am (gout and asthma excepted) very well.

DANIEL WEBSTER.

(*To Mrs. Grote, London*, 1839.) The "Great Western" turns out very well — grand, simple, cold, slow, wise, and good.

[When Mr. Webster, says Lady Holland (Mem. p. 252), was Secretary of Foreign Affairs for the United States, my father heard it reported from America that an accidental mistake he had made, in introducing Mr. Webster, on his coming to this country some time before (I believe to Lord Brougham), under the name of Mr. Clay, was intentional, and by way of joke. Annoyed that so much impertinence and bad taste should be imputed to him, he wrote a few lines of explanation to Mr. Webster, to which he received the following answer.]

"*Washington*, 1841. My Dear Sir: Though exceedingly delighted to hear from you, I am yet much pained by the contents of your note; not so much, however, as I should be, were I not able to give a peremptory denial to the whole report. I never mentioned the incident to which you refer, as a joke of yours — far from it; nor did I mention it as anything extraordinary.

"My dear, good friend, do not think me such a —— as to quote or refer to any incident falling out between you and me to your disadvantage. The pleasure of your acquaintance is one of the jewels I brought home with me. I had read of you, and read you for thirty years. I was delighted to meet you, and to have all I know of you refreshed and brightened by the charms of your conversation. If any son of —— asserts that either through ill-will, or love of vulgar gossip, I tell such things of you as you suppose, I pray you, let him be knocked down *instanter*. And be assured, my dear sir, I never spoke of you in my life but with gratitude, respect, and attachment. "D. WEBSTER."

To this Smith wrote in reply:—

"Many thanks, my dear sir, for your obliging letter. I think better of myself, because you think well of me. If, in the imbecility of old age, I forgot your name for a moment, the history of America will hereafter be more tenacious in its recollections— tenacious because you are using your eloquent wisdom to restrain the high spirit of your countrymen within the limits of justice, and are securing to two kindred nations, who ought to admire and benefit each other, the blessings of peace. How can great talent be applied to nobler ends, and what existence can be more truly splendid? Ever sincerely yours,

"SYDNEY SMITH."

CHARLES DICKENS.*

(*To Sir George Philips, about* 1838.)—Nickleby is very good. I stood out against Mr. Dickens as long as I could, but he has conquered me.

(*To Charles Dickens, June* 11, 1839.) My dear Sir: Nobody more, and more justly, talked of than yourself.

The Miss Berrys, now at Richmond, live only to become acquainted with you, and have commissioned me to request you to dine with them Friday, the 29th, or Monday, July 1st, to meet a Canon of St. Paul's, the Rector of Combe Florey, and the Vicar of Halberton—all equally well known to you; to say nothing of

---

* Dickens has paid a genial tribute to the memory of Sydney Smith, in a paper in his happiest vein of irony, in Household Words, Sept. 8, 1855. He treats the biography as a myth, a story of impossible virtue, a satire on the whig party who left such fabulous merits so long unrewarded.

other and better people. The Miss Berrys and Lady Charlotte Lindsay have not the smallest objection to be put into a Number, but, on the contrary, would be proud of the distinction; and Lady Charlotte, in particular, you may marry to Newman Noggs. Pray come; it is as much as my place is worth to send them a refusal.

(*May* 14, 1842.) My dear Dickens: I accept your obliging invitation conditionally. If I am invited by any man of greater genius than yourself, or one by whose works I have been more completely interested, I will repudiate you, and dine with the more splendid phenomenon of the two.

(*To Charles Dickens, Esq., January* 6, 1843.) My dear Sir: You have been so used to these sort of impertinences, that I believe you will excuse me for saying how very much I am pleased with the first number of your new work. Pecksniff and his daughters, and Pinch, are admirable — quite first-rate painting, such as no one but yourself can execute.

I did not like your genealogy of the Chuzzlewits, and I must wait a little to see how Martin turns out; I am impatient for the next number.

Pray come and see me next summer; and believe me ever yours.

P. S. — Chuffey is admirable. I never read a finer piece of writing; it is deeply pathetic and affecting. Your last number is excellent. Don't give yourself the trouble to answer my impertinent eulogies, only excuse them. Ever yours.

(*To Charles Dickens, Esq.,* 56 *Green Street, July* 1, 1843.) Dear Dickens: Excellent! nothing can be better! You must settle it with the Americans as you can, but I have nothing to do with that. I have only to certify that the number is full of wit, humour, and power of description.

I am slowy recovering from an attack of gout in the knee, and am very sorry to have missed you.

(*To Charles Dickens,* 56 *Green Street, Feb.* 21, 1844.) Dear Dickens: Many thanks for the "Christmas Carol," which I shall immediately proceed upon, in preference to six American pamphlets I found upon my arrival, all promising immediate payment! Yours ever.

A BREAKFAST.

(*To Mrs.* ——, *Green Street, April* 8, 1840.) Dear Mrs. ——: I wish I may be able to come on Monday, but I doubt. Will you come to a philosophical breakfast on Saturday — ten o'clock precisely? Nothing taken for granted! Everything (except the Thirty-nine Articles) called in question — real philosophers!

INVITATION TO THE OPERA.

(*To Mrs. Meynell, Green Street, June*, 1840.) Thy servant is threescore-and-ten years old; can he hear the sound of singing men and singing women? A Canon at the Opera! Where have you lived? In what habitations of the heathen? I thank you, shuddering; and am ever your unseducible friend.

GOUT.

(*To the Countess of Carlisle*, 1840.) What a very singular disease gout is! It seems as if the stomach fell down into the feet. The smallest deviation from right diet is immediately punished by limping and lameness, and the innocent ankle and blameless instep are tortured for the vices of the nobler organs. The stomach having found this easy way of getting rid of inconveniences, becomes cruelly despotic, and punishes for the least offences. A plum, a glass of Champagne, excess in joy, excess in grief — any crime, however small, is sufficient for redness, swelling, spasms, and large shoes.

VISIT TO AMERICA.

(*To the Countess Grey*, 1841.) I hear Morpeth is going to America, a resolution I think very wise, and which I should decidedly carry into execution myself, if I were not going to **Heaven.**

BOMBARDING THE ASIATICS.

(*To the Countess Grey, Oct.* 1841.) The news from China gives me the greatest pleasure. I am for bombarding all the exclusive Asiatics, who shut up the earth, and will not let me walk civilly and quietly through it, doing no harm, and paying for all I want.

ST. ANTHONY.

(*To Lady Ashburton*, 1841.) You have very naturally, my dear Lady Ashburton, referred to me for some information respecting St. Anthony. The principal anecdotes related of him are, that he was rather careless of his diet; and that, instead of confining himself to boiled mutton and a little wine and water, he ate of side-dishes, and drank two glasses of sherry, and refused to lead a life of great care and circumspection, such as his constitution required. The consequence was, that his friends were often alarmed at his health; and the medical men of Jerusalem and Jericho were in constant requisition, taking exorbitant fees, and doing him little good.

CORRESPONDENCE — SUSAN HOPLEY — PUSEYITE.

(*To Mrs. Crowe,* Combe Florey, Jan.* 31, 1841.) Dear Mrs. Crowe: I quite agree with you as to the horrors of correspondence. Correspondences are like small-clothes before the invention of suspenders; it is impossible to keep them up.

That episode of Julia [in Susan Hopley] is much too long. Your incidents are remarkable for their improbability. A boy goes on board a frigate in the middle of the night, and penetrates to the captain's cabin without being seen or challenged. Susan climbs into a two-pair-of-stairs window to rescue two grenadiers. A gentleman about to be murdered is saved by rescuing a woman about to be drowned, and so on. The language is easy, the dialogue natural. There is a great deal of humour; the plot is too complicated. The best part of the book is Mr. and Mrs. Ayton; but

---

* Mrs. Catherine Crowe, author of the Adventures of Susan Hopley, Lilly Dawson, The Night-Side of Nature, and other works.

the highest and most important praise of the novel is that you are carried on eagerly, and that it excites and sustains a great interest in the event, and therefore I think it a very good novel and will recommend it.

It is in vain that I study the subject of the Scotch Church. I have heard it ten times over from Murray, and twenty times from Jeffrey, and I have not the smallest conception what it is about. I know it has something to do with oat-meal, but beyond that I am in utter darkness. Everybody here is turning Puseyite. Having worn out my black gown, I preach in my surplice; this is all the change I have made, or mean to make.

There seems to be in your letter a deep-rooted love of the amusements of the world. Instead of the ever-gay Murray and the never-silent Jeffrey, why do you not cultivate the Scotch clergy and the elders and professors? I should then have some hopes of you.

PUSEYISM.

(*To Lady Ashburton*, 1841.) Still I can preach a little; and I wish you had witnessed, the other day at St. Paul's, my incredible boldness in attacking the Puseyites. I told them that they made the Christian religion a religion of postures and ceremonies, of circumflexions and genuflexions, of garments and vestures, of ostentation and parade; that they took up tithe of mint and cummin, and neglected the weightier matters of the law — justice, mercy, and the duties of life, and so forth.

(*To Lady Davy*, 1842.) I have not yet discovered of what I am to die, but I rather believe I shall be burnt alive by the Puseyites. Nothing so remarkable in England as the progress of these foolish people. I have no conception what they mean, if it be not to revive every absurd ceremony, and every antiquated folly, which the common sense of mankind has set to sleep. You will find at your return a fanatical Church of England, but pray do not let it prevent your return. We can always gather together, in Park Street and Green Street a chosen few who have never bowed the knee to Rimmon.

A BORE.

(*To Mrs. ——, Green Street, Grosvenor Square, March 5, 1841.*) My dear Mrs. ——: At the sight of ——, away fly gayety, ease, carelessness, happiness. Effusions are checked, faces are puckered up; coldness, formality, and reserve, are diffused over the room, and the social temperature falls down to zero. I *could* not stand it. I know you will forgive me, but my constitution is shattered, and I have not nerves for such an occurrence.

AVERSIONS AND ARGUMENTS.

(*To Mrs. ——, March 6, 1841.*) My dear Mrs. ——: Did you never hear of persons who have an aversion to cheese? to cats? to roast hare? Can you reason them out of it? Can you write them out of it? Would it be of any use to mention the names of mongers who have lived in the midst of cheese? Would it advance your cause to insist upon the story of Whittington and his Cat?

BLUECOAT THEORY.

(*To the Countess of Morley. No date.*) Dear Lady Morley: Pray understand me rightly: I do not give the Bluecoat theory as an established fact, but as a highly probable conjecture; look at the circumstances. At a very early age young Quakers disappear, at a very early age the Coat-boys are seen; at the age of seventeen or eighteen young Quakers are again seen; at the same age, the Coat-boys disappear: who has ever heard of a Coat-man? The things is utterly unknown in natural history. Upon what other evidence does the migration of the grub into the aurelia rest? After a certain number of days the grub is no more seen, and the aurelia flutters over his relics. That such a prominent fact should have escaped our naturalists is truly astonishing; I had long suspected it, but was afraid to come out with a speculation so bold, and now mention it as protected and sanctioned by you.

Dissection would throw great light upon the question; and if our friend —— would receive two boys into his house about the time of their changing their coats, great service would be rendered to the cause.

Our friend Lord Grey, not remarkable for his attention to natural history, was a good deal struck with the novelty and ingenuity of the hypothesis. I have ascertained that the young Blue-coat infants are fed with drab-coloured pap, which looks very suspicious. More hereafter on this interesting subject. Where real science is to be promoted, I will make no apology to your Ladyship for this intrusion.

Yours truly,   SYDNEY SMITH.

(*From the Countess of Morley. No date.*) Had I received your letter two days since, I should have said your arguments and theory were perfectly convincing, and that the most obstinate skeptic must have yielded to them; but I have come across a person in that interval who gives me information which puts us all at sea again. That the Bluecoat boy should be the larva of the Quaker in Great Britain is possible, and even probable, but we must take a wider view of the question; and here, I confess, I am bewildered by doubts and difficulties. The Bluecoat is an indigenous animal —not so the Quaker; and now be so good as to give your whole mind to the facts I have to communicate. I have seen and talked much with Sir R. Kerr Porter on this interesting subject. He has travelled over the whole habitable globe, and has penetrated with a scientific and scrutinizing eye into regions hitherto unexplored by civilized man; and yet *he* has never seen a Quaker baby. He has lived for years in Philadelphia (the national nest of Quakers); he has roamed up and down Broadways and lengthways in every nook and corner of Pennsylvania; and yet he never saw a Quaker baby; and what is new and most striking, never did he see a Quaker lady in a situation which gave hope that a Quaker baby might be seen hereafter. This is a stunning fact, and involving the question in such impenetrable mystery as will, I fear, defy even your sagacity, acuteness, and industry, to elucidate. But let us not be checked and cast down; truth is the end and object of our research. Let us not bate one jot of heart and hope, but still bear up and steer our course right onward.

Yours most truly,   F. MORLEY.

ACKNOWLEDGEMENT OF GAME.

(*To the Rev. R. H. Barham, London, about* 1842.) Many thanks, my dear Sir, for your kind present of game. If there is a pure and elevated pleasure in this world, it is that of roast pheasant and bread sauce;—barn-door fowls for dissenters, but for the real churchman, the thirty-nine times articled clerk—the pheasant. the pheasant!*

ALLEN—OLD AGE.

(*To Lady Holland, Combe Florey, Sept.* 13, 1842.) I am sorry to hear Allen is not well; but the reduction of his legs is a pure and unmixed good; they are enormous—they are clerical! He has the creed of a philosopher and the legs of a clergyman; I never saw such legs—at least, belonging to a layman.

It is a bore, I admit, to be past seventy, for you are left for execution, and are daily expecting the death-warrant; but, as you say, it is not anything very capital we quit. We are, at the close of life, only hurried away from stomach-aches, pains in the joints, from sleepless nights and unamusing days, from weakness, ugliness, and nervous tremors; but we shall all meet again in another planet, cured of all our defects. —— will be less irritable; —— more silent; —— will assent; Jeffrey will speak slower; Bobus will be just as he is; I shall be more respectful to the upper clergy; but I shall have as lively a sense as I now have of all your kindness and affection for me.

INVITATION TO "SEMIRAMIS."

(*To Lady Holland, November* 6, 1842.) My dear Lady Holland: I have not the heart, when an amiable lady says, "Come to 'Semiramis' in my box," to decline; but I get bolder at a distance. "Semiramis" would be to me pure misery. I love music very little—I hate acting; I have the worst opinion of Semiramis herself, and the whole thing (I can not help it) seems so childish and so foolish that I can not abide it. Moreover, it would be rather out of etiquette for a Canon of St. Paul's to go to an opera; and

* Memoir of Barham.

where etiquette prevents me from doing things disagreeable to myself, I am a perfect martinet.

All these things considered, I am sure you will not be a Semiramis to me, but let me off.

DYING SPEECHES.

(*To Miss Berry*, 1843.) I am studying the death of Louis XVI. Did he die heroically? or did he struggle on the scaffold? Was that struggle (for I believe there was one) for permission to speak? or from indignation at not being suffered to act for himself at the last moment, and to place himself under the axe? Make this out for me, if you please, and speak of it to me when I come to London. I don't believe the Abbé Edgeworth's "Son of St. Louis, *montez au ciel!*" It seems necessary that great people should die with some sonorous and quotable saying. Mr. Pitt said something not intelligible in his last moments: G. Rose made it out to be, "Save my country, Heaven!" The nurse on being interrogated, said that he asked for barley-water.

EDWARD EVERETT — AMERICAN DEBTS.

(*To Mrs. Holland, Combe Florey, Jan.* 31, 1844.) Everett, the American Minister, has been here at the same time with my eldest brother. We all liked him, and were confirmed in our good opinion of him. A sensible, unassuming man, always wise and reasonable. * * * * * * * * *

[This visit appears to have called forth some comments from a portion of the American Press which were met by the following from Sydney Smith.]

(*Letter to the Editor of the Morning Chronicle.*) Sir: The Locofoco papers in America are, I observe, full of abuse of Mr. Everett, their minister, for spending a month with me at Christmas, in Somersetshire. That month was neither lunar nor calendar, but consisted of forty eight hours — a few minutes more or less.

I never heard a wiser or more judicious defence than he made to me and others of the American insolvency; not denying the injustice of it—speaking of it, on the contrary, with the deepest feeling, but urging with great argumentative eloquence every topic that could be pleaded in extenuation. He made upon us the same impression he appears to make universally in this country; we thought him (a character which the English always receive with affectionate regard), an amiable American, republican without rudeness, and accomplished without ostentation! "If I had known that gentleman five years ago," said one of my guests, "I should have been deep in the American funds; and as it is, I think at times that I see 19s. or 20s. in the pound, in his face."

However this may be, I am sure we owe to the Americans a debt of gratitude for sending to us such an excellent specimen of their productions. In diplomacy a far more important object than falsehood is to keep two nations in friendship. In this point, no nation has ever been better served than America has been served by Mr. Edward Everett.

I am, sir, your obedient servant,   SYDNEY SMITH.

APRIL, 17, 1844.

TABLE-TALK — ANECDOTES.*

JEFFREY AND THE NORTH POLE.

The reigning bore at this time in Edinburgh (at the beginning of the century), was ———; his favourite subject, the North Pole. It mattered not how far south you began, you found yourself transported to the north pole before you could take breath; no one escaped him. My father declared he should invent a slip-button. Jeffrey fled from him as from the plague, when possible; but one day his arch-tormentor met him in a narrow lane, and began instantly on the north pole. Jeffrey, in despair and out of all patience, darted past him, exclaiming, "Damn the north pole!"† My father met him shortly after, boiling with indignation at Jeffrey's contempt of the north pole. "Oh, my dear fellow," said my father, "never mind; no one minds what Jeffrey says, you know, he is a privileged person; he respects nothing, absolutely nothing. Why, you will scarcely believe it, but it is not more than a week ago that I heard him speak disrespectfully of the equator!"

LINES ON JEFFREY.

Among our rural delights at Heslington (says Lady Holland), was the possession of a young donkey, which had been given up to our tender mercies from the time of its birth, and in whose

---

* Except where otherwise credited, the following anecdotes of Sydney Smith's conversation are derived from the Memoir by Lady Holland.

† "I see this anecdote," says Lady Holland, "in Mr. Moore's Memoirs attributed to Leslie, but I have so often heard it told as applying to a very different person, that I think he was mistaken."

education we employed a large portion of our spare time; and a most accomplished donkey it became under our tuition. It would walk up-stairs, pick pockets, follow us in our walks like a huge Newfoundland dog; at the most distant sight of us in the field, with ears down and tail erect, it set off in full bray to meet us. These demonstrations on Bitty's part were met with not less affection on ours, and Bitty was almost considered a member of the family.

One day, when my elder brother and myself were training our beloved Bitty, with a pocket-handkerchief for a bridle, and his head crowned with flowers, to run round our garden, who should arrive in the midst of our sport but Mr. Jeffrey. Finding my father out, he, with his usual kindness toward young people, immediately joined in our sport, and, to our infinite delight, mounted our donkey. He was proceeding in triumph, amidst our shouts of laughter, when my father and mother, in company, I believe, with Mr. Horner and Mr. Murray, returned from their walk, and beheld this scene from the garden-door. Though years and years have passed away since, I still remember the joy-inspiring laughter that burst from my father at this unexpected sight, as, advancing toward his old friend, with a face beaming with delight and with extended hands, he broke forth in the following impromptu:—

> "Witty as Horatius Flaccus,
> As great a Jacobin as Gracchus;
> Short, though not as fat, as Bacchus,
> Riding on a little jackass."

These lines were afterward repeated by some one to Mr. ——, at Holland House, just before he was introduced for the first time to Mr. Jeffrey, and they caught his fancy to such a degree that he could not get them out of his head, but kept repeating them in a low voice all the time Mr. Jeffrey was conversing with him.

SENSIBILITY OF CHILDHOOD.

ONCE, when we were on a visit at Lord ———'s, we were sitting with a large party at luncheon, when our host's eldest son, a fine boy of between eight and nine, burst into the room, and, running up to his father, began a playful skirmish with him; the boy, half in play, half in earnest, hit his father in the face, who to carry on the joke, put up both his hands, saying, "Oh, B——, you have put out my eye." In an instant the blood mounted to the boy's temples, he flung his little arms around his father, and sobbed in such a paroxysm of grief and despair, that it was some time before even his father's two bright eyes beaming on him with pleasure could convince him of the truth, and restore him to tranquillity.

When he left the room, my father, who had silently looked with much interest and emotion on the scene, said, "I congratulate you; I guarantee that boy; make your hearts easy; however he may be tossed about the world, with those feelings, and such a heart, he will come out unscathed."

The father (continues Lady Holland), one of those who consider their fortune but as a loan, to be employed in spreading an atmosphere of virtue and happiness around them as far as their influence reaches, is now no more, and this son occupies his place; but his widowed mother the other day reminded me how true the prophecy had proved; and the scene was so touching that I cannot resist giving it.

STAGE-COACH TRAVELLING.

In 1820, my father (writes Lady Holland) went on a visit of a few days to Lord Grey's; then to Edinburgh to see Jeffrey and his other old friends; and returned by Lord Lauderdale's house at Dunbar. Speaking of this journey, he says, "Most people sulk in stage-coaches, I always talk. I have had some amusing journeys from this habit. On one occasion, a gentleman in the coach with me, with whom I had been conversing for some time, suddenly looked out of the window as we approached York and said, 'There is a very clever man, they say, but a d— odd fellow, lives near here — Sydney Smith, I believe.' 'He may be a very odd fellow,' said I, taking off my hat to him and laughing, 'and I dare say he is; but odd as he is, he is here, very much at your service.' Poor man! I thought he would have sunk into his boots, and vanished through the bed of the carriage, he was so distressed; but I thought I had better tell him at once, or he might proceed to say I had murdered my grandmother, which I must have resented, you know.

"On another occasion, some years later, when going to Brougham

Hall, two raw Scotch girls got into the coach in the dark, near Carlisle. 'It is very disagreeable getting into a coach in the dark,' exclaimed one, after arranging her bandboxes; 'one can not see one's company.' 'Very true, ma'am, and you have a great loss in not seeing me, for I am a remarkably handsome man.' 'No, sir! are you really?' said both. 'Yes, and in the flower of my youth.' 'What a pity!' said they. We soon passed near a lamp-post: they both darted forward to get a look at me. 'La, sir, you seem very stout.' 'Oh no, not at all, ma'am, it's only my great coat.' 'Where are you going, sir?' 'To Brougham Hall.' 'Why, you must be a very remarkable man, to be going to Brougham Hall.' 'I am a very remarkable man, ma'am.' At Penrith they got out, after having talked incessantly, and tried every possible means to discover who I was, exclaiming as they went off laughing, 'Well, it is very provoking we can't see you, but we'll find out who you are at the ball; Lord Brougham always comes to the ball at Penrith, and we shall certainly be there, and shall soon discover your name.'"

DINNER IN THE COUNTRY.

Though it was the general habit in Yorkshire to make visits of two or three days at the houses in the neighborhood, yet not unfrequently invitations to dinner only came, and sometimes to a house at a considerable distance.

"Did you ever dine out in the country?" said my father; "what misery human beings inflict on each other under the name of pleasure! We went to dine last Thursday with Mr. ———, a neighbouring clergyman, a haunch of venison being the stimulus to the invitation. We set out at five o'clock, drove in a broiling sun on dusty roads three miles in our best gowns, found Squire and parsons assembled in a small hot room, the whole house redolent of frying; talked, as is our wont, of roads, weather, and turnips; that done, began to grow hungry, then serious, then impatient. At last a stripling, evidently caught up for the occasion, opened the door and beckoned our host out of the room. After some moments of awful suspense, he returned to us with a face of much distress, saying, 'the woman assisting in the kitchen had mistaken the soup for dirty water, and had thrown it away, so we must do without it;' we all agreed it was perhaps as well we should, under the circumstances. At last, to our joy, dinner was announced; but oh, ye gods! as we entered the dining-room what a gale met our nose! the venison was high, the venison was uneatable, and was obliged to follow the soup with all speed.

" Dinner proceeded, but our spirits flagged under these accumulated misfortunes: there was an ominous pause between the first and second course; we looked each other in the face—what new disaster awaited us? the pause became fearful. At last the door burst open, and the boy rushed in, calling out aloud, 'Please, sir, has Betty any right to leather I?' What human gravity could stand this? We roared with laughter; all took part against Betty, obtained the second course with some difficulty, bored each other the usual time, ordered our carriages, expecting our post-boys to be drunk, and were grateful to Providence for not permitting them to deposit us in a wet ditch. So much for dinners in the country!"

A DOG DIFFICULTY.

DURING one of his visits to London, at a dinner at Spencer House, the conversation turned upon dogs. "Oh," said my father, "one of the greatest difficulties I have had with my parishioners has been on the subject of dogs." "How so?" said Lord Spencer. "Why, when I first went down into Yorkshire, there had not been a resident clergyman in my parish for a hundred and fifty years. Each farmer kept a huge mastiff-dog, ranging at large, and ready to make his morning meal on clergy or laity, as best suited his particular taste; I never could approach a cottage in pursuit of my calling, but I rushed into the jaws of one of these shaggy monsters. I scolded, preached, and prayed, without avail; so I determined to try what fear for their pockets might do. Forthwith appeared in the county papers a minute account of a trial of a farmer, at the Northampton Sessions, for keeping dogs unconfined; where said farmer was not only fined five pounds and reprimanded by the magistrates, but sentenced to three months' imprisonment. The effect was wonderful, and the reign of Cerberus ceased in the land." "That accounts," said Lord Spencer, "for what has puzzled me and Althorp for many years We never failed to attend the sessions at Northampton, and we never could find out how we had missed this remarkable dog case."

SMALL MEN.

An argument arose, in which my father observed how many of the most eminent men of the world had been diminutive in person, and after naming several among the ancients, he added, "Why, look there, at Jeffrey; and there is my little friend ——, who has not body enough to cover his mind decently with; his intellect is improperly exposed."

LOCAL MORALITIES.

When I took my Yorkshire servants into Somersetshire, I found that they thought making a drink out of apples was a tempting of Providence, who had intended barley to be the only natural material of intoxication.

A NEW ZEALAND ATTORNEY.

There is a New Zealand attorney arrived in London, with 6s. 8d. tattooed all over his face.

NIEBUHR'S DISCOVERIES.

Have you heard of Niebuhr's discoveries? All Roman history reversed; Tarquin turning out an excellent family man, and Lucretia a very doubtful character, whom Lady —— would not have visited.

TELEMACHUS.

How bored children are with the wisdom of Telemachus! they can't think why Calypso is so fond of him.

A LIFE.

Yes, he has spent all his life in letting down empty buckets into empty wells; and he is frittering away his age in trying to draw them up again.

A REBUKE.

At a large dinner party the death of Mr. Dugald Stewart was announced. The news was received with so much levity by a lady of rank, who sat by Sydney Smith, that he turned round and said, " Madam, when we are told of the death of so great a man as Mr. Dugald Stewart, it is usual, in civilized society, to look grave for at least the space of five seconds."

BEAUTY OF THE STYLE OF THE BIBLE.

"What is so beautiful as the style of the Bible? what poetry in its language and ideas!" and taking it down from the bookcase behind him, he read, with his beautiful voice, and in his most impressive manner, several of his favourite passages; among others I remember—" Thou shalt rise up before the hoary head, and honour the face of an old man;" and part of that most beautiful of Psalms, the 139th: " O Lord, thou hast searched me, and known me. Thou knowest my downsitting and mine uprising; thou understandest my thoughts afar off. Thou compassest my path and my lying down, and art acquainted with all my ways. . . . Whither shall I go from thy spirit, or whither shall I flee from thy presence? If I ascend up into heaven, thou art there; if I make my bed in hell, behold thou art there. If I take the wings of the morning, and dwell in the uttermost parts of the sea; even there shall thy hand lead me, and thy right hand shall hold me. If I say, Surely the darkness shall cover me, even the night shall be light about me; yea, the darkness hideth not from thee; but the night shineth as the day; the darkness and the light are both alike to thee"— putting the Bible again on the shelf.

FIREPLACES.

Never neglect your fireplaces; I have paid great attention to mine, and could burn you all out in a moment. Much of the cheerfulness of life depends upon it. Who could be miserable with that fire? What makes a fire so pleasant is, I think, that it is a live thing in a dead room.

ANTI-MELANCHOLY.

Never give way to melancholy; resist it steadily, for the habit will encroach. I once gave a lady two-and twenty receipts against melancholy: one was a bright fire; another, to remember all the pleasant things said to and of her; another, to keep a box of sugar-plums on the chimney-piece, and a kettle simmering on the hob

BLUE-STOCKINGS.

KEEP as much as possible on the grand and common road of life; patent educations or habits seldom succeed. Depend upon it, men set more value on the cultivated minds than on the accomplishments of women, which they are rarely able to appreciate. It is a common error, but it is an error, that literature unfits women for the every-day business of life. It is not so with men; you see those of the most cultivated minds constantly devoting their time and attention to the most homely objects. Literature gives women a real and proper weight in society, but then they must use it with discretion; if the stocking is *blue*, the petticoat must be *long*, as my friend Jeffrey says; the want of this has furnished food for ridicule in all ages.

DRESS AND BEAUTY.

NEVER teach false morality. How exquisitely absurd to tell girls that beauty is of no value, dress of no use! Beauty is of value; her whole prospects and happiness in life may often depend upon a new gown or a becoming bonnet, and if she has five grains of common sense she will find this out. The great thing is to teach her their just value, and that there must be something better under the bonnet than a pretty face for real happiness. But never sacrifice truth.

A UTILITARIAN.

SOME one, speaking of the utility of a measure, and quoting ——'s opinion: "Yes, he is of the Utilitarian school. That man is so hard you might drive a broad-wheeled wagon over him, and it would produce no impression; if you were to bore holes in him with a gimlet, I am convinced saw-dust would come out of him. That school treat mankind as if they were mere machines; the feelings or affections never enter into their calculations. If everything is to be sacrificed to utility, why do you bury your grandmother at all? why don't you cut her into small pieces at once, and make portable soup of her?"

THE HOUSE OF COMMONS.

YES, it requires a long apprenticeship to speak well in the House of Commons. It is the most formidable ordeal in the world. Few men have succeeded who entered it late in life; Jeffrey is perhaps the best exception. Bobus used to say that there was more sense and good taste in the whole House, than in any one individual of which it was composed.

TWENTY-FOUR HOURS AFTER.

WE are told, "Let not the sun go down on your wrath." This, of course, is best; but, as it generally does, I would add, Never act or write till it has done so. This rule has saved me from many an act of folly. It is wonderful what a different view we take of the same event four-and-twenty hours after it has happened.

LIGHT AND SHADE.

I LIKE pictures, without knowing anything about them; but I hate coxcombry in the fine arts, as well as in anything else. I got into dreadful disgrace with Sir George Beaumont once, who, standing before a picture at Bowood, exclaimed, turning to me, "immense breadth of light and shade!" I innocently said, "Yes; about an inch and a half." He gave me a look that ought to have killed me.*

A ONE-BOOK MAN.

YES, it was a mistake to write any more. He was a one-book man. Some men have only one book in them; others, a library.

* Smith furnished his house once with a set of daubs, and invented names of great masters for them :—"a beautiful landscape by Nicholas de Falda, a pupil of Valdeggio, the only painting by that eminent artist." He consulted two Royal Academicians as to his purchases, and when he had set them considering what opportunities were likely to occur, added, by way of afterthought; "Oh, I ought to have told you that my outside price for a picture is thirty-five shillings."

COMPOSITION.

In composing, as a general rule, run your pen through every other word you have written; you have no idea what vigour it will give your style.

MATHEMATICS.

The most promising sign in a boy is, I should say, mathematics.

FACTS AND FIGURES.

Oh, don't tell me of facts—I never believe facts: you know Canning said nothing was so fallacious as facts, except figures

HAND-SHAKING.

On meeting a young lady who had just entered the garden, and shaking hands with her: 'I must,' he said, 'give you a lesson in shaking hands, I see. There is nothing more characteristic than shakes of the hand. I have classified them. Lister, when he was here, illustrated some of them. Ask Mrs. Sydney to show you his sketches of them when you go in. There is the *high official*—the body erect, and a rapid, short shake, near the chin. There is the *mortmain*—the flat hand introduced into your palm, and hardly conscious of its contiguity. The *digital*—one finger held out, much used by the high clergy. There is the *shakus rusticus*, where your hand is seized in an iron grasp, betokening rude health, warm heart, and distance from the Metropolis; but producing a strong sense of relief on your part when you find your hand released and your fingers unbroken. The next to this is the *retentive shake*—one which, beginning with vigour, pauses as it were to take breath, but without relinquishing its prey, and before you are aware begins again, till you feel anxious as to the result, and have no shake left in you. There are other varieties, but this is enough for one lesson.

A JOKE IN THE COUNTRY.

A joke goes a great way in the country. I have known one last pretty well for seven years. I remember making a joke after a meeting of the clergy, in Yorkshire, where there was a Rev. Mr. Buckle, who never spoke when I gave his health; saying, that he was a buckle without a tongue. Most persons within hearing laughed, but my next neighbour sat unmoved and sunk in thought. At last, a quarter of an hour after we had all done, he suddenly nudged me, exclaiming, "I see *now* what you meant, Mr. Smith; you meant a joke.' "Yes," I said, " sir; I believe I did." Upon which he began laughing so heartily, that I thought he would choke, and was obliged to pat him on the back.

SALAD RECIPE.

THAT pudding! yes, that was the pudding Lady Holland asked the recipe for when she came to see us. I shook my head and said it could not be done, even for her ladyship. She became more urgent; Mrs. Sydney was soft-hearted, and gave it. The glory of it almost turned my cook's head; she has never been the same since. But our forte in the culinary line is our salads; I pique myself on our salads. Saba always dresses them after my recipe. I have put it into verse. Taste it, and if you like it, I will give it you. I was not aware how much it had contributed to my reputation, till I met Lady —— at Bowood, who begged to be introduced to me, saying, she had so long wished to know me. I was of course highly flattered, till she added, 'For, Mr. Smith, I have heard so much of your recipe for salads, that I was most anxious to obtain it from you.' Such and so various are the sources of fame!

> " 'To make this condiment, your poet begs
> The pounded yellow of two hard-boiled eggs;
> Two boiled potatoes, passed through kitchen sieve,
> Smoothness and softness to the salad give.
> Let onion atoms lurk within the bowl,
> And, half-suspected, animate the whole.
> Of mordant mustard add a single spoon,
> Distrust the condiment that bites so soon;
> But deem it not, thou man of herbs, a fault,
> To add a double quantity of salt.
> Four times the spoon with oil from Lucca brown,
> And twice with vinegar procured from town;
> And, lastly, o'er the flavored compound toss
> A magic soupçon of anchovy sauce.

Oh, green and glorious! Oh, herbaceous treat!
'Twould tempt the dying anchorite to eat:
Back to the world he'd turn his fleeting soul,
And plunge his fingers in the salad bowl!
Serenely full, the epicure would say,
"Fate cannot harm me, I have dined to-day."

[The above is the famous recipe as given by Lady Holland in her Memoir. We have before us printed on the first page of a letter-sheet (on the back of which is the second note to Captain Morgan on the American Debts previously given, p. 72), the following with some variations, and as the date of the letter is 1844 it has good pretensions to the latest edition. The affectionate friend solicitously adds with his own hand: "Let me beg you not to alter the proportions in the salad." Such are the well-known anxieties of salad-makers.]

A Recipe for Salad.
LAST EDITION.

Two large potatoes, passed through kitchen sieve,
Unwonted softness to the salad give:
Of mordant mustard, add a single spoon,
Distrust the condiment which bites so soon;
But deem it not, thou man of herbs, a fault,
To add a double quantity of salt:
Three times the spoon with oil of Lucca crown,
And once with vinegar, procured from town;
True flavour needs it, and your poet begs
The pounded yellow of two well-boiled eggs;
Let onion atoms lurk within the bowl,
And scarce suspected, animate the whole;
And lastly, on the flavoured compound toss,
A magic teaspoon of anchovy sauce:
Then though green turtle fail, though venison's tough,
And ham and turkey are not boiled enough,
Serenely full, the epicure may say—
"Fate cannot harm me,—I have dined to-day"

To this is added in print:

A Winter Salad.

Two well boiled potatoes, passed through a sieve: a teaspoonful of mustard; two teaspoonfuls of salt; one of essence of anchovy; about a quarter of a teaspoonful of very finely-chopped onions well bruised into the mixture, three tablespoonfuls of oil:

one of vinegar; the yolk of two eggs, hard boiled. Stir up the salad immediately before dinner, and stir it up thoroughly.

N. B. As this salad is the result of great experience and reflection, it is hoped young salad-makers will not attempt to make any improvements upon it.

PARODY ON POPE.

HAVE you heard my parody on Pope?

>Why has not man a collar and a log?
>For this plain reason — man is not a dog.
>Why is not man served up with sauce in dish?
>For this plain reason — man is not a fish.

TRANSIT OF A SOVEREIGN.

BY-THE-BY, it happened to be a charity sermon, and I considered it a wonderful proof of my eloquence, that it actually moved old Lady Cork to borrow a sovereign from Dudley, and that he actually gave it her, though knowing he must take a long farewell of it. I was told afterward by Lady S—— that she rejoiced to see it had brought "iron tears down Pluto's cheek" (meaning by that her husband), certainly little given to the melting mood in any sense.*

VENUS MILLINARIA.

I ONCE saw a dressed statue of Venus in a serious house — the Venus Millinaria.

---

*This story is told somewhat differently in Dyce's Recollections of the Table-Talk of Rogers: "Lady Cork was once so moved by a charity sermon, that she begged me [Smith] to lend her a guinea for her contribution. I did so — she never repaid me and spent it on herself." Jekyll, the great wit of the lawyers, said at one of Lady Cork's parties where she wore an enormous plume, "she was exactly a shuttlecock — all cork and feathers."

Lady Cork was the veteran of London society. Her parties to literary celebrities were famous from the days of Dr. Johnson who visited her gatherings. She was the Miss Monkton of Boswell's Johnson; daughter of Viscount Galway; married in 1786 to the Earl of Cork. She held on among the London literati bravely to the last, dying in 1840, at the age of ninety four.

THE VANILLE OF SOCIETY.

Ah, you flavour everything; you are the vanille of society.

SEWING FOR MEN.

I wish I could sew. I believe one reason why women are so much more cheerful, generally, than men, is because they can work, and vary more their employments. Lady —— used to teach her sons carpet-work. All men ought to learn to sew.

DOGS.

No, I don't like dogs; I always expect them to go mad. A lady asked me once for a motto for her dog Spot. I proposed, "Out, damned Spot!" but she did not think it sentimental enough. You remember the story of the French marquise, who, when her pet lap-dog bit a piece out of her footman's leg, exclaimed, "Ah, poor little beast! I hope it won't make him sick." I called one day on Mrs. ——, and her lap-dog flew at my leg and bit it. After pitying her dog, like the French marquise, she did all she could to comfort me, by assuring me the dog was a Dissenter, and hated the Church, and was brought up in a Tory family. But whether the bite came from madness or Dissent, I knew myself too well to neglect it; and went on the instant to a surgeon and had it cut out, making a mem. on the way to enter that house no more.

MANNERS.

Manners are often too much neglected: they are most important to men, no less than to women. I believe the English are the most disagreeable people under the sun; not so much because Mr. John Bull disdains to talk, as that the respected individual has nothing to say, and because he totally neglects manners. Look at a French carter; he takes off his hat to his neighbour carter, and inquires after "La santé de madame," with a bow that would not have disgraced Sir Charles Grandison; and I have often seen a French soubrette with a far better manner than an English duchess. Life is too short to get over a bad manner; besides, manners are the shadows of virtue.

FURNITURE OF A COUNTRY-HOUSE.

I THINK no house is well fitted up in the country without people of all ages. There should be an old man or woman to pet; a parrot, a child, a monkey; something, as the French say, to love and to despise. I have just bought a parrot, to keep my servants in good-humour.

TOWN AND COUNTRY.

THE charm of London is that you are never glad or sorry for ten minutes together: in the country you are the one and the other for weeks.

TEA AND COFFEE.

AT the tea-table: " Thank God for tea! What would the world do without tea? how did it exist? I am glad I was not born before tea. I can drink any quantity when I have not tasted wine, otherwise I am haunted by blue-devils by day, and dragons by night. If you want to improve your understanding, drink coffee. Sir James Mackintosh used to say, he believed the difference between one man and another was produced by the quantity of coffee he drank.

CLASSES OF SOCIETY.

I HAVE divided mankind into classes. There is the Noodle — very numerous, but well known. The Affliction-woman — a valuable member of society, generally an ancient spinster, or distant relation of the family, in small circumstances: the moment she hears of any accident or distress in the family, she sets off, packs up her little bag, and is immediately established there, to comfort, flatter, fetch, and carry. The Up-takers — a class of people who only see through their fingers' ends, and go through a room taking up and touching everything, however visible and however tender. The Clearers — who begin at the dish before them, and go on picking or tasting till it is cleared, however large the company, small the supply, and rare the contents. The Sheep-walkers —

those who never deviate from the beaten track, who think as their fathers have thought since the flood, who start from a new idea as they would from guilt. The Lemon-squeezers of society—people who act on you as a wet blanket, who see a cloud in the sunshine, the nails of the coffin in the ribands of the bride, predictors of evil, extinguishers of hope; who, where there are two sides, see only the worst—people whose very look curdles the milk, and sets your teeth on edge. The Let-well-aloners—cousins-german to the Noodle, yet a variety; people who have begun to think and to act, but are timid, and afraid to try their wings, and tremble at the sound of their own footsteps as they advance, and think it safer to stand still. Then the Washerwomen—very numerous, who exclaim, "Well! as sure as ever I put on my best bonnet, it is certain to rain," etc. There are many more, but I forget them.

Oh, yes! there is another class, as you say; people who are always treading on your gouty foot, or talking in your deaf ear, or asking you to give them something with your lame hand, stirring up your weak point, rubbing your sore, etc.

MRS. SIDDONS.

I never go to tragedies, my heart is too soft. There is too much real misery in life. But what a face she had! The gods do not bestow such a face as Mrs. Siddons's on the stage more than once in a century. I knew her very well, and she had the good taste to laugh heartily at my jokes; she was an excellent person, but she was not remarkable out of her profession, and never got out of tragedy even in common life. She used to *stab* the potatoes; and said, "Boy, give me a knife!" as she would have said, "Give me the dagger!"

SHAM SYDNEY SMITHS.

I have heard that one of the American ministers in this country was so oppressed by the numbers of his countrymen applying for introductions, that he was obliged at last to set up sham Sydney Smiths and false Macaulays. But they can't have been good counterfeits; for a most respectable American, on his return home, was heard describing Sydney Smith as a thin, grave, dull old fellow:

and as to Macaulay," said he, "I never met a more silent man in my life."*

CANVAS-BACK DUCKS.

I FULLY intended going to America; but my parishioners held a meeting, and came to a resolution that they could not trust me with the canvas-back ducks; and I felt they were right, so gave up the project.

FRIENDSHIP.

TRUE, it is most painful not to meet the kindness and affection you feel you have deserved, and have a right to expect from others; but it is a mistake to complain of it, for it is of no use: you can not extort friendship with a cocked pistol.

* In the summer of 1844, in the list of passengers, on the arrival of the Great Western at New York, was advertised Sydney Smith. It created some paragraphing in the papers, and quite a flutter among the genuine Sydney's church friends. In a letter to the Countess Grey, Smith alludes to the affair: "There arrived, the other day, at New York, a Sydney Smith. A meeting was called, and it was proposed to tar-and-feather him; but the amendment was carried, that he should be invited to a public dinner. He turned out to be a journeyman cooper! My informant encloses for me an invitation from the Bishop of the Diocese to come and see him, and a proposition that we should travel together to the Falls of Niagara."

The author of the article in the Edinburgh Review, on Smith (July, 1855), caps the "sham Sydney Smiths and false Macaulays" with the following:— " Sophie Arnault actually played off a similar trick on a party of Parisian fine ladies and gentlemen who had expressed a wish to meet Rousseau. She dressed up a theatrical tailor who bore some likeness to the author of 'Emile,' and placed him next to herself at dinner, with instructions not to open his mouth except to eat and drink. Unluckily he opened it too often for the admission of champagne, and began talking in a style befitting the *coulisses*; but this only added to the delusion, and the next day the noble faubourg rang with the praises of the easy sparkling pleasantry of the philosopher. According to another well-authenticated anecdote, there was a crazy fellow at Edinburgh, who called himself Doctor, fancied that he had once been on the point of obtaining the chair of Moral Philosophy, and professed the most extravagant admiration for a celebrated poet. Some wag suggested that he should pay a visit to his idol. He did so, and stayed two days, indulging his monomania, but simultaneously gratifying his host's prodigious appetite for adulation; and the poet uniformly spoke of him as one of the most intelligent and well-informed Scotchmen he had ever known. When this story was told to Sydney Smith, he offered the narrator five shillings for the exclusive right to it for a week. The bargain was struck, and the money paid down."

THREE SEXES.

Don't you know, as the French say, there are three sexes— men, women, and clergymen.

SOCINIAN.

Some one naming —— as not very orthodox, "Accuse a man of being a Socinian, and it is all over with him; for the country gentlemen all think it has something to do with poaching."

DOME OF ST. PAUL'S.

We were all assembled to look at a turtle that had been sent to the house of a friend, when a child of the party stooped down and began eagerly stroking the shell of the turtle. "Why are you doing that, B——?" said my father. "Oh, to please the turtle." "Why, child, you might as well stroke the dome of St. Paul's, to please the Dean and Chapter."

PRAISE.

Some one observing the wonderful improvement in —— since his success; "Ah!" he said, "praise is the best diet for us, after all."

SAMARITANS.

Yes! you find people ready enough to do the Samaritan, without the oil and twopence.

HAPPINESS.

The haunts of Happiness are varied, and rather unaccountable; but I have more often seen her among little children, home fire sides, and country-houses, than anywhere else; at least I think so

DANIEL WEBSTER.

Daniel Webster struck me much like a steam-engine in trowsers.

PRESCOTT THE HISTORIAN.

WHEN Prescott comes to England, a Caspian Sea of soup awaits him.

SAMUEL ROGERS.

IN 1823, having received a presentation to the Charterhouse from the Archbishop of York, for his second son, Wyndham, Sydney Smith took him there in the spring. While he was in town, Mr. Rogers says, "I had been ill some weeks, confined to my bed. Sydney Smith heard of it, found me out, sat by my bed, cheered me, talked to me, made me laugh more than I ever thought to have laughed again. The next day a bulletin was brought to my bedside, giving the physician's report of my case; the following day the report was much worse; the next day declaring there was no hope, and England would have to mourn over the loss of her sweetest poet; then I died amidst weeping friends; then came my funeral; and lastly, a sketch of my character, all written by that pen which had the power of turning everything into sunshine and joy. Sydney never forgot his friends."

ADDRESSING Rogers: "My dear R., if we were both in America, we should be tarred and feathered; and, lovely as we are by nature, I should be an ostrich and you an emu."

"How is Rogers?" "He is not very well." "Why, what is the matter?" "Oh, don't you know he has produced a couplet? When our friend is delivered of a couplet, with infinite labour and pain, he takes to his bed, has straw laid down, the knocker tied up, expects his friends to call and make inquiries, and the answer at the door invariably is, 'Mr. Rogers and his little couplet are as well as can be expected.' When he produces an Alexandrine he keeps his bed a day longer."

SYDNEY SMITH mentioned having once half-offended Sam. Rogers, by recommending him, when he sat for his picture, to be drawn saying his prayers, with his face in his hat.*

* Diary of the Rev. Richard Harris Barham, Oct. 2, 1831—in Memoir. The *tête morte* anecdotes of Rogers are numerous. That pleasant book

TALLEYRAND.

ONE evening, at his house (in London in later life), a few friends had come in to tea; among others, Lord Jeffrey, Dr. Holland, and his sister. Some one spoke of Talleyrand. "Oh," said Sydney, " Lady Holland labored incessantly to convince me that Talleyrand was agreeable, and was very angry because his arrival was usually a signal for my departure; but, in the first place, he never spoke at all till he had not only devoured but digested his dinner, and as this was a slow process with him, it did not occur till everybody else was asleep, or ought to have been so; and when he did speak he was so inarticulate I never could understand a word he said." "It was otherwise with me," said Dr. Holland; "I never found much difficulty in following him." "Did not you? why it was an abuse of terms to call it talking at all; for he had not teeth, and, I believe, no roof to his mouth — no uvula — no larynx — no trachea — no epiglottis — no anything. It was not talking, it was gargling; and that, by-the-by, now I think of it, must be the very reason why Holland understood him so much better than I did," turning suddenly round on him with his merry laugh.

"Yet nobody's wit was of so high an order as Talleyrand's when it did come, or has so well stood the test of time. You re-

The Clubs of London, tells us "it was the fashion to liken the pale visage of the poet to all sorts of funereal things—*Tristissima mortis imago!* But Ward's (Lord Dudley) were the most felicitous resemblances. Rogers had been at Spa, and was telling Ward that the place was so full, that he could not so much as find a bed to lie in, and that he was obliged, on that account, to leave it. 'Dear me,' replied Ward, 'was there no room in the *church*-yard?' At another time, Murray was showing him a portrait of Rogers, observing that 'it was done to the *life*.' 'To the *death*, you mean,' replied Ward." Among other sallies of the same kind, was his asking Rogers —"Why don't you keep your hearse, Rogers? you can well afford it." Fraser's Magazine, in 1830, had a severe caricature—"There is Sam. Rogers, a mortal likeness—painted to the very death." Byron's terrible lines are well known :—

> Nose and chin would shame a knocker;
> Wrinkles that would puzzle Cocker.
>   *   *   *   *
> Is't a corpse stuck up for show,
> Galvanized at times to go?

The corpse, however, long survived all the satirists, Ward, Byron, Maginn

member when his friend Montrond* was taken ill, and exclaimed, 'Mon ami, je sens les tourmens de l'enfer.' ' Quoi! déjà?' was his reply. And when he sat at dinner between Madame de Staël and Madame Récamier, the celebrated beauty, Madame de Sta-l, whose beauties were certainly not those of the person, jealous of his attentions to her rival, insisted upon knowing which he would save if they were both drowning. After seeking in vain to evade her, he at last turned toward her and said, with his usual shrug, " Ah, madame, *vous savez nager.*" And when —— exclaimed, " Me voilà entre l'esprit et la beauté," he answered, " Oui, et sans posséder ni l'un ni l'autre." And of Madame ——, " Oui, elle est belle, très-belle; mais pour la toilette, cela commence trop tard, et finit trop tôt." Of Lord —— he said, " C'est la bienveillance même, mais la bienveillance la plus perturbative que j'ai jamais connu." To a friend of mine he said on one occasion, " Milady, voulez-vous me prêter ce livre?" "Oui, mais vous me le rendrez?" " Oui." " Parole d'honneur?" " Oui." " Vous en êtes *sûr?*" " Oui, oui, milady; mais, pour vous le rendre, il faut absolument d'abord me le prêter."

* "I find," says Lady Holland, "that Talleyrand used to tell this story as having passed between Cardinal De la Roche-Guyon, a celebrated epicure, and his confessor."

Moore in his Diary (April 2, 1833) has a similar mót of Talleyrand in connection with the above: " On some occasion when M. very ill, had fallen on the floor and was grasping at it violently with his hands ' *Il veut absolument descendre,*' said T. His friend Montrond took his revenge in the style of his master — Madame Flamelin reproached M. de Montrond with his attachment to Talleyrand: 'Heavens,' he replied, 'who could help liking him, he is so wicked!' "

A few of the neat sayings of Talleyrand, current in London society with the above and of a similar character, also from Moore's Diary:—

"At breakfast at Lord Lansdowne's, Madame Durazzo, in talking of poor Miss Bathurst (who was drowned at Rome), mentioned that Talleyrand in reading an account of it (in which it was said that her uncle plunged in after her, and that M. Laval was in the greatest grief), said, '*M. de Laval aussi s'est plongé, mais dans la plus profonde douleur.*'

To some notorious reprobate (said to be Rivarol) who remarked to him, '*Je n'ai fait qu'une seule méchanceté dans ma vie;*' Talleyrand answered, '*Et celle là, quand finira-t-elle?*'

Of a lady who was praised for her *beaucoup d'esprit:* ' Oui, beaucoup d'esprit, beaucoup; elle ne s'en sert jamais.' "

Jerdan in his Autobiography has the following:—

MACAULAY.

To take Macaulay out of literature and society, and put him in the House of Commons, is like taking the chief physician out of London during a pestilence.

"OH yes! we both talk a great deal, but I don't believe Macaulay ever did hear my voice," he exclaimed laughing. "Sometimes, when I have told a good story, I have thought to myself, Poor Macaulay! he will be very sorry some day to have missed hearing that."

I ALWAYS prophecied his greatness from the first moment I saw

"When an inquisitive quidnunc who squinted, asked Talleyrand how he thought certain measures would go, he replied '*comme vous voyez.*'

"A council of the ministry having sat upon some question an eminent nobleman met him as he came from the meeting: ' Que s'est-il *passé dans ce conseil?*' to which he replied, ' *Trois heures!*'

"In a period of rapid political change in Paris he was asked what he thought of it: 'Why,' he replied, 'in the morning I believe; in the afternoon I change my opinion, and in the evening, I have no opinion at all.'

When he was Minister for Foreign Affairs and there was a report in Paris of the death of George III., a banker, full of speculative anxieties, asked him if it was true. 'Some say,' he replied, 'that the King of England is dead, others say that he is not dead; but do you wish to know my opinion?' 'Most anxiously, Prince!' 'Well, then, I believe neither! I mention this in confidence to you; but I rely on your discretion; the slightest imprudence on your part would compromise me most seriously!"

To these may be added a brace of anecdotes from the recently-published Journal of Thomas Raikes:—

"A certain Vicomte de V——, friend of Talleyrand, who with him frequented some distinguished soirées, where high play was encouraged, had incurred some suspicions not very creditable to his honour. Detected one evening in a flagrant attempt to defraud his adversary, he was very unceremoniously turned out of the house, with a threat, that if he ever made his appearance there again, he should be thrown out of the window. The next day he called upon M. de Talleyrand to relate his misfortune, and protest his innocence: 'Ma position est très embarrassante,' said the Vicomte, 'donnez moi donc un conseil.' 'Dame! mon cher, je vous conseille de ne plus jouer qu'au rez de chaussée' (the ground floor).

"When the Duchesse de Berri had disappeared from La Vendée in 1832 there were reports that she had been seen in various places in France but always disguised. Talleyrand remarked: 'Je ne sais pas si vous la trouverez en la Vendée, ou en Italie, ou en Hollande, mais ce qu'il y a de sur, c'est, que vous la trouverez *en homme.*'"

him, then a very young and unknown man on the Northern Circuit. There are no limits to his knowledge, on small subjects as well as great; he is like a book in breeches.

YES, I agree, he is certainly more agreeable since his return from India. His enemies might have said before (though I never did so) that he talked rather too much; but now he has occasional flashes of silence, that make his conversation perfectly delightful. But what is far better and more important than all this is, that I believe Macaulay to be incorruptible. You might lay ribbons, stars, garters, wealth, title, before him in vain. He has an honest genuine love of his country, and the world could not bribe him to neglect her interests.

LORD DUDLEY.

OH don't read those twelve volumes till they are made into a *consommé* of two. Lord Dudley did still better; he waited till they blew over.

Lord Dudley was one of the most absent men I think I ever met in society. One day he met me in the street, and invited me to meet myself. "Dine with me to-day; dine with me, and I will get Sydney Smith to meet you." I admitted the temptation he held out to me, but said I was engaged to meet him elsewhere. Another time, on meeting me, he turned back, put his arm through mine, muttering, "I don't mind walking with him a little way; I'll walk with him as far as the end of the street." As we proceeded together, W——— passed: "That is the villain," exclaimed he, "who helped me yesterday to asparagus, and gave me no toast." He very nearly overset my gravity once in the pulpit. He was sitting immediately under me, apparently very attentive, when suddenly he took up his stick, as if he had been in the House of Commons, and tapping on the ground with it, cried out in a low but very audible whisper, "Hear! hear! hear!"*

---

* There is a more famous anecdote of Lord Dudley's absence of mind. He was Secretary of State for Foreign Affairs in Canning's Administration, when, at an important moment too, shortly before the battle of Navarino, he addressed a letter intended for the French Ambassador Polignac, to the Russian Ambassador, Prince Lieven. The latter took it for a hoax, and promptly

LUTTRELL.

I THINK it was Luttrell who used to say ———'s face always reminded him of boiled mutton and near relations.

returned it. He remarked it was a good trick, but he was "*trop fin,*" and a diplomatist of too high a standing to be so easily caught. Lord Dudley's habit of soliloquizing in company probably furnished the original of a character in Theodore Hook's Gilbert Gurney, the East India Nabob, Mr. Nubley, who carries on polite conversations with his friends, with a *sotto voce* accompaniment of his real and less complimentary opinions. Lockhart, in an admirable sketch of Dudley in the Quarterly Review, relates one of these adventures: "He had a particular dislike to be asked to give any one a lift in his carriage, in which he thought over the occurrences of the day, more, perhaps, than half the members of the Royal College of Physicians. An ingenious tormento of Brookes's begged him to give a cast to a homeward bound, unconscious victim. It could not be refused. The unhappy pair set out in their chariot, and arrived, silently, near Mount street, when Lord Dudley muttered audibly, 'What a bore! It would be civil to say something. Perhaps I had better ask him to dinner. I'll think about it.' His companion, a person of infinite fancy, and to whom Lord Dudley afterward took a great liking, re-muttered, after a due pause, 'What a bore! Suppose he should ask me to dinner! What should I do? I'll think about it.'"

Moore, in his diary, has frequent mention of Ward. He notices "his two voices; squeak and bass; seeming, as some one remarked, as if 'Lord Dudley were conversing with Lord Ward.' Somebody who proposed a short walk with him, heard him mutter to himself, introspectively, "I think I may endure him for ten minutes." One day that he had Lord Lansdowne to dinner with him, Lord Dudley took the opportunity to read to himself Hume's History of England.

Lord Dudley was, in his youth, at Edinburgh, in the family of Dugald Stewart, studied at Oxford, and entered Parliamentary life early. The family estate, derived from the coal and iron mines of Worcester, was enormous. Lord Dudley's income was some eighty thousand pounds a year. With this extraordinary wealth at command, and a fine classical culture, endeared, by his virtues, to the best London society, and fond of gathering its members about him, he passed much of his time unhappily, in consequence of an organic malformation of the brain, which he traced to an early neglect of physical training. "Melancholy marked him for her own." His "Letters" to his friend Copleston, the Bishop of Llandaff, published after his death, afford many proofs of this.

As a speaker in Parliament, where, with a few exceptions, he was always on the strong conservative side, he was celebrated for his fine, studied speeches. Rogers burlesqued his method in an exceedingly neat, malicious epigram, which Byron, in conversation with Lady Blessington, pronounced "one of the best in the English language, with the true Greek talent of expressing, by implication what is wished to be conveyed:"—

Was not —— very disagreeable? "Why, he was as disagreeable as the occasion would permit," Luttrell said.

Luttrell used to say, I hate the sight of monkeys, they remind me so of poor relations.

Mrs. Sydney was dreadfully alarmed about her side-dishes the first time Luttrell paid us a visit, and grew pale as the covers were lifted; but they stood the test. Luttrell tasted and praised. He spent a week with us, and having associated him only with Pall Mall, I confess I was agreeably surprised to find how pleasant an inmate he made of a country-house, and almost of a family party; so light in hand, so willing to be pleased. Some of his Irish stories, too, were most amusing, and his manner of telling them so good. One: "Is your master at home, Paddy?" "*No*, your honour." "Why, I saw him go in five minutes ago." "Faith, your honour, he's not exactly at home; he's only there in the back-yard a-shooting rats with cannon, your honour, for his *devarsion*."

Luttrell came over for a day (writes Smith, to Lady Holland,

"Ward has no heart, they say, but I deny it;
He has a heart, and gets his speeches by it."

Dudley, (as Lockhart remarks), took capital revenge, in a review of Rogers' Columbus, in the Quarterly, a specimen of cool, exhausting criticism. Rogers comes out of it like a cat taken, at the last gasp, from the receiver of an air-pump. There are several other examples of Dudley's powers as a reviewer, in his articles in the *Quarterly*, on Horne Tooke, Charles James Fox, and Miss Edgeworth.

Luttrell, by the way, had his couplet on "the joke about Lord Dudley's speaking by heart." Moore preserves it in his Diary:—

"In vain my affections the ladies are seeking:
If I give up my heart, there's an end to my speaking."

Lady Blessington also tried an adaptation of it:—

"The charming Mary has no mind they say;
I prove she has — it changes every day"

It was Lord Dudley who made the remark, when he heard of Sir Walter Scott's pecuniary disasters: "Scott ruined! the author of Waverley ruined! Let every man to whom he has given months of delight give him a sixpence, and he will rise to-morrow morning richer than Rothschild."

The Earl of Dudley died, unmarried, at the age of fifty-two, in 1833.

from Combe Florey, in 1829), from whence I know not, but I thought not from good pastures; at least, he had not his usual soup-and-pattie look. There was a forced smile upon his countenance, which seemed to indicate plain roast and boiled; and a sort of apple-pudding depression, as if he had been staying with a clergyman.

I was at Bowood last week (says Smith in another letter about the same); the only persons there were seashore Calcott and his wife—two very sensible, agreeable people. Luttrell came over for the day; he was very agreeable, but spoke too lightly, I thought, of veal-soup. I took him aside, and reasoned the matter with him, but in vain; to speak the truth, Luttrell is not steady in his judgments on dishes. Individual failures with him soon degenerate into generic objections, till, by some fortunate accident, he eats himself into better opinions. A person of more calm reflection thinks not only of what he is consuming at that moment, but of the soups of the same kind he has met with in a long course of dining, and which have gradually and justly elevated the species. I am perhaps making too much of this; but the failures of a man of sense are always painful.

Again, in 1843:—
Luttrell is staying here. Nothing can exceed the innocence of our conversation. It is one continued eulogy upon man-and-woman-kind. You would suppose that two Arcadian old gentlemen, after shearing their flocks, had agreed to spend a week together upon curds and cream, and to indulge in gentleness of speech and softness of mind.*

* Luttrell's couplets, epigrams, puns, and parodies, his *vers de société*, were always of the neatest. He "talks more sweetly than birds can sing," writes Sydney Smith. Rogers said none of the talkers whom he met in London society could "slide in a brilliant thing with such readiness." Luttrell wrote verses of the day, for the Times Newspaper. His "Letters to Julia in Rhyme," a third improved edition of which appeared in 1822, brought him to the notice of the public. It is a vehicle for the description of London manners and ideas. Julia is an ambitious coquette, a widow, to whom the epistles are addressed by a friend of her lover. The sufferings of the inamorato, and the amusements of the town, from which he is driven by the lady's ill-treatment, furnish the themes, which are elegantly presented in a pure witty strain of verse. Luttrell wrote also " Crockford House, a Rhapsody,"

A NOVEL BY SYDNEY SMITH.*

WHEN Smith lost a few hundreds by the Pennsylvania Bonds, a publisher called on him offering to retrieve his fortunes, if he would get up a three-volume novel.

in two cantos, in trochaic eight syllable catalectic. It appeared in 1827, when Crockford established his magnificent "hell" in James street. The moral is well-pointed, but the verse is feeble for the satiric demand of the occasion. It was accompanied by a little poem, "A Rhymer in Rome."

Byron, as reported in the Conversations with Lady Blessington, describes the traits of Luttrell: "Of course," he said, "you know Luttrell. He is a most agreeable member of society, the best sayer of good things, and the most epigrammatic conversationist I ever met with. There is a terseness and wit mingled with fancy, in his observations, that no one else possesses, and no one so peculiarly understands the apropos. His Advice to Julia is pointed, witty, and full of character, showing in every line a knowledge of society, and a tact rarely met with. Then, unlike all or most wits, Luttrell is never obtrusive: even the choicest *bon-mots* are only brought forth when perfectly applicable, and then are given in a tone of good-breeding which enhances their value."

Moore has a number of Luttrell's "felicities" in his Diary. Walking with him one day, the poet remarked a saying on Sharp's very dark complexion, that he looked as if the dye of his old trade (hat-making), had got engrained into his face, "Yes," said Luttrell, "darkness that may be *felt*." He gave this illustration of the English climate: "On a fine day, like looking up a chimney; on a rainy day, like looking down it." He told a capital story of a tailor, who (we follow Moore's words) used to be seen attending the Greek lectures constantly; and when some one noticed it to him as odd, the tailor saying modestly, that he knew too well what became his station, to intrude himself, as an auditor on any of those subjects of which, from his rank in life, he must be supposed to be ignorant; but "really," he added, "at a *Greek* lecture, I think we are all pretty much on a par."

Rogers pronounced Luttrell's epigram on Miss Tree, the singer, "quite a little fairy tale."

"On this tree when a nightingale settles and sings,
The tree will return her as good as she brings."

We are indebted to Mr. Washington Irving for the following anecdote, not hitherto in print. He was walking in company with Moore and Luttrell, at the former's suburban residence, La Butte, near Paris, when the conversation fell on a female aeronaut, who had not been heard of since her recent ascent. Moore described her upward progress — the last seen of her she was still ascending, ascending, "Handed out," slipped in Luttrell, "by Enoch and Elijah."

Henry Luttrell died at his London residence, in December, 1851, in his eighty-first year.

* This and the three following passages are from the Memoir of Rev. Richard Harris Barham, by R. H. D. Barham, the author of the " Ingoldsby

"Well, sir," said the Rev. Sydney, after some seeming consideration, "if I do so, I can't travel out of my own line, *ne sutor ultra crepidam;* I must have an archdeacon for my hero, to fall in love with the pew-opener, with the clerk for a confidant—tyrannical interference of the churchwardens—clandestine correspondence concealed under the hassocks—appeal to the parishioners, etc."

"All that, sir," said the publisher, "I would not presume to interfere with; I would leave it entirely to your own inventive genius."

"Well, sir, I am not prepared to come to terms at present, but if ever I do undertake such a work you shall certainly have the refusal."

THE BISHOP OF NEW ZEALAND.

On the departure of the Bishop of New Zealand for his diocese Smith recommended him to have regard to the minor as well as to the more grave duties of his station—to be given to hospitality—and, in order to meet the tastes of his native guests, never to be without a smoked little boy in the bacon-rack, and a cold clergyman on the sideboard. "And as for myself," my lord, "he concluded, "all I can say is, that when your new parishioners *do* eat you, I sincerely hope you may disagree with them."

WILD CURATES.

Of Dean C—— he said his only adequate punishment would be to be preached to death by wild curates.

VIRGILIAN PUN.

Smith told me of the motto he had proposed for Bishop Burgess's arms, in allusion to his brother, the well-known fish-sauce projector.

"*Gravi* jampridem *saucia* curâ.*

Legends," whose Diary furnishes us with several choice specimens of Smith's pleasantry. He was a Minor Canon of St. Paul's, and of course had good opportunity to study his friend's humour.

* Æneid, iv

DOUBLING THE CAPE.

Puns are frequently provocative. One day, after dinner with a Nabob, he was giving us Madeira—

"London — East India — picked — particular,"

then a second thought struck him, and he remembered that he had a few flasks of Constantia in the house, and he produced *one*. He gave us just a glass apiece. We became clamorous for another, but the old qui-hi was firm in refusal. "Well, well," said Sydney Smith, a man for whom I have a particular regard, "since we can't double the Cape, we must e'en go back to Madeira." We all laughed—our host most of all—and he too, luckily, had his joke. "Be of Good Hope, you shall double it;" at which we all laughed still more immoderately, and drank the second flask.*

SPECIE AND SPECIES.

Sydney Smith, preaching a charity sermon, frequently repeated the assertion, that, of all nations, Englishmen were most distinguished for generosity and the love of their species. The collection happened to be inferior to his expectations, and he said, that he had evidently made a great mistake, and that his expression should have been, that they were distinguished for the love of their specie.†

A CONVERSATIONAL COOK.

Moore set Sydney Smith at home in a hackney-coach after a pleasant dinner-party at Agar Ellis's. On his remarking "how well and good-humouredly the host had mixed us all up together," Smith said, "That's the great use of a good conversational cook, who says to his company, 'I'll make a good pudding of you; it's no matter what you came into the bowl, you must come out a pudding.' 'Dear me,' says one of the ingredients, 'wasn't I just now an egg?' but he feels the batter sticking to him now."‡

---

* Maginn's Maxims of Odoherty, Number Twenty Blackwood's Mag., 1824.
† The World We Live In. Blackwood, June, 1837.
‡ Moore's Diary, May 30, 1826.

A FALSE QUANTITY.

THERE is a current remark attributed to him, that a false quantity at the commencement of the career of a young man intended for public life, was rarely got over; and when a lady asked him what a false quantity was, he explained it to be in a man the same as a *faux pas* in a woman.

A DISPUTANT.*

He said that —— was so fond of contradiction, that he would throw up the window in the middle of the night, and contradict the watchman who was calling the hour.

MEDICAL ADVICE.

WHEN his physician advised him to "take a walk upon an empty stomach," Smith asked, "Upon whose?"

THE ARTICLES AND THE MUSES.

"I HAD a very odd dream last night," said he; "I dreamed that there were thirty-nine Muses and nine Articles; and my head is still quite confused about them."†

APOSTOLICAL SUCCESSION.

SMITH said, "The Bishop of —— is so like Judas, that I now firmly believe in the apostolical succession.

---

* This and the three following are from Dyce's Recollections of the Table-Talk of Samuel Rogers.

† There is a better version of this in Lady Holland's Memoir: "Now I mean not to drink one drop of wine to-day, and I shall be mad with spirits. I always am when I drink no wine. It is curious the effect a thimbleful of wine has upon me; I feel as flat as ——'s jokes; it destroys my understanding: I forgot the number of Muses, and think them thirty-nine of course; and only get myself right again by repeating the lines, and finding 'Descend, ye thirty-nine,' two feet too long."

SENTENCE ON AN ALDERMAN.

Sydney Smith was asked what penalty the Court of Aldermen could inflict on Don-Key for bringing them into contempt by his late escapade. He said, "Melted butter with his turbot for a twelvemonth instead of lobster-sauce."*

BOOKED.

When the great Nestor of our poets (Rogers) advanced as a great truth, at his own table, that no man became great but by getting on the shoulders of another, Sydney Smith, who was present, was so pleased with the remark, that his favourite expression, when he heard anything very good, "booked" was uttered by him very emphatically on this occasion. By "booked" Sydney meant to imply—accepted, endorsed, and to be repeated."†

YOUTH AND FAMILIARITY.‡

One evening, at a dinner party, he was excessively annoyed by the familiarity of a young fop, who constantly addressed him as "Smith"—"Smith, pass the wine," and so forth. Presently the young gentleman stated that he had received an invitation to dine with the Archbishop of Canterbury, and asked the reverend canon "what sort of a fellow" he was.

"A very good sort of a fellow, indeed," replied the satirist; "only, let me give you a piece of advice—don't call him Howley."

This rebuff vastly amused the company, but the object of it, being a fool at all points, did not see this point, and talked on in happy unconsciousness. Soon afterward, one of the company rose to depart, pleading an engagement to a soiree at Gore House.

"Take me with you," roars young Hopeful.—" I've the greatest possible desire to know Lady Blessington."

This request was very naturally demurred to, on the ground that a visitor was not authorized to introduce uninvited guests.

* Letter of Jekyll to Lady Blessington, Sept. 1833. Sir John Key, alderman and mayor, a notoriety of the times.

† Town and Table Talk. Illus. Lond. News, Feb. 25, 1854.

‡ This and the four following are waifs and strays, to which we can assign no particular credit.

"Oh!" said Sydney Smith, "never mind; I'm sure that her Ladyship will be delighted to see our young friend: the weather's uncommonly hot, and you can say that you have brought with you *the cool of the evening.*"

"I HOPE, my friend," he said, kindly, to a brilliant young man, who had freely exhibited his opinions to the company, on a variety of subjects, "that you will know as much ten years hence as you do now!"

DR. WHEWELL.

SMITH is reported to have have said of Dr. Whewell, of Cambridge, whose universality in authorship is one of the marvels of the time, that omniscience was his forte, and science his foible.

TWELVE-PARSON POWER.

SITTING by a brother clergyman at dinner, he afterward remarked, that his dull neighbour had a twelve-parson power of conversation.

ASSUMPTIONS.

THERE are three things which every man fancies he can do—farm a small property, drive a gig, and write an article for a review.

A VESTRY.

AT a church conference on the expediency of securing the new street pavement of wooden blocks, he gave it as his opinion that the thing might be accomplished if the vestry would lay their heads together.

DUNCES.

If men (writes Smith) are to be fools, it were better that they were fools in little matters than in great: dullness, turned up with temerity, is a livery all the worse for the facings; and the most tremendous of all things is a magnanimous dunce.

PRACTICAL JOKING.*

On one occasion, when some London visitors were expected, he called in art to aid nature, and caused oranges to be tied to the shrubs in the drive and garden. The stratagem succeeded admirably, and great was his exultation when an unlucky urchin from the village was detected in the act of sucking one through a quill. It was as good, he said, as the birds pecking at Zeuxis' grapes, or the donkeys munching Jeffrey's supposed myrtles for thistles. Another time, on a lady's happening to hint that the pretty paddock would be improved by deer, he fitted his two donkeys with antlers, and placed them with their extraordinary headgear immediately in front of the windows. The effect, enhanced by the puzzled looks of the animals, was ludicrous in the extreme.

But in his most frolicsome moods, he never practised what is called practical joking, agreeing in opinion on this topic with the late Marquis of Hertford, who checked a party of ingenious tormentors at Sudbourn with the remark, that the human mind was various, and that there was no knowing how much melted butter a gentleman would bear in his pocket without quarreling. There was one practical joke, however, which Sydney admitted he should like to see repeated, if only as an experiment in physics and metaphysics. It was the one played off in the last century on a Mr. O'Brien, whose bedroom windows were carefully boarded up, so that not a ray of light could penetrate. When he rang his bell in the morning, a servant appeared, half dressed and yawning with a candle, and anxiously asked if he was ill. Ashamed of the fancied irregularity, the patient recomposed himself to sleep, but at the end of a couple of hours rang again, and again the same pantomime was enacted. "Open the shutters." They were opened, and all without was as dark as a wolf's mouth. He was kept in bed till driven to desperation by hunger, when rushing out upon the landing-place, he found that he had only just time to dress for a late dinner.

CLERICAL ANGLING

In an argument with a serious baronet, who objected to clerical sporting in the abstract, he stood up for angling. "I give up fly-

* This and the five following paragraphs are from an article on Sydney Smith in the Edinburgh, Review, July, 1855.

fishing: it is a light, volatile, dissipated pursuit. But ground-bait, with a good steady float that never bobs without a bite, is an occupation for a bishop, and in no ways interferes with sermon-making." He once discovered some tench in a pond at Sandhill Park (a seat of the Lethbridges close to Combe Florey) and kept the secret till he had caught every one of them (an exploit requiring several days), when he loudly triumphed over the fisherman of the family. Writing to Lady Grey, he says: "his [John Grey's] refusal of the living of Sunbury convinces me that he is not fond of gudgeon-fishing. I had figured to myself, you and Lord Grey, and myself, engaged in that occupation upon the river Thames."

DINNER-TABLE CONVERSATION.

"Eloquence," says Bolingbroke, "must flow like a stream that is fed by an abundant spring, and not sprout forth a little frothy water on some gaudy day, and remain dry the rest of the year." So must humour, and Sydney Smith's was so fed; yet it was seldom overpowering, and never exhausting, except by the prolonged fits of laughter which it provoked. Although in one of his letters already quoted he calls himself a diner-out, he had none of the prescriptive attributes of that now happily almost extinct tribe. He had no notion of talking for display. He talked because he could not help it; because his spirits were excited, and his mind was full. He consciously or unconsciously, too, abided by Lord Chesterfield's rule, "Pay your own reckoning, but do not treat the whole company; This being one of the very few cases in which people do not care to be treated, every one being fully convinced that he has wherewithal to pay." His favourite maxim (copied from Swift) was "Take as many half-minutes as you can get, but never talk more than half a minute without pausing and giving others an opportunity to strike in." He vowed that Buchon, a clever and amiable man of letters, who talked on the opposite principle, was the identical Frenchman who murmured as he was anxiously watching a rival, "S'il crache ou tousse, il est perdu." Far from being jealous of competition, he was always anxious to dine in company with men who were able and entitled to hold their own; and he was never pleasanter than when some guest of congenial turn of mind assisted him to keep up the ball. On the occasion of the first attempt to bring him and Theodore Hook together, the late Mr. Lockhart arrived with the information, that Hook was priming himself (as was his wont), at the Athenæum Club, with a tumbler or two of hot punch. "Oh," exclaimed Sydney, "if it comes to that, let us start fair. When Mr. Hook is announced, announce Mr. Smith's Punch." When they did meet, they contracted a mutual liking, and Sydney ran on with his usual flow and felicity; but poor Hook had arrived at that period of his life when his wonderful powers required a greater amount of stimulants than could be decently imbibed at an ordinary London dinner with a clergyman.

A SCOTCH GARDENER.

When he stopped to give directions to his servants or labourers he was well worth listening to. On it being pointed out to him that his gardener was tearing off too many of the leaves of a vine, he told him to desist. The man, a Scotchman, looked unconvinced. "Now, understand me," he continued; "you are probably right, but I don't wish you to do what is right; and as it is my vine, and there are no moral laws for pruning, you may as well do as I wish."

MEDICAL PRACTICE.

Sir Henry Holland's high authority is adduced in favour of Sydney's medical knowledge; but we have our doubts whether the health of either Foston or Combe Florey was improved by the indulgence of his hobby in this particular. A composition of blue-pill which he was glad to "dart into the intestines" of any luckless wight whom he could induce to swallow it, sometimes operated in a manner which he had not anticipated. One morning, at Combe Florey, a regular practitioner from Taunton, who had been going his weekly round and was considerately employed to overlook the serious cases, came in with rather a long face, and stated that an elderly woman, who had been taking the pill during several consecutive nights for the lumbago, complained that her gums were sore, and he therefore advised the discontinuance of it. A London visitor, who had tried it once, began to titter; and Sydney, after attempting a weak apology for his practice, heartily joined in the laugh, exclaiming: "What a story you will make of this, when you next breakfast with Rogers, and how he and Luttrell will triumph in it!"

A BISHOP'S COURTSHIP.

Some one asked if the Bishop of —— was going to marry. "Perhaps he may—yet how can a bishop marry? How can he flirt? The most he can say is, 'I will see you in the vestry after service.'"

TITHES.

It is an atrocious way of paying the clergy. The custom of tithe in kind will seem incredible to our posterity; no one will believe in the ramiferous priest officiating in the cornfield.

ILLUSIONS.

We naturally lose illusions as we get older, like teeth; but there is no Cartwright to fit a new set into our understandings. I have, alas! only one illusion left, and that is the Archbishop of Canterbury.

INDEX.

Acknowledgment of Game, 414.
Affectations of Knowledge, 197.
Affection and the Thermometer, 404.
Affections, Uses of the Evil, 246.
Age, Benefits of Knowledge to, 152.
Airy, G. P., Epigram on, 403.
Allen, John, Notices of, 20, 91, 414.
America, Articles on, 184–194.
————, Travellers in, 396.
————, Visit to, 409.
American Debts, 415.
———————— Letters on, 69, 353–362.
Angling, Clerical, 449.
Antediluvian Authorship, 120.
Anti-Cholera, 403.
Anti-Melancholy, 423.
Anti-War, 399.
Apologue of the Village, 307.
Apostolical Succession, 446.
Argillaceous Immortality, 398.
Articles, the, and the Muses, 446.
Assumptions, 448.
Athenæum, London, quoted, 396.
Aurungzebe, 240.
Austin, Sarah, Edits Correspondence, 10; Notice of Smith's Preaching, 98.
Aversions and Arguments, 412.
Ballot, the, 68.
Banks, Sir Joseph, 172.
Barham, R. H., Diary of, quoted, 101, 435, 443.
Barn-door Fowl, 133.
Barrow, Dr., Sermons, 33.
Beach, Mr. Hick, 17; Letters of Smith to, 18.
Beautiful, Incentives of the, 237; Action of the, 239.
Bell, Robert, Life of Canning, quoted, 310.

Bentham, Jeremy, 160; Book of Fallacies, 162.
Berkeley, Hon. G. F., 119
Bernard, Sir Thomas, Notices of, 30, 35.
Bible, Beauty of the Style of, 423.
Bishop, a Real, 375.
———— Sacrifice of, on a Railroad, 350.
Bishop's Courtship, 452.
Bishops, Advice to, 331.
———— and Patronage, 329.
———— Saturday Night, 337.
Blair, Hugh, 22.
Blessington, Lady, Conversations, quoted, 443.
Blind, the, 263.
Bloomfield, Bishop, 65.
Bluecoat Theory, 412.
Blue-stockings, 424.
Bobus Smith, see Robert.
Body, of the, 278.
Bombarding the Asiatics, 410.
Booked, 447.
Bore, a, 412.
Borough System, the, 318.
Botany Bay, Description of, 157–159
Bourne, Sturges, 305.
Breakfast, a, 409.
Brougham, Henry, 19; Ed. Review 27; the Court of Chancery, 320.
Brown, Isaac Hawkins, 302.
Brown, Thomas, 21, 27.
Buffoonery, 231.
Bull's Charity Subscriptions, 162.
Bulls, Irish, 232.
Bunch, 48. 54.
Burges, James Bland, 24.
Burlesque, 232.
Burning Alive on Railroads, 350

Byron, Lord, Notice of "The Exodiad," 24; of Lady Holland, 89; Notices of Smith in his Poems, 93; 436.
Campanero, the, 168.
Campbell, Thomas, Anecdotes of, 22, 89; Lochiel, quoted, 221.
Canning, George, 10, 160; his Parasites, 301; Character of, 309.
Canvas-Back Ducks, 433.
Carlisle, Lord, Notice of Robert Smith, 14; Notice of, 52;
Carlyle, Thomas, 92.
Castlereagh, Lord, 160.
Cathedral Revenue Bill, 329.
Catholic Church Question, 363–378; see Peter Plymley.
Catholic Toleration, &c., 41–3; 64.
Caucus, 185.
Caution, in Use of Talent, 2??.
Ceylon, Inhabitants of, 11?.
Channing, Dr., Sermon p?·?hed at St. Paul's, 33.
Charades, 233.
Cheerfulness, of, 282.
Chemistry, 135.
Chesterfield, Lord, quoted, 450.
Childhood, Sensibility of, 418.
Chimney-Sweepers, 159.
Christian Charity, 261.
Church in Danger, 299.
Claphamites, the, 301.
Classes of Society, 431.
Classical Education, 121–131.
Club Life, 38.
Cobbett, Notice of Netheravon, 18.
Combe Florey, Life at, 61–63.
Common Sense for 1810, 46.
Commons, House of, 425.
Composition, 426.
Conquerors, Use of, 157.
Conversational Cook, 445.
Conversation and Books, 212.
Conversation, Educated, 150.
Cool of the Evening, 447.
Copleston, Bishop of Llandaff, Reply to Ed. Review, 45; Smith's Reply to, 131–136; Letters of Ward, 440.
Cork, Lady, 429.
Country House, 431.
Courage in the Use of Talent, 201.
Cranzius and Ernesti, 124, 132.
Crashaw, Epigram of, 221.
Crowe, Mrs., Letter to, 410.
Crumpet's Ascent to St. Paul's, 333.
Curates, 338, 340, 341.
Delphine, Analysis of 113.
Demerara, 168.

D'Epinay, Madame, 154–156.
De Quincey, Notice of Robert Smith, 12.
De Stael, Madame, Delphine, 113.
Diary, Reflections from, 292–4.
Dickens, Charles, Letters to, 407–9.
Digestion and the Virtues, 404.
Dinner in the Country, 420.
Dinner Table Conversation, 450.
Discussing, Habit of, 203.
Disputant, A, 446.
Dogs, 421, 430.
Dome of St. Paul's, 434.
Dort, Chronicle of, 332.
Doubling the Cape, 445.
Doyle, Dr., 367.
Dress and Beauty, 424.
Drunkenness, 289.
Dunces, 448.
Dwight, Timothy, 187.
Dying Speeches, 415.
Edinburgh, Visit to, 398.
Edinburgh Review, Early History of, 25; Attack on Oxford, 45; Passages from, 107–194.
Edinburgh Society, 19.
Edmonton, Living of, 67.
Education, Classical, 121–131.
———— Female, 136–154.
———— Popular, 274–5.
Elephant, Anecdote of, 243.
Ellis, George, 309.
Emulation, 207.
England in an Invasion, 304.
Erin go Bragh, 366.
Erskine, Lord, Anecdote of, 39.
Essays and Sketches, 278–296.
Everett, Edward, 72; Letter on, 415.
Facts and Figures, 426.
Fagging System, 16.
Fallacies, 283–5.
False Quantities, 115.
Fearon, H. B., 185.
Female Education, 136–154.
Fireplaces, 423.
Foolometer, a, 337.
Foston-le-Clay, 47–57.
Fox, C. J., Saying of, 337.
Fragment on the Irish Roman Catholic Church, 363–378.
Franklin, Benjamin, 62, 315.
Fraser's Gallery of Portraits, 94.
———— Magazine cited, 119, 436.
Frere, John Hookham, 10.
Friendship, of, 281.
Friendship, 433.
Fuller, Dr. Thomas, 102, 259.

INDEX.

Gardener, Scotch, 451.
Gladstone, W. E., 373.
God save the King, 311.
Goderich, Lord, 373.
Good Man and a Bad Minister, 299.
Gout, 409.
Granby, Novel of, 176–9.
Grant, Sir William, 395.
Grattan, Visits Mickleham, 36.
—— Character of, 161.
Gravity and License, 95–102.
Great Western Railway, 344.
Green, Duff, 71; 359.
Grenville, Thomas, 371.
Grey, Earl, 61; Conduct of the Reform Bill, 321; 394, 402.
Habit, Force of, 248; Orbit of, 251; Superiority to, 251; Effect of, 253.
Half-Measures, 285.
Hallam, Henry, 21.
Hamilton, Alexander, 27.
Handshaking, 426.
Happiness, 434.
Happiness, Past, 248.
Hardness of Character, 286.
Hardships of Public Schools, 154.
Hare, James, 81.
Hawkesbury, Lord, 300.
Haydon, B. R., 36; 73.
Hay-Fever, the, 403.
Heptarchy of the Press, 323.
Hobbes and his Pipe, 248.
Hodgson, Dr., 374.
Holland House, 22, 30; Historical Notices of, 86–88; Anecdotes of, 90; Dinner Party, 395.
Holland, Lady (Saba, daughter of Sydney Smith), Memoir of her Father, 10; Birth, 30; Marriage to Sir Henry H., 64.
Holland, Lord (Henry Richard Vassall), Notices of, 88; Lady Holland, 89, 103.
Holland, Sir Henry, Notice of, 64.
Holoplexia, 258.
Hook, Theodore, 450.
Hope, Charles, 21.
Horned Cattle and the Lion, 336.
Horner, Francis, 20; Notice of Smith's Preaching, 25; Notice of Lectures, 35; Recollections of, 387–391.
Howick, Lord, 306.
Hoyle, Charles, Poem Exodus, 101.
Humour, Nature of, 227–231.
Hunt, Leigh, Notices of Holland House, 86.

Illusions, 452.
Immortality of a Book, 116.
Individual Peculiarities and Genius, 213.
Inflictions on Youth, 284.
Inglis, Sir Robert, 371.
Insects of the Tropics, 175.
Instinct and Talent, 241; Change of Instinct, 242.
Irreligion and Impiety, 400.
Irving, Edward, 402.
—— Washington, Original Anecdote of Luttrell, 443.
Jameson, Mrs., Notice of Sydney Smith. 10; Character of his Wit, 85.
—— to Lady Blessington, 446.
Jeffrey, Francis, 26; Marriage, 46.
—— and the North Pole, 417; Lines on, ib.
Jeffre's Analysis, 393; Hints to, ib.; His ljectives, 400.
Jekyll , Witticism of, 429.
Jenkins 1, Lord Hawkesbury, 300.
Johnson, Samuel, quoted, 102.
Joinville, Prince de, 370.
Joke in the Country, 426.
Judge, Taylor, and Barber, 186.
Kay, Annie, 50, 55.
Key, Sir John, 446.
King of Clubs, the, 38.
Kinglake, Dr., 317.
Kingsley, Rev. Charles, quoted, 262.
Knowledge, Rewards of, 206; Pleasures of, 216.
Labour and Genius, 195.
Lamb, Charles, 97.
Landseer, Sir Thomas, Anecdote, 102.
Langford, W., Anniversary Sermon, 108.
Lapdogs, 430.
Law, Cheapness of, in America, 186.
Letters, Passages from, 392–416.
Lewis, Frankland, 324.
Leyden, John, 21.
Leyden's Sonnet on the Sabbath, 238
Licensing of Ale-Houses, 179–183.
Life of a Parent, 392.
Light and Shade, 425.
Lister, T. H., 177.
Literature of America, 187–8.
Local English Morals, 156.
Local Moralities, 422.
Lockhart, J. G., 450.
Locking-in on Railways, 344–352
Longevity and Wisdom, 243
Lucretius, quoted, 390

Luttrell, H., Smith's Notices of, 440; Epigram by, 441; Witticisms of, 443; Account of, ib.
Lynch, Judge, 193.
Lyndhurst, Lord, 321.
——— ——— and Lady, 52, 60.
Macaulay, T. B., 43; Tribute to Holland House, 91.
——— ———, an Illustration from Smith, 120.
——— ———, Sayings of Sydney Smith on, 438-9.
Mackenzie, Henry, 22.
Mackintosh, Sir Æneas, 82.
———, Sir James, Character and Anecdotes of, 379-386.
———, ——— Memoirs, quoted, 38.
Malays, the, 112.
Malthus, T. R., 401.
Manners, 430.
Mathematics, 426.
Maxims, 394.
——— of Life, 292-4.
Medical Advice, 446.
——— Statesmanship, 312.
———Practice of Sydney Smith, 451.
Melbourne, Lord, Character of, 334.
Methodism, Articles on, 119.
Microcosm, the, 10.
Military Glory, 187.
Modern Changes, 295.
Monk, Dr., Bishop of Gloucester, 65, 341.
Montrand and Talleyrand, 437.
Moore, Thomas, Sydney Smith's Memoir, 10; Notice of Robert Smith, 13; Anecdote of Newton's Studio, 75; Anecdotes of Smith, 84 98; of Holland House, 90; Poetical Compliment, 93; Letter to, 401; Diary, quoted, 437, 445.
Moral Philosophy — Passages from Lectures, 195-255.
Morgan, Capt. E. E., Correspondent of Smith, 71-2; Portrait of Smith, 75.
Morley, Countess of, 413.
Murray, John A. (Lord Murray), 21, 27.
Musæ Etonenses, 11.
Napier, Sir Charles, History quoted, 313.
New Song to an Old Tune, 70.
Newton, Gilbert Stuart, Portrait of Smith, 75.
New Zealand Attorney, 422.

New Zealand, Bishop of, 444.
Nice Person, a, 285.
Niebuhr's Discoveries, 422.
Noah, M. M., Anecdote of, 191.
Noctes Ambrosianæ, 94.
Noodledom, 143.
Noodle's Oration, 164.
No-Popery Outcry, 183-4.
Notes and Queries, cited, 316.
Novel by Sydney Smith, 443.
Occupation, of, 279.
O'Connell, 326, 365, 369.
Old Age to be Passed in the City 404, 414
Olier, Miss, Birth and Character, 9 Mother of Sydney Smith, 15.
One-Book Man, 425.
Opera, Invitation to, 409, 414.
Oratorio, an, 399.
Oxford UniversityEducation, 121-136.
——— visited, 392.
Paris visited by Smith, 58-60.
Parishioners, Advice to, 287.
Parody, 232.
——— of Milton, 405.
Parr, Dr., Tributes to Robert Smith, 13.
———, Spital Sermon, 107; Philopatris, 120.
Partington, Mrs., 64, 315.
Passions, the, 253.
Paying in Turbot, 394
Peel, Sir Robert, Letter to, 352, 370.
Pennsylvania, Public Debt, 353.
Perceval, Spencer, 297, 299, 300, 302, 310, 311.
Percival, R., Account of Ceylon, 111.
Persecutions, Catholic and Protestant, 298.
Peter Plymley, Passages from, 297-313.
Petition of Sydney Smith to Congress, 353.
Philips, Sir George, Notice of, 73.
Pictures, Smith's Purchase of, 425.
Pilpay, Fable from, 360.
Playfair, John, 22.
Plymley Letters, 40, 297-313.
Pope, Parody on, 429.
Porson's Review of the Sovereign, 24; Epigram, ib.
Portrait of Sydney Smith, 404.
Practical Joking, 448.
Praise, 434.
Prancing Indenture, 108.
Preferment at Court, 401.
Prescott, W. H., 435.

INDEX.

Private Cellars and Public Houses, 182.
Professional Education, 121-131.
Ptochogony, a, 339.
Puns, 85, 124.
Public Eye, the, 330.
Public Houses and Drinking, 179.
Public Schools, 154.
Puseyism, 411.
Pybus, Catherine Amelia, wife of Smith, 23.
—— Charles Small, 23.
Pye, Henry James, 24.
Quantity, False, a, 446.
Raikes, T., Journal quoted, 438.
Railway, Letters on, 344-352.
Randolph, John, on the Ballot, 68.
Reading, Art of, 208.
—— in Age, 402.
Rebuke by Sydney Smith, 423.
Redesdale, Lord, 306.
Reform Speeches, 314-328.
Religious Liberty, 190.
Riches, on, 267.
Ridicule, Superiority to, 226; Use of 119.
Rogers, Henry, Notice of Smith's Lectures, 37.
——, Samuel, Notice of Robert Smith, 14; Anecdote of Lord Holland, 16: of Lady Holland, 89; Dining-room Anecdote, 101 and Note; 394; Witticisms of Smith, 435; Anecdotes of, ib.; Epigram on Ward, 441.
Romilly, Sir Samuel, Tribute to, 273.
Round Man in the Round Hole, 206.
Rousseau and D'Epinay, 153.
Rumford, Count, 30, 35.
Russell, Lord John, Smith's Description of, 65.
—— —— —— and the Bishops, 335.
Salad Recipe, 427-8.
Samaritans, 434.
Sarcasm, 226.
Science, Claims of, 129.
Scotland and the Catholic Question, 303.
Scott, Sir Walter, 305, 395.
Seduction, 290.
Sentence on an Alderman, 447.
Selwyn, George, 309.
Semiramis, Invitation to, 414.
Sermons, of, 256.
—— Passages from, 256-277.
Servants, Treatment of, 262.

Sewing for Men, 430.
Seymour, Lord Webb, 20.
Sham Sydney Smiths, 432-3.
Sharp, Richard, Notice of, 35.
——, Mot by Luttrell.
She is not Well, 364.
Shillaber, B. P., Mrs. Partington, 317
Shyness, 245.
Siddons, Mrs., 432.
Sign of the State in Difficulty, 394.
Simon of Gloucester, 333, 343.
Simond, Louis, Notice of, 46.
Simonides, Danae, 11.
Singleton, Archdeacon, Letters to, 64 66, 329-343.
Skepticism, 205.
Slavery, American, 194.
Sloth of Cruelty and Ignorance, 311.
Sloth, the 173.
Small Men, 422.
Smith, Cecil, 14.
Smith, Courtenay, 14, 72.
Smith, Douglas, at Westminster, 16; Death, 61; Letter to, 397.
Smith, Maria, 15.
Smith, Robert (father of Sydney), 9, 15.
Smith, Robert (Bobus) at Eton, 10; at Cambridge, 11; Verses "Ex Simonide" ib.; Marriage, ib.; in India, 12; in the House of Commons, ib.; death, ib.; tributes to, 13.
Smith, Sir Sidney, 9, 59, 382.
Smith, Sydney, Association of the Names, 9.
Smith, Sydney: Birth and Family, 9; School-Days, 15; in Normandy, 17; at Oxford, 17; enters the Church, ib.; at Netheravon, ib.; at Edinburgh, 18; Projects the Edinburgh Review, 25; Sermons at Edinburgh, 29; in London, 30; Chapel Preaching, 30-2; Character of Sermons, 33; Charge of Plagiarism, ib.; Lectures on Moral Philosophy, 34; Plymley Letters, 40; in Yorkshire, 43; Controversy with Oxford, 45; Justice of the Peace, 56; Visits France, 57-60; at Bristol, ib.; Canon of St. Paul's, 61; Combe Florey, 61-3; Reform Speeches, 64; Letters to Archdeacon Singleton, 64-66; the Ballot, 68; Letters on American Debts, 69-72; Death, 74; Personal Appearance, ib.; Characteristics, 75-79; Intellectual Habits, 79-81; Wit and Humour

20

INDEX.

81–85; Letters, 86; Contemporary Notices, 93–4; License and Gravity Considered, 95–102; Summary, 104.
Smoking, Habit of, 250.
Smythe, George Sydney, 9.
Smythe, Sir Thomas, 9.
Socinian, 434.
Soldiers and Theology, 300.
Solvent States, 361.
Somerville, Lord, 305.
Sonnet on the Sabbath, 238.
Sovereign, the, a poem, 23.
Sovereign, Transit of, 429.
Specie and Species, 445.
Spirits, Consumption of, 182.
St. Antony, 410.
Stage-Coach Travelling, 419.
Stephen, James, 302.
Stewart, Dugald, 21; Death of, 423.
Study, Habits of, 209.
Styles, Rev. John, 119.
Sublimity, 235.
Supplies for the Mind, 195.
Susan Hopley, 410.
Swing, Mr., Letter to, 291.
Table-Talk of Sydney Smith, 417, 452.
Talfourd, Serjeant, 336.
Talleyrand, Witticism on Robert Smith, 14; Madame De Stael, 115; Anecdotes of, 436.
Tarring and Feathering, 362.
Taste, Certainty of, 236.
Taunton, Reform Speeches, 314.
Taxes, 187–8.
Tea and Coffee, 431.
Telemachus, 422.
Temperance, 400.
Thackeray, W. M., Allusion to Lord Carlisle, 52.
Thomson, John, 21, 27.
Thomson, Thomas, 27.
Three Sexes, 434.
Tickell, Richard, 309.
Ticknor, George, 72.
Tithes, 452.
Town and Country, 405, 431.
Travel, Books of, and Travellers, 109, 156.

Triumph of Civilized Life, 393.
Truth, 199, 264.
Tuckerman, H. T., Article in N. A Review, 92.
Twelve Parson Power, 448.
Twenty-Four Hours after, 425.
Twiss, Horace, 324.
Understanding, Conduct of the, 195.
Union of America, 192.
Utilitarian, a, 424.
Vampire, the, 174.
Vanille of Society, 430.
Vellum and Plumpkin, 319.
Venus Millinaria, 429.
Versailles Railway Accident, 344.
Vestry, a, 448.
Victoria, Sermon on the Accession of, 274.
Village, the, an Apologue, 307
Virgilian Pun, 444.
War, 276, 399.
War and Credit, 358.
Ward (Lord Dudley), Witticisms on Rogers, 436; Anecdotes of, 439; Account of, 440.
Waste of Life, 422.
Waterton, Charles, Wanderings in South America, 166–176
Webster, Daniel, Correspondence with Smith, 406, 434.
Well-Informed Women, 392.
Wellington, Duke of, 324, 327.
Wet Clothes, 288.
Whewell, Dr., 35, 448.
Whip-poor-Will, 171.
Whishaw, John, 395.
Who Reads an American Book? 188.
Wild Curates, 444.
William IV. and the Reform Bill, 322, 328.
Wisdom of our Ancestors, 162.
Wit, Essentials of, 217–224; a Cultivable Faculty, 224; Dangers and Advantages of, 233.
Words, Abuse of, 199.
Wourali Poison, 168.
Youth and Familiarity, 447.

THE END.

www.ingramcontent.com/pod-product-compliance
Lightning Source LLC
Chambersburg PA
CBHW031956300426
44117CB00008B/784